BMP WORKS

*21 Award Winning Case Histories
from BMP DDB Needham*

Edited and introduced by

Paul Feldwick
Executive Director of Planning
BMP DDB Needham

NTC PUBLICATIONS LIMITED

First published in 1992 by
NTC Publications Limited
Farm Road
Henley-on-Thames
Oxfordshire RG9 1EJ
United Kingdom
Telephone: 0491 574671

The permission of the Institute of Practitioners in Advertising to
reproduce the case histories from its Advertising Effectiveness Awards
is gratefully acknowledged

A CIP catalogue record for this book is available
from the British Library

ISBN 1-870562-07-0

Produced by NTC Publications Ltd
Printed and bound in Great Britain by
Biddles Ltd, Guildford and King's Lynn

The case history pages in this book have been photographically reproduced
from volumes in the IPA's *Advertising Works* series, therefore readers are
asked to excuse some variation in reproduction quality

For Stanley Pollitt

Contents

"*I throw a spear into the dark. That is intuition.*
Then I send an army to find the spear. That is intellect."

Ingmar Bergman

About this Book

Advertising is a part of business. It must be approached in a scientific, disciplined way. Its effects must be carefully monitored. The risk of failure must be minimised.

Advertising has at its disposal all the resources of art, music, and language. It can make people laugh, cry, and see the world in a different way. Great advertising defies analysis. It is at its most powerful when it breaks rules and takes risks.

Both statements, of course, are true.

This book is an advertisement for BMP DDB Needham. But more than just a record of our success in the IPA Advertising Effectiveness Awards.

We hope that these twenty-one papers are also an advertisement for our ways of working, and our beliefs about advertising.

They show that disciplined thinking and creative originality need not be in conflict.

This book is a tribute to all those people in the agency who helped create the advertising featured here. Among many different roles the creative department are usually, and rightly, the heroes. But this volume belongs perhaps most of all to the account planners - who, mostly, wrote it, and whose work here receives a rare public exposure.

It shows how we believe research is best used - in planning strategies, in developing creative executions, and in evaluating and learning from the campaign itself.

THE IMPORTANCE OF STRATEGY

The Greek word στρατηγια signified "the art of generalship", so strategy means *a plan for winning*. A military commander needs to understand, as well as he can, three things:

- his own side's strengths and weaknesses;
- the environment in which the conflict will take place; and
- the position and intentions of the enemy.

Each of these has a parallel for the planner of advertising :

- the current status of the brand, its equity and product performance;
- the consumer's attitudes and behaviour, and other "things that are around";
- the performance and plans of the competition.

INTRODUCTION

As these papers often show, the process of planning strategy requires a detailed understanding of the product itself and the resources available to the client. It also involves many different types of research; analysis of the market, purchasing behaviour, usage and attitude studies, pricing studies, competition, and importantly, qualitative research which in the vast majority of these cases was carried out by agency planners.

But all this intelligence on its own is not enough to define the best plan of action. The best strategies, in war or advertising, are decisive, elegant, and often unexpected. Strategic thinking is in itself a creative process.

Strategy is about making choices. It is better to achieve one objective than attempt and fail at several. And it is also true that one decisive victory may change the course of the whole conflict.

So the first decision is the choice of an objective. The more precise the better. And in advertising, a precise objective will mean defining exactly who we are to address and exactly what we would like them to do.

page 327 –	**An overall objective of reducing crime was refined into a more specific campaign to reduce burglaries by urging householders to fit window locks.**
page 339 –	**A campaign to reduce calls to the Fire Brigade focussed on chip pan fires as the biggest cause of call outs. People were resistant to warnings telling them to be careful - no one thinks they are going to have an accident! Instead the advertising showed them how to cope with a fire should it happen.**
page 95 –	**Consumers were inhibited in their use of Hellmann's mayonnaise because it was seen as only for special occasions. Advertising focussed on changing their behaviour to everyday usage on simple foods.**
page 313 –	**The Conservative government proposed to abolish the Greater London Council, at that time under Labour control. Labour supporters were naturally opposed to this; the objective of the advertising was to influence *Conservative* voters by presenting the abolition of the GLC as an undemocratic act, outside of party politics.**

The other major element of an advertising strategy, after defining the target and what we want them to do, is *how* best to persuade them to do it. Sometimes this will involve factual information about the product, very often it will not. But in either case the consumer must take out of the advertisement a belief that there will be some benefit to them when they take the desired action. This may be very vague; the enhanced security associated with a known, rather than an unknown, name. Usually it is much more specific .

In many cases the benefit is conferred by intangible values of the brand, rather than a specific product based claim. The satisfactions that people obtain from even the most mundane products nearly always go beyond the merely functional. We choose paint to express our pride in our homes; we choose a brand of beer partly as a statement about ourselves. "Others sell cosmetics", said Charles Revlon; "I sell hope." Good advertising starts by understanding the real needs that the manufacturer's product can satisfy.

When I ask for Hofmeister in the pub, I'll be one of the lads.	*– page 65*
When I treat my child with Karvol, we'll all sleep well.	*– page 137*
When I buy Kia-Ora, I'll be giving my children fun.	*– page 41*
When I get my mortgage from the Alliance & Leicester, I can get it arranged before I start house-hunting.	*– page 275*

CREATIVE DEVELOPMENT

Psychologists have shown that there is a clear division of functions between the two hemispheres of the brain. The left side processes language, logic and analysis; the right deals with visual recognition, pattern and rhythm, creativity, our sense of humour, and, interestingly, long-term memory. It is demonstrably easier to remember things if we can associate them with pictures, and the more unusual or absurd these are, the better. Some of the ways in which creativity enhances the impact and memorability of advertising may be easily explained on the same principle.

However there is more to great advertising than creating effective mnemonics. In the words of Bill Bernbach,

"Properly practised creativity can lift your claims out of the swamp of sameness and make them accepted, believed, persuasive, urgent."

Creative inspiration can break down barriers of credibility; can create from nothing a desirable brand image; can make a simple fact into a profound and motivating statement.

The commonest mistake in advertising is to focus on what is put *into* an ad, rather than what the target market will take *out* of it. The most powerful communications are generally not in words; things can be implied which could never be said. If the Clarks Desert Boots campaign had read "The latest thing in fashion.", the target market would never have been seen dead in them. But the non-verbal message of the enigmatic Helmut Newton photography had this effect.

There is a danger of course with any communication that the message received may not be what the sender meant. Fortunately it is relatively easy to find out if this is the case. You can ask people.

Just about all these campaigns were exposed to their target markets in group discussions at an early stage. In many cases they were severely altered as a result. George, the Hofmeister bear, only came right at the fourth attempt. This may seem a rather messy way of getting to the right answer - and at the time it felt like it. But the result was advertising that not only transformed the brand for a long-term future, but actually paid for itself in the first year. Remember also that two previous Hofmeister campaigns (by other agencies) had expensively sunk without trace.

Too often creative research does more harm than good because of the heavy-handedness of its methods. It looks at aggregated data instead of understanding individuals, and it judges advertisements against artificial and often irrelevant criteria. For these reasons we prefer the flexibility of qualitative research, which properly should be conducted by the account planner. When this happens the findings can be fully integrated with all the other research and thinking on the brand, and interpreted and actioned in ways which creative people can use.

EVALUATION

Campaign evaluation has two slightly different purposes.

One is to estimate the contribution advertising has made to the client's business.

The other is to learn how the advertising is, or isn't, working, and provide direction for the future.

The IPA Advertising Effectiveness Awards were set up to encourage both of these, but especially the first. That is why each of these papers puts emphasis on evaluating the advertising's business effects.

Having said that, such estimates can rarely be precise. It is a truism that sales can be affected by many factors besides advertising, and therefore need to be analysed with great care. Even econometric techniques, which are represented here in several papers, do not always capture the full benefits of advertising, as they may explain short-term variations without measuring longer-term effects. The difficulty of measuring a sales response has led to the extensive use of other, intermediate measures of advertising effect - brand or advertising awareness, or changes in attitudes. These are of enormous help in understanding campaign effects, and appear throughout these papers. But it always needs to be remembered that a measure of attitude or awareness may not have any relationship to actual purchasing behaviour (as the paper on Hofmeister demonstrates). Evaluation is a process of detective work, piecing together many strands of evidence, not all of which is reliable. That is one reason why these case histories often run to 4,000 words.

Also there are many reasons for advertising, and many kinds of advertising effects on a business. Some advertising creates a short-term uplift in sales and pays for itself within the year. Some advertising launches, or relaunches, a brand to create longer-term income. And other campaigns exist primarily to defend an established position. Like many other continued investments, their real value only becomes apparent in the long-term, or else in their absence.

page 41 – Kia-Ora was third brand in its market and about to be delisted by major retailers. Within eighteen months of starting to advertise it was brand leader.

page 65 – Hofmeister spent £1.7m on advertising in the first year and over the same period earned incremental profit due to the advertising of £1.9m.

page 275 – Alliance & Leicester advertising increased profit from mortgage business by £2.5m in a declining market by attracting customers direct rather than through commission-taking intermediaries.

page 137 – Karvol invested a share of its profit in advertising in order to establish a dominant position in the "over-the-counter" pharmaceuticals market.

page 177 – PG Tips remained brand leader in the tea market for thirty-five years despite heavy competition. One possible estimate of the long-term benefit of the advertising is £2 billion in extra sales.

The other purpose of evaluation is to learn how the advertising is performing. Who exactly is buying, whether they are behaving as expected, how awareness and attitudes have changed, what the advertising is really communicating.

The interesting thing is that despite all the best laid plans, campaigns are often successful in a slightly different way from what was anticipated. Sometimes, more successful than anyone had thought possible.

page 339 – The Chip Pan Fire campaign did reduce call outs because more householders were dealing with the crisis themselves. But it also reduced the actual number of fires. Giving advice turned out to be an effective way of making people think about the danger.

page 95 – The Hellmann's campaign did widen usage away from salads, but most of the growth was still salad usage. Nevertheless by popularising the product, growth was achieved well above the most optimistic estimates.

page 253 – The Alliance & Leicester corporate campaign was planned as an investment in long-term brand awareness. No short-term extra business was expected. Nevertheless the advertising paid for itself in profit from incremental deposits.

Of course, campaign results can be disappointing as well as pleasantly surprising. Even when the advertising development process has been above criticism, changes in the market-place can effectively move the goalposts. But either way campaign evaluation is a vital process as it is also the beginning of the strategic planning for future advertising. For this to be effective it needs to take place in an atmosphere of security where people regard failure as something to be learnt from, rather than just something to find a scapegoat for.

However valuable it may be to study disappointing results, the papers in this book all deal with success. Here is a collection of some of the best of what we have done over the last twelve years. But we do not intend to rest on these laurels. When the composer Darius Milhaud was asked which of his compositions was his favourite, he replied "The next one." It should be in the same spirit that we look back over these past achievements.

THE IPA ADVERTISING EFFECTIVENESS AWARDS

The Institute of Practitioners in Advertising has held its Advertising Effectiveness Awards every other year since 1980. The objectives of the scheme are to demonstrate that advertising can make a significant contribution to business success, and to encourage improved standards of evaluation. Agencies are invited to submit written papers of up to 4,000 words which are judged on how convincing a proof they offer of advertising effect, relative to the difficulties inherent in each case.

Over 120 winning case histories have now been published in the six volumes of *Advertising Works*, from which the present papers have been reprinted by the kind permission of the IPA.

1

How Advertising Helped Make Krona Brand Leader

INTRODUCTION

This case history analyses the launch of Krona margarine, a new product from Van den Berghs, into the Harlech and Westward TV areas.

The brand was sold in from 9th October 1978 and TV advertising broke on 20th October 1978. The case history covers a period of twelve months from launch in the two test areas.

Krona was launched to exploit the widening gap in price between butter and margarine and to attract butter users who were trading down. The brand succeeded beyond all expectations and by the end of the first year was established as brand leader in the launch areas with a national equivalent turnover of £32m at RSP.

Following this successful test market Krona has been extended to other areas. In all but one of these Krona is now brand leader or Number 2 brand.

Substantial problems existed in promoting Krona but these were wholly overcome by an extremely unusual advertising campaign. Very rapid trial was achieved and consumers identified advertising as their prime motivation. Subsequent research showed that the advertising had become an important element in the continuing satisfaction provided by Krona to its users.

BUSINESS BACKGROUND

The Yellow Fats Market

Krona operates within the Yellow Fats Market, which comprises butter, margarine and low fat spreads.

This is a huge market worth £600m at RSP in 1979, but it is not showing many signs of real growth. Indeed, it has declined by about one per cent since 1975.

Within this total picture there have been major shifts in the consumption of butter and margarine. A number of factors are at work here. After the war and with the ending of rationing, consumers switched back to butter in a big way, a trend which reached its peak in the 1960s (although per capita consumption never reached the prewar level). Since then the picture has gradually been reversed so that, by the end of 1979, butter and margarine shared the market equally. The trend to margarine has continued strongly in 1980.

The reasons for this are partly the major improvements in the quality of margarine, in particular the development of soft margarine in tubs, partly the development of specialist margarines and low fat spreads designed to tap concerns about health and diet but, most of all, changes in relative price.

Movements in relative price are quite clearly the dominant influence on sector shares of the Yellow Fats Market. Since a period of roughly level-pegging in the early 1970s, the rate of increase of butter prices has been significantly ahead of that of margarine. Because butter does not operate in a free market but is subject to import quotas and subsidies the precise movement of prices is difficult to predict, but all forecasts assume that a substantial premium for butter over margarine will remain.

Van den Berghs in the Market

Van den Berghs are the leading manufacturers in the market with a share well in excess of 50 per cent. They have the long established brand leader in Stork and have pioneered most of the major technical developments both in soft margarine - with Blue Band - and in opening up the specialist sectors with Flora and Outline.

With a substantial share of the market already, Van den Berghs see the best prospects for profit growth as being, therefore, the further development of the more profitable premium brands but, more importantly, increasing the size of the total sector by maximizing gains from butter.

Market Opportunity

The motivation and mechanism of the move to margarine from butter can vary. The major reason will inevitably be economy and any brand priced below butter may benefit. But there are other triggers too. The softness and ease of spreading of tub margarines are attractive to housewives who have a lot of spreading to do and in cookery too. In some families the taste of margarine becomes preferred to that of butter. The health and slimming claims of Flora and Outline obviously work on certain minority sections of butter users.

But the inescapable common element of all these examples is the fact that butter users are moving - indeed, until Krona, are forced to move - to very different products, which match neither the physical characteristics, the taste, nor the texture of butter. Now while, as explained above, this may be the precise reason for the move for some consumers, it does leave unsatisfied that large potential group of consumers who find the increasing price of butter a problem but are unwilling to sacrifice what they see as the unique qualities of butter. So as the price gap widened, a major opportunity was seen to exist for a margarine which duplicated the characteristics of butter but at a significantly lower price.

The search for a genuine butter substitute is not new. For many years Stork claimed to be indistinguishable from butter and, while arguably falling short of this in practice, was built to brand leader. More recently, Unigate launched St Ivel Gold: not strictly a margarine but a mixture of butter and vegetable oils offering a close-to-butter taste and texture. But it came in semi-soft form in a tub, did not have a generally acceptable taste and was limited to use as a spread. So there existed both a technical problem in making an acceptable product and a considerable credibility problem in persuading consumers that such a product could exist.

The margarine that raised questions in an Australian parliament.

In Sydney Australia, several years ago, an extraordinary rumour started amongst housewives.

It grew to such proportions that the New South Wales Government became involved. And it all began over something as simple as a margarine.

So successful did this margarine become, that housewives were even buying it by the caseful. People were taking it off lorries when it was delivered at supermarkets, to be certain of buying some.

All this activity led to the Minister of Agriculture being asked questions about the product in parliament.

For the rumour was that it wasn't margarine at all. Its taste was that good.

The counterpart of this Australian Margarine is on sale in Britain.

It's called Krona.

Krona press advertisement.

NEW PRODUCTS

The Background to Krona

A few years ago a Unilever Company in Australia, E.O.I., had a considerable success with a margarine called Fairy. This was a hard block margarine which bore a remarkable likeness to butter. Samples of the product were tested by Van den Berghs in the UK. In a blind product test 40 per cent of the sample thought Fairy was butter, compared with only 7 per cent for Stork. A lengthy development process then ensued to match Fairy using UK production facilities and in due course this was more than achieved. Launch date was then finally determined by a judgement on the optimum price gap between butter and margarine. The brand was launched as Krona margarine in 1978 with TV advertising breaking in October 1978. It was a block margarine in a foil wrapper initially selling at around 20p for $\frac{1}{2}$ lb, compared with the average butter price of 30p.

MARKETING AND ADVERTISING OBJECTIVES

Marketing Objectives

To increase the Company's market share in the premium sector by securing for Krona a share of at least 5 per cent.

Advertising Objectives

To encourage trial of new Krona margarine by establishing that it is the first margarine with a taste and texture indistinguishable from butter.

CREATIVE STRATEGY AND EXECUTION

Prime Target Group

Housewives currently spreading salted butter, who are being forced to trade down because of the increasing price of butter, but who do not wish to sacrifice the taste and texture of butter.

Basic Consumer Benefit

Krona margarine has a taste and texture indistinguishable from butter.

Supporting Evidence

When the counterpart of Krona was on sale in New South Wales, housewives could not believe it was margarine and a rumour that in fact it was New Zealand butter re-wrapped as margarine spread round the State. The result was the brand became brand leader within weeks.

A brief word of explanation is needed both for the strategy and the execution. Any brand with a claim and a position such as Krona faces two substantial problems in putting these across:

(a) The Margarine Regulations, which are Government regulations prohibiting any presentation of a margarine which either implicitly or explicitly compares it to, likens it to, or refers to butter. Thus there is no legal way in which Krona's benefit can be directly expressed to the consumer.
(b) There exists a legacy of distrust of claims of butter parity deriving from Stork. In addition, Stork has pre-empted a number of possible advertising routes to the extent that they are closed to Krona.

Out of a number of possible creative routes identified, a campaign was therefore developed in which a long established and well respected reporter – René Cutforth – talked about the astonishing success of the Fairy brand in Australia: how a rumour spread that it was not margarine at all and how it became an almost overnight brand leader. The counterpart of this Australian product was now on sale in the UK and called Krona margarine. No direct claim was made for Krona itself. The implication was, however, that a similar success might occur in the UK. Three commercials were produced for the launch campaign, each explaining different aspects of the 'Fairy Story'.

The campaign had been pretested in rough video form and qualitative research was also carried out on the finished commercials. This confirmed that the commercials communicated strongly that Krona would be very like butter. Respondents were certainly very willing to try the product although there was a degree of disbelief that the product would live up to its claim and therefore that Krona would be used as a butter substitute for spreading. There was also a strong, positive response to what was seen as the original 'documentary' style of the advertising.

MEDIA STRATEGY AND PLAN

Budget

The national equivalent launch budget was set at £1.5m. This figure was based on an assessment of what the brand could afford in Year 2, assuming targets were met, upweighted by 20 per cent for the launch year. Company experience on necessary weights for launching premium brands was also influential.

Target Group

The target consumers were seen primarily as housewives trading down from butter and secondly as soft margarine spreaders who still preferred the taste of butter. This definition was not of value in media selection. In fact the profile of margarine and butter users closely matches the population as a whole and demographics were expected to be less significant in selecting Krona users than attitude of mind. For the launch period the target group was therefore defined for media purposes as All Housewives.

Area Choice

Westward and Harlech (82 per cent Test Market Area) were selected for the launch of Krona for the following reasons:

1. Approximately 10 per cent of the UK would be covered – a sample judged to be large enough to assist in network forecasting, yet small enough to minimize capital investment.
2. The area was strong for butter and relatively poor for all margarine. If Krona achieved target, then it was likely to be successful elsewhere.
3. The area is strong for sweet cream (salted) as opposed to lactic (unsalted) butter.
4. St Ivel Gold had begun testing in the same region – consumer acceptance of the two new yellow fat concepts (Krona, a butter grade margarine; St Ivel Gold, a butter/margarine spread) could therefore easily be monitored.
5. The area is strong for packet margarine: it therefore provided the best opportunity to assess whether housewives would perceive Krona as a conventional packet margarine or a butter substitute.

Media Group Selection

Television was the most appropriate medium for announcing Krona. Its various advantages, in combination, were judged to outweigh the disadvantages associated with its sole use:

1. It was felt that the recommended creative approach would be less effective in any other medium.
2. High coverage of the broad target audience of all housewives could be attained (90 per cent).
3. Fast coverage could be achieved.
4. Television is intrusive: important when advertising a basic commodity.
5. Other media groups could not supply appropriate regional test market facilities (unsatisfactory coverage and/or high cost).
6. Test market discounts offered by ITV contractors are helpful.
7. Television advertising tends to be seen by the retail trade as a confident sign of marketing intention.
8. The facility to upweight advertising at short notice was a plus point.

The disadvantage associated with television is that of inadequate coverage/frequency against the light- and non-ITV housewife viewing group. Figures suggested that housewives responsible for a sizeable proportion of total butter and margarine consumption would receive a disproportionately low measure of advertising weight.

The problem was noted, but the recommendation for the solus use of television remained for the launch year. Additional media in the test area would have to be funded from the (National Equivalent) budget, and this would have meant a disproportionate reduction in weight for the preferred medium. It was proposed that a secondary medium, press, would be employed once relatively low weight ITV continuation bursts were bought in Year 2.

Rate of Strike

The theoretical budget would buy approximately 2400 TVR (45 seconds) during the launch year. High and rapid awareness of the new product amongst housewives was considered to be vital to the success of the brand.

It was therefore proposed that the ratings be deployed in short bursts rather than spread over a longer period at a much reduced rate of strike. The launch burst target was set at 1000 H/W TVRs over four weeks to minimize the coverage problems associated with light- and non-ITV viewers and achieve adequate exposure of the three launch commercials.

CAMPAIGN EVALUATION

Brand Performance

DELIVERIES

Despite two major interruptions, Krona deliveries during the first twelve months exceeded expectations and by the end of the period were running at four to five times initial levels.

The pattern was affected by two industrial disputes, the lorry drivers' strike (2nd January to 5th February 1979) and a dispute at Van den Berghs' Bromborough factory. The former sharply reduced deliveries in cycles 1 and 2 1979 while the latter meant that there were no deliveries of Krona (or of other of Van den Berghs' brands) between the beginning of April and the beginning of May 1979.

The resumption of deliveries after the strike was not uniform across all Van den Berghs' brands and Krona received priority. This, to a degree, explains a peak in deliveries in cycles 12 and 13 1979. However, this was not, as might have been expected, a temporary pheno- menon and Krona sales were established at a new high level up to cycle 20.

Overall, the figures show a pipe-line filling phase at the end of 1978, a confused period in the first quarter of 1979, a further pipe-line filling phase in cycle 11 but then evidence of very substantial sales when normal deliveries could be resumed.

DISTRIBUTION

Figures are available only for sterling weighted distribution in the two areas combined, in Multiples and Co-ops only (Table 1.1).

Very strong distribution was thus achieved within two or three months and growth in distribution cannot fully explain the growth in deliveries.

TABLE 1.1: KRONA STERLING DISTRIBUTION, HARLECH AND WESTWARD

October/November 1978	78%
December 1978/January 1979	95%
February/March	95%
April/May	89%
June/July	95%
August/September	86%
October/November	93%

Stats MR.

CONSUMER SALES/SHARE

Within three TCA periods, Krona had achieved a 10 per cent share, making it Number 2 brand in the market (Table 1.2).

TABLE 1.2: KRONA VOLUME BRAND SHARE

1978						4 w/e:		1979				
14/10	11/11	9/12	6/1	3/2	3/3	31/3	28/4	26/5	23/6	21/7	18/8	15/9
–	5	10	9	5	8	12	5	3	14	15	18	16

TCA.

This was a time of rapid sampling. Cumulative penetration had reached 24 per cent by November (see below).

There was a temporary set-back as a result of the lorry drivers strike but share recovered strongly by March, only to be hit again by the Van den Berghs strike. As explained earlier, Krona benefited by a shortage of other Van den Berghs brands in June, but, far from falling back when normal supplies were resumed, it actually made large volume gains in subsequent periods. By the end of the first twelve months, Krona was brand leader, with around twice the share of the next brand.

The Consumer

AWARENESS

The first post-check showed that awareness after only five weeks of advertising had already reached a high level and this was then maintained in subsequent months despite the interruptions in supply caused by strikes early in 1979. Considering the very substantial brand shares achieved, the level of spontaneous awareness could seem on the low side. However, viewed in the context of the lowish figures for long established brands such as Stork and Blue Band, Krona's achievement may be judged satisfactory. Certainly prompted awareness was at a very high level for a new brand (Table 1.3).

TABLE 1.3: KRONA AWARENESS (SPONTANEOUS/PROMPTED)

November	February	July/August
20/79	22/86	25/80

Quick Read

TRIAL

To be tried by one quarter of all housewives within little more than a month was obviously an exceptional achievement and the brand continued to gain trial in the succeeding months (Table 1.4).

TABLE 1.4: KRONA TRIAL (% BOUGHT IN LAST SIX MONTHS)

November	February	July/August
24%	38%	43%

Quick Read.

Obviously, the advertising cannot take sole credit for initial trial. A door-to-door coupon was dropped during October and there were a number of in-store demonstrations. By the end of 1978, distribution in Multiples and Co-ops exceeded 90 per cent sterling. However, there is good evidence that advertising played a major role:

INFLUENCES ON FIRST PURCHASE

The November Quick Read Survey showed:

Coupon received or not
No. of respondents aware of Krona:	248
Yes	47%
No	50%
Don't know, etc.	3%

Whether coupon first encouraged trial
No. of respondents	44
Yes	34%
No	66%
Don't know, etc.	–

Awareness of Krona TV advertising
No. of respondents aware of Krona:	248
Yes	91%
No	7%
Don't know, etc.	2%

A separate survey was carried out at the end of November 1978 among Krona buyers in the two areas:

Source of awareness of Krona
No. ever bought	186
TV advertising	66%
Leaflet/Coupon	13%
Friend told me	13%
In-Store	11%

Seen Krona advertised on TV
No. not mentioning TV above	63
Yes	68%
No	17%
Don't know	14%

Combined with those mentioning TV previously this gives a total of 89 per cent who claimed to have seen Krona advertising on TV, while only a small percentage related their awareness of Krona to the coupon.

Similar information was sought in the March/April Taylor Nelson Survey. This showed that among trialists a majority of both acceptors (59 per cent) and rejectors (63 per cent) gave TV advertising as the main reason for trying Krona in the first place. Obviously, by this time, some while had elapsed since the coupon drop, while there had been a substantial weight of TV advertising, but at the very least it demonstrates the importance advertising was seen to have as a source of information on the brand.

This information should be seen against the context of the general reluctance of consumers to admit advertising as an influence on their behaviour.

REPEAT PURCHASE

The Quick Read Monitors show a steady increase in the numbers of housewives intending to purchase Krona next time (17 per cent of respondents by July/August). By July/August, more than two thirds of buyers had bought more than one pack. Obviously the recruitment rate of new users shows a sharp drop over the period of the surveys, although sampling was still going on. As long after the launch as July/August 1979, over one third of housewives who had ever bought Krona had bought Krona as their last purchase. The November 1978 Krona Buyers' Survey confirmed that, within not much more than a month, 50 to 60 per cent of buyers had bought more than one pack.

The March Taylor Nelson Survey showed that 50 per cent of buyers said that they would definitely buy again and a further 29 per cent would probably buy again. Outright rejection was at a minimal level. Over two thirds of buyers had at that point bought more than one pack.

PRODUCT POSITIONING

The aim of Krona advertising was to present the brand as a high quality spreading margarine, indistinguishable from butter. Was this being borne out in practice in the market-place?

The November 1978 Buyers' Survey indicated that even in the earliest stage of the brand's life, when sampling was at its peak, around half of current Krona buyers felt they had stopped buying other brands or cut down on them. In each case the largest single source of Krona business was butter.

The March 1979 Taylor Nelson Study confirmed this picture, around half acceptors and a quarter of rejectors who had substituted Krona for another product having switched from butter.

Switching from other margarine brands at this point did not show any clear pattern, but certainly there was no demonstrable association of Krona with cheap packet cooking margarine.

HOW THE ADVERTISING WORKS

The brand, then, in its first twelve months in the two areas was clearly highly successful in sales and share terms. A high level of trial had been achieved in a short period and the brand had largely been received by consumers in the way intended. It had lived up to or exceeded expectation for a substantial body of consumers and good levels of repeat purchase were achieved.

Advertising had been identified by consumers as the primary influence on their initial purchase and this is confirmed by the most sensible interpretation of the sales and attitude data discussed.

A fair amount of evidence exists to explain how the Krona launch campaign works.

Sources

We derive our understanding of how the advertising works, as opposed to the influences it has on purchasing behaviour, from several sources:

(a) The various quantitative surveys already quoted.
(b) Qualitative research into the finished commercials prior to transmission and two qualitative studies carried out to assist creative development.

Communication

Our analysis can be divided into two sections: communication and persuasion.

We know from a lot of past research that the concept of a margarine identical to butter (and at a lower price) is highly appealing.

The problem, as we discussed earlier, is to overcome the hurdles provided by restrictive regulation and credibility and communicate the concept effectively and persuasively.

It is clear from the evidence that the communication was understood. In the qualitative studies the main message was seen as:

'It's as good as butter'
'Closer to butter than other margarines'
'Tastes more like butter'
'Alternative to butter'
'Implying it was as good as butter'

The March Taylor Nelson Study showed that over half of acceptors and 42 per cent of rejectors expected either a new brand of butter or something similar.

Persuasion

In terms of persuasion, we have the evidence of image statements from the various Quick Read Studies. These show that:

(a) Despite the legacy of incredibility and the current status of packet margarines, communication *and* persuasion that Krona was a high quality margarine with a butter-like taste was well achieved.
(b) Levels of agreement were high, even in November 1978 *when a substantial majority had only the evidence of the advertising to go on.*

Not surprisingly, acceptance or otherwise of this message became a touchstone of trial of Krona and subsequent repurchase, and in research carried out after the launch there is a substantial division on this issue between acceptors and rejectors.

The advertising had clearly established the pretensions of Krona. It was up to the brand itself to live up to the claims or not.

How was persuasion achieved to the point of trial? The following interpretation is a distillation of the findings of the various qualitative studies mentioned earlier:

STYLE AND TONE

The novel 'documentary' style of the commercials was liked because:

(i) It was different from other, particularly margarine, advertisements.
(ii) The tone was 'telling not selling'. It left the choice to the consumer; it treated her as an adult; it did not talk down to her. The personality of René Cutforth was important here.
(iii) The tone was serious and gave stature to the product.

All combined strongly to enhance credibility.

LOCATION

The Australian context worked in a number of ways:

(i) It was interesting and different.
(ii) It took Krona out of the conventional margarine context.
(iii) It had definite 'dairy' connotations.
(iv) It was related to the UK, though not part of it.
(v) It was a desirable place to be – redolent not so much of affluence, but of a good, healthy, open-air life.

Trial and Repeat Purchase

Finally, the evidence suggested that the campaign was trial *and* repeat purchase orientated. While for some people it clearly on its own could not overcome rooted scepticism about margarine claims, for the majority it provided a strong inducement to try. Once people had tried and accepted the product, the advertising was seen as a confirmation of their experience. They too had made this discovery. They too could not believe it was a margarine. What had happened in Australia was only to be expected. In addition, the intelligent tone of the commercials complimented them as consumers and confirmed the good sense of their choice of Krona. It is quite reasonable on the evidence, then, to claim that the Krona advertising, far from simply conveying a highly desirable message, has by its distinctive character become an essential part of the brand's character and therefore a crucial element in the success of this very major grocery brand.

CONCLUSION

That Krona represented a major marketing success in Harlech and Westward over the period under review is amply demonstrated by the facts. Nor was it a temporary phenomenon. Krona is achieving similar results in other areas as it is extended and has more than maintained its dominance in its original test areas.

We say 'marketing success' deliberately because, as we all know, the successful launch of a new product depends on many related factors. In the case of Krona these were:

1. TIMING

The increasing price premium of butter over margarine provided the opportunity for a brand aimed at people forced to trade down.

2. PRODUCT QUALITY

Krona was the first margarine successfully to simulate butter. It exceeds expectations and arouses almost a religious fervour among converts.

3. NAMING AND PACKAGING

The presentation of the brand communicates the required positioning and reinforces the belief of users that Krona is closer to butter than margarine.

4. PRICING

While Krona is clearly a premium-priced margarine, it is sufficiently cheaper than butter to make the incentive to switch as strong as possible.

5. MARKETING INVESTMENT

Van den Berghs recognized the potential of the brand and were prepared to spend heavily behind it, above and below the line, in its first year. Significantly, the bulk of this money was spent on the consumer in order to encourage the critically important first purchase and not to reduce price at point-of-sale.

6. ADVERTISING

Because of these factors it would be easy to argue that almost any advertising would have worked for Krona. This is not the case, for these reasons:

1. The problem in persuading housewives to accept Krona was formidable. Conventionally, packet margarines were cheap cooking media. Yet here was a premium-priced brand. Previous claims of butter-parity had proved to be excessive. Yet here was a brand ringing the same bell again. Regulations forbade explicit or implicit comparisons with butter, yet here was a brand whose whole raison d'être was that it was indistinguishable from butter.

    Krona achieved not only very rapid and high awareness, which could be put down to the substantial TV expenditure, but rapid trial too.

    While hard evidence of precise cause and effect is unavailable and indeed unattainable to apportion credit between advertising, coupon drop and POS, the view of housewives expressed repeatedly in quantitative and qualitative studies puts advertising as the major influence.

2. Krona's role is to be a cheap substitute for butter. Knowing the strong emotional aura surrounding butter, this role is one which legitimately might be expected to reach the housewife's pocket, but not her heart. In fact there is growing evidence that Krona is on the way to becoming a 'religion' for its users. There is a sense of a 'miracle', that the housewife has made 'a discovery' which she wants to pass on to others.

There is no doubt that the advertising, with its serious and intelligent tone and the story which it tells, is contributing importantly to this.

APPENDIX: DATA USED IN KRONA ADVERTISING EVALUATION

Sales

1. Van den Bergh delivery figures
2. TCA
3. Stats MR Distribution Check: Multiples and Co-ops

Consumer

QUICK READ MONITORS

A series of quantitative studies based on the Quick Reading method developed by Unilever Marketing Division was carried out.

Research was among margarine users (who form around 80 per cent of the population) in Harlech and Westward, quota-ed by age and class.

KRONA BUYERS' SURVEY

187 housewives who had ever bought Krona were interviewed in-home in Harlech (95) and Westward (92). Interviewing was conducted between 27th November and 1st December 1978.

KRONA MARKET MONITOR: HARLECH AND WESTWARD (TAYLOR NELSON & ASSOCIATES) MARCH/ APRIL 1979

Main Objectives:

1. Evaluate Krona's success in terms of awareness and penetration.
2. Investigate Krona's future in terms of likelihood of repurchase or trial (non-users).
3. Evaluate effects of experience on perceived product acceptability and positioning.

Method:

Area: Harlech and Westward TV areas.
Sample: Based on contact interviews with a quota sample of 945 housewives, three subsamples were identified, who were taken through an extended interview:

(a) Respondents who had bought Krona and would definitely or probably buy again in the future (acceptors).
(b) Respondents who had bought Krona but did not know or were unlikely to buy again in the future (rejectors).
(c) Respondents who were aware of Krona and had seen a pack in-store (aware non-buyers).

QUALITATIVE RESEARCH: QUICKSEARCH 1979

30 individual interviews: 15 trialists who either had Krona at home at the time of interview or would have had it if it were available. 15 non-trialists. All aware of Krona advertising with a spread by weight of ITV viewing.

Objectives:

(a) To evaluate response to the launch campaign after four months' exposure.
(b) To elicit response to a possible follow-up campaign.

QUALITATIVE RESEARCH: GREGORY LANGMAID ASSOCIATES (MARCH 1979)

This research consisted of four groups and 16 depth interviews in Swansea and Bristol. All respondents were from the BC1C2 social grades, aged between 20 and 55.

Half were users (bought twice or more) of Krona, half were non-users and non-rejectors of the brand. These latter were women who had heard of Krona but who had not bought or tried it.

Objectives:

(a) To examine attitudes to Krona in the test market area among users and non-users as a background to exploring the acceptability and comprehension of two new Krona commercials in terms of their effects on users and non-users.
(b) To examine the continuity of the new films leading on from the earlier Australian films.
(c) To probe the suitability and effectiveness of René Cutforth as a presenter.

2
The Launch of Miller Lite

INTRODUCTION

There have been beer prizewinners in three of the previous four IPA Advertising Effectiveness Competitions. On each occasion advertising has been shown to have had a positive and profitable effect on sales. However, all three previous winners have concentrated on the draught beer market and as far as we are aware no one has yet 'proved' advertising effectiveness in the highly competitive and overcrowded canned-beer market.

In this paper we seek to demonstrate the effectiveness of Miller Lite advertising in the launch of the lager in *both* the draught and canned form.

BUSINESS BACKGROUND

Lager Market

The lager market is the most dynamic sector of the British beer market. Over the past ten years it has consistently outgrown a static total beer market and now accounts for 45 per cent of all beer sales. It is even more important to the brewers than its volume share would suggest because it has a higher margin per barrel than ales.

Within the lager market there are several industry-defined sectors which contain brands of similar alcoholic strength. By and large this division into sectors is

TABLE 1: LAGER MARKET SUB-SECTORS

Alcoholic strength	Draught	Canned
1060° o.g. +	—	Super strength
1040°–1050° o.g.	Premium strength	Premium strength
1030°–1040° o.g.	Standard strength	Standard strength
Very low or zero	Low/no alcohol	Low/no alcohol

o.g. = original gravity.

acknowledged by the consumer and represents a framework from which brand selection is made.

Historically the standard sector has dominated the market, and continues to do so. Not only does it represent approximately 75 per cent of all lager sales but it also contains the majority of the most famous brands — Heineken, Carling Black Label, Hofmeister, Harp, Carlsberg Pilsner, Skol, Foster's and Castlemaine XXXX.

Position of Courage

Throughout the 1970s and early 1980s Courage as a brewer had been reactive to market changes rather than proactive. Only in 1977 when the lager market was already well established did Courage launch their own major standard lager in the shape of Hofmeister.

By 1985, when the majority of the other large brewers had already launched a second standard lager, Courage were battling on with Hofmeister, their lead brand, and a series of regionally available alternatives. As a consequence Courage sales were biased towards the less profitable and declining ales sector, particularly so in the canned market (see Tables 2 and 3).

TABLE 2:   COURAGE DRAUGHT 'MIX' VERSUS
MARKET

	Courage %	Market %
Draught ales	63	61
Draught lagers	35	39

Source: Stats MR, 1985—86, England and Wales

TABLE 3:   COURAGE CANNED 'MIX' VERSUS
MARKET

	Courage %	Market %
Canned ales	51	34
Canned lagers	49	66

Source: Stats MR, 1985—86, England and Wales

Clearly then Courage needed to launch a new lager alongside Hofmeister which would contribute to a gain in share for the company in the standard lager market, particularly in the canned sector.

WHY LAUNCH MILLER LITE?

Miller Lite is an unusual lager. It is brewed using a special process which means that a higher percentage of sugars than is the case for 'normal' standard lager are converted to alcohol. This results in a lager that is 10 per cent lower in calories and is less dense than any other standard lager. Yet it has the same alcoholic content as other standard lagers. Why should Courage want to launch such a brew?

Pros

The standard lager market is overcrowded. This is less obvious in the draught sector because a large proportion of the distribution channels (the 'tied' outlets representing over 50 per cent of draught lager sales) are controlled to some extent by the brewers.

On the other hand, the bulk of canned lager is sold in off-licences, and increasingly in supermarkets and grocers. In stark contrast to the draught market, as many as 16 standard canned brands may be stacked up next to each other in the same shop. In addition own-label and a whole new sector of 'cheapie' brands (Skona, Norseman etc.), which are unavailable on draught, has developed. They compete solely on price and are not supported with advertising. This has resulted in a very tight squeeze on margins. Even the largest, most well-known brands are unable to raise prices in line with the rises they achieve in the draught sector.

The average price of a 16-oz can for the five best-selling brands of lager fell from 62.1p in April–May 1986 to 62p in April–May 1987. But for the five biggest-selling standard brands of draught beers, the average price rose from 87p a pint in April–May 1986 to 91.6p in April–May 1987 (source: Stats MR).

There would be little point therefore in launching a new canned standard lager that represented a 'me-17th'! Why would retailers stock it? And why would consumers buy it if it were stocked?

Miller Lite's unique product qualities appeared to provide an opportunity to provide real differentiation in this market; and, if this difference could be positioned as a desirable benefit, to offer a valid reason for retailers to stock and consumers to purchase, and perhaps at a premium price!

... And Cons

To say that Miller Lite possessed some potential weaknesses is to underestimate the difficulties that developing the product into a potentially successful brand represented.

Unfortunately, lagers with 'lite' in their brand names had been launched in the UK before, and had all failed, as is illustrated by Table 4.

TABLE 4:   PREVIOUS 'LITE' LAGER LAUNCHES

Hemeling Lite	Launched 1977, repositioned as Hemeling, now very small volume.
Arctic Lite	Launched 1978, now withdrawn except in bottles and cans.
Carlsen Lite	Launched 1979, now only available in packaged form.
Heldenbrau	Launched 1979, draught now withdrawn, can repositioned as very cheap standard.
Kalback	Launched 1980, now only available in bottles.

Each of these brands had originally been positioned as low in calories or carbo-hydrates and they had failed for three reasons.

First of all, lager drinkers in the late 1970s had rejected the idea of an overtly 'healthy' lager. The male-dominated atmosphere of the pub ensured that even those who might secretly have found the proposition motivating were unwilling to be *seen* with such a product. 'Liteness' implied 'reduced' in some way and given that at the time one's pint was perceived as almost an extension of one's manhood, 'reduced' pints tended to be avoided!

Secondly, 'liteness' also conveyed 'weakness'. If something had been removed then alcohol was a strong contender and few drinkers were prepared to be seen with a reduced alcohol lager.

Thirdly, no attempt was made to provide any of the brands with a 'heritage'. The 'lite' lagers all lacked origins — where did Arctic Lite come from? — and history — for how many years had Hemeling Lite been brewed? Qualitative research revealed this to be a signficant weakness. The bulk of drinkers were found to require some kind of evidence of a brand's 'credentials', and a lager that drinkers thought had been invented last year in a laboratory was at a considerable disadvantage.

Hence, if we were now intending to make 'liteness' a positive characteristic we had both to undo the work of the previous 'lites' and redefine what Miller's new 1986 'liteness' meant.

As if redefining 'liteness' were not enough, we also had to contend with Miller Lite's American origins. America is a complex image for British lager drinkers to assimilate. In particular we found that the concept of American lager had a negative connotation that was likely to prove a very major concern. Qualitative research revealed that drinkers believed Americans drank weaker beer than the English, and hence that an American lager would necessarily be weak — American lite lager was only one stage removed from water. However, if Miller Lite was to be successful, then we believed it needed a heritage, which meant communicating its American origins, and countering the inevitable weak imagery that this would stimulate.

DEVELOPING THE BRAND

Qualitative research was conducted to develop a positive expression of 'lite'. During this research it was discovered that drinkers were generally less satisfied with the quality of canned lagers than with the draught equivalent.

In a sample of 1700 male lager drinkers (RBL U & A) it was found that 76 per cent agreed with the statement: 'Most lagers taste better on draught than in cans', with only 15 per cent disagreeing. The concern was centred around the claimed 'tinny' flavour and the perceived gassiness of canned lager. The 76 per cent who preferred draught lager were asked whether it was less gassy, and 68 per cent agreed that it was. The remaining 32 per cent disagreed.

Interestingly for us, Miller Lite's unique product qualities seemed to offer a solution to this last point. Combined with the word 'lite', Miller Lite's product delivery enabled us to imply that the product was less gassy than usual. We had to be cautious however because an overtly 'less gassy' claim would reinforce the 'reduced' thoughts that lite already conjured up. The most positive way to express the 'less gassy' benefit was found to be to combine the concept of lite with the words 'smoother' and 'easier to drink', and to avoid saying 'less gassy' directly.

It was also decided that even though American pedigree was thought likely to lessen perceived alcoholic strength, it was vital to provide a heritage and a belief that Miller was a genuine brewer rather than an invented one.

Hence we finally arrived at the following positioning:

'Miller Lite is a genuine standard strength lager from America which is smoother and easier to drink.'

In this way we hoped that liteness might become a positive benefit rather than the 'reduced' apology that it currently was.

MARKETING OBJECTIVES

In the light of the brand's likely consumer appeal the marketing objectives set for the first year of launch were as follows:

Canned format
1. To gain 65 per cent sterling distribution.
2. To reach approximately 5 per cent of the standard lager sector (excluding cheapies) by end of year one.
3. To do so while maintaining a price as high as any other canned standard lager.
4. To avoid causing delisting of Hofmeister and Harp (which Courage were still selling in canned form at the time).

Draught format
1. To grow Courage's total draught standard lager share.
2. To achieve sales approximately equal to $\frac{1}{3}$ of Hofmeister's current sales (weighted for distribution), a subtstantial proportion of which should be incremental for Courage rather than substitutional.

DEVELOPING THE ADVERTISING

Role for Advertising

Advertising had two roles to play:

1. To create very high levels of awareness for the brand.
2. To develop a distinctive brand identity and in particular to define consumer perceptions of Miller's 'liteness'.

Target Audience

In a sense the choice of target audience was out of our hands! The bulk of standard lager is drunk by 18−24-year-old, C1C2, males. They also represent the future of the market and hence seem to be the main target audience for all standard lagers. If Miller Lite was to be a large profitable brand we had to attract these young heavy drinkers.

However, having said that, qualitative research had revealed that Miller Lite's promise was more likely to attract a certain type of young male drinker. Our core target audience was likely to be slightly more interested in personal appearance − whether clothes, hair or physique. Hence it was important that the advertising recognised this while not alienating the remainder of young drinkers.

To summarise, the target audience was 18−24-year-old, C1C2, male standard lager drinkers, particularly those more interested in personal appearance.

Developing Creative Executions

In developing advertising we had both to develop an appealing identity for the brand, and also to communicate more rational product qualities. To do so TV seemed essential. Two 40-second TV commercials were developed by BMP, both of which employed a technique which cleverly enabled us to communicate product detail and to reinforce it through displaying an appropriate and appealing image for the brand and its potential drinkers. The ads were based on showing the differences between a dull, 'heavy' world populated by people who drank products other than Miller Lite, and a bright, 'lite' world where everyone drank Miller Lite. In this way we were able to suggest that Miller Lite drinkers were regular lager drinkers but smarter, sharper and more fashionable, and that they tended to look livelier and perhaps at least aspire to being fitter. Comparison with the stodgy, slow-moving, grey inhabitants of the grey world heightened this communication.

Use of the words 'It has a cleaner taste because most of the sugar's been turned to alcohol and goes down smooth' in the voice-over was intended to communicate Miller's definition of 'liteness', while reinforcing its standard strength positioning.

The American origins of the product were reinforced in the voice-over and in the use of sound-track music based on music taken from the American Blues Brothers movie. The endline 'It ain't heavy, it's Miller Lite' was intended both to summarise the executions and their communication, and to become a permanent branding device used across all future promotional and advertising material.

Testing of a final animatic qualitatively, and quantitatively in hall tests, led us to believe that we had produced an advertising vehicle that would succeed in communicating the required brand identity and product differences, while also gaining empathy and generating appeal for the brand. In the hall tests three matched samples of male lager drinkers were exposed to a variety of stimuli. Cell 1 were given a can of Miller Lite. Cell 2 were given a can of Miller Lite and were shown the animatic. Cell 3 were given a can of Heineken and were shown a Heineken commercial. Although the absolute numbers in the results are difficult to interpret, the differences between cells confirmed our qualitative findings that the animatic, and hence probably the finished films, were likely to succeed in meeting the objectives set for it. The results are summarised in Tables 5−7.

TABLE 5: COMPARISON WITH USUAL LAGER

(1 = much worse, 5 = much better)

Miller Lite (*Can, no animatic*)	Miller Lite (*Can and animatic*)	Heineken (*Can and commercial*)
2.83	2.95	2.88

Source: Millward Brown Hall Test
Base: 3 x 150 male lager drinkers

TABLE 6: 'FOR PEOPLE LIKE ME'

Miller Lite (*Can, no animatic*) % agreeing	Miller Lite (*Can and animatic*) % agreeing
29	42

Source: Millward Brown Hall Test
Base: 2 x 150 male lager drinkers

TABLE 7: COMMUNICATION

	Miller Lite (*Can, no animatic*) % agreeing	Miller Lite (*Can and animatic*) % agreeing
Strong in alcohol	40	46
Weak in alcohol	45	30
Strong in taste	40	45
Weak in taste	45	38
Not filling or bloating	53	57
Rather gassy	44	39

Source: Millward Brown Hall Test
Base: 2 x 150 male lager drinkers

In addition to the two TV commercials a series of outdoor and bus-side posters were developed to the theme of 'It ain't heavy, it's Miller Lite'. Tactical use of poster sites was exploited whenever possible to add originality and a further degree of novelty to the campaign. Finally, the sound-track to the TV commercial was also developed into radio commercials to be used where feasible.

LAUNCH ACTIVITY

Advertising

The brand was launched on draught and in 16 oz cans in March 1986. The advertising and promotional support are described here.

The launch was conducted on a 'rolling' basis, gradually extending across the

Courage trading regions. By March 1987 the brand was available throughout England and Wales. Although the Courage trading regions do not match TV regions exactly, they are approximately similar, hence it was possible to support the roll-out with TV advertising in the appropriate TV regions. On each occasion a similar TV advertising schedule was deployed. A relatively heavy 'announcement' burst was shown during the first four weeks, followed by a second burst four weeks later. Approximately five weeks after that a longer 'maintenance' burst was shown lasting for up to six weeks. A follow-up burst was then shown approximately six months after launch.

Anglia region did not, however, receive any TV coverage because negotations failed to produce an acceptable cost. In its place a low-cost cinema campaign (using the TV commercials) was aired. Where there was local availability, and acceptable cost-effectiveness, radio, posters and bus-sides were used in addition to the TV campaign. In all areas outside Anglia, TV received over 85 per cent of the budget.

Promotions

In addition to the various forms of advertising a series of promotions was arranged for both the draught and canned formats. In pubs, a Miller Lite evening was arranged in each area when a further free pint was given away with purchase of the first, in order to encourage trial. At the same time a proportion of the cans, during launch into each area, carried a voucher entitling the holder to 60p off the next purchase of a four-pack.

LESSONS LEARNT AS THE BRAND ROLLED OUT

The staggered nature of the launch presented us with an opportunity to improve any aspect of the launch package that was found to be operating ineffectively. Feedback from qualitative and quantitative post-testing revealed the following two findings, which were subsequently acted upon:

1. The positive response to the TV advertising so outweighed response to posters and radio that it was decided to drop them in favour of more TV in the remainder of the country.
2. Its American origins were found to be having a far more damaging effect on the brand's perceived alcoholic strength than expected. (See 'How the Advertising Worked', p. 36.) It was decided therefore to delete the words 'from America' from all future TV advertising after the second burst in London. We hoped that this would allow the standard strength communication to have more effect, and this later proved to be so. A verbal reference to the brand's American origins was never made in advertising outside London.

First Year TV Commercial No. 2

MUSIC...MVO: There's a
new beer around

that's so light, everything
else seems just --

3 MEN: Heavee!

MVO: It's called Miller
Lite.

The new pilsner from America.
It has a cleaner taste,

because most of che sugar's
been turned to alcohol, and

goes down so smooth, anything
else seems just 3 MEN: Heavee!

CHORUS : The taste is clean,
it's Miller Lite. It goes
down clean, it's

Miller Lite. It's my baby,
Miller Lite.

in't

heavy,

it's Miller Lite.

RESULTS

To present data in a relatively simple fashion the various TV areas' data have been aggregated into the following four regions, and performance discussed over the launch year in each region:

> Region A : London, launched in March 1986;
> Region B : HTV, TSW and TVS, launched in October 1986;
> Region C : Central, Granada, Yorkshire and Tyne Tees,
>   launched in March 1987;
> Region D : Anglia, launched in March 1987 with no TV
>   support.

Canned Results

In all regions where the brand was supported with TV advertising, by the end of the first year sales share exceeded expectations, as can be seen in Table 8 (and Figures 1, 2, 3 and 4).

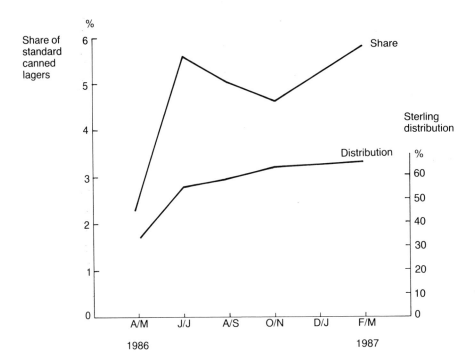

Figure 1. *Region A*
Source: Stats MR

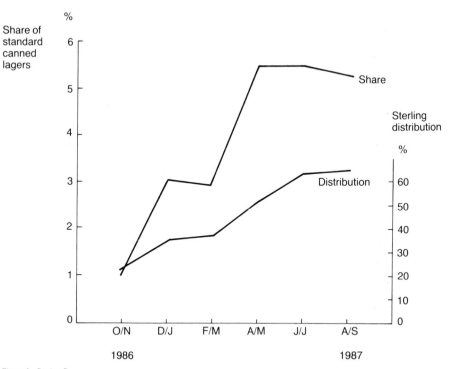

Figure 2. *Region B*
Source: Stats MR

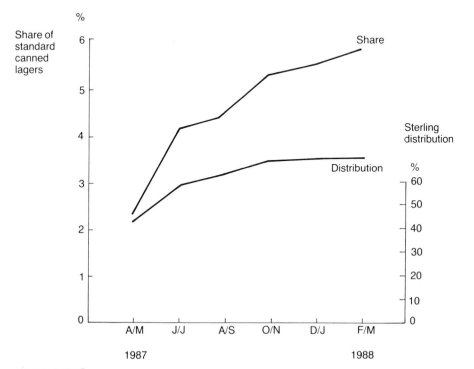

Figure 3. *Region C*
Source: Stats MR

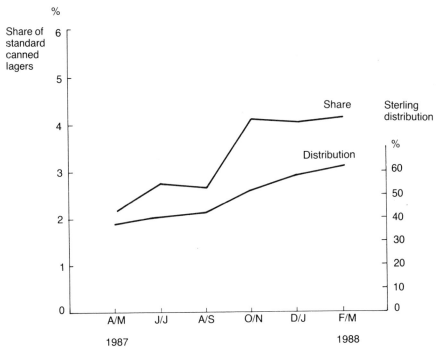

Figure 4. *Region D*
Source: Stats MR

TABLE 8:   MILLER LITE SHARE OF STANDARD CANNED LAGERS
ONE YEAR AFTER LAUNCH IN EACH REGION

Region	%
A	5.8
B	5.3
C	5.8
D	4.1

Source: Stats MR

Overall, canned Miller Lite sales during the first year of launch totalled approximately 55 000 bulk barrels (bbs), representing sales of over £8.5 million. Considering that Hofmeister, Courage's lead standard brand since 1977, which has continually received heavy advertising support, achieved canned sales of less than £9 million in 1987, Miller Lite's first-year performance was outstanding.

In terms of distribution the objectives set for the brand were again met in every region except Anglia, as can be seen in Figures 1 to 4.

The difficulty of achieving such high distribution figures should not be underestimated – Hofmeister has not achieved 50 per cent distribution in England and Wales since 1985! Achieving 65 per cent in TV advertised regions within one year of launch, compared with 48 per cent in Anglia, suggests that Miller Lite's advertising was as potent as expected. We investigate this in detail later.

First Year Poster No. 1

Not only did canned Miller Lite achieve its sales and distribution targets (in advertised areas) but it did so while maintaining a price premium over the other canned standards, as can be seen in Table 9.

TABLE 9: AVERAGE RETAIL PRICE OF 16 OZ
STANDARD LAGER CANS

Standard brands	
Miller Lite	54.4p
Heineken	53.3p
Carlsberg Pilsner	52.3p
Carling Black Label	51.7p
Skol	51.1p
Tennents Pilsner	48.9p
Hofmeister	47.4p
Harp	46.4p
Kestrel	43.3p
Standard 'cheapie' brands	
Heldenbrau	42.0p
Top Brass	37.3p
Royal Dutch	36.9p
Own-label Brands	34.8p
Skona	33.3p
Norseman	32.7p

Source: Stats MR. April 1986–March 1988

Having said that, it should be noted that the data in Table 9 does not take account of promotional offers, and unfortunately data detailing the 'real' price paid for each can of each lager is not available. However, we believe that Miller Lite was not subject to more promotional activity than the other brands on the market over this period. This is supported by the fact that Miller Lite share was buoyant even at times when no promotional cans were available. Hence we conclude that Miller Lite did achieve its objectives while maintaining a premium price — at least in advertised regions.

One might wonder whether Miller Lite's success in cans was having a damaging effect on Courage's other standard lagers. Encouragingly, Hofmeister's share actually increased over this period. Harp on the other hand, which at the time was also handled in canned form by the Courage sales force, did suffer some decline in share over the period of Miller Lite's launch, falling from 12.7 per cent in April 1986 to 10.7 per cent in January 1988 (Stats MR). Over this period, however, its distribution fell by only 3 per cent and hence we can conclude that the bulk of the sales decline was due to falls in consumer rate of purchase, and not delistings at the expense of Miller Lite.

Draught Results

In general, Miller Lite's sales in draught form exceeded expectation, but the situation is muddied by the fact that Courage were purchased by Elders IXL during 1987, and that in August 1987 Foster's was launched into all Courage outlets supported by heavy advertising spends. As a consequence both Miller Lite and Hofmeister sales inevitably suffered. Unfortunately the first-year launch period for Miller Lite in two of the regions (C and D) covers this unexpected occurrence. Therefore, in attempting to show the draught results of the Miller Lite launch it has only been possible to analyse a full year's data in detail in regions A and B.

In regions A and B, which account for over 43 per cent of all draught lager sales in the UK, it is clear that Miller Lite's introduction did result in a substantial increase in Courage's share of the draught standard market (see Table 10).

TABLE 10:   COURAGE SHARE OF DRAUGHT STANDARD LAGER

Region	12 Months pre-launch	12 Months post-launch
A	13.3% *	14.6%
B	13.8%	14.3%

Source: Stats MR.
* only 6 months' data available

In this market a 1 per cent share is equivalent to sales of approximately £25 million p.a. Hence although the gains suggested by Table 10 may look relatively small, they actually represent very large increases in sales revenue.

The second marketing objective for draught Miller Lite was to achieve a sales target equal to one-third of Hofmeister current sales when weighted for distribution. This was almost reached in all TV-advertised regions (see Table 11).

TABLE 11: HOFMEISTER AND MILLER LITE SALES

Region	Annual sales of Hofmeister in year before Miller Lite's launch* (bulk barrels)	First-year Miller Lite sales	
A	88 000	28 000	32%
B	95 000	36 000	38%
C	135 000	61 000	45%
D	4 000	1 000	25%

* This excludes outlets where Miller Lite was not introduced

Region A, London, was the weakest performer of the TV-advertised areas. It is plausible that the inclusion of 'from America' in the TV commercials may have caused some of this underperformance. In addition London received slightly fewer TVRs than other advertised areas.

So, in TV-advertised regions, Miller Lite exceeded its sales targets and Courage's share of the market increased. At the same time Hofmeister's volume remained flat in most areas and fell slightly in others, indicating that Miller Lite was the brand responsible for Courage's share growth.

Year Two Performance

At the time of writing Miller Lite has been available in London for almost exactly two years; in HTV, TSW and TVS for 18 months; and in the remainder of England and Wales for one year. Analysis of its year two performance is largely confined therefore to its performance in London.

In the canned sector the brand has gone from strength to strength. Share has continued to grow and Miller Lite now accounts for between 6.5 per cent and 7 per cent of the standard market. Retailers continue to stock the brand and distribution is now at 77 per cent, making Miller Lite the third most available standard canned brand in London − a substantial achievement for a late entrant into a crowded market (see Figure 5).

In terms of draught performance Miller Lite has been less successful in London in its second year. However, this would appear to be primarily due to the appearance of Foster's in the Courage portfolio. Foster's is generally regarded as one of the most desirable brands in the market and it is not surprising that Miller Lite's sales have been held in check. Whereas Miller Lite represented approximately 15 per cent of Courage's draught standard sales in its first year in London, it now accounts for approximately 10 per cent of their sales since the introduction of Foster's.

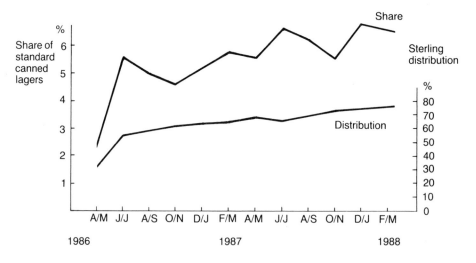

Figure 5. *London*

HOW THE ADVERTISING WORKED

Why Consumers Choose to Buy

There is little doubt that Miller Lite's advertising, particularly the TV advertising, succeeded in generating high levels of awareness for the brand. Levels of spontaneous advertising awareness were quickly as high as for any established lager brands in all TV areas where data was available (see Table 12).

TABLE 12:   SPONTANEOUS ADVERTISING AWARENESS

	Miller Lite %	Foster's %	Carling Black Label %	Castlemaine XXXX %	Heineken %
London	35	22	20	19	15
HTV/TSW	23	17	22	17	18
TVS	23	20	20	20	16

Sources: Millward Brown, PAS Tracking Studies. All scores taken approximately 8 weeks after launch of Miller Lite in each area

It is not possible to 'prove' that the advertising was responsible for the high brand awareness, but it is true that the advertising generated high levels of awareness and at the same time the brand became well known (see Tables 13 and 14). In addition only 40 per cent of lager drinkers claimed to have seen the brand on sale, suggesting that familiarity was not just due to presence.

TABLE 13: SOURCE OF ADVERTISING AWARENESS
FOR MILLER LITE

Claimed to have seen:	
TV	91%
Posters	20%
Radio	7%
Bus sides	2%

Source: Millward Brown,
London, June 1986

TABLE 14: PROMPTED BRAND AWARENESS

London	84%
HTV/TSW	69%
TVS	75%
Granada	79%
Yorkshire	69%

Sources: Millward Brown, PAS.
All scores taken approximately
8 weeks after launch in each
area

The tracking research also suggested that the desired brand benefits had largely been communicated to the consumer. It appeared that we had overcome many of lite's potential weaknesses and conveyed the desired messages of smoothness, ease of drinking and not bloating. The only concern was that the American origins of the brand seemed to be affecting the product's perceived alcoholic strength more negatively than expected. The fact that this only occurred in London indicates perhaps the importance of the TV advertising in establishing the brand's image (see Tables 15 and 16).

TABLE 15: PROMPTED BRAND IMAGE

	London	HTV/TSW/TVS
Easy to drink	1.0	1.2
Smooth	0.9	1.0
Different to ordinary lagers	0.7	0.7
Not filling or bloating	0.6	0.5
Rather gassy	−0.3	−0.5
American	1.4	0.8
Weak in alcohol	0.2	−0.1
Strong in alcohol	−0.3	−0.1
Weak in taste	0.1	0

2 = agree strongly, −2 = disagree strongly
Source: Millward Brown, PAS
Base: All those aware of Miller Lite. All scores taken 8 weeks after launch
in each area

TABLE 16: PROMPTED ADVERTISING COMMUNICATION

	London	TVS/HTV/TSW
Agreeing that the TV advertising gave the impression of:		
New type of lager	51%	40%
American	45%	18%
Easy to drink	37%	35%
Smooth	32%	25%
Weak in alcohol	17%	11%

Source: Millward Brown, PAS. All scores taken 8 weeks after launch in each area

We concluded therefore that the advertising had helped generate high levels of brand awareness, while also establishing the desired positioning and that this had generated purchase.

Why Retailers Chose To Sell

Feedback from the Courage sales force suggested that retailers were also responding well to the brand. The advertising was admired, was successful in establishing Miller Lite's positioning with retailers, and thought by them to be successful at communicating the brand's benefits with consumers and likely to lead to high sales.

As a consequence retail buyers were keen to stock the brand. The importance of the *advertising* in generating this distribution is clearly demonstrated in the econometric model (discussed later) where it is shown that distribution levels responded directly to the amount of TV advertising. Therefore, it appears to have been the advertising itself and not the promise of advertising, or simply the brand itself, that led to such high levels of distribution.

Confirmation of the success with retailers came in a study entitled 'New Products in Grocers' conducted by KAE in 1987. In it 85 retailers were questioned about recently launched new products. In answer to the question 'which of the following beer launches were successful?' only Kaliber (a non-alcohol brand) scored higher (51 per cent) than Miller Lite (38 per cent), with Castlemaine XXXX in third place with 25 per cent. Other brands that scored less were Skol 1080, Red Stripe Crucial Brew, Harp Premier, Swan Export and Swan Special Light.

ISOLATING THE ADVERTISING EFFECT

In order to explore and isolate the contribution that the advertising made, two analyses were conducted: a regional test comparing Anglia, the non-TV-advertised area, with a TV supported area; and an econometric study.

Regional Test

Anglia is a weak area for Courage, which has only 3 per cent of the draught standard market because it has few outlets. In order to analyse Miller Lite's performance there, the TV area which is most similar to Anglia from Courage's point of view has been selected as a comparison. Granada, the chosen area, is also a weak area for Courage. The brewer has few outlets there, and share of the draught standard market was also around 3 per cent before Miller Lite's launch.

Launch activity in the two areas was similar: promotional activity was the same, radio support was provided in both areas and the retail price of Miller Lite on draught and in cans was the same in both areas. The only difference between the areas was the advertising activity: in Granada 2180 male TVRs were delivered in the launch year, in Anglia there was no TV but £15 000 was spent on a low-key cinema support campaign. This campaign achieved very low coverage.

In terms of performance Granada significantly out-performed Anglia on all measures. In the canned market 33 per cent more distribution was gained in Granada than in Anglia during the launch year. Canned Miller Lite achieved a share almost 70 per cent higher in Granada than in Anglia, and consequently in terms of share per distribution point Granada out-performed Anglia by over 27 per cent (see Table 17).

TABLE 17:   ANGLIA, GRANADA CANNED PERFORMANCE

	Anglia	Granada
Average distribution	48%	64%
Brand share	3.3%	5.6%
Share per distribution point (indexed)	100	127

Source: Stats MR. April 1986–March 1987

We concluded therefore that, since all other non-advertising activity was equal, the Miller Lite TV advertising had had a pronounced effect on the canned product's distribution and rate of sale. The relationship between advertising, distribution and rate of sale was later explored more fully in the econometric model.

In the draught market the regional test was disturbed by the introduction of Foster's into Courage outlets five months into the launch year in both areas. We have therefore analysed the performance of Miller Lite in both areas in only the four months from launch until Foster's introduction. Consequently, the reliability of the data is questionable. However, the sheer size of the out-performance of Granada over Anglia suggests that even if the data is inaccurate to a certain extent then Miller Lite still performed significantly better in Granada than in Anglia (see Table 18).

Given that all other activity was equal, again we concluded that the TV advertising had had a pronounced effect on the draught Miller Lite performance. (Selection of any other TV advertising area would have produced similar results: Granada was not abnormal in its high level of success.)

NEW PRODUCTS

TABLE 18:   ANGLIA, GRANADA DRAUGHT PERFORMANCE

	Anglia	Granada
Average distribution	2%	1%
Total sales share	0.3%	0.6%
Share per distribution point (indexed)	100	400

Source: Stats MR. April 1986–July 1986

Econometrics

Ideally we would have performed an econometric analysis of both canned and draught Miller Lite performance. Unfortunately, sales, share and distribution data in the draught market proved too unreliable to model – the Stats MR audit (which is the only source of share and distribution data) has only been in existence in the draught market for two and a half years and the early data had not yet 'settled down' when Miller Lite was launched. We did however perform an econometric analysis on the canned market.

While detailed explanation of the procedure is included in the appendix, the following summary of results confirms the important contribution that the TV advertising made to the canned performance:

1. The TV advertising was shown to have generated distribution for the canned product. In all TV-advertised areas the model suggested that the TV advertising was directly responsible for at least 27 per cent extra distribution (see Table 19).

TABLE 19:   ADVERTISING EFFECT ON DISTRIBUTION

Region	TVRs delivered	Predicted distribution with no advertising	Actual distribution	Distribution gain due to advertising (*percentaged*)
A	1900	59%	75%	27%
B	2300	53%	75%	42%
C	2100	48%	70%	46%
D	0	57%	57%	–

Source: Econometric study

In the light of our findings concerning retailer reaction to the advertising this makes sense.

2. The TV advertising directly affected sales of the brand, raising them by at least 34 per cent over levels which would have been achieved with no advertising support (see Figure 6, illustrating London, Figure 7 and Table 20).

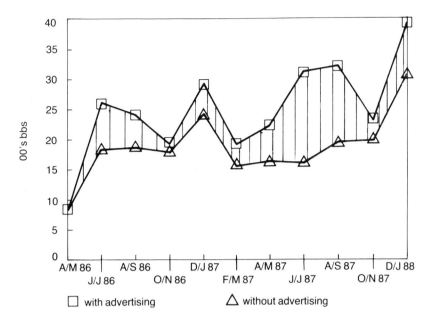

Figure 6. *Miller Lite sales in London. Actual v. projected without advertising*

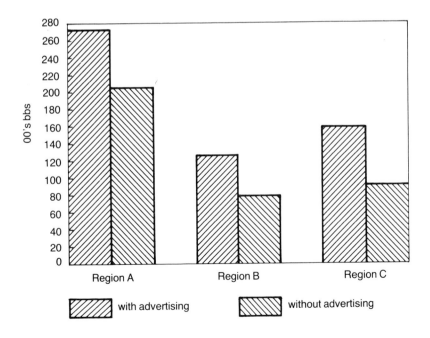

Figure 7. *Miller Lite sales comparison. Actual v. projected without advertising*

TABLE 20: ADVERTISING EFFECT ON SALES

Region	TVRs delivered	Predicted sales with no advertising (indexed)	Actual sales (indexed)	Sales gain due to advertising
A	1900	100	134	34%
B	2300	100	160	60%
C	2100	100	174	74%
D	0	100	100	—

Source: Econometric study

Interestingly, in Region A, London, the TV advertising appeared to have had least effect — we hypothesised that it is possible that the inclusion of 'from America' in the advertising in that region alone had contributed to this under-performance, as well as the fact that Region A received less TVRs.

3. Analysis of the results in Tables 19 and 20 revealed that, in all TV-advertised areas, advertising had generated sales at a greater rate than distribution. This suggested that the TV advertising generated not only distribution but also rate of sale gains.

We went on to investigate a direct correlation between rate of sale and TV advertising, and found strong evidence that this existed (see Table 21).

TABLE 21: RATE OF SALE

Region	TVRs delivered	Rate of sale with no advertising (indexed)	Rate of sale with advertising (indexed)
A	1900	100	107
B	2300	100	118
C	2100	100	128
D	0	100	100

Source: Econometric study

4. Miller Lite TV advertising possessed a very high adstock retention value, indicating that its effect on the brand's performance was sustained long after each burst of advertising. The retention value was 80 per cent over each bi-monthly period, which seems very high and is perhaps indicative of the advertising's potency. Yet it does make sense if one considers the relatively high saliency that the advertising and brand have achieved since launch, and the relatively quick 'payback' that the advertising achieved (as is shown in the next section); after all, high retention levels suggest high levels of 'effect' per pound spent on media.

COST-EFFECTIVENESS OF THE ADVERTISING

Cost-effectiveness has been examined as follows:

We calculated the volume of Miller Lite sales attributable to the advertising, using the econometric model and regional test. Then we established the profit generated by this volume taking into account *all* costs except advertising. This 'profit before advertising' figure equals approximately 80 per cent of the total advertising production and media costs in the first year in each area.

On this basis, even assuming no further growth in Miller Lite's volume and an advertising budget of the same size as in year 1, advertising would have recovered its total cost within two years of launch.

CONCLUSIONS

We have pointed out the difficulties of launching a new 'lite' lager into a market where 'liteness' had already been tried and had failed. We have demonstrated that nevertheless Miller Lite has been a success. In doing so we have established that the advertising was instrumental in defining to the public and to retailers the new interpretation of 'liteness', in gaining awareness for the brand and ultimately in generating high levels of distribution and sales. Without advertising it seems likely that Miller Lite might have been received by trade and consumer alike as another 'lite' lager in the old vein. With advertising the brand has been established as a sizeable and profitable force in a highly competitive market.

We conclude therefore that advertising can be proven to work in the launch of a new lager in both draught and canned markets, and that Miller Lite advertising is a case in point.

3

Going for the Heart of a Market — Kia-Ora Orange Squash 1983–86

INTRODUCTION

In 1981, trade research indicated that the squash market would be rationalised by the major multiples to two brands plus own-label. This case study examines the role played by advertising in moving Kia-Ora from precarious third brand to brand leader in the orange squash market, thus avoiding almost certain and rapid decline.

Market Background 1971–81

During the 1970s the growth in importance of the major supermarket groups, and the increased availability of cheaper own-label products, radically changed the patterns of trading in the squashes market. Until this time grocers had accounted for less than 60 per cent of squash purchases, with outlets such as CTNs and off-licences also important. By 1981, grocers accounted for 90 per cent of sales and the six major multiple groups for over 50 per cent. Market volume grew healthily by 35 per cent between 1971 and 1981, own-label share increased towards 50 per cent and the manufacturers' brands were under severe pressure to maintain share and profitability.

The Brands' Position in 1981

Of the three brands in the market-place, Robinsons from Colmans of Norwich adapted best to the changing market and trading environment. In 1979 their standard range was relaunched in the increasingly popular large sizes of plastic packaging. The savings generated from the cheaper plastic were used to fund aggressive pricing and modest, but consistent, advertising support. As a result Robinsons were able to offer consumers the best price per litre of all the branded squashes and through advertising focused on the Wimbledon associations of their premium Lemon Barley Water brand, succeeding in creating a 'halo' effect of quality and tradition for their standard range. Robinsons overtook Quosh as brand leader in the market.

Quosh, marketed by the Beecham Groups Food Division, had also moved to larger-size plastic packs but the majority of its volume continued to come from its wide flavour range, which remained in its original 26 oz glass packaging. The brand enjoyed a strong distribution base with good consumer awareness and trial of its many flavours, but had difficulty establishing itself in the growing large-pack sector (by 1981, plastic one-litre and over-size packs accounted for two thirds of volume sales).

Finally, Kia-Ora trailed in third place behind Robinsons and Quosh, as shown in Table 1.

TABLE 1:   VOLUME SHARE (%)

	1980	1981
Robinsons	18.9	16.6
Quosh	14.5	13.8
Kia-Ora	8.0	8.2

Source: Nielsen

Kia-Ora: The Third Brand

Kia-Ora has a very long history, stretching back to 1930 when Schweppes Ltd bought a 51 per cent interest in an Australian company called Kia-Ora Ltd (its name means 'good health' in Maori). In the 1970s, Kia-Ora was one of four brands of squash marketed by Schweppes Ltd., the drinks division of Cadbury Schweppes.

By 1977, Schweppes revised its strategy in order to improve profitability and concentrate sales and marketing effort more efficiently. Production was brought in-house and the four brands were rationalised to two, with the strongest brands, Schweppes and Kia-Ora retained, each to perform a specific role, Schweppes for the licensed trade and Kia-Ora as the mainstream grocery brand.

Kia-Ora was a brand name familiar to most squash purchasers, but for mothers, the most regular purchasers, Kia-Ora was the kind of brand that they remembered from their childhood, visits to the cinema ('on sale here') and small corner shops where the small dumpy 'milk bottle' (20 oz) Kia-Ora was sometimes found and bought as a top-up or emergency purchase. The following is a typical quote from a mother at the time:

'you don't often see Kia-Ora. It's in dumpy bottles, smaller and fatter than Ribena .... You can only get it in the V.G.'

By 1981 the changing strength of the competition and the policies of the retail trade had left Kia-Ora in an extremely vulnerable position. A new 30 oz size had failed to achieve the level of distribution that had been expected, and without the pack range to compete in the growing large-size sector or the production capability to produce plastic and generate the associated cost savings, Kia-Ora was unable to compete on price without seriously eroding brand profitability.

Schweppes commissioned Stats MR to conduct a trade survey among multiple and co-op. head office buyers. The results were alarming. They showed that sales of squashes did not increase significantly with an increase in number of lines (brand, sizes and flavours) on display and they showed that a strong-selling orange squash was the trade's key measure of a brand's performance. The research indicated that without dramatic and immediate improvement in Kia-Ora's position in the market, the brand would die.

> The research suggests that only two major brands plus own-label should be stocked. Kia-Ora in its current form is obviously vulnerable in this situation. Unless Kia-Ora's position is strengthened, the brand will suffer from declining volume and consequent loss of profitability. (Schweppes Marketing Plans, 1981)

Schweppes' experience suggested that the trade was already beginning to act along these lines. In July 1981, Tesco rationalised their soft drinks listings. Kia-Ora was delisted.

The Importance of the Squash Sector to Schweppes

Within grocers, squashes accounted for 25 per cent of soft drinks sales value. Without a strong brand in this sector Schweppes' position versus other soft drinks competitors would have been severely weakened. More importantly Schweppes could not achieve their corporate objective of being the *total* soft drinks company without a strong squash brand.

In 1981 Schweppes responded to the trade research by taking the decision to plan for the relaunch of Kia-Ora and thus to invest significantly in its future growth.

THE RELAUNCH STRATEGY

The relaunch of Kia-Ora required a heavy investment programme by Schweppes. The key elements were:

1. Building of a new factory and investment in latest plant and equipment that would be capable of producing the necessary range of pack sizes that the consumer required.
2. Production in OPVC plastic which would give Schweppes a distinct advantage over the competitors in PVC (OPVC was cheaper, had a longer shelf life, and greater clarity and strength).
3. To utilise the savings from moving to plastic to fund competitive pricing and advertising.

The new range of pack sizes comprised the 20 oz, a new one-litre (the single most frequently purchased pack in the market) and a two-litre (the most popular of the larger sizes). In the year of relaunch (1983) production constraints resulted in the 20 oz size remaining unchanged in glass, which provided us with a useful means of isolating the effects of advertising without packaging or pricing change.

The Kia-Ora product remained unchanged, with orange as the most popular, staple flavour available in all three pack sizes.

The final element in the relaunch strategy was consumer support.

Schweppes knew that they needed to build awareness further for Kia-Ora and develop a differential positioning for the brand — a reason for the trade to stock it and the consumer to buy it. They approached BMP with a clear brief to develop advertising that would achieve maximum impact as quickly as possible.

IDENTIFYING THE OPPORTUNITY

Initial Research

A comprehensive mix of desk and qualitative research was conducted to both educate us about the market and to assess whether an opportunity for Kia-Ora existed.

The key findings of the desk research were:

— Orange was the dominant flavour, accounting for 62 per cent of the market volume. (No other flavour — except lemon — accounts for more than 5 per cent.)
— Orange was the *only staple flavour* for the majority of consumers.
— Children were the major consumers, with over 60 per cent of volume consumed by 2 to 15-year-olds.
— Mothers were the purchasers.

Our qualitative research provided us with an understanding of both mothers' and children's attitudes towards squash. The key findings of this exploratory qualitative research were:

— Squash was a non-controversial, everyday product generally viewed as 'flavoured water for kids'.
— There was little distinct brand imagery (other than Robinsons having an association with Wimbledon via its Lemon Barley advertising. This gave Robinsons an adult and very 'English' image).

But, crucially, there were definite feelings towards specific areas:

— Concern over own-label weaknesses, in particular, poor taste acceptance by children and poor value for money. Own-label squashes were cheaper than branded squashes but much weaker. Hence, the number of glasses per bottle was far lower.
— Concern that children will like the product.
— A clear view of what the 'good squash' would be 'like.

The 'Good Squash'

The 'good squash' satisfied two distinct sets of requirements: those of the purchaser and those of the consumer. For the purchaser, the main requirements were:

— Trust that children will like it.
— Value for money based on the strength of the product, its price and the pack size.
— Reassurance on the content. In particular, the fruitiness of the product.

For the consumer, the requirements were largely centred on instant gratification, although there was also an underlying need for 'brandedness':

— Tastes good.
— Quenches thirst.
— Satisfying, i.e. 'It's the one for me'.

The Kia-Ora Taste Advantage

The final piece of research carried out was a blind taste test of Kia-Ora versus the major brands and own-label. Kia-Ora emerged as the clear winner.

The Opportunity For Kia-Ora

On pulling together the strands of the desk, qualitative and taste test research, it became apparent than an opportunity for Kia-Ora did exist.

— The orange sector was dominant in volume terms and, as the only staple flavour in the market, it offered the greatest potential to develop brand loyalty.
— There were clear generic benefits that were currently 'unowned' by any of the brands.
— Kia-Ora was the best-tasting squash.

It was from these three major findings that we identified the opportunity:

> Capture the generic benefits of the 'good squash' exclusively for Kia-Ora orange.

Marketing Objectives

Once Schweppes and BMP were convinced that this opportunity existed, it became clear that exploiting the opportunity would involve considerable investment in communication. In addition, Schweppes' trade research had indicated that without dramatic and immediate improvement in Kia-Ora's position in the market, the brand would die. To summarise:

> The research suggests that only two major brands plus own-label should be stocked. Kia-Ora in its current form is obviously vulnerable in this situation.

Unless Kia-Ora's position is strengthened, the brand will suffer from declining volume and consequent loss of profitability. (Schweppes Marketing Plans, 1981)

So the marketing objectives set for Kia-Ora were ambitious — they had to be both to justify the investment and to avoid the likely death of the brand. They were:

— To move Kia-Ora from third brand to brand leader in the orange-squash market.
— To increase distribution for Kia-Ora orange squash.

THE ADVERTISING STRATEGY

The dual nature of the product's target market (i.e. mothers and their children) raised some interesting questions about the advertising strategy. The most central of these questions was, who should the advertising target and what, realistically, could we expect the advertising to do both attitudinally and behaviourally?

Further qualitative research was carried out to try and clarify the role of the mother/child relationship in squash purchasing. We went into this research with an hypothesis that the advertising opportunity was to generate direct child request of Kia-Ora. The research was to prove us wrong, but not completely wrong.

Children

In general, children are aware that they have a finite number of direct requests that will be granted. This number is not fixed and may vary according to how good they've been or whether 'mum is in a good mood'. However, in general, children have a fairly good idea of what they can get away with. Thus, products will be requested by children if and only if they come above a certain point in some loose ranking of desirability. This is where the idea of direct child request of an orange squash ran into difficulties. Children were being given orange squash fairly freely anyway — it was an everyday product. In addition, even though Kia-Ora was the best-tasting orange squash, its main competitors were still more than acceptable, meaning that there were three brands that came above the threshold of general child taste acceptance.

Finally, once this everyday product was about to be consumed, i.e. in a glass, it was virtually indistinguishable from its branded competition and also, effectively, unbrandable.

We concluded that whilst child request would probably play some part in the mother/child purchase decision for orange squash, its role was not a dominant one and it was unreasonable to expect the advertising to change this fundamentally.

We then talked further to some mothers.

Mothers

The research amongst mothers led us to develop a simple generalised model of the way in which they chose brands when purchasing non-controversial products for their children.

Be a good Home Economist

Value for money
Name I trust
Readily available

Be a 'nice' mum

↙   ↘

Give them what they like   Give them what they ask for

We had already decided that the potential for direct child request was likely to be limited. So we believed the primary route to purchase was through generating a perception amongst mothers that Kia-Ora is the squash their children will like, and the secondary route was via direct child request of Kia-Ora.

The Differential Positioning

It was from this that we developed the positioning for Kia-Ora as 'The squash for kids'. This positioning statement had a dual meaning reflecting the dual target audience. It implied both 'The one kids want' and 'The one mums think their kids want'.

The Role for Advertising

Primary: To generate a perception amongst mothers that Kia-Ora orange squash is the one their children will like *even if they don't actively ask for it.*

Secondary: To realise the potential child request for Kia-Ora.

Advertising Objectives

These were (1) to communicate that Kia-Ora is the 'good orange squash' thereby convincing mothers that Kia-Ora is the squash their kids will like; and (2) to establish Kia-Ora as 'the squash I want' thereby generating child request of Kia-Ora.

Target Market

Primary: Mothers of children aged 2−12.

Secondary: Children aged 5−15.

How the Advertising Should Work

By the end of this second stage of qualitative research and the development of the strategy, we had a clear view of how we hoped the consequent advertising would work (see Figure 1).

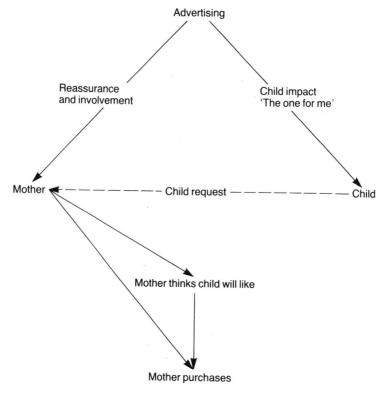

Figure 1. *How the advertising should work*

This pathway from advertising to purchase hinged crucially on the creative execution. There is a subtle but vital distinction between producing advertising for children and producing advertising that mothers think is for children whilst ensuring that it appeals to and influences both mothers and children. The closest we could get to expressing this difference was that the ads for Kia-Ora had to be 'charming'. This tonal requirement was a key component of the creative brief, as will be seen shortly.

THE MEDIA STRATEGY

Objectives

The objectives were (1) to relaunch Kia-Ora into all areas of distribution opportunity; (2) to build awareness: The relaunch must be seen to go off with a bang, not a whimper; and (3) to build awareness *as* the summer season takes off.

Why We Chose TV

— In order to maximise the potential for mother-perceived child appeal of Kia-Ora, we wanted the ads to be seen if possible by mother and child *at the same time*.

— Children like TV advertising and mothers know this.
— We needed to maximise the impact of the relaunch and build awareness quickly.

The media target audience was mothers (BC1C2D) watching TV in the presence of their children aged 2−12.

THE RELAUNCH 1983 AND 1984: THE CREATIVE BRIEF

The proposition needed to refine the benefits of the 'good squash' into a single attribute. What we came up with was the word 'orangeyist'. This attribute captured in full or in essence all of the requirements of the 'good squash' amongst both mothers and children (see 'The Good Squash' p. 101).

Proposition: Kia-Ora is the orangeyist squash.

Primary target: Mothers with children aged 2−12.

Secondary target: Children aged 5−15.

Mood and tone: Charming, fun.

Guidelines: Avoid contradicting the non-controversial nature of squash.

MEDIA 1983 AND 1984

In both 1983 and 1984 we deployed the budget in two bursts separated by a gap of a few weeks. In this way we effectively covered the key summer season from late May to mid-August. In 1983 we bought a total of 632 40″ housewife-with-children ratings and in 1984, 653 housewife-with-children ratings.

THE ADVERTISING FOR 1983 AND 1984

'Fedora', the first film for Kia-Ora, was written with the central idea of cartoon crows following a little boy and his 'dawg', desperate to get some Kia-Ora. It went down extremely well in research. The general initial response was that the ad was 'catchy' with the atmosphere created being very appropriate to the product category − sunny, lively, carefree, happy-go-lucky. Children in particular became highly involved in the action and absorbed an incredible amount of detail from just one showing. The statement 'I'll be your dawg' became part of playground language by the end of the first year and was commonly quoted whenever BMP carried out groups on children.

The strong orange ground and sky and the line that justified why the crows couldn't have any Kia-Ora ('It's too orangey for crows') strongly communicated

"Fedora" - The First Film

the association of Kia-Ora with orangeyness. With minor alterations, the film was commissioned and drawn up.

EVALUATION OF 1983 AND 1984

The total orange-squash market was reasonably constant across 1983 and 1984, rising from 166 000 litres in 1983 to 173 000 litres in 1984 (Nielsen).

The key marketing objective was for Kia-Ora to move from third brand to brand leader in this mature and static market. The advertising was expected to help in two ways; one short term and one long term. Short term, the advertising had to generate demand and thus increase the rate of sale. In the longer term, this advertising effect was to play its part in generating additional listings, thus achieving the second marketing objective of increased distribution.

Short-term Effect on Sales Share, 1983

The initial effect was far more dramatic than we had expected. Volume share jumped by 48 per cent for the bi-monthly period covering August and September (see Table 2).

TABLE 2: SHORT-TERM EFFECT OF ADVERTISING ON SALES SHARE

	1982			1983		
	APR.	AUG.	DEC.	APR.	AUG.	DEC.
Kia-Ora share (%)	8.5	8.5	8.4	8.5	12.6	13.9

↑
Advertising

Source: Nielsen

By April–May 1984, Kia-Ora's share had dropped to 11.0 per cent, still 29 per cent up on April–May 1983. Then we ran 'Fedora' again: the result is shown in Table 3.

TABLE 3: EFFECT OF ADVERTISING ON SALES SHARE (1983–84)

	1983			1984		
	APR.	AUG.	DEC.	APR.	AUG.	DEC.
Kia-Ora share (%)	8.5	12.6	13.9	11.0	14.5	14.0

↑ Advertising ↑ Advertising

Source: Nielsen

This time, volume share jumped to 14.5 per cent for the August–September period, a full 71 per cent up on the April–May 1983 figure and 15 per cent above the August–September 1983 figure. The share had decayed following the 1983 advertising but, as we shall see throughout, the decayed level was consistently higher each year.

Performance against the Primary Marketing Objective

For the year ending April 1983, Kia-Ora orange squash was the distant third brand at just over half the size of the brand leader. By year ending April 1984, Kia-Ora was clear second brand, and by year ending April 1985 the objective had been met. In an albeit more even-looking branded market (with only 4.7 share points separating first and third brand versus 7.6 share points in 1982), Kia-Ora had achieved brand leadership of the orange-squash market (see Table 4).

TABLE 4: VOLUME SHARE

	Pre-advertising	1st Year	2nd Year
Kia-Ora	8.5	13.1	14.5
Robinsons	16.1	15.2	13.4
Quosh	11.7	11.3	9.8

Source: Nielsen

Performance against the Secondary Marketing Objective

A full econometric analysis of the market has been carried out to elicit the precise relationship between sales and the independent variables. However, it seems fair to point out here that, certainly in the first two years of advertising, the secondary marketing objective was not achieved and distribution gains played a minimal role in the share growth detailed above, as can be seen from Table 6.

What we did have by the end of the second year was an extremely powerful sales force argument for the future based on rate of sale (see Table 5).

TABLE 5:   RATE OF SALE

	Pre-advertising	1st Year	2nd Year
Kia-Ora	13.3	19.6	21.0
Robinsons	19.9	18.8	16.7
Quosh	15.2	14.1	12.6

Source: Nielsen

Eliminating the Effect of the packaging Change

There are three facts which led us away from believing the packaging change to OPVC caused the dramatic sales effect in 1983.

1. The new packs were on shelf during the April−May period prior to the advertising when Kia-Ora's share remained at 8.5 per cent.
2. There was an almost equally dramatic effect on share after the second year's advertising, when there was obviously no packaging change.
3. We carried out a Nielsen special analysis which measured the change in Kia-Ora's share after the advertising in shops which *only* stocked the unchanged glass 20 oz bottle. The results showed that these shops responded in the same way to advertising as the market as a whole.

CONSOLIDATION − 1985 AND 1986

By the end of the second year of advertising, Kia-Ora was brand leader in the orange-squash sector. Any plans the major multiples had had to delist Kia-Ora as the third brand in the squash market simply disappeared. Both the Schweppes sales force and Kia-Ora trade advertising made it very plain that Kia-Ora was now both the brand leader and the fastest-selling orange squash in the market − to delist made no sense at all.

In addition, Kia-Ora now had a strong and relevant differential positioning. As 'the squash for kids', Kia-Ora had a distinct role to play on the shop shelf that could not be filled by Robinsons or Quosh.

Marketing Objectives

The primary objective was to maintain brand-leader status in the orange sector, and the secondary objective was to increase distribution.

With the weapons mentioned above, the Schweppes sales force went to the trade and achieved the secondary marketing objective, as shown in Table 6.

TABLE 6: £ DISTRIBUTION

	Pre-1983	1st Year	2nd Year	3rd Year	4th Year
Kia-Ora	64	67	69	74	85
Robinsons	81	81	82	82	84

Source: Nielsen

The Advertising in 1985 and 1986

Qualitative post-testing of the first ad amongst mothers and children clearly indicated that the current strategy was still relevant and showed that Kia-Ora and the characters were now very strongly associated with orange squash. For 1985 and 1986 we wrote a new ad to support orange and other flavours.

Media 1985 and 1986

The budgets for both years were again deployed across the key summer season. The arrival of TVAM gave us a new opportunity to catch mums and kids watching TV together, and around 25 per cent of the total ratings went on this new service. In 1985 we bought a total of 645 40″ housewife-with-children ratings and in 1986, 630 housewife-with-children ratings.

The Advertising for 1985 and 1986

The second film for Kia-Ora, 'Fruity Crows', again featured the central idea of the cartoon crows following a little boy and his dog, and trying desperately to get some Kia-Ora. Once again, qualitative research endorsed the creative approach with both mums and kids showing high levels of involvement and enjoyment. As with the first film, mothers expressed a strong feeling that 'my kids will love it', possibly more so in this case since they knew their children had loved the first ad.

Evaluation of 1985 and 1986

The market remained fairly constant in volume terms, as shown in Table 7.

TABLE 7: MARKET FOR KIA-ORA IN VOLUME TERMS

	1983	1984	1985	1986
Volume (M litres)	166	173	162	160

Source: Nielsen

"FRUITY CROWS" – THE SECOND FILM

As has already been seen from the first two years, we had evidence (in market-share terms) that the advertising had a dramatic short-term effect in addition to a long-term effect that manifested itself in a higher share prior to advertising each year. We hoped for the new advertising to continue this trend.

Once again the effect of advertising was dramatic, as shown in Tables 8 and 9.

TABLE 8:   SHORT-TERM EFFECT ON SALES SHARE, 1985

| | 1984 | | | 1985 | | |
	APR.	AUG.	DEC.	APR.	AUG.	DEC.
Kia-Ora share %	11.0	14.5	14.0	13.9	16.2	13.8
		↑			↑	
		Advertising			Advertising	

Source: Nielsen

TABLE 9:   SHORT-TERM EFFECT ON SALES SHARE, 1986

| | 1985 | | | 1986 | | |
	APR.	AUG.	DEC.	APR.	AUG.	DEC.
Kia-Ora share %	13.9	16.2	13.8	13.9	17.2	15.2

Advertising   Advertising

Source: Nielsen

For the fourth year in succession, the dramatic short-term effect followed by a decline to a higher level than the previous year was apparent (see Figure 2).

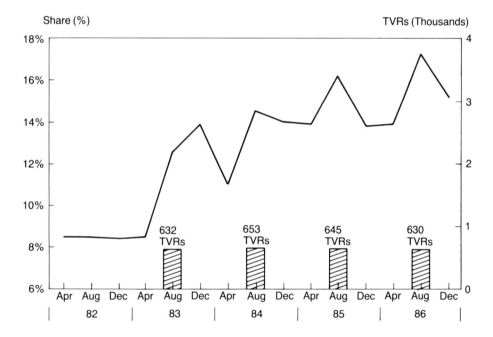

Figure 2. *Kia-Ora share of orange market, April 1982–December 1986*

It is difficult to decide conclusively how much of this effect is attributable to advertising without recourse to the econometric analysis (see later) but we know of no variable that consistently altered between April and August of each year (1983–86) other than the presence of advertising. Table 10 illustrates the change in market share over this period.

TABLE 10: SHARE OVER THE FOUR YEARS

	Pre-advertising	1st Year	2nd Year	3rd Year	4th Year
Kia-Ora	8.5	13.1	14.5	15.2	15.6
Robinsons	16.1	15.2	13.7	13.9	13.8
Quosh	11.7	11.3	9.8	9.3	11.5

Source: Nielsen

Clearly, the marketing objective of consolidating Kia-Ora's brand leadership in the orange-squash sector had been achieved (see Figure 3).

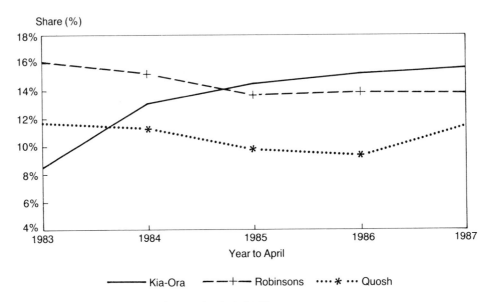

Figure 3. *Standard orange-squash market shares, April 1982–April 1987*

DID THE ADVERTISING WORK THE WAY IT WAS SUPPOSED TO?

We believe the answer is 'yes'.

Firstly, the advertising appeared to greatly boost top-of-mind awareness of Kia-Ora amongst mothers, as Table 11 shows.

TABLE 11: AWARENESS OF KIA-ORA AMONGST MOTHERS

	Pre-1983 %	Post-1983 %	Post-1984 %	Post-1985 %	Post-1986 %
Kia-Ora first brand mentioned	12	18	25	22	24
Spontaneous awareness	41	53	58	61	61

Source: Millward Brown tracking study

Secondly, the ad was clearly perceived by mums to be appealing to children. Table 12's comparison with the Robinsons advertising (at similar weight and timing) makes this point very clearly.

TABLE 12: 'IT APPEALS TO THE CHILDREN' (%)

	1983	1984	1985	1986
Kia-Ora	78	81	68	70
Robinsons	5	2	11	16

Source: Millward Brown tracking study

Thirdly (although the data only exists for 1985 and 1986: see Table 13), more children requested Kia-Ora than either of the other two brands.

TABLE 13: REASON FOR PURCHASE:
'IT'S THE ONE THE CHILDREN ASK FOR' (%)

	1985	1986
Kia-Ora	33	34
Robinsons	16	21
Quosh	24	19

Source: Millward Brown tracking study

Finally, reprofiling the remaining responses to the 'reason for purchase' question shows that the key objective of building a perception of child desire in mums was also achieved:

Reason for Purchase

'It's the one I think the children will particularly like
even though they haven't asked for it'

	1985	1986
Kia-Ora	74%	65%

(Source: Millward Brown tracking study)

In addition, periodic exploratory qualitative research showed conclusively how popular and enjoyable the ad was amongst children (Figure 4).

QUANTIFYING THE ADVERTISING EFFECT

The Econometric Model

An econometric analysis of the data was carried out to help to isolate and to quantify the effect of advertising on sales. A full explanation of the econometric

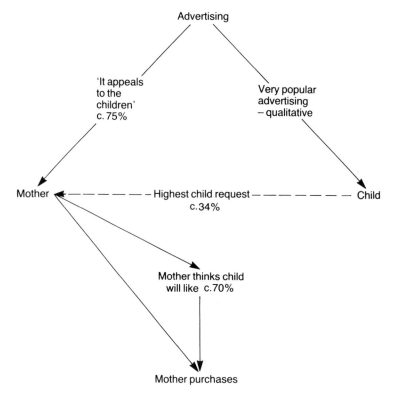

Figure 4.

analysis is included in the Appendix, but an outline description and summary of results will be detailed here.

The Model

A two-tier model has been estimated, one for Kia-Ora orange market share, and a second which explains movements in Kia-Ora's distribution feeding into it. Factors included in the initial share model for Kia-Ora and competitors were:

— Volume sales (litres)
— Price per litre
— Sterling distribution
— Out of stock
— TV advertising (housewife-with-children TVRs)
— Retail price index

Data sources used were A. C. Nielsen, BARB and the CSO. The models were estimated using 29 bi-monthly observations from December 1982 to September 1987.

Both models predict the data very well, the share model explaining 92 per cent of the variations in market share (see Figure 5), the distribution model 97 per cent of those in distribution. Both also behaved very satisfactorily against a range of other statistical tests which are reported in the Appendix.

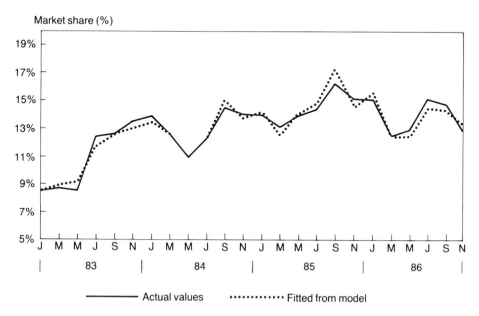

Figure 5. *Kia-Ora share of standard orange-squash market: actual v. fitted values*

RESULTS OF THE ANALYSIS

Most results have been produced by using the model to run simulations, e.g. what level of sales would have been achieved had distribution remained at its original level.

Price

Kia-Ora is less price-sensitive than might be expected given the degree of competition in this market and the close substitutability of products one for another. A sustained 1 per cent rise in Kia-Ora's price relative to a competitive average leads to a 2.45 per cent reduction in market share (NB: not 2.45 share points). We would like to hypothesise that Kia-Ora's relatively low price elasticity is a result of branding through advertising. Unfortunately, there was insufficient data prior to the relaunch to explicitly test whether the price elasticity was indeed higher then.

Distribution

Kia-Ora's sterling distribution has risen from 65 per cent to 85 per cent since the relaunch. All else remaining equal, the model shows that this rise has added 1.3 points to share.

Advertising

Advertising has *two* effects on Kia-Ora's market share, one a *direct* consumer effect on sales (Table 14) and one *indirect* via its influence on distribution.

Advertising during both campaigns has also had reasonably long-term effects on sales. Sixty per cent of any one month's advertising continues to increase sales in the following month (i.e. Kia-Ora's advertising works with an adstock effect).

TABLE 14:   DIRECT CONSUMER EFFECT ON MARKET SHARE

	Estimated additional sales (M litres)
1983	1.05
1984	1.28
1985	1.79
1986	0.96
TOTAL	5.08

The effect of advertising on distribution differs between the campaigns. Every 100 TVRs generated 0.54 sterling distribution points throughout the first campaign but 0.89 points during the second. Undoubtedly, as a result of many of the factors explained above, the trade environment was much more favourable by the time the second campaign came on air, so distribution gains came more easily.

Any estimate of the total sales effect of Kia-Ora's advertising must clearly take account of both the direct and indirect effects of advertising. Although we have a very good estimate of the effect that given distribution changes have on sales, we do not know for certain to what level of distribution Kia-Ora would have continued to sink in the absence of advertising and therefore what the final indirect effect might be. We can however make a very educated projection.

The central reason for supporting Kia-Ora in 1983 was the belief that unless Kia-Ora could move away from being third brand in the market it would die at the hands of the major multiples. Kia-Ora's relaunch shook up the branded market and made a natural candidate for delisting difficult to find. For the last four years Quosh have settled down in third place and the signs are that what we feared would happen to Kia-Ora is happening to Quosh instead.

Quosh's distribution declined steadily from 84 per cent in 1983 to 76 per cent in 1986. In the second half of 1987 distribution slipped to 66 per cent. (Kia-Ora's distribution took a similar dive in 1982, dropping from 74 per cent to 64 per cent just prior to relaunch.)

Our trade sources and the Kia-Ora sales force inform us that Quosh was delisted by some of the major multiples for 1988. (Quosh's share of the market for May 1988 was below 5 per cent.)

On the basis of this information we present three scenarios of what might have happened to distribution, and hence final sales, in the absence of advertising.

We believe Scenario 3, although the most dramatic of the possible scenarios, to be the most likely. We have assumed here that trade rationalisation after the 1983 summer (with Kia-Ora still third brand) would have resulted in an immediate drop to 40 per cent sterling distribution. We have assumed that from 1984 to 1987 distribution would then have gradually declined to 25 per cent. In fact, if Kia-Ora had lost distribution in the major multiples, it is more likely that Schweppes would eventually have stopped production altogether so even this scenario of 'what would have happened' may be optimistic.

The scenarios are:

Scenario 1 Kia-Ora's distribution remained at 65 per cent (its level in 1983). (This scenario represents the very *minimum total* effect that advertising could have had.)

Scenario 2 Kia-Ora's distribution declined gradually to 40 per cent by 1987.

Scenario 3 Kia-Ora's distribution drops to 40 per cent in 1983 and thereafter declines to 25 per cent.

Table 15 summarises the overall result of the advertising for Kia-Ora between 1983 and 1986.

TABLE 15: TOTAL EFFECT OF KIA-ORA's ADVERTISING

| (Additional volume in millions of litres) | | |
	Scenario 1	Scenario 2	Scenario 3
1983	1.25	1.34	3.80
1984	1.95	2.89	6.14
1985	3.30	4.61	7.70
1986	3.00	4.78	7.35
Total	9.50	13.62	24.99
% volume increase	8.6	14.1	29.4

FINANCIAL EFFECTIVENESS OF THE ADVERTISING

The gross margin on Kia-Ora is approximately 20 p per litre. The total advertising spend from 1983 to 1986 was £3.1 million. We can calculate the incremental profit based on the advertising-related incremental volume from the three scenarios:

Incremental profit

Scenario 1	£1.9 m
Scenario 2	£2.7 m
Scenario 3	£5.0 m

Judging whether the advertising has been profitable is thus a matter of deciding what would have happened to Kia-Ora if we had done nothing in 1983. The agency/client belief is that something close to, if not more dramatic than, Scenario 3 is the most likely. If so, then the advertising has paid for itself plus an additional £1.9 million profit on top. And, as each year goes by, the mere fact that Kia-Ora is still distributed through most major multiples adds to this advertising-generated profit.

SUMMARY

The main points are as follows:

1. Trade research indicated that Kia-Ora as third brand was on the verge of rapid decline through trade rationalisation to two brands plus own-label.
2. An ambitious relaunch programme involving repackaging and advertising commenced in 1983.
3. The advertising concentrated on the main opportunity in the market – orange squash.
4. The strategy was to position Kia-Ora as 'the squash for kids', creating a belief in mothers that Kia-Ora is the one their children will like, as well as getting children to ask for it.
5. Over the four years there was a consistently dramatic short-term effect on share during and after the advertising.
6. The share declined to a higher level each year, demonstrating a long-term effect of advertising.
7. Kia-Ora achieved brand leader status in 1984.
8. Kia-Ora's share increased each year of the campaign, maintaining brand leadership throughout.
9. The mechanism via which the advertising worked seemed to be on strategy. This is based on evidence from an annual Millward Brown survey as well as qualitative research of the ads.
10. If we believe that the advertising did save the brand from virtually disappearing then we can prove that, after removing the effect of other variables, the advertising generated at least £1.9 million additional gross profit after paying for itself.

CONCLUSION

We believe this case study demonstrates the role advertising played in moving Kia-Ora from a precarious position as third brand to brand leader by using an innovative strategy and inspired creative work. By identifying the key sector of the squash market and an understanding of the purchase motivations we developed a differential positioning for Kia-Ora and communicated it through advertising.

Over four years, the campaign met all its objectives and played a major role in helping Schweppes meet their marketing objectives.

With a corporate objective of being the *total* soft drinks company, Schweppes needed a major brand in the squash market. In 1983, advertising first appeared that ensured that they would have that major brand.

APPENDIX: RECENT CHANGES IN THE MARKET

Towards the end of 1985 and through 1986, the squash market began to change. The issue of additives in food and the general media interest and consumer trend towards healthier eating affected squash. As a product consumed mostly by children, it was a prime area for potential maternal guilt, and the presence of the 'nastiest of the nasties', tartrazine, in orange squash caused a good deal of publicity (through *That's Life, E for Additives* etc.).

The main effects of this were the removal of tartrazine from branded orange squash and the emergence of a new sector in the squash market − the high-juice sector. A high-juice squash contained around four times as much juice as standard squash and no artificial colours, flavours or sweeteners. The first high-juice squash was made by St Clements and was closely followed by products from Robinsons, Quosh and then Kia-Ora in 1987.

By 1986, the high-juice sector accounted for around 12 per cent of the total orange market and was still growing. Schweppes, in 1987, reacted to these market changes and moved support away from standard Kia-Ora to tetrapaks and high-juice.

Hence this paper concentrates on the period 1983−86 inclusive. All share figures quoted refer to the standard orange-squash market.

4

Hofmeister: a Study of Advertising and Brand Imagery in the Lager Market

INTRODUCTION

In 1983 brewers spent £44 million advertising lager brands. The market has experienced steady growth for some years, and brands are both big – up to £300 million at retail value – and profitable in relation to ales. Yet the bulk of lager volume goes through the brewers' tied pub trade. People tend to choose pubs as places to drink, rather than for the brands they serve, and even when in the pub will usually ask for 'a pint of lager' rather than a brand by name.

On face value, then, this enormous investment might well appear to be superfluous – why advertise to a captive market? What is the real role and value of all this advertising?

This case history attempts to answer both questions. It looks at Hofmeister, Courage's mainstream lager brand, which came late to the market, suffered a shaky start and subsequently struggled to catch up with the bigger lager brands it was launched to rival.

In simple terms, we will try to demonstrate that a major new advertising campaign for Hofmeister generated profit over and above its costs. In a wider context, we hope to say something more fundamental about the importance of brand imagery, even to a captive market, and the role advertising plays in creating it. We therefore confine ourselves to the tied-pub trade and exclude clubs and off-licences, where Hofmeister is also sold. The pub trade accounts for more than 70 per cent of the brand's sales.

We should make it clear at this point that we are not at liberty in this paper to disclose share or volume figures for Courage brands. These data have therefore been indexed.

SALIENT FEATURES OF THE LAGER MARKET

For the past two decades lager has been the most dynamic sector of the British beer market, growing to capture one-third of it. Sales of draught lager alone are now worth nearly £2 billion, and even during the recent market recession lager volume has kept increasing. This trend has been to the benefit of the brewers, who derive a 20 per cent higher margin from lagers than from ales.

Lager has achieved this growth through its appeal to young drinkers: 18–34s consume two-thirds of total volume. This further enhances its importance to the brewers: not only is it their market's most dynamic and profitable product sector, it also represents the future. Drinkers tend to carry preferences established when young through the rest of their lives. It is therefore vital to a brewer to have a strong lager brand.

Not surprisingly, the brewers have responded to this opportunity by distributing and promoting a plethora of brands. To ensure the appeal of their pubs, most brewers now offer a portfolio of alternatives on the bar. New contenders frequently appear and some 30 lagers enjoy TV support. Yet, as in most markets, the first brands in have remained the leaders: 60 per cent of draught lager sales are held by the big six brewers' original mainstream brands – Carlsberg, Carling Black Label, Harp, Heineken and Skol.

In part, this persistence is explained by the major brewers' distribution muscle, but the nature of lager and its drinkers' needs also play their part. Mainstream lagers are much of a muchness in product terms, and the low temperatures at which they are served usually mask any differences that may exist between them. In blind product tests, most drinkers cannot consistently discriminate between brands. They differentiate between them on image.

Brand images are crucial in determining choice, a feature of the market highlighted in our qualitative research. And the nature of those images is bound up with the lifestyle of lager drinkers. They tend to be young, sociable and fashion-conscious. They drink in public, amongst their peer group. They prefer lager to bitter not only because its blander taste is more readily accessible, but because it is seen to be a more modern, youthful drink, with a higher price that demonstrates its higher status value.

Successful brands tend to reflect these generic market-place demands. They may have a specific product or heritage story, but they also establish an image around this story. Almost invariably, they demonstrate through the portrayal of their 'ideal' drinkers that they are contemporary, confident and sympathetic to a young man's outlook on life. Drinkers want to be sure that the brands they choose are popular and thus that they themselves are 'doing the done thing'. Big is beautiful.

Media advertising is crucial in creating and sustaining these images of success. Indeed, respondents in lager group discussions often talk of their brands primarily by reference to their advertising. In a market where products are so simple and so similar, advertising-created images provide consumers with the only means to differentiate.

COURAGE AND HOFMEISTER

Hofmeister was a late entrant to the market. Courage already had a standard lager in Harp, whose ownership was shared amongst a consortium of brewers. Growth in the market and a desire for greater control led to the launch of Hofmeister in 1977, with a 'continental' positioning considered complementary to Harp. By 1981, the new brand had become Courage's main draught lager, replacing Harp in the majority of tied outlets.

During these years, Courage's lager sales performance did not keep up with that of its ales. Thus, on an indexed basis, Courage's 1983 ales market share was 106 compared with 100 in 1977, but its lagers share was 93 compared with 100 in 1977 (see Figure 1).

Courage lagers consistently lost ground in every year except 1981. In that year, ale

Figure 1. *Courage's retail trade share of major brewers market*
Source: BMS, Courage

marketing activity increased pub traffic; total pub sales increased, including lager. However, lager sales resumed their downward path thereafter. The movements shown may seem small, but it is worth reiterating their significance for two reasons: the market is huge and the figures, derived from a census of sales returns contributed by each major brewer, are very accurate.

Courage had a problem. In the important lager sector it was losing share. Lagers were 'letting the side down'. Hofmeister was a £100 million brand, available in over 85 per cent of Courage's pubs, but it was underperforming.

The key marketing objective was therefore to reverse Courage's declining lager share. It was the inadequate performance of Hofmeister, the mainstream lager brand with near-universal tied-trade distribution, which had apparently led to the decline; it was up to Hofmeister to bring about its reversal. It was important to discover why Hofmeister was underperforming and, when Boase Massimi Pollitt was appointed to the brand early in 1983, we set out to answer this important question. We needed to explore the nature and position of the brand and to discover whether advertising could play a role in its revitalisation.

UNDERSTANDING THE BRAND'S PROBLEMS

Qualitative research was illuminating in suggesting reasons for the brand's sales problem. Hofmeister drinkers showed little enthusiasm for the brand. The only reason they gave for drinking it was that it was served in their local. To them the brand was unremarkable, low key and, because they could say little about it, faceless. They even felt that Hofmeister was unpopular amongst men who didn't drink it.

Non-drinkers were indeed critical. The brand was criticised for being 'weak' and 'having no head'. Its symbol – the bear – was mischievously abused, with the brand all too frequently being referred to as 'bear's piss'! All this, when in blind tests it was shown that the brand matched its key competitors. The justification for this criticism was perhaps that the brand had experienced early product shortcomings, but these had been rectified as early as 1981; the real problem lay elsewhere.

Quantitative research added to the understanding of the brand's problems. Hofmeister's weaknesses were apparent in a number of ways.

Drinker Commitment

Compared with other major lager brands, Hofmeister had the lowest level of drinker commitment (see Table 1).

TABLE 1:   DRINKERS' COMMITMENT TO BRANDS

commitment = drink regularly ÷ drink nowadays

	%
Carling Black Label	55
Carlsberg	45
Heineken	42
Skol	42
Harp	38
Hofmeister	36

Source: Millward-Brown Jan–Feb 1983

Brand Awareness

Hofmeister's prompted brand awareness was comparable with other brands. However, its spontaneous awareness was very low. The brand lacked 'front-of-mindness' (see Figure 2).

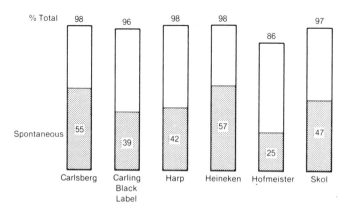

Figure 2. *Hofmeister brand awareness vs. the Big 5*
Source: Millward Brown Jan/Feb 1983

Quantitative Attitude Measures

The brand had a weak image profile compared to the other leading brands (see Figure 3).

Conventional market research interpretation would suggest that the cause of the brand's problem arose through these image weaknesses, and presumably could be put right by rectifying them. As we shall see, in the real world advertising did not work in this neat way.

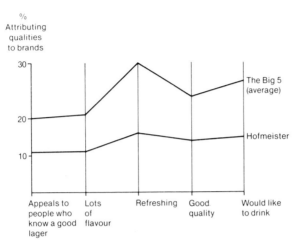

Figure 3. *Brand images: Hofmeister vs. the Big 5 competitors*
Source: Millward Brown Jan/Feb 1983

THE ADVERTISING BRIEF

If Courage's lager performance was to be revitalised, then the new advertising had two essential tasks. In the short term, it had to boost the saliency and appeal of Hofmeister amongst lager drinkers exposed to the brand, primarily Courage pub-goers. In the long term, it had to raise the reputation of Hofmeister alongside that of the market leaders, amongst the wider universe of all lager drinkers.

The initial advertising objective was therefore to raise Hofmeister's profile in the market-place and to increase its franchise of frequent drinkers. Brand loyalty is weak in the standard lager market, but if the advertising could create an aura of popularity and success around Hofmeister, it could bolster the confidence of its drinkers in their choice and thus build their commitment to the brand.

The mechanism by which we believed this could be achieved was the creation of a new brand image for Hofmeister which was not only distinctive, but of genuine appeal and relevance to young drinkers.

The creative brief emerging from this initial research and thinking requested a campaign that would position Hofmeister as 'cool' and fashionable. It suggested a number of guidelines, the most important of which was to bring back 'The Bear'. Our qualitative work had consistently found this to be Hofmeister's only brand asset. Although drinkers were confused as to what the bear did, looked like, or represented, they knew Hofmeister as the 'beer with the bear' and some even claimed to ask for 'a pint of bear'. Despite its two-year absence from Hofmeister advertising, this animal symbol remained potent. What it needed was direction, a purpose and a relevance. If a new bear was to embody the brand or personalise its drinkers, it clearly had to do so in a way that those drinkers found admirable and sympathetic.

A strong character, we felt, could personify the 'cool' aspect of the brand and carry the secondary elements of intended communication, notably Hofmeister's satisfying product qualities and German heritage. It should also provide a long-term brand theme capable of translation into point-of-sale and promotional material – significant elements in drinks marketing.

MEDIA PLANNING

The Reason for Choosing TV

It was clear from our consumer research that a strong TV presence was an integral part of drinkers' confidence in a lager brand; to compete with the market leaders, we had to match them on that battle ground. More importantly, TV was also the natural choice for the job. Given the need to create a new, confident image for the brand, TV provided the most intrusive and influential way to reach our young drinkers. The budget of £1.7 million set for the draught product was a realistic reflection of the brand's share and less than any of our major competitors' anticipated spend. Rather than dilute this presence further, we therefore decided to put all the money into TV.

The Media Strategy

Although Courage's pubs are distributed throughout England and Wales, 70 per cent of them are concentrated in six TV areas: London, TVS, Yorkshire, Harlech, TSW and Central. We therefore concentrated our advertising in these areas alone. Advertising for canned Hofmeister ran in these areas alongside the draught commercials.

DEVELOPING THE CAMPAIGN

The development of the new advertising revolved around the development of a character, George the Bear. This took four stages of qualitative animatic testing, during which his personality evolved to meet young drinkers' need for a figure whom they could admire, identify with and be amused by.

The agency's original embodiment of 'cool' was a classically sophisticated, somewhat haughty bear in a dinner jacket; by the final stage, George had emerged as a stylish, 'Fonz'-type, street-smart bear, the leader of his young peer group. Trendy, extrovert, witty, fun to be with and slightly anarchic, George reflected the aspirations of young drinkers. He became at once both brand and drinker and, through this dual role, tied Hofmeister to a set of positive values that the drinkers themselves demanded of the advertising.

Bear: Life in a Bavarian forest was boring.
A big event was me and Ronnie Rabbit watching a leaf fall down.
Rabbit: (excitedly) a leaf! A leaf!
Bear: Hey . . .

Bear: Then one day I discovered Hofmeister lager with a picture of my Grandpa on it.
It had a cool cut on the back of the throat that was so good I decided to leave the forest.

And so I found . . .
companionship.

I found the left hand screw to kiss onto the pink. (SFX kiss)
But most of all I found Hofmeister on draught.

The moral is: If you want poetry stand and stare

But if you want great lager –
follow the bear, hey!

Bear: So the cold Hofmeister is sliding down like a dream

When this girl comes up and asks me what I do.

So I tell her I'm a dispensing chemist, which really impresses her for a bear,

And I'll read her prescription any time.

Sometimes I think the medical profession is misunderstood. I prescribe Hofmeister twice nightly, hey.

Hofmeister. For great lager, follow the bear.

RESULTS: SALES EFFECT

The year following the launch of the new campaign was a record one for lager: the hot summer of 1983 helped standard lager sales in pubs rise by 9 per cent. Over the same period, Hofmeister's pub sales increased by 25 per cent (see Figure 4). This dramatic

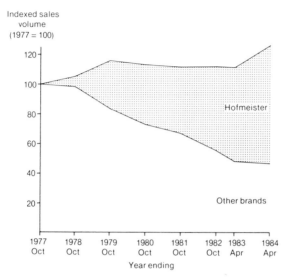

Figure 4. *Courage sales of lager to the pub trade*
Source: Courage

growth was not caused by a wider availability of the brand: its pub distribution only grew by 1.5 per cent. Hofmeister's rate of sale thus rose by 13 per cent more than the market. Furthermore, the brand's growth was incremental to Courage's total lager sales, rather than substitutional as it had been before. The company's share of the pub lager market therefore rose after two years of consistent decline, at a time when its ales share was static (see Figure 5). Hofmeister's brand share performance within the standard lager market in pubs was impressive, increasing by 1.24 per cent, worth no less than £10 million in this huge market.

We examined some possible causes of Hofmeister's improved performance:

1. *Product* There was no change in product specification over the period.
2. *Price* Hofmeister's price actually increased in relation to its competitors at this time.
3. *Distribution* As mentioned above, Hofmeister's pub distribution grew by less than 1.5 per cent.
4. *Promotions* There was no change in the level of below-the-line support for Hofmeister, although new promotions and promotional material were designed to complement the advertising. Indeed, enthusiasm for the advertising led to demand for branded 'George the Bear' T-shirts that surpassed all such previous offers.
5. *Presentation* The draught fount remained unchanged.
6. *Pubs* There was no change in pub investment policy over the period.

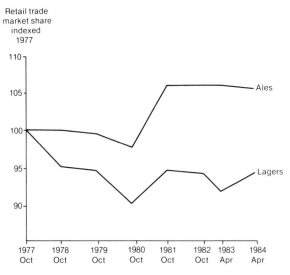

Figure 5. *Courage's retail trade share of major brewers market*
Source: BMS, Courage

The reasons for the uplift in sales had to lie elsewhere. The strongest indication as to the cause came from an area analysis of the sales increase, which demonstrated its association with the advertising activity. In those Courage pubs which saw no change in the lagers on offer between the summers of 1982 and 1983, *Hofmeister sales grew at almost twice the rate in the advertised areas as in the non-advertised ones* (see Table 2).

TABLE 2: HOFMEISTER PUB SALES IN UNCHANGED CONFIGURATIONS*

		1982	1983
advertised areas	Hofmeister	100	139
	the market	100	121
non-advertised areas	Hofmeister	100	120
	the market	100	121

period: July–Aug 1983 vs. 1982
* in pubs where the range of lagers on offer did not change
Source: Courage, BMS

RESULTS: CONSUMER BEHAVIOUR

This uplift in Hofmeister's sales was explained by marked shifts in claimed consumer behaviour relating to the brand. Over the year following the new campaign's launch, claimed trial of Hofmeister rose by 13 per cent in the advertised areas: non-advertised areas showed no rise at all (see Table 3). 'Nowadays' drinkers on the survey also increased, whilst the proportion within those who claimed to be regular Hofmeister drinkers rose as well, indicating a new commitment to the brand. The behavioural data is thus consistent with the observed increase in Hofmeister's sales *in advertised areas*. We will now attempt to explain the link between behaviour and advertising.

TABLE 3:   HOFMEISTER TRIAL AND DRINKING IN ADVERTISED AREAS

	Pre %	Post %
trial	45	51
drink nowadays	17	21
drink regularly	6	9
'commitment'	36%	43%

commitment = drink regularly ÷ drink nowadays
period: Jan–Feb 1984 vs. 1983
Source: Millward Brown

RESULTS: CONSUMER ATTITUDES

That advertising had played some part in Hofmeister's improved performance appeared evident from both quantitative and qualitative research. The new campaign was unmistakably noticeable and well branded. Advertising recall shot up in response to the first burst, to levels never previously achieved by the brand (see Figure 6).

This level of awareness, moreover, was greater than for any of the 'Big Five' lager brands' campaigns, despite media expenditure lower than any of theirs. Similarly, brand awareness in advertised areas rose to higher levels than had been seen at the height of the

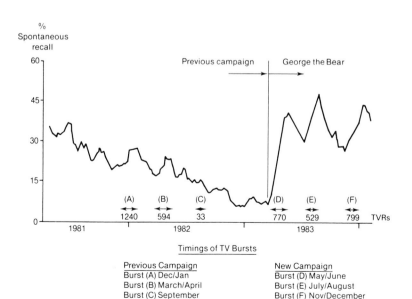

Figure 6. *Hofmeister claimed advertising recall*
Source: Millward Brown

1982 campaign, so that Hofmeister's consumer 'stature' came more closely in line with the other major brands (see Table 4).

TABLE 4: HOFMEISTER BRAND AWARENESS IN ADVERTISED AREAS

	Pre %	Post %
	spontaneous/total awareness	
Hofmeister	31/90	38/92
the 'Big Five' brands	48/97	48/98

period: Jan–Feb 1984 vs. 1983
Source: Millward Brown

We sought to establish the link between Hofmeister's new consumer saliency and its observed sales increase, by examining the brand's consumer image. We found this link in qualitative research, but *not* in the quantitative brand imagery data.

Qualitative Findings

Our findings were based on qualitative research conducted in February 1984. We found that the advertising had altered drinkers' perceptions of the brand. A faceless brand had been given a positive, desirable identity – that of George the Bear: confident, popular and enviable.

> 'He doesn't have to try'.
> 'He's cool'.
> 'He can do anything'.

Drinkers, moreover, had readily identified with George, bear or not:

> 'I don't really see him as a bear'.
> 'He's the sort of bloke I'd like to be'.

Drinkers were happy to drink Hofmeister because they perceived it to be popular and trendy, rather than because it was a superior product. Indeed, product perceptions – always low key amongst lager drinkers – had changed little; the advertising, after all, had deliberately provided little more than basic product reassurance. Non-drinkers of Hofmeister, on the other hand, were now reluctant to criticise the brand. Many of them referred to it as second best to their brand.

Quantitative Findings

When we turned to the quantitative data, however, we were surprised to find that there had been no significant shift in Hofmeister's consumer standing.

To attempt to understand this anomaly, Boase Massimi Pollitt conducted a series of in-depth interviews among lager drinkers who had beforehand completed the lager tracking study questionnaire. We found that brand image and brand usage could not be separated in the way the questionnaire attempted to. This is because when answering a structured questionnaire the majority of lager drinkers will not express an opinion of a brand they have not tried or do not drink regularly. This observation has been made for other product fields.[1]

Regular drinkers of Hofmeister were content with the brand and rated it accordingly. However, because of Hofmeister's relatively small presence in the market, they were swamped by non-drinkers of the brand who were reluctant to rate it. Average ratings were thus low and pegged down by the brand's low absolute availability. Its non-drinkers were now happy with the brand, but still unwilling to praise it extravagantly on *product* grounds against better-known competitors, as they were perfectly well aware that the product was nothing special.

The in-depth interviews supported the earlier qualitative research in suggesting that Hofmeister's new appeal lay in drinkers' perceptions of it as a popular, fashionable lager; thus, the link between the brand's advertising-born saliency and its sales increase was confirmed.

SUMMARY AND FINANCIAL EVALUATION

In the year following the new advertising, Hofmeister's sales increased at over twice the market rate on a very small distribution increase. This increase was confined to advertised areas; elsewhere the brand's sales simply rose in line with the market. This strong performance almost single-handedly reversed Courage's declining lager share; given no other variables, it seems hard to avoid the conclusion that the new advertising was primarily responsible for Hofmeister's change of fortune, and the achievement of the marketing objectives.

In an IPA competition there may be an expectation for the case history to demonstrate a massive profit payback from advertising investment. Unfortunately the vast majority of advertised brands are not afforded this opportunity. In Hofmeister's case, once the 'natural' market growth has been subtracted from the sales increase (setting aside the fact that the brand had previously performed consistently below the market rate), the incremental wholesale profit on the sales increase achieved was £1.9 million, against an advertising spend of £1.7 million over the same period.

It is worth remembering that the lager market, like many, is one in which heavy expenditure is always expected, simply to *maintain* share, and in which advertisers look gradually to recoup their initial advertising investment in following years. Yet this campaign generated incremental profit greater than the cost of the advertising in the first year alone. Nor have we considered here either the additional effect of the advertising on draught sales in the club trade, which also outstripped the market, or the considerably enhanced retail profit secured by Courage pubs at the same time.

We hope we have shown a 'real world' case where advertising has succeeded in making a significant contribution to sales and a solid contribution to profits.

CONCLUSIONS

The tied-pub trade is a captive market, yet advertising can be shown to have a significant effect on sales within it. Even where consumer purchase can be guaranteed, advertising has a role to play. Rate of sale depends on consumer commitment to outlet and product, and a key to this is brand imagery; in the absence of any grounds for rational discrimination, advertising must play a crucial part in creating a strong brand image.

This case history suggests that the increased consumer confidence in a brand through a strong brand image *can* bring about a sales increase, even in a captive market, which more than justifies the financial investment involved.

REFERENCES

1.   Bird, M., Channon, C. and Ehrenberg, A. S. C., *Journal of Marketing Research*, August 1970.

5

The 'Big John' Campaign

Advertising in the beer market

INTRODUCTION

This paper attempts to show how the 'Big John' advertising campaign boosted John Smith's Bitter's brand share amongst Yorkshire beers and helped to increase sales at a time of market decline.

It is notoriously difficult to isolate the effect of advertising on beer sales, owing to the complexity of the business and the sheer size of the brands involved, which together mitigate against radical, and therefore easily measurable, changes. The attempt is nonetheless well worth making. As the £6 billion beer market has fallen into decline under the effects of the recession, the fight for brand share has intensified and the brewers have increased their advertising expenditure. In 1981 they spent well over £40 million on television alone, of which more than £12 million went to promote bitters such as John Smith's, an increase over 1980 of some 60 per cent. While this expenditure does not appear to expand the market, it is clearly believed to influence drinkers' brand choice; to determine whether it can do so is the aim of this paper.

With John Smith's Bitter we were fortunate. The number of variables was fewer than usual. Courage and John Smith's have good data from a wide variety of sources over several years, so we were able to measure sales (and consumer response) before the advertising and after, and in the advertised area against non-advertised areas. Thus we were able to estimate the incremental sales stimulated by advertising.

The study is chiefly concerned with brand sales through John Smith's 'tied' public houses. This is for three reasons: retail (pub) sales account for the bulk of brand volume at a secure margin; the brand's problems were most evident in this sector; and better data are available to us for the tied trade than for the 'free' (club) trade.

This analysis is interesting because it represents a first step towards a more thorough understanding of what advertising can do for pub sales in general. We have gained a clearer idea of how advertising can be used and evaluated, and hope we show that, although there are several ways for a brewer to stimulate sales, in this case advertising was the most efficient in that it produced extra sales more cheaply than the alternatives. This experience and the evaluative techniques used will be useful, we believe, in planning future marketing investment.

BACKGROUND

The Brewery

John Smith's Brewery was founded in 1758 and taken over by Courage in 1970. It still produces all its own beers at Tadcaster, Yorkshire. John Smith's 1500 pubs are widespread across the North of England, and account for 15 per cent of all pubs in the heartland of Yorkshire. Tied houses account for some 60 per cent of total sales; the remainder goes through the free trade (mainly clubs). These proportions are roughly in line with those of other major brewers.

The Brand

John Smith's Bitter accounts for about half of the Company's total sales and is sold in every John Smith's pub. It is a well-established Yorkshire beer, whose formulation was last altered in the mid-1970s. It is a medium-strength, session bitter with an original gravity of 1036°. Ales of this type are known as 'Bitter Is' in brewery definitions; they are stronger and more expensive than 'Bitter IIs' or 'Milds', weaker and cheaper than 'Premiums', and constitute the single largest sector in the whole beer market.

The Market

The Bitter I market in the North East was worth some £350 million in 1980 (at retail prices). Bitter Is account for almost half of all draught beers in Yorkshire, though nationally the proportion is nearer one-quarter.

Yorkshire consumers are thus committed bitter drinkers, averaging over 13 pints of bitter a week, and tend to judge brewers by their Bitter Is rather than by their strongest beer or the standard of their pubs. Pub traffic is materially affected by the status of the brewer's Bitter I. The sector therefore is of primary importance.

The Competition

John Smith's chief rivals among the major brewers, who account for some 80 per cent of the Yorkshire market, comprise: Tetley (Allied), with 14 per cent of Yorkshire pubs and a massive free trade presence; Stones (Bass), 16 per cent; Whitbread, 11 per cent; and Webster (Grand Metropolitan), 7 per cent. Competition is fierce: draught bitters accounted for some 30 per cent of all Yorkshire TV beer advertising, against some 20 per cent in England and Wales (1981).

THE PROBLEM

John Smith's Bitter's volume sales started to fall in 1979, even though the Bitter I market was static.

 ˙The decline was due to lost pub sales. Sales in the so-called free trade (the largely finance-dependent clubs) continued to grow, reflecting distribution increases (Table 1.1).

TABLE 1.1   JOHN SMITH'S BITTER TRADE PERFORMANCE, 1976-1980 (1976 = 100)

| John Smith's volume share of: | 12 months to December | | | 6 months to June |
	1977	1978	1979	1980
Pubs	100.7	100.7	95.4	95.4
Free trade	99.5	107.4	113.8	127.4

Source: BMS (see Appendix)
Base: major brewers, north east.

The pub share decline in 1979 represented a loss of 5.7 million pints (worth some £1.9 million at 1979 retail prices). But there is a multiplier effect: bitter drinkers (accompanied by friends) also spend money on fruit machines, bar food and games, so that non-beer sales account for some 30 per cent of pub turnover. Thus the total revenue loss caused by a mainstream bitter's decline is hard to estimate, but may be double the value of its own lost sales.

The BMS 'North East' region includes Yorkshire and Tyne-Tees. Company sales figures, collected on a regional basis from 1979, show that the 1980 sales decline was in Yorkshire. Non-Yorkshire sales were growing, reflecting pub acquisitions (Table 1.2).

TABLE 1.2:   JOHN SMITH'S BITTER VOLUME SALES (PUBS) BY REGION, 1979–1980

12 months to October 1979 (fiscal year)	Percentage change 1980 v. 1979
Yorkshire (75%)	−4
Non-Yorkshire (25%)	+7

Source: Courage (see Appendix)

Several explanations for the sales decline were examined and rejected:

1. *Product*. No change.
2. *Price*. In line with competition (cf. Wyman-Harris LTM, see Appendix).
3. *Pub standards*. No evidence of deterioration. No change in rate of investment in estate. No unusual staff or recruitment problems.
4. *Distribution*. No loss in the universe of tied pubs.
5. *Industrial relations*. No problems of production or availability.
6. *Share of mix*. No product in the portfolio promoted at the expense of John Smith's Bitter.

The fount design was slightly modified in the late 1970s, but this was not thought to be a significant factor.

We turned to consumer research to understand what appeared to be a consumer problem with the brand.

UNDERSTANDING THE CONSUMER PROBLEM

We conducted ten group discussions in June 1980 when reappointed to the brand. The sample comprised regular drinkers of both John Smith's and competitive bitters, in five Yorkshire towns covering strong and weak John Smith's trading areas.

Findings were consistent across locations. Essentially, John Smith's Bitter lacked character. Although acceptable to most drinkers, it did not arouse enthusiasm among its users. It was known to be local and long-established (both positive attributes), but so were its competitors. It was regarded merely as 'one of' Yorkshire's bitters, while Tetley's was the paradigm, especially among young drinkers, who saw John Smith's as an 'old boy's drink'. Younger drinkers in particular spoke highly of handpumped Tetley's (the consumer symbol for cask-conditioned, traditional 'real ale'). We deal with this important point in more detail later.

Survey data corroborated these findings (Table 1.3). The measures reflected but exaggerated the sales loss among drinkers in general, and young drinkers in particular.

TABLE 1.3:   CLAIMED 'MOST OFTEN' DRUNK BRAND OF BITTER
($\neq$) = 18–24-year-olds

	1974	1978	1980
Base: total sample	449	314	264
		Percentage of total sample	
John Smith's	10 (13)	9 (10)	6 (5)
Tetley	19 (19)	27 (34)	29 (32)
Trophy	–	9 (9)	11 (9)
Stones	–	9 (6)	112 (14)

Source: Marplan, Yorks (see Appendix)
Base: All male bitter drinkers weekly or more often

The 'most often' drinkers appeared to decline much more than sales. This, we believe, is because the 'most often' claim measures both behaviour and consumer preference – a greater propensity to think of the brand as 'my brand' when asked a market research question like this. Thus the loss of 'most often' drinkers reflected the loss of commitment to the brand among its users, evident in the group discussions.

We seemed to have a particular problem with young drinkers in Yorkshire (see Table 1.4).

TABLE 1.4:   18–24-YEAR-OLDS AS PROPORTION OF 'MOST
OFTEN' PLUS 'REGULAR' DRINKERS

	Yorkshire		Non-Yorkshire*
	1978	1980	1980
	%	%	%
John Smith's	21	14	22
Tetley	16	23	22

Source: Marplan
* Non-Yorks. = North West/Lancs plus Tyne-Tees.

Image measures also showed a decline, especially among young drinkers; Tetley, however, improved among this group on overall imagery (Table 1.5). The scales in this table have been selected as the most descriptive of drinkers' attitudes to bitter brands on product and user imagery.

TABLE 1.5:   MEAN SCORES ON THREE ATTITUDE SCALES

Base: heard of brands		1976 (223/221)	1978 (179/119)	1979 (157/115)
'Good value for a bitter'				
John Smith's	All	3.43	3.49	3.23
	18–24	3.51	3.72	3.22
Tetley	18–24	3.65	3.99	3.93
'Lots of flavour'				
John Smith's	All	3.48	3.54	3.37
	18–24	3.49	3.48	3.23
Tetley	18–24	3.67	3.90	4.11
'For knowledgeable drinkers'				
John Smith's	All	3.26	3.52	3.34
	18–24	3.24	3.37	3.16
Tetley	18–24	3.28	3.89	4.21

Source: Marplan, Yorks.
Scale: +5 to +1.

The importance of the younger drinkers is threefold. They tend to consume more bitter than older people; they go to more pubs and are more willing to try different drinks; and they represent the market's future and will retain, in later years, the tastes they now develop.

Reasons for Loss of Young Drinkers

There seemed to be two factors affecting the decline in young drinkers. First, there was a change in the market. This period saw the northern revival of handpumped, cask-conditioned 'real ales' from major brewers, of whom Tetley's were in the forefront. Handpumped Bitter Is showed significant share growth: +3 per cent year on year (Table 1.6).

TABLE 1.6: HANDPUMPED BITTER I'S SHARE OF TOTAL PUB SALES IN THE NORTH OF ENGLAND

	1979				1980	
Quarter	1	2	3	4	1	2
Percentage share	n/a	8.1	10.9	11.5	11.9	11.1

Sources: LTM (Wyman-Harris)

The demand for handpumped ales is most prevalent among young drinkers. The effect of young drinkers on pub beer sales is shown in Table 1.7.

TABLE 1.7:   EFFECT OF UNDER-25s ON HANDPUMPED BITTER'S SHARE OF PUB SALES

	Proportion of Under-25s in Bar		
	Under 10%	11–20%	21–40%
Handpumped bitter's percentage share of all sales (excluding lager)	12.9	14.6	20.6

Source: LTM (Wyman-Harris)

But John Smith's Bitter was not available in handpumped form; John Smith's brewery only produces 'bright' (keg) beers, so the brand could not profit from the new trend amongst young drinkers.

The second factor was a decline in John Smith's Bitter share of advertising voice (see Table 1.8). Moreover its advertisements had stressed the brand's 'Yorkshire heritage' during the 1970s, and similar claims had been adopted by other bitters, so that confusion existed in consumer recall of particular brands' campaigns. Too many competitors had jumped on the same bandwagon.

TABLE 1.8:   JOHN SMITH'S BITTER SHARE OF DRAUGHT BITTER ADVERTISING ON
YORKSHIRE TV

	1977	1978	1979	1980
Share of Yorkshire's major brands	34	27	22	15
Share of all brewers' brands	26	18	19	12

Source: MEAL (Media Expenditure Analysis Limited)

In conclusion, we believed that sales were down because the brand had declined in appeal, particularly to young drinkers, who had lost interest. It lacked handpumps, and the advertising had failed to offer something new in the face of heavy competition from similar bitter campaigns and more exciting lager commercials.

THE CASE FOR ADVERTISING

The marketing objective was to increase volume sales. Various options were assessed.

Installing cask-conditioned capacity at the brewery and handpump facilities in the pubs was not judged to be financially justifiable. Substantial increases in the rate of investment in the Yorkshire estate (or increasing the size of the estate) were not affordable within budget plans. However, advertising offered a cost-effective way of restoring share, by revitalizing the brand in the eyes of consumers.

The 18–24s appeared to be the most volatile group in terms of brand imagery and choice, and produced the greatest volume return for a given proportional change. If brand advertising could regain the loyalty of only a small proportion of these drinkers, share would be regained, and with that would follow benefits for total pub revenue.

It is worth stating here the rationale for putting media support behind a brand rather than outlets. Direct pub advertising is impractical, because of the infinite variations within the estate: all pubs are different, in size, location, style or 'atmosphere'; that is their charm. Virtually the only elements common to all the pubs are the John Smith's name and the beer on sale. By advertising the mainstream bitter, we could support the brewer whose name endorsed it, as well as his biggest single product, and could promote its sales in both pubs and clubs.

THE ADVERTISING

The Task

The task was to create a more relevant brand image for John Smith's Bitter (without any changes to the product or its presentation at point of sale), which would give the brand greater appeal in the face of increasingly aggressive competition.

Objectives

PRIMARY

The main objective was to restore the commitment of John Smith's Bitter drinkers to the brand, thus increasing their frequency of purchase.

SECONDARY

The secondary objective was to attract lapsed drinkers, both those who had switched to other pubs and those who had adopted other brands in the free trade.

The Role of Advertising

These objectives were realistic because of the significance of brand imagery in brand choice, particularly among younger drinkers. Beer drinking is essentially social and group pressures can be strong. The public selection of a brand of beer reflects the buyer's self-image in the same way as choice of cigarettes, clothes or car. Buyers want to feel that they are making a sensible, defensible choice that reflects well upon them as knowledgeable beer drinkers. This can override actual taste preference; the brewery adage that 'people drink with their eyes' has been repeatedly confirmed by blind and branded product tests, where the brand-names can reverse the preferences expressed 'blind'.

The under-30s tend not to be beer experts: they are too young. Their drinking is more influenced by what is popular and fashionable among their peer group. With them, the problem was to find a brand personality for John Smith's Bitter which could match the appeal of handpumped rivals, be talked about in the pubs, and revive their confidence in the brand.

TARGET MARKET

The primary target market was defined as young bitter drinkers (18–30, C1C2D). They were the most frequent buyers, the future market, the least enthusiastic about John Smith's Bitter and the most interested by advertising.

The proviso was attached that the advertising should not alienate the brand's older drinkers.

THE BRIEF

Alternate strategies to achieve the advertising objectives were investigated in group discussions, in the form of concept boards. Consumer reactions forced us to acknowledge that no single, strong, product-based platform existed. As a mainstream brand in the biggest sector of the beer market, John Smith's Bitter had, to some extent, to be all things to all men; its advertising had to express the essential qualities of a major Yorkshire bitter, and attach them unmistakably to John Smith's.

John Smith's Bitter
'The Forester'

(To the tune of 'Big John')

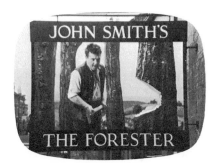

I wish I could get down from chopping these trees, 'cause a John Smith's pub is below my knees.

Now forestry is a worthy career, but stuck up on this sign I miss the big bitter beer that's Big John.

(Chorus) Big John, Big John, Great Big John.

Now don't get me wrong 'cause this job is OK ... I like trees a lot if they fall the right way.

There's advantages too with Big John Smith's beer – 'cause of the simple fact they've got branches everywhere.

(Chorus) Big John, Big John, Big John (fades)

John Smith's Bitter
'The Cricketer'

(To the tune of 'Big John')

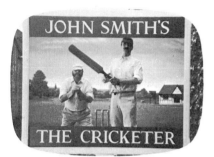

I've had a long innings on this John Smith's sign. In fact I've been here since 1909.

And I wish that bowler there could knock off these bails, 'cause I reckon I deserve a pint of Big John Smith's Ale; that's Big John.

(Chorus) Big John, Big John, Great Big John.

Now that brings my score to 5 million and two. My faithful old bat is nearly worn through.

Hmmm ... must be woodworm, well who'd have thought that!

Now for the big bitter taste of John Smith's. Howzat!

(Chorus) Big John, Big John (fades)

The execution, therefore, needed to be masculine, sociable, working-class and pub-based; drinkers in the commercials must really want the beer and be seen to enjoy it.

The tone should be assertive and the style contemporary, so that it could rival lager advertising in its appeal to young drinkers.

The communication, most importantly, should be that while John Smith's remained proud of its Yorkshire heritage, it was nonetheless as successful, popular and right today as it had ever been. Drinkers of the brand, we wanted consumers to believe, were not the 'old boys' of current criticism, but admirable drinking men who knew their beer.

THE CAMPAIGN

The creative solution was the 'Big John' idea. This stemmed from the fact that drinkers often ask for 'a pint of John's' at the bar.

The advertising aimed to create the impression of John Smith's Bitter as a 'big' pint – popular, widespread, drunk by everyone. 'Big' also implied a flavourful and strong pint.

The ingenuity of the campaign came from the blend of brand and drinker: 'Big John' was also a character, a real drinking man.

Classic values were expressed through the pubs and their signs, the traditional occupations of the characters, and the role of the beer as reward and refreshment after labour. 'Yorkshireness' was not overt – a reversal of earlier campaigns and a distinction from most competitors.

The modern elements of the 'Big Bad John' music, humour and special effects, gave the idea its freshness and strong branding.

Key frames from the two draught commercials are on pp. 18–19, the music track was faithful to the original Country and Western song, well-known by drinkers when tested.

MEDIA

Choice

Television was chosen as the sole medium. This was not only for reasons of cost-efficiency (although heavy drinkers do tend to be heavy ITV watchers too), but because of the nature of the advertising task. First, in a market dominated by brands spending heavily on television, John Smith's Bitter needed to establish a major advertising presence. Second, the chosen strategy involved a change to the brand's perceived character, which only television was felt able to achieve quickly.

Buying

Four bursts ran in Yorkshire. Timing was related to market seasonality and to cost-efficient time periods. Weight was determined by the media budget available (£250 000) and deemed sufficient at over 1500 men TVRs during 1981. Granada received one burst in November/December. Advertising for canned John Smith's was on air with the draught commercials.

Weight

With the launch of the new campaign, John Smith's Bitter's weight and share of advertising expenditure in Yorkshire rose substantially, returning to historic levels (see Table 1.9).

TABLE 1.9   JOHN SMITH'S BITTER SHARE OF DRAUGHT BITTER ADVERTISING SPEND ON
YORKSHIRE TV

	1977 %	1978 %	1979 %	1980 %	1981 %
Share of Yorkshire's major bitters	34	27	22	15	34
Share of all brewers' bitters	26	18	19	12	26

Source: MEAL

RESPONSE TO THE ADVERTISING

Three stages of qualitative research were carried out by BMP (see Appendix) to confirm the relevance and appeal of the strategy, and to develop the executions.

Post-campaign qualitative research revealed that the desired communications were being achieved (as they were during the pre-testing). The following verbatim quotations from the group discussions illustrate the consumer response to 'Big John'.

The beer:
   'It's a big pint, it's good value with a good taste.' (Leeds 18–30)
   'It goes down big and it sells a lot.' (Doncaster 25–40)
   'It says the beer's strong, a man's drink.' (York 18–24)

The drinker:
   'It's drunk by big and manly chaps.' (Leeds 30–45)
   'It's a masculine ad, all macho.' (York 25–40)
   'They're aimed at a big lad who's been knocking down a tree and wants to get down to tap room.' (Leeds 18–30)

The brewer:
   'It shows that John Smith's are still in business, still as good as ever was, as traditional as ever was.' (Leeds 30–45)
   'It's big John Smith.' (Leeds 18–30)
Source: BMP Qualitative

The post-campaign research also indicated positive improvements in the brand's status. A year before, John Smith's was simply overlooked, and placed among the crowd of lesser brands, behind Tetley's. But now its drinkers displayed considerable enthusiasm for the brand, and even most Tetley drinkers acknowledged it as an acceptable choice. Nor was it seen particularly as an 'old boy's drink' – it was for everyone, young and old.

This is not to say that among all drinkers the brand matched Tetley's, but our drinkers now felt justified in stating their preference. It had risen above the competitive brands into clear second place and the renewed commitment of its buyers (our target) had reduced Tetley's predominance.

The 'Big John' campaign seemed to have affected this attitudinal shift more than any other factor. Drinkers vastly enjoyed the advertising and saw the advertiser (John Smith's) in a new light:

   'They're new and something different, not run of the mill adverts like the others.' (Leeds 18–30)
   'The Woodman one was brilliant. They're trendy and they're always bringing them up to date.' (York 18–24)
Source: BMP Qualitative

THE EFFECTS OF ADVERTISING: SALES

The campaign appeared to work in terms of increased sales, and also the intermediate measures we would expect.

The brand's volume sales in its Yorkshire pubs rose in 1981 by 4.8 per cent, even though the Bitter I market there declined by 7.7 per cent. Market share thus increased to its highest ever level, increasing from 97.2 in 1980 to 105.5 in 1981 (1976 = 100).

Year on year, the share improvement continued throughout 1981, although the greatest growth was seen in the first quarter, when the heaviest advertising took place (Table 1.10).

TABLE 1.10:   JOHN SMITH'S BITTER TRADE PERFORMANCE IN 1981 (1980 = 100)

		1981		
	1st quarter	2nd quarter	3rd quarter	4th quarter
John Smith's volume share of pubs	116	106	105	108

Source: BMS
Base: major brewers, north east.

The difference between the 1979 and the 1981 shares represented additional sales of 10.3 million pints, worth some £5.1 million at 1981 retail prices.

The additional effect of the campaign on free trade sales is hard to measure as distribution increased, but the brand's share rose from 100 in 1980, to 114 in 1981.

Comparing sales in the advertised area with those in John Smith's other trading regions, the turn-around in Yorkshire looked all the more remarkable, as sales-growth slowed elsewhere (Table 1.11).

TABLE 1.11:   JOHN SMITH'S BITTER VOLUME SALES (PUBS) BY REGION, 1980–1981

12 months to October 1980 (fiscal year)	% Change year-on-year 1980	1981
Yorkshire (75%)	−4	+5
Non-Yorkshire (25%)	+7	+3

Source: Courage

We examined other possible explanations for the rise in sales:

1. Distribution. Static in Yorkshire; volume improvements were attributable to increased consumer offtake.
2. Pub standards. Investment in the estate and improvements in licensee selection continued, and both are probably more significant than advertising in the long term. But Yorkshire pubs did not receive proportionately more attention than non-Yorkshire ones.
3. Price. In line with competition.

THE EFFECTS OF ADVERTISING: CONSUMER BEHAVIOUR

Consumer research helped us identify a causal link between the advertising and increased sales (see Table 1.12).

TABLE 1.12:   CLAIMED 'MOST OFTEN' DRUNK BRAND OF BITTER ( ) =
18–24s

| | Yorkshire | | Non-Yorkshire | |
	1980	1982	1980	1982
Base: total sample	264	412	540	797
		Percentage of total sample		
John Smith's	6 (5)	19 (19)	3 (3)	4 (3)
Tetley	29 (32)	30 (32)	11 (12)	13 (8)
Trophy	11 (9)	9 (10)	5 (6)	4 (4)
Stones	12 (14)	10 (11)	4 (3)	7 (6)

Source: Marplan
Non-Yorks. = North West/Lancs plus Tyne-Tees.

As with the decline, the rise in claimed 'most often' brand share reflects the Yorkshire sales increase but exaggerates it, suggesting an increase in preference as well as actual consumption. This is also implied by the increase in the proportion of 'most often' drinkers among those who had ever tried John Smith's Bitter (see Table 1.13).

TABLE 1.13:   'MOST OFTEN' DRINKERS AS
PROPORTION OF 'EVER TRIED' 1980–1982

	1980 %	1982 %
John Smith's – Yorkshire	13	36
– Non-Yorkshire	10	9
Tetley	47	47
Trophy	21	22
Stones	21	21

Source: Marplan
Base: ever tried brand

Such a large increase may seem incredible, but our confidence that the measures reflect a real change in our drinkers' loyalty to John Smith's was confirmed by the stability of the non-Yorkshire John Smith's and the competitive brand figures.

In claimed behaviour, it seemed that the advertising had more effect on the younger drinker. The proportion of loyal drinkers who were aged 18–24 came back into line with other brands (see Table 1.14).

TABLE 1.14:   18–24s AS PROPORTION OF
'MOST OFTEN' PLUS 'REGULAR' DRINKERS

	1980 %	1982 %
John Smith's – Yorkshire	14	21
– Non-Yorkshire	22	20
Tetley	23	23
Trophy	23	23
Stones	24	21

Source: Marplan

Attitudes to John Smith's

These also showed improvement within the advertised Yorkshire area and, while young drinkers still lagged behind their elders, it appeared that the movements were encouraging (Table 1.15).

TABLE 1.15:   MEAN SCORES ON THREE ATTITUDE SCALES

| | Yorkshire | | North West/Lancs | |
	1980	1982	1980	1982
'Good value for a bitter'				
John Smith's All	3.23	3.60	3.34	3.13
18–24	3.22	3.56		
'Lots of flavour'				
John Smith's All	3.37	3.66	3.39	3.35
18–24	3.23	3.41		
'For knowledgeable drinkers'				
John Smith's All	3.34	3.50	3.45	3.24
18–24	3.16	3.34		

Source: Marplan
Scale: $+5$ to $+1$

It is interesting that, despite our success with our primary target, the younger age group, we in fact achieved a turn-round in loyalty and attitudes among John Smith's Bitter drinkers of all ages in Yorkshire. The advertising seemed to have a broader appeal than we anticipated and older drinkers were perhaps more susceptible to brand imagery than they were prepared to admit.

Thus the consumer measure revealed significant improvements both in claimed drinking of John Smith's Bitter and in attitudes towards the brand, improvements which did not occur in non-advertised areas. Moreover, the loyalty and age profiles of drinkers only improved significantly for John Smith's, while other brands and John Smith's in non-advertised areas remained the same.

So the sales turn-round was accompanied by improvements on the same measures that had first prompted us to identify the brand's problem as essentially one of consumer commitment. This, we felt, indicated that the analysis had been sound and that the advertising had addressed the key area in need of change, namely the brand image.

SUMMARY

In a market where advertising can seldom be confidently shown to have an effect on volume, this campaign seems to have succeeded in restoring sales-growth to John Smith's Bitter cost-efficiently.

Whereas in 1980, drinkers appeared to be losing their confidence in the brand and transferring their loyalty to competitors, sales and their claimed behaviour in 1982 indicated renewed commitment to John Smith's Bitter. This turn-round was reflected in drinkers' improved attitudes to the brand on scales relevant to the advertising content.

These improvements in sales, claimed drinking and brand imagery were largely confined to Yorkshire, the only area to receive substantial media support throughout 1981. Competitive brands did not enjoy similar improvements, and indeed the bitter market as a whole declined in the area, in contrast to John Smith's growth.

Qualitative and quantitative consumer research studies underline the role of advertising in stimulating the brand's success. The absence of any identifiable changes in the marketing mix or retail environment, apart from advertising investment and content, help to confirm this role. A total investment of some £300 000 in television advertising thus contributed to a revenue increase for John Smith's draught bitter of some £5 million in the pub trade alone, whilst free trade growth continued, all in a declining market. The profitability of such a return on investment in the tied trade alone is assured.

We believe that, by rejuvenating the brand's imagery amongst younger bitter drinkers in particular, so that they could confidently claim it as their pint in a sales-environment where social pressures predominate, the 'Big John' campaign played a significant part in this improved performance.

CONCLUSIONS

1.   Causal relationships can only be inferred, never demonstrated. But the weight of evidence suggests to us that the Big John advertising caused incremental sales.
2.   Other marketing investments could have had the same effect, but we doubt whether they would have been so cost-efficient. Within a year, investment in advertising resulted in revenue over fifteen times greater than the investment.
3.   It is impossible to judge whether it was the advertisement's content, or merely the increased weight of advertising, that was mainly responsible. Our judgement is that both worked together. A lower weight would have reduced the brand's consumer presence. Inappropriate content would not have regained the loyalty of drinkers. But we still lack measures relating weight to response. That may be the next subject for research.

APPENDIX: MAJOR DATA SOURCES

Beer Market Survey (BMS)   A census of major brewers' sales. Each brewer contributes his sales figures by trade and beer type confidentially. Thus each can monitor market trends and his own share.

Marplan U & A Survey   A regular consumer study commissioned by Courage, covering drinking behaviour and brand imagery. Structured to represent the universe of men drinking bitter once a week or more often. Regional upweights of specific groups (including the 18–24s).

Wyman-Harris Licensed Trade Monitor (LTM)   Quarterly audit of retail trade sales. Data collected by auditor observation in pubs.
   The Northern sample is over 300 pubs.

Courage Sales   Ex-brewery production.

BMP Qualitative   Source, 40 group discussions in Yorkshire over two years.

6

The Repositioning of Hellmann's Mayonnaise

INTRODUCTION

Most of the classic studies of advertising effectiveness start with a sluggish or declining sales graph, which is then dramatically reversed by the new campaign. Hellmann's is different: it was already a healthily growing brand and the need for a new initiative was not immediately obvious, though we believe and hope to show it was crucially necessary. And, of course, it presents a particular challenge to demonstrate advertising effectiveness under these circumstances.

BACKGROUND

Hellmann's importance to CPC

CPC Best Foods Division is one of three divisions of CPC (UK) Ltd, the others dealing with catering supply and industrial starch technology. Best Foods (the retail division) currently turns over some £45 million at manufacturer's selling price and the business is comprised of Mazola Corn Oil, Brown & Polson cornflour, Dextrosol, Knorr cubes, soups and sauces, Frank Cooper, and Hellmann's Mayonnaise.

In 1981 divisional strategy was thoroughly reappraised, among other issues addressing the problem of how a finite total marketing budget should be apportioned among a large number of small- to medium-sized brands. One influential tool in the analysis was the matrix originally developed by the Boston Consulting Group, by which each brand is evaluated in two dimensions: market growth and brand dominance.

Dominant brands in growing markets become 'stars' – the opportunities on which the future of the business depends and therefore priorities for investment. Dominant brands in static or declining markets are regarded as 'cash cows', which can be 'milked' to provide investment for the 'stars'. Weak brands in declining markets are described as 'dogs' (for apparent reasons); and weak brands in growth markets must be treated on their individual merits. (This is inevitably an oversimplistic description and the results are rarely as unequivocal as this sounds; it can be, nevertheless, and was here, a useful aid to decision making, as can be seen in Figure 1.)

As a result, Hellmann's (hitherto regarded as a relatively minor part of the portfolio)

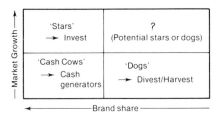

Figure 1. *The BCG matrix*

emerged as a prime candidate for investment: it dominated the mayonnaise market with a 60 per cent volume share, and the market itself had been growing for some years by 10–20 per cent per annum, being worth in 1981 some £7 million (see Figure 2).

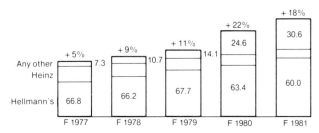

Figure 2. *Mayonnaise market trends (000/jars) & Hellmann's share*
(NB: F 1977, etc., refers to CPC fiscal years which end
30 September. Thus, F 1977 refers to 12 months ending
30 September 1977)

Source: Nielsen

Hellmann's: Early History

Hellmann's Real Mayonnaise, originally an American brand, was launched in this country in the 1960s. At first it was very much a delicatessen product in limited distribution and continued for a number of years to develop a small but discriminating following.

It is important to understand that at the time of Hellmann's original launch, 'real' mayonnaise – ie a thick, spoonable, subtle-tasting emulsion of egg yolks and oil – was virtually unknown to the majority of the British public. The word 'mayonnaise' was widely used, erroneously, as a synonym for salad cream (a peculiarly British product with a pourable texture and highly flavoured with vinegar and sugar). This may be due to the fact that Heinz marketed until 1981 a product called 'Heinz Mayonnaise' which was very similar in taste and texture to salad cream.

Two significant circumstances followed from this. Firstly, mayonnaise became known exclusively as a salad dressing. This may still seem unsurprising to the British reader, until we remember that we are probably the only country in the world where this statement would be true: in the USA or on the Continent, there is no particular link between mayonnaise and salad.

Secondly, the early advertising history of Hellmann's was devoted by one means or another to explaining how the 'real' mayonnaise differed from salad cream expectations. By drawing these comparisons, of course, the salad usage positioning was reinforced.

Hellmann's Position in 1981

By 1981, Hellmann's had achieved reasonable distribution throughout the grocery trade (85 per cent £). The brand had been advertised, but not nationally or consistently: the best remembered campaign was that featuring 'Mrs Hellmann' which ran from 1976–79, mostly in London and the South. Penetration was still low and even awareness of the brand continued to be patchy. Year-on-year growth rates were encouraging (see Figure 2); but against this, it could be seen that much of this growth was simply a factor of improved distribution (see Figure 3). Calculating the actual rate of sale, this was much flatter – indeed in certain areas rate of sale could be shown to be in decline.

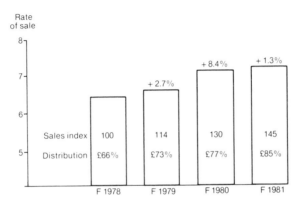

Figure 3. *Hellmann's Rate of Sale (000 jars/% £ distribution)*

Source: Nielsen

The original portfolio analysis had taken account of historical growth rates, but had not attempted to predict the future. Yet the logic of investing in the brand depended on the assumption that the market would, or could be made to, continue to grow. At £3.7 million (MSP), Hellmann's was not a large enough brand to justify heavy advertising expenditure simply for maintenance purposes. Its share of market was unlikely to increase, being so high already; indeed, it was almost inevitably foreseen to decline as own-label products became available, retailing considerably cheaper than Hellmann's, yet of highly acceptable quality. Before committing large sums of money, therefore, we had to address the question: what were the prospects of continued market growth?

Our analysis suggested strongly that Hellmann's, as it was at that time perceived and used, could not expect to grow indefinitely and indeed as distribution plateaued, might not grow much further. At its simplest this was predictable from the fact that the amount of salad served, while showing some growth, is finite; therefore Hellmann's would continue to compete with salad cream, and increasingly with other dressings such as French dressing which were – and are – growing from a small base even faster than mayonnaise.

The naive assumption that people would forsake salad cream as soon as mayonnaise became available to them was not borne out by the facts. Loyalty to salad cream was, and is, enormously strong. Most mayonnaise buyers were buying it in addition to, not instead of, salad cream. In fact mayonnaise was seen by the majority of its users as a 'special occasion' salad product, an occasional but not a routine substitute for salad cream.

This 'special occasion' imagery had in the past been recognised by client and agency as an important part of the Hellmann's brand: it grew out of the delicatessen origins of the brand and, in one campaign at least, had been explicitly reflected in an upper-class setting and a suggestion that Hellmann's was 'superior' or 'posh'.

However, we now began to consider whether this imagery was not a limitation as well as a strength. For users it inhibited everyday use of the product, which in any case was unlikely to take the place of salad cream totally. For non-users it was even a disincentive to purchase, especially to the C2D groups: the profile of Hellmann's at this time still being strongly AB (Table 1).

TABLE 1:   HELLMANN'S PENETRATION BY SOCIAL CLASS

(Base: all housewives)	AB	C1	C2	D	E
Claim to buy Hellmann's nowadays:	33%	20%	10%	5%	7%

Source: TGI

It seemed likely then that once Hellmann's Mayonnaise had achieved a certain share of salad cream occasions, and a certain penetration among ABCls, and allowing for the fact that about a quarter of all potential buyers reject the product on taste grounds, it would not have much further room to grow. And this point seemed to be not far off. If this were to be the case, it was difficult to justify the level of expenditure which were being contemplated.

THE NEW STRATEGY FOR HELLMANN'S

All these limitations derived from the fact that mayonnaise was seen exclusively as a salad dressing. This had other limitations as well, in terms of regionality and seasonality. Salad consumption is heavily biased, of course, to the summer. For Hellmann's, with a relatively short shelf-life, this meant plant standing idle in the off-season. Also, salad consumption is greater in the South than the North. Hellmann's historical Southern bias was not a case of the South being ahead of the North; it was largely the same regional pattern as salads, or indeed salad cream.

On the other hand, if it were possible to re-present mayonnaise as a product with a wider range of uses and to divorce it from salad cream, the potential for growth would be very much greater. This would entail consumers seeing mayonnaise more in the way it is seen in the USA or Europe: as a versatile condiment. At the same time, it could be made more accessible and everyday: a condiment for snacks as well as formal meal occasions, associated with good food but not pretension.

Whether or not this aspiration was realistic or not was a difficult question for research to predict before the event. In the end, we decided on a major piece of qualitative research to probe, using individual interviews, people's attitudes to and experience of mayonnaise. This was very encouraging in that it showed little resistance to extending the versatility of mayonnaise usage, though there were clear 'no go' areas such as red meat or meals with gravy. One of the most interesting findings was that the heaviest users of mayonnaise were *already* using it in many different ways, but with considerable guilt because this was not 'proper', and almost disrespectful to a product which had positioned itself on a pedestal.

In addition to this, the new strategy seemed to fit well with some broad trends in eating habits; in particular the long-term growth in all pickles and sauces, the increase of snacking and the decline of the formal meal occasion, and an increasing willingness of the consumer to experiment and try new things.

Advertising Development

On this basis, we proceeded to a creative brief. The objectives of the new campaign were defined as:

ADVERTISING OBJECTIVES

1. To encourage trial of Hellmann's (especially in areas of low salad consumption).
2. To stimulate a wider range of applications among existing trialists.

At the time, we considered two ways of approaching the objective. Either we could maintain our existing salad base and add new suggestions gradually, or we could abandon all the precedents and talk about mayonnaise as if it were a new product, with no salad antecedents. We decided fairly soon that the second approach was the only viable one: we needed to force a complete revaluation of the brand, and to do this we had to be radical, even shocking. The creative strategy was formulated as follows.

CREATIVE BRIEF

1. Redefine Hellmann's as a versatile, everyday 'condiment/ingredient'.
2. Divorce Hellmann's from any association with salad cream.
3. Brand Hellmann's strongly.

Guidelines:

— Feature a range of usage occasions (rather than a 'recipe' approach).
— Hellmann's is not just for good cooks – it's idiot proof.
— Hellmann's is a natural, simple product (parallel: whipped cream).

TARGET MARKET

1. Current Hellmann's users.
2. Non-users of mayonnaise.

The campaign that was produced was certainly different (see page 91). Not only did burgers and jacket potatoes replace delicate salads: but the black ties and silver candlesticks gave way to a Northern working-class kitchen where Mum was an awful cook and ran off with the coalman, leaving our hero (an overgrown schoolboy) to transform her inedible, boring food with the addition of a little Hellmann's.

Neither the client nor the agency could ignore the dangers of this radical approach if it misfired. Would we jeopardise all Hellmann's traditional brand strengths by debunking it like this? The campaign was extensively researched, both qualitatively as an animatic, and quantitatively as a finished film. The research showed a campaign with great impact which clearly communicated its objective of extended usage, and forced a revaluation of mayonnaise, but which also had no detectable effects on the quality perception of the brand. Indeed, intentions-to-buy scores were improved and the campaign was much liked by users and by non-users (Table 2).

TABLE 2:   INTENTION TO BUY
'How likely would you be to buy Hellmann's Mayonnaise?'

Base: housewives exposed to:	Previous Commercial %	New Commercial 'Kitchen' %	Control (pack) %
very likely (+ 5)	30	38	34
quite likely	37	31	19
neither likely nor unlikely	6	7	8
not very likely	17	14	9
not at all likely (+ 1)	10	9	31
mean score	3.62	3.74	3.17
n =	(161)	(159)	(160)

Source: Millward Brown

The following verbatims give examples of how consumers responded in group discussions to the new campaign at the animatic stage; the first group are C2D non-users from Cheshire.

'Terrific.'
'Really amusing.'
'It gets you to look at it.'
'Not like some dreary ones.'
'Trying to tell you you can use it on all types of food – more than you think.'
'Some of these things I would never have thought of but I'll try them.'

The second group, from Hampton, Middlesex, are BC1 users:

'I like the Hellmann's brightening the food.'
'Goes with things you would never have dreamt of, like chips.'
'Encouraging other members of the family to help themselves.'
'I like the message that you can use it on things all the year round.'

And the final group, from Oldham, Lancashire, are also BC1 users:

'That's very good.'
'I'd forgotten I'd had it on baked potatoes!'
'There's nothing extraordinary: it's food you eat anyway.'
'Salad cream's just for salad – with that one, it points out that you can use it with all these different things so you get your money's worth.'

Media

TV was chosen for its impact, and also because it addresses a family audience; we emphatically did not want a recipe campaign addressed to housewives, but a campaign to stimulate demand from all members of the family. Research suggested, for example, that teenagers making themselves snacks would be part of the opportunity.

Mayonnaise, as we have mentioned, was and still is a market with distinct regional strengths and weaknesses. A number of factors could be identified:

— the historical weight of advertising and distribution in London and the South;
— high salad consumption in the South;
— for an up-market product, the slightly different demographic profile of the South vs. the North.

Given the new strategy, however, we did not feel any of these factors constrained the opportunity. Indeed it was part of our objective to build a broader national brand than we inherited, which would not be limited by regional bias of salad consumption, nor so rigorously confined to AB purchasers.

Accordingly, the campaign was planned nationally and, in fact, the relatively cheaper airtime costs in the North of the country resulted in those areas being upweighted to the consumer. This was in line with our view that a higher weight of advertising was needed to build penetration and awareness in these areas.

The campaign was planned to break around the end of May 1982, the peak season for mayonnaise, followed by another burst in August–September. It was, however, part of our objective to develop counter-seasonal usage for Hellmann's. There had historically been a slight Christmas sales peak associated with cold turkey and seasonal indulgence: we decided to build on this by creating a special Christmas commercial (see page 93) to run for two weeks before and after Christmas, followed by two weeks of the original 'Kitchen' commercial retitled with a new end-line 'Don't save it for the summer'.

This regional pattern was essentially repeated the second year of advertising. To add new life to the campaign we made three new 20-second commercials, each tackling one new type of usage occasion: chips, coleslaw, and sandwiches (one example is shown on page 95).

THE PROGRESS OF THE BRAND: 1982-84

At the time of writing, (May 1984), exactly two years have passed since the new Hellmann's campaign began. Let us describe first of all what has happened in the marketplace and evaluate Hellmann's progress against our objectives, which may be summarised as:

— *Primary*: major volume growth (while maintaining price).
— *Secondary*: development of weaker areas and development of counter-seasonality to be achieved by increased penetration and increased weight of purchase.

HELLMANN'S MAYONNAISE
"KITCHEN"

When I was a lad my mother was a dreary cook.

Her string beans tasted of real string.

Then one day she ran off with the coalman's humper.

Left with a wedge of rubber and one of mother's doorsteps.

I was lucky enough to spot a forgotten jar of Hellmann's.

Quickly I mixed 'em up and bingo!

It were stupendous.

I spread Hellmann's on her carpetburgers.

They were magic.

And mixed with tuna thick creamy Hellmann's transformed the limpest cloth lettuce.

Never again would her humble spud taste like it had a woolly on under its jacket.

Hellmann's. Don't save it for the salad.

Volume Growth

It is clear that Hellmann's has seen accelerated volume growth (Figure 4). It is true that the brand has also lost some share, but only at the same rate as we have observed for some years previously (about 3 per cent per annum): starting from such a high base this is perhaps not surprising. The share has been lost partly to own-label – in early 1983

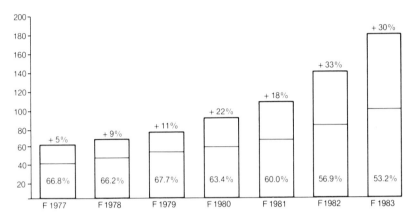

Figure 4. *Mayonnaise market trends (000 jars) and Hellmann's share*
Sources: Nielsen, 1977-81, MGS 1982-83

Tesco launched own-label mayonnaise for the first time – and to a lesser extent to Heinz, who relaunched a mayonnaise in spring 1983. This product has taken about 10 per cent of the market, although much of this replaces the share taken by Heinz Slimway Mayonnaise, on sale during 1981 and 1982. Both the own-label and Heinz products are considerably cheaper than Hellmann's, which commands a premium of some 60 per cent by weight at RSP.

Under the circumstances, it is a tribute to the strength of the Hellmann's brand that the rate of share loss has been so low: and for the last 12 months has shown signs of plateauing at around 50 per cent volume share.

What we did not predict was the rate at which the market could grow, with the result that Hellmann's ex-factory sales for the 1983 financial year were considerably in excess of the most ambitious internal forecasts made in 1981. (A 56 per cent increase compared with a 27 per cent forecast increase.)

Development of Weak Areas

Here the pattern is less clear cut, and complicated by problems in accurate regional measurement. Progress in Lancashire and especially Yorkshire seems to have been disappointing and all our attempts to explain this have been unsatisfactory; but other areas where mayonnaise was formerly very weak such as Harlech and the West, the Midlands and, in particular, Scotland, have shown very high levels of growth so that the profile of the brand is now more nationally based than it was (see Table 3).

HELLMANN'S MAYONNAISE
"TURKEY"

I'll never forget the Christmas we won turkey in raffle...

it were July before we had to feed the cat again...

Luckily Santa left me a jar of thick creamy Hellmans OOH OOH.

It were best Christmas ever.

Gran said if Dad...
ate anymore turkey, he'd end up looking like one.

Hellmanns. Don't save it for the summer.

TABLE 3:   REGIONAL BREAKDOWN OF HELLMANN'S SALES BY VOLUME

	1981 Apr–Oct %	1983 Apr–Oct %	Population, ISBA regions %
London	42	33	20
Southern	7	8	9
Wales and West	6	9	11
Midlands	11	11	16
Anglia	5	7	6
Lancashire	11	10	13
Yorkshire	7	6	10
North-East	3	4	5
Scotland	8	12	10

Source: Mars Group Services

Development of Counter-Seasonality

This is the most difficult area to evaluate. We have had two winter seasons and two very different experiences. The first winter showed an unprecedented rate of market growth, and one moreover in which Hellmann's participated fully (Table 4). This result is also remarkable for the fact that there is a high correlation between the rate of growth achieved by TV area, and the level of TVRs which our 'net homes' allocation enabled us to buy, making a strong case that this sales peak was in response to advertising (Figure 5).

The second winter, however, shows minimal year-on-year growth. Admittedly, this is starting from a high base, but in view of the continuing high rates of summer growth it means that progress towards making the brand less seasonal has apparently been wiped

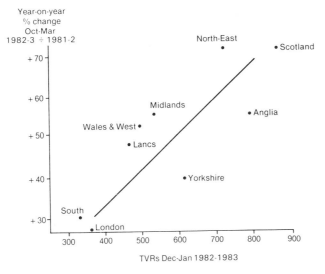

Figure 5. *Hellmann's volume growth: Winter campaign*
Sources: MGS, BARB

**HELLMANN'S MAYONNAISE
"SANDWICH"**

In mother's absence

hunger drove me to the four distant corners of the fridge where I discovered a 'ham frisbee'.

With my trustee jar of delicious creamy thick Hellmanns

and a trick I learned with an egg. . .

I fast became expert in the art of the sarnie.
OOH magic.

Hellmanns. Don't save it for the summer.

TABLE 4: SUMMARY OF HELLMANN'S PERFORMANCE – CHANGE ON PREVIOUS YEAR BY VOLUME

	Summer 1982 (Apr–Oct)	Winter 82–83 (Nov–Mar)	Summer 1983 (Apr–Oct)	Winter 1983–84 (Nov–Mar)
market	+35.8%	+43.0%	+24.5%	+7.7%
Hellmann's	+30.7%	+41.5%	+13.6%	−4.2%

Source: Mars Group Services

out. Weights of advertising each year were similar, but in the second year the campaign did not break until after Christmas, while in the first year it started on 18th December. Whether this made any difference is a matter for debate, but it seems unlikely it could have accounted for such a wide discrepancy.

THE CONTRIBUTION OF ADVERTISING

As we have seen, our primary objective – major volume growth for the brand – has been achieved. We have yet to make the case that advertising was a major factor in this growth, and that without the advertising it would have been less (we guess the market would have grown, but at a lower rate). Unfortunately the obvious demonstration of this is not available to us as the campaign has been national from the outset and hence no control exists. Given, however, that we have seen an acceleration in the rate of growth, we can build our case on the following evidence:

1. A discussion of the other factors that might have caused an increased rate of growth.
2. Measures of the campaign's impact on the consumer.
3. Changes in usage pattern and user profiles which would reflect the advertising strategy.

Other Possible Factors in Generating Growth

Let us review and, where possible, discount other factors which might have affected Hellmann's growth.

— Distribution
— Pricing
— Trade stocking and display
— Promotional activity
— Product development

DISTRIBUTION

Gains in distribution were a considerable factor in Hellmann's volume growth up to the end of the 1981 financial year. The growth since has, however, come from a much more static distribution base. A calculation of rate-of-sale shows the increase in offtake post-advertising (Figure 6).

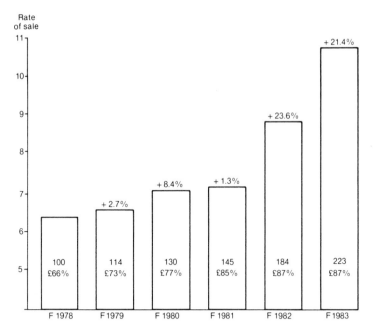

Figure 6. *Hellmann's rate of sale (000 jars/% £ distribution)*
Sources: Nielsen, MGS

PRICING

There was indeed a slight reduction in the retail price between 1981 and 1983, a consequence of increasing volumes being sold through the major multiples (Table 5). However, while this may well have helped, it did little to reduce the very considerable premium of Hellmann's over salad cream (Table 6).

Having conducted price elasticity research since, it seems unlikely that these modest

TABLE 5:   HELLMANN'S PRICE APRIL–SEPTEMBER

	1981 £	1982 £	1983 £
200 g	0.576	0.567	0.572
400 g	1.04	1.00	0.982

Source: Mars Group Services

TABLE 6:   PRICE PER 100 g: HELLMANN'S AND HEINZ SALAD CREAM

	1981 p	1983 p
Hellman's	28.8	28.6
Heinz salad cream	19.4	20.6
premium	9.2	8.0

Source: Mars Group Services

reductions would effect 30 per cent sales increases. The market is clearly not dominated by price: if it were, Hellmann's would hardly be able to command the premium it does over own-label.

STOCK LEVELS AND TRADE SUPPORT

With increasing availability of own-label and pressure on the 'salad sector' from other brands, the amount of Hellmann's on-shelf has not increased nearly as much as the actual sales to the consumer. Mars Group Services (MGS) audit the amount of stock in the forward area: taking the period April–September 1981–83 gives us the following figures expressed as indices (Table 7).

TABLE 7:   HELLMANN'S PERFORMANCE (INDEXED)

	Front Stocks	Sales
1981	100	100
1982	112	131
1983	113	148

Source: Mars Group Services

PROMOTIONAL ACTIVITY

Compared with the considerable advertising spend over this period, there was very little promotional activity and the pack design and copy remained unchanged for most of the period. An on-pack recipe book offer, while it achieved good levels of redemption, does not explain the observed rates of growth.

PRODUCT DEVELOPMENT

During the second year of advertising, in May 1983, two flavour variants of Hellmann's (lemon and garlic) were launched and had achieved a 6 per cent share of the market by September. The rationale behind the flavours is to differentiate the brand from own-label and to stimulate re-trial among lapsed users who find ordinary mayonnaise too 'bland'. As such, they may be expected to have contributed something to the brand's growth, though the extent of straight substitution for the base product is very hard to estimate. It is worth noting also that the launch of flavours has not been reflected in increased total Hellmann's facings in the retail trade. Our best conclusion must be that the addition of flavours to date has been a contribution – but not *the* major factor – in the growth picture, and this in any case applies to the last 12 months only.

    We conclude that no other factor or combination of factors can conceivably explain Hellmann's rate of volume growth.

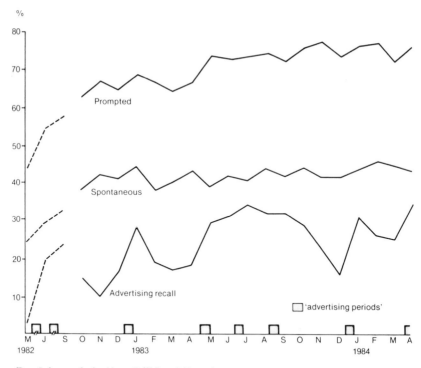

Figure 7. *Awareness & advertising recall of Hellmann's Mayonnaise*

Sources: ──── NOP

─────── Millward Brown

Consumer Reactions to the Advertising

While the following data does not necessarily equate to purchasing behaviour, there is considerable evidence that the campaign has been widely seen, recalled, understood, and liked by the consumer (see Figure 7).

— Brand awareness has improved significantly since the campaign began.
— The campaign has achieved consistently high recall levels. (To put these figures into context, the high points are the highest figures (with one exception) recorded on the CPC tracking study, which includes not only all CPC's own brands but heavily and successfully advertised competitors such as Heinz and Oxo.)
— Related recall is accurate and recall of the main message is on strategy (Table 8).

TABLE 8:   RELATED RECALL OF HELLMANN'S CAMPAIGN

(average 11 months to April 1984)	%
use of different things/not just salad	38
livens up boring meals/revives them	24
makes things taste better	24
adds flavour to ordinary food/makes more interesting	27

Base: all recalling Hellmann's advertising
Source: Millward Brown

TABLE 9: PROMPTED COMMENTS ON HELLMANN'S
          CAMPAIGN

(average 11 months to April 1984)	%
it gave the impression the product would be very good	40
I liked it	38
it made me more interested in buying the product	15
it was no different from most other commercials	7
it was hard to believe	9
I'm getting fed up seeing it	3
it put me off buying the product	1
I don't like it	2

Base: all recalling Hellmann's campaign
Source: Millward Brown

On a standard set of statements, the campaign is clearly liked and appreciated. Again, these figures are high compared with company norms (Table 9). These types of responses are also found in qualitative research where the campaign is characteristically received with recognition and enjoyment.

He was lovely . . . human . . . you really felt sorry for him . . . it's just how men are on their own.
He's a bit scruffy . . . the lazy type . . . had his mum to run around for him and in a bit of a mess until he found the Hellmann's.
He is quite nice . . . down to earth type . . . it somehow makes you think that anyone can have Hellmann's . . . it's not just for posh people.
It's the versatility of the product - it's not like a salad cream, you can use Hellmann's on anything . . .
It's quite stunning with him in it.

— Image ratings over time have shown increases in 'versatility' and 'everyday usage' without any loss in traditionally high-quality ratings (Table 10).

These quantified image ratings also reflect a profound change in the way people talk about mayonnaise in qualitative research. Two years ago mayonnaise was widely seen as having strong class connotations which, for many, were a real inhibition to trial. The following statements from C2 non-users in Cheshire illustrate this point:

My husband's boss - he wouldn't have salad cream, only mayonnaise.
We buy salad cream, they buy mayonnaise.

These barriers are now very much a thing of the past, and there is now a much more relaxed acceptance of mayonnaise as an accessible product among all social classes. This is reflected in consistent figures that show the new market entrants in the last two years to come increasingly from C2s and Ds (Table 11).

So much for the accessible image of the product, but how have usage patterns actually changed? We measured this in July 1983 and were able to make some comparisons with a survey conducted in 1980 (Table 12). While it is clear that salad remains a common denominator (though to a lesser extent than for salad cream), there have been increases in most non-salad uses. Also, the specific uses shown in the advertising (eg burgers,

TABLE 10: IMAGE STATEMENTS

| | agree % | |
| | disagree % | |
Accessibility:	1980	1983
'I would only serve mayonnaise on special occasions'	25	13
	63	83
'Mayonnaise is too expensive to use all the time'	34	27
	51	68
'There's no point in giving mayonnaise to children, they wouldn't enjoy it'	15	17
	55	66
	Hellmann's buyer	own-label buyer
Versatility: (*not asked in 1980*) 'Mayonnaise is something the family will help themselves to for snacks'	48	43
	41	47
'I think of mayonnaise mainly as an ingredient'	37	38
	54	56
'Mayonnaise has more use than salad cream'	57	55
	27	31

Source: ICI

TABLE 11: INCREASE IN PENETRATION 1980–83

AB	C1	C2	D	E
+3%	+12%	+22%	+117%	+15%

Source: TGI

potatoes, cheese on toast), while not comparable with 1980, have attained respectable levels. Also, it can be shown that while in 1980 mayonnaise was less versatile than salad cream, the positions are now reversed (Table 13).

A more sophisticated analysis segments mayonnaise users into four categories: traditionalists, combination salad makers, 'new' types of users, and combination plus 'new' users. This indicates that 40 per cent of Hellmann's users are using the product in at least one of the ways shown in the advertising. Interestingly, too, this proportion is significantly higher among Hellmann's users than it is among users of own-label mayonnaise (Table 14).

TABLE 12:   HELLMANN'S USERS: WAYS OF USING MAYONNAISE

	(mayonnaise)	(mayonnaise)	(salad cream)
	1980 %	1983 %	1983 %
with a lettuce type of salad	N/A	84	97
with tomatoes	N/A	57	69
salad sandwich	24	51	63
egg mayonnaise	52	64	36
prawn cocktail	34	46	30
cold meat without salad	16	19	24
chips without salad	5	14	18
hot meat without salad	8	14	3
fish without salad	8	15	11
savoury dip	8	23	15
bread & butter without salad	0	12	18
with:			
hamburgers	N/A	11	7
tuna fish	N/A	34	23
cheese on toast	N/A	10	8
jacket potatoes	N/A	20	15
potato salad	47	46	43
coleslaw	42	41	41
cucumber salad	10	14	11
rice salad	14	15	8
Russian salad	8	10	5
Waldorf salad	6	10	4
prawn salad	1	27	18
mixed vegetable salad	2	22	24
sweetcorn salad	0	11	8
other made salad	9	12	8

Source: 1980–PAS
        1983–ICI

TABLE 13:   AVERAGE NUMBER OF CLAIMED USES PER RESPON-
            DENT

	1980	1983
salad cream	3.1	6.1
mayonnaise	2.8	6.7

Source: 1980–PAS
        1983–ICI

(Note: The increase 1980 to 1983 is considerably exaggerated by a
       longer list of uses: the object of the chart is the relative position
       of salad cream vs. mayonnaise.)

TABLE 14:   TYPES OF USE MEASURED

salad	combination salad	new uses
lettuce type	cucumber salad	cold meat without salad
tomatoes	rice salad	chips without salad
salad sandwich	Russian salad	hot meat without salad
	Waldorf salad	fish without salad
	prawn salad	bread & butter without salad
traditional recipe	mixed vegetable salad	hamburgers without salad
	sweetcorn salad	cheese on toast without salad
egg mayonnaise	savoury dip	jacket potatoes without salad
tuna fish		
potato salad		
coleslaw		

MAYONNAISE USAGE SEGMENTS

	all %	Hellmann's users %	own-label users %
1. salad/traditional only	31	27	30
2. salad/traditional + combination salad	23	23	28
3. salad/traditional + 'new uses'	17	19	11
4. salad/traditional + combination salad + 'new uses'	27	29	28

Source: ICI

CONCLUSION

In summary then we can show that the advertising has made an impression; that perceptions of mayonnaise have been changed in the way we intended: that ways of using the product reflect that change. These findings, and the otherwise unexplained acceleration in volume growth from a static distribution base, lead us to conclude that the advertising has been effective in achieving our main objective.

We hope to have shown that the growth we have seen would not have taken place without the advertising. It would be wrong, however, to leave the argument there without admitting that the nature of that growth has not been entirely what we anticipated, and that more remains to be achieved in the future.

We expected growth to come from two sources – from attracting new users to the market, and also from increasing the average weight of purchase which, for most mayonnaise users, has always been very low. In the event, as extensive TCA analyses have shown, the weight of purchase has hardly increased: the brand and market growth has instead largely come from new trialists including, as we have seen, many from social classes hitherto unfamiliar with mayonnaise. Inevitably, not all these trialists will become regular users: hence our strategic focus for the future will be increasingly on creating more weight of purchase.

What, then, have we achieved? We have taken mayonnaise off its pedestal and made it accessible to a whole new market; we have reduced its exclusive association with special occasion salads and encouraged experimentation and a more relaxed attitude towards it. This has increased penetration for the brand: it has also, without a doubt, endorsed the existing behaviour of a core of heavy, versatile users who have always been important to our sales. At the same time, we have not devalued the brand, which retains very high loyalty among its users even at a considerable premium price (TCA shows very little direct switching to own-label or to Heinz).

7

The Repositioning of Mazola

INTRODUCTION

This paper demonstrates how advertising helped to change the fortunes of Mazola corn oil. It describes a campaign which has begun to move Mazola from a position of weakness in one sector of a market to a position of strength in another. It is a classic example of a brand moving from 'problem child' status to that of a 'star', and it shows how alertness to underlying change in the environment can be capitalised on through the right advertising.

In the case of Mazola, we shall demonstrate how such a combination of forces turned the brand's major historical impediment into a unique competitive advantage. Our conclusions are based on observations of sales, attitudes and usage of Mazola in advertised versus non-advertised regions.

BACKGROUND

Mazola is a brand of cooking oil which has been sold in the UK since the 1960s. It is marketed in this country by the Best Foods Division of the American Corn Products Corporation.

Mazola is 100 per cent corn oil. In practice, this means that Mazola's price is based on a much higher commodity price than its competitors – which are mostly blended vegetable oils – and hence sells at a premium. Furthermore, it is at the mercy of fluctuations in the world price of corn, while competitors can be cushioned from this by changing their source of supply or altering their mix of ingredients.

An understanding of the historical development of the cooking oil market will clearly illustrate the difficulty in justifying a price premium in this market.

BRIEF HISTORY OF THE COOKING OIL MARKET – 1965–1982

The market for cooking oils has largely developed in the last 25 years and is still growing. This reflects a trend of substituting oil for solid fat (e.g. lard), especially for deep frying. The main factors behind this trend are:

— A trend from using animal fats to using vegetable substitutes, on health grounds.
— An increasing aversion to 'fatty foods', partly connected with the above, but also with
  weight watching.
— A belief, fostered by advertising, that oil represents a more modern, cleaner and con-
  venient way of frying, and produces drier, crisper results.
— The very pronounced decline in the real price of oil.

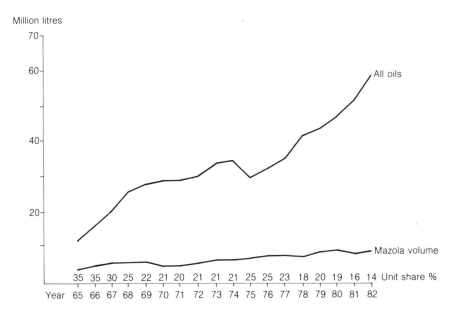

Figure 1. *Market volume growth*
Source: Nielsen/MGS

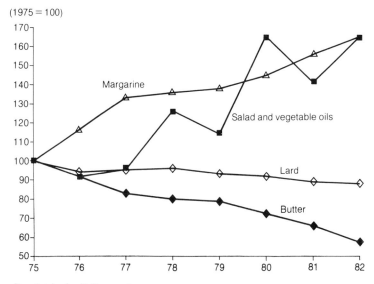

Figure 2. *Index of weekly fat consumption*
Source: National Food Survey

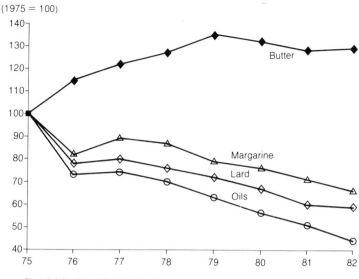

Figure 3. *Index of price of fats (RPI adjusted)*
Source: NFS

The tendency to substitute oils for solid fats had been strongest in London and the South East (where the advertising was historically concentrated) so that the market for oil became skewed towards the south, not because more frying was done there, but because less lard was used.

Throughout this period, we believe that advertising played an important part in establishing the perceived benefits of oil versus lard. In the sixties, Mazola ran various TV campaigns attacking lard overtly. In the seventies, Spry Crisp n' Dry (launched in 1969) dominated the share of voice reinforcing the values present in their brand name, such as the famous 'towel test' demonstrating non-greasy food.

What was notable about all this advertising was its emphasis on deep fat frying or, less often, straightforward shallow frying (e.g. eggs). In this context the oil is used as a cooking medium rather than as an ingredient, and the advertising increasingly made this into a virtue. Thus a good oil was portrayed as having no positive 'food' values.

TABLE: 1: CONVERSION FROM SOLID FAT: LONDON Vs. ELSEWHERE

			GB		London and South	
		1965 (%)	1976 (%)	1979 (%)	1976 (%)	1979 (%)
Deep	Oil	27	36	40	45	46
	Fat	51	46	37	34	24
Shallow	Oil	20	21	27	24	35
	Fat	71	63	53	57	45

% housewives using oil or fat for frying

Base: Total sample

Source: CPC Omnibus

TABLE 2: REGIONAL BREAKDOWN

		London	Southern	Wales/South West	Mids	Lancs	Yorks	N. East	Scotland
A	Population %	23	7	10	21	13	10	5	10
	% housewives who deep fry	70	66	81	[86]	[82]	[89]	[91]	[92]
	% use oil for deep frying	[51]	35	[42]	[47]	[45]	39	29	44
B	Oil location of sales	31	7	13	19	11	7	3	9
	Index (B/A)	135	100	130	90	85	70	60	90

Source: MGS 1982
  CPC Omnibus 1979

However, despite the importance of Mazola and Spry's advertising in developing the oil market, neither achieved a dominant share of it. About two-thirds of the market volume went to own-label. This is not surprising, since most users of cheaper oils were satisfied with the frying results they were getting. And indeed, as we had found in qualitative research, there were many own-label users who had tried Mazola and noticed no difference. We appeared to have a situation where the essential benefit of Mazola – that it was corn oil – was irrelevant to the large majority of oil users.

As a result of our inability to combat cheaper oils on the basis of better frying results (i.e. more invisible!) CPC stopped advertising Mazola in 1979. Share at this time was 20 per cent. Not surprisingly, in the absence of support the brand began to lose users and its share fell in the ensuing four years to 14 per cent.

TABLE 3: MAZOLA PENETRATION

	1978	1979	1980	1981	1982	1983
Cooking oil	55.1	56.3	57.5	59.3	64.0	65.6
Mazola	21.1	19.6	19.1	18.9	16.1	14.6

Source: TGI

TABLE 4: REASONS FOR NO LONGER USING MAZOLA

	(All no longer using) %
Too expensive	53
Prefer other brand	8
Prefer other type	7
Health reasons	5
Dislike it	3

Source: CPC U + A 1985

DEVELOPMENT OF THE PURITY STRATEGY

In 1983 the future for Mazola looked unpromising. As a brand with a small share in a market still growing, Mazola was a 'problem child', as described by the Boston matrix.

Generally, there are two courses for such a brand. One is to do little to reverse its trend, simply managing its decline. The only role for advertising in this scenario would be a sort of rearguard action. But to CPC this would prove unacceptable. Mazola was one of their largest brands and, as brand leader in the oil market for many years, it had been a useful trade 'lever'. Allowing Mazola to decline could harm CPC's overall position considerably.

With this in mind, Boase Massimi Pollitt began to examine the market to try to find a new strategy for the brand which could reverse its decline. We knew that the majority of oil growth had come from deep frying. But Mazola, or indeed any premium oil, was ill-placed to compete in the deep frying sector, the natural tendency of which is to become largely a commodity market. But what if we were to look outside the deep frying sector?

We considered all the ways in which oil was currently being used.

TABLE 5: MARKET SEGMENTS – CURRENT USAGE

	Deep fry	Shallow fry	Recipe fry	Roasting	Grilling	Baking	Salads (Summer months)
Ever	71	87		94	80	77	22
Use oil	41	31		14	13	1	100
Use fat	40	60		68	30	75	–

Source: CPC Omnibus 1979

The first point to note is that the proportion of people who were ever deep frying was smaller than the proportion of people doing any of the other things. This suggested that there could be an opportunity outside deep frying.

Using omnibus data and estimates from a home economist of how much oil was used on each occasion we arrived at a volumetric breakdown of oil usage – see Table 6. As we suspected, the bulk of oil was used in deep frying.

TABLE 6: CURRENT OIL USAGE OCCASIONS AND VOLUME

	Total	Deep fry	Shallow fry	Recipe fry	Roast	Grilling	Baking	Salads
Oil usage occasions (million)	1890	680	704		164	248	9	84
Estimated volume per occasion (ml)		125	50		30	7	100	50
Yearly Volume (million litres)	132	85	35		5	1.5	9	5
% Total oil volume	100	65	25		4	1	1	4

Source: CPC Omnibus 1979; BMP Calculations

But given that the deep frying sector had become so large because of *conversion* from solid fats, we considered the volume opportunities which could be realised if people began to convert from solid fat in the *other* usage occasions – recipe frying and so on. The result of this calculation was a picture of the market much less dominated by deep frying, although it remained a large sector.

But we had evidence at the time that deep frying as a sector was in decline, and there would come a point where this decline in deep frying would cancel out the effect of lard – oil conversion, resulting in a static or declining market for oil in deep frying.

We also felt that shallow frying was declining because of the growth in grilling (although grilling often uses little or no fat). We felt recipe frying would increase, as 'casseroles' and similar dishes were becoming preferred to 'fry-ups'. And salads were also seen to be an area of opportunity.

What we were observing was the start of a change in the environment for Mazola. The market was moving away from the dominance of deep frying.

TABLE 7:   COOKING METHODS – OIL USAGE (All Housewives)

	1976 %	1979 %	% change
Deep frying			
use oil	40	43	+ 8
use fat	50	40	– 20
Shallow frying (all – including recipe)			
use oil	27	34	+ 26
use fat	68	60	– 18
Salad dressing	16	22	+ 38
Grilling			
use oil	10	14	+ 40
use fat	37	30	– 19

Source: CPC Omnibus

We then looked at what people wanted from an oil in each of these sectors, to see whether any of them offered a better context than deep frying in which to create a competitive advantage for Mazola.

Consider Figure 4. We set up a spectrum, from deep frying to salads. For deep frying, as we had found, the ideal is for none of the oil to be eaten – it is just a neutral medium. At the other end of the spectrum are the salads, where the entire object of the oil is to be eaten. We christened the two ends of this spectrum 'the medium' and 'the message'.

The other types of usage were ranged between these points. For example, in shallow frying such as bacon and eggs, one is probably a little more conscious of eating the oil than in deep frying – but in recipe frying the oil becomes part of the finished dish.

We knew from qualitative work that as you move along the spectrum from 'medium' to 'message', two factors became more important:

— The taste of the oil.
— Concern about what it is and where it comes from, which included an implied concern about healthy eating.

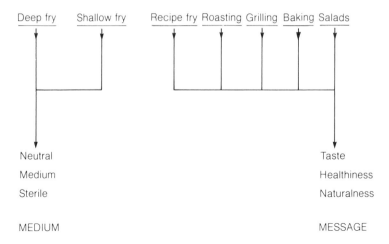

Figure 4. *What people want from an oil*

If we consider the example of using oil in a salad dressing, the sense of this becomes apparent.

The concept which tied together all these relevant aspects of using Mazola as a 'message' was '100% Pure Corn Oil'. And the key element of this, although it loses its meaning when taken out of context, is that of PURITY.

We had known for some time of the emotional power of purity when applied to Mazola. Where attempts to turn it into advertising had failed was in the difficulty of trying to make it directly relevant to deep frying. In contrast to this, featuring use of Mazola in salads was seen by consumers as a *very* powerful demonstration of 'purity' in action. It immediately differentiated Mazola from its cheaper competitors (and even Crisp n' Dry) which were seen as being quite unsuitable for salad usage.

To sum up therefore, we believed that the very nature of the Mazola product – and the thing that made it distinctive from other oils – implied all the values which were relevant to expanding the oil market in directions other than deep frying: taste, naturalness, and healthy eating. At the same time, purity would not contradict current deep frying usage. Our users found the pure corn oil story a perfectly plausible explanation for the results that they believed they were getting from Mazola.

We formulated the marketing plan.

MARKETING PLAN, FISCAL 1984

Marketing Objectives

To increase Mazola's volume while maintaining or improving price premium.

Strategy

To foster increased use of Mazola in areas where it offers a distinctive benefit to users – recipe use, roasting and grilling, and salads – without discouraging other uses such as deep frying.

Proposition

Because Mazola is 100 per cent *pure* corn oil it is ideal for all your culinary needs.

Target Market

1. Existing users of Mazola.
    — To maintain their loyalty as their use of oil broadens.
2. Users of fat for recipe frying, roasting or grilling.
    — Who may be included in No.1.
3. Makers of French dressing.
    — Again, firstly Mazola users who were using other oils too.

CREATIVE DEVELOPMENT

Having chosen TV as the primary medium, a 40-second script ('Good Earth') was written to the above brief and filmed as an animatic for research. The nature of the script demanded a very accurate visual representation of the characters and their surroundings, and so we used very highly finished paintings as the basis of the animatic.

In the qualitative research, the animatic produced a very boisterous response in all groups. The hero prompted a flood of associations: from Adam, to Tarzan, to a Soviet peasant. The visual imagery was extremely powerful and sparked off similar associations.

Purity was successfully communicated, meaning 'no additives', absolutely unadulterated and therefore natural – a single source oil which would be used instead of olive oil on salads. The idea of using Mazola on salads was again seen as a very powerful demonstration of Mazola's worthiness.

Here are some quotes from the pre-test qualitative research which illustrate the favourable response to the animatic:

I thought of Adam in the Garden of Eden first of all, with all the things growing and them giving thanks to God for the food.

C1C2, Oldham

I found it quite comforting that one. It made me think that I should be using 100% Pure Corn Oil. The feeling of getting back to the land and eating things that are good for you.

BC1, Oldham

It's from the earth . . . its pure goodness.

Be sure your oil is as good as the food you cook.   C1C2, Hampton

With it being pure corn . . . you could just buy one bottle of oil and use it for frying as well as for salads. Other oils you can only fry and you have to buy olive oil for a salad.   BC1, Hampton

Another thing that struck me . . . I use Mazola, but I never use Mazola on a salad. They're saying it can be used.

BC1, Oldham

With some executional changes, the script was progressed and shot during the summer of 1983. Ten-second cutdowns (featuring one food usage situation in each one) were also made from the final film.

If the food be pure then so should the oil

Pure corn oil, that's Mazola

Transform the humble trout . . . make potatoes to be praised
Turn onions into pure gold, for casseroles

Make salads, dressed for the Gods

With the oil as pure as the food it cooks.
Mazola 100% pure corn oil

Client:	CPC (UK) LIMITED	*Title:*	THE GOOD EARTH
Product:	MAZOLA	*Job No:*	CPC/40/5150
Date:	14 September 1983	*Length:*	40 seconds
Producer:	BARNABY SPURRIER		

VISION	SOUND
The opening series of images are stylised, like a Russian poster. The figures are almost in silhouette, against stunning, dramatic skylines.	1½ seconds silence MUSIC UNDER THROUGHOUT
Open on a peasant man stripped to the waist, about to pull a potato plant from the earth.	
Dissolve through to C/U of the plant being lifted out of the ground. Loose earth falls from its roots.	
Dissolve to man holding the cluster of potatoes up to the skies, admiring it.	
Cut to a peasant figure at a lakeside. He has his hand in the lake.	
Dissolve to the man's hands as he thrusts a trout upwards.	*V/O:* If the food should be pure
Cut to a group of peasant women harvesting Maize.	then so should the oil.
Dissolve to one of the women admiring a perfect cob.	Pure corn oil that's Mazola.
Cut to three trout sizzling in an underlit frying pan surrounded by vegetables.	Transform the humble trout . . .
Cut to a shallow frying pan full of sauté potatoes, also under-lit.	. . make potatoes to be praised.
Cut to side shot of a beautiful salad arrangement.	Make salads,
Mazola is poured onto the salad from vinegrette bottle.	dressed for Gods.
Cut to a frying pan, cooking sliced onions.	Turn onions into pure gold, for casseroles.
Cut to woman carrying steaming casserole over fields followed by children.	with the oil as pure as the food it cooks.
Cut back to peasant woman admiring the cob, against the sun.	
We see the cob dissolve through to a bottle of Mazola.	Mazola 100 per cent pure corn oil.

MEDIA PLAN

The budget available (£340 000 for the first burst) led us to a regional media strategy. The reasons for selecting the areas were:

London/Southern Important areas for oil and Mazola (50 per cent of volume), and we needed to protect volume in these areas.

Tyne Tees A test of the strategy in a northern area.

Central (fiscal 1984 onwards): added to the schedule as the first stage in the roll-out process, being the third largest market area.

TABLE 8: MAZOLA ADVERTISING FISCAL 1983–FISCAL 1985 (TVR)

	Fiscal 1983	Fiscal 1984	
	Sept/Oct	April	Sept
Primary			
London	600	500	450
Southern	600	500	–
Tyne Tees	600	500	–
Central	600	500	–
	£340.000	£316.000	£160.000

EVALUATION OF THE ADVERTISING EFFECTIVENESS

In this part of the paper, I have looked a two time periods. The first, dealing with 1983 and 1984, was a time when Mazola's price was fairly stable (it rose about 10 per cent between 1984 and 1983) and we were able to monitor sales regionally using:

1. MGS – a retail audit – monitoring volume sales, price, distribution etc., by TV region.
2. Millward Brown – a consumer survey conducted monthly which was split: advertising regions vs. non-advertised regions during 1984, so that we could monitor the advertising effect.

During the last half of 1985, there was a severe shortage of raw material causing a price rise of nearly 25 per cent for Mazola. The effect on sales was disastrous and, although such an experience was traumatic for the brand, it did give us an insight into the effect of advertising during a severe price rise. This is the second period we look at.

PERIOD 1. SEPTEMBER 1983 TO DECEMBER 1984

Given that we were aiming to gain volume by changing perceptions of Mazola, we shall start by examining consumer attitudes to the brand during the campaign. Unfortunately, the

Millward Brown study to monitor the brand only began in February 1984 and so genuine 'pre' advertising benchmarks are unavailable.

However, we can consider a subsequent burst and look at its effect. Table 9 shows spontaneous awareness of Mazola before and after the April 1984 burst.

TABLE 9:   MAZOLA AWARENESS (All Housewives)

	Advertised regions			Non-advertised regions		
	Pre	Post		Pre	Post	
Spontaneous awareness						
– first mention	29%	41%	(+41%)	17%	17%	(–)
– total	45%	51%	(+13%)	32%	32%	(–)
TV ad awareness						
spontaneous	1%	11%		1%	4%	

Source: Millward Brown
       'Pre': 26.3 to 22.4.84
       'Post':21.5 to 17.6.84

In the advertised regions, spontaneous awareness rose significantly after the second burst – although it was already higher. We do not know if this original difference was due to the first burst (which ought to have had a similar effect) or other area effects; probably it was a combination of the two.

As for the communication of the advertising, we are able to look at attitudes which were likely to be altered by the advertising message. Firstly, we look at the statement 'Mazola is made from pure corn oil'. Agreement with this statement was already quite high but rose during 1984 in the advertised regions, and fell everywhere else (Figure 5). A feature of these

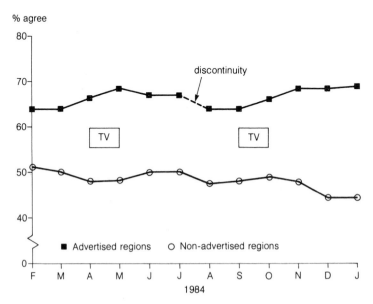

Figure 5. 'Mazola is pure corn oil'
Source: Millward Brown

charts is the 'discontinuity' in July/August when Midlands was added to the schedule. This would have had the effect of 'tipping in' a further 10 per cent of the population who had not seen the advertising into our 'advertised regions' sample, so some diluting of the attitudes could be expected. Hence, one should really look at the direction of the trend during 1984 rather than the absolute scores. Even when the discontinuity is ignored, by the end of 1984 agreement with the statement was nearly 60 per cent higher in advertised regions than in the rest of the country. At the beginning of the year it was only 23 per cent higher.

Other associated dimensions were also changing. We had found from our qualitative work that 'Purity' prompted a whole gamut of positive feelings towards the brand. We were beginning to see this in practice. Consider Figure 6, which shows agreement with the statement 'Mazola is high quality'.

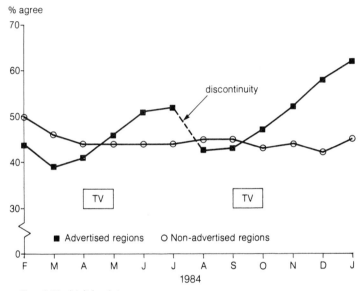

Figure 6. 'Mazola is high quality'
Source: Millward Brown

Here the trend is even more marked. While the non-advertised regions show a slow decline in Mazola's perceived quality, the advertising was having a dramatic effect. Starting below the non-advertised regions, the agreement levels rose sharply during 1984 (note the effect of adding in the Central sample in August).

Another example of attitudinal change is with respect to how 'light' Mazola is felt to be. Corn oil is actually darker in colour than other vegetable oils and so the level of agreement with this question is understandably lower than the attributes we have looked at! But 'light' also means lighter in consistency, an attribute of healthier oils (from our own qualitative). In Figure 7 we see how the advertising is beginning to change this perception of Mazola. The picture that was emerging was a very encouraging one. The advertising was raising the saliency of the brand and changing people's attitudes to it in the way we wanted.

But what of usage? We knew we needed to improve Mazola's worthiness for use in occasions where it was more the 'message' and less the 'medium'. Again using Millward Brown, consumers were asked whether they felt that Mazola was suitable for frying. We

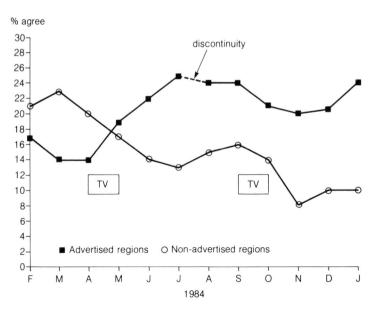

Figure 7. *Mazola is a light oil*
Source: Millward Brown

know that the nature of frying is changing slightly, with deep frying declining in importance and recipe frying growing. Figure 8 shows the level of agreement with this question. The sample includes non-users of Mazola, and so we are looking at attitudes rather than usage.

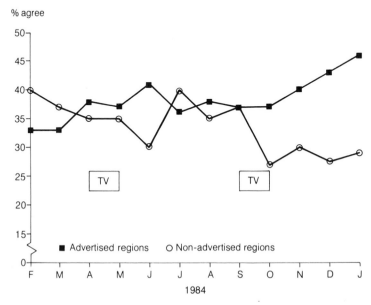

Figure 8. *Mazola is good for frying*
Source: Millward Brown

From similar ratings at the start of the year, the advertised regions had significantly different opinions of Mazola by the end of 1984. In fact, the positions had reversed from earlier in the year. We would have expected this attribute to decline in the absence of support as the brand lost saliency.

And now for salads. Using Mazola in a salad dressing represented the ultimate acceptance of our purity strategy. Although we knew that salad usage was only a part of the new volume potential, if we could convince people that Mazola was suitable for salad use it could trigger off the other 'message' uses where the oil is actually consumed. Figure 9 shows agreement with the statement 'Mazola is good for salads'.

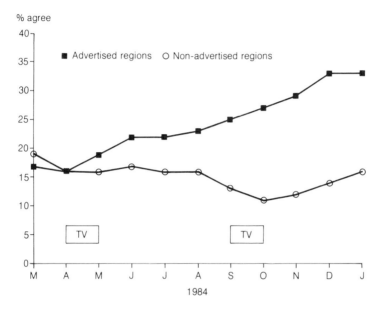

Figure 9. 'Mazola is good for salads'
Source: Millward Brown

There were very encouraging trends in the advertised regions, whereas in the non-advertised regions people were slowly losing any feelings they had for Mazola in the salad usage area. Obviously, for our strategy to work, these attitudes needed to be converted into action. Again using the Millward Brown survey, we asked users of Mazola whether they found it good for salads. Figure 10 shows the findings.

As well as short-term effects of the two bursts of advertising, over the total observed period our users were increasingly of the opinion that Mazola was suitable for salads. By the end of 1984, over twice as many felt this way as had done at the beginning of the year.

So the evidence suggested that our users were being affected in the way we had hoped. As an example of 'message' usage, salad usage was being successfully communicated by the advertising and being adopted by our users. We believed it would trigger wider use of Mazola and give us extra volume. But did it work?

The first thing to consider is our slow loss of users. Penetration of Mazola had been falling for many years but, as Figure 11 shows, although only a regional campaign (albeit the

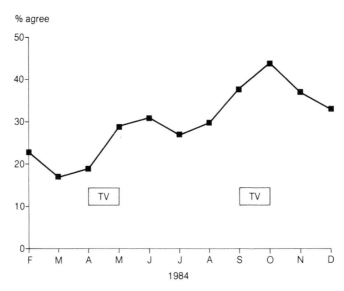

Figure 10. *Good for salads – Mazola users*
Source: Millward Brown

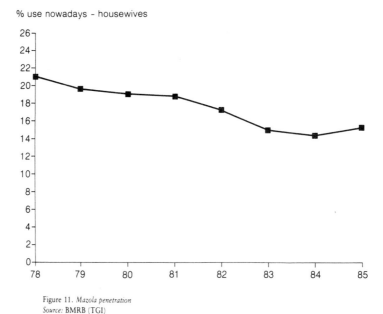

Figure 11. *Mazola penetration*
Source: BMRB (TGI)

majority of our sales areas) the advertising period did coincide with a cessation of penetration decline. 1985 (actually 1984 fieldwork) shows a slight reversal in the trend.

So we had stopped losing users. But had we affected our volume? Using MGS data, we considered brand sales as a share of the total market before and after the advertising. Although we considered the advertised regions as one area in the attitudinal/usage monitoring, we separated out each TV region's sales data. Also, to avoid short-term effects of the advertising, we considered the difference in market share between the whole of 1984 (12 months data) with the whole year up to the beginning of the advertising (another 12 months data). Figure 12 shows the percentage change in brand share between these periods and the percentage change in retail price (also measured regionally by MGS).

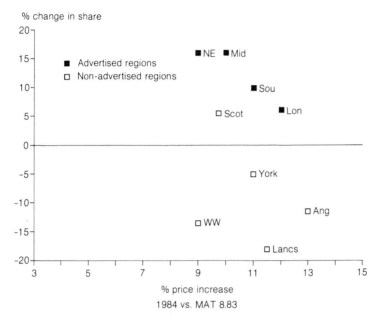

Figure 12. *Mazola share and price movements*
Source: MGS

As we can see, *the advertised regions all gained share* (about +12 per cent on average) over the period, a dramatic reversal of the four-year trend. The rest of the country continued on its decline. Aside from Scotland – where there were regional promotions during 1983 and 1984 in Co-ops and Independents (see Appendix) – the non-advertised regions lost, on average, 12 per cent of their share – a difference of nearly 25 per cent. Aside from Scotland, there were no large-scale regional promotions during 1984 and, as can be seen, a fairly constant price rise of about 10 per cent at RSP.

Packaging and presentation were constant and, in any case, are unlikely to have varied regionally. Distribution was also fairly constant during 1984, with only minor variations at the 'fringe' of listings. These would not explain the differences found.

It seems highly probable that it was the advertising which caused these regions to fare so well by changing attitudes and usage in the way described above.

PERIOD 2. INTO 1985

The last section dealt with a period when Mazola was 'behaving itself'. Its price rose only moderately between the end of 1982 and the end of 1984. It was a time when, as we have shown, advertising was able to reverse the decline in the brand's fortunes. But 1985 was very different.

The first change, at our instigation, was a change in the candidate list for TV support the following autumn. Following an analysis at the end of 1984, Scotland was added to the schedule and Tyne Tees was dropped. Although Tyne Tees had responded very well to advertising, the absolute size of our business there was small, even after a 16 per cent growth in share. The consumption of oils is virtually half the national per capita average in Tyne Tees, and so money was diverted to Scotland where we expected a more immediate payback.

But then disaster struck. Midway through the year there was a worldwide shortage of corn oil and stocks of Mazola declined considerably. The price was put up from around £1.07 to £1.35 per litre; some shops sold Mazola for £1.40. The brand lost share throughout the country, and in some areas began to lose distribution because of supply shortage. Tyne Tees, for example, went from £70 per cent distribution to £56 per cent between March and April. But throughout this traumatic period, those areas that had received TV advertising fared better than those that had been unsupported.

In Figure 13 we have repeated the share/price exercise, but taken out the effects of the stock shortage on distribution – we divided the share by the distribution at the time.

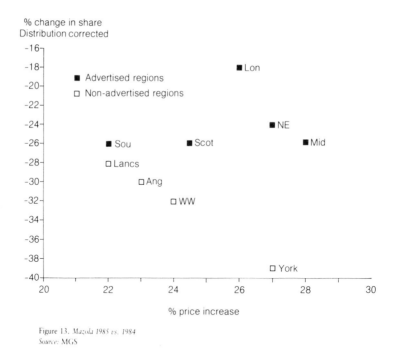

Figure 13. *Mazola 1985 vs. 1984*
Source: MGS

As one can see, the advertised regions fared better than the other regions (in the shops where it was sold), clearly showing the long-term stability advertising builds into a brand.

CONCLUSIONS

Mazola is an important brand to CPC and has great historical strength with the consumer.

However, its cost structure – based on the commodity price of corn – has always created marketing problems, against Van den Bergh's heavily supported Spry Crisp n' Dry and against much cheaper own-label blended oils. Both marketing funds and price flexibility are constitutionally limited.

Within these constraints, the 'Good Earth' campaign has turned Mazola's corn oil sourcing into a benefit increasingly relevant to changing consumer attitudes and behaviour. On fairly modest levels of expenditure a measurable effect has been achieved.

The advertising has worked:

1. By 'moving the goalposts' to enable Mazola to compete in those market sectors where it has a competitive advantage.
2. By creating 'added value' for the brand in attaching important emotional reassurance to a very simple product.

It would be hard to demonstrate that the advertising paid back directly in incremental profit over this short period. The calculation is clouded by CPC's internal sourcing of raw material. However, it reversed a decline in brand share which, if continued, could have led to delistings and a consequent effect on other CPC business. It has also invested in a valuable brand property which may have other applications in the future. What it could not do is reverse large trends in the other elements of the marketing mix. Huge price inreases, whatever the cause, can have disastrous effects which advertising can only temper. But such eventualities are not expected this year or next, and the 'Purity' strategy will again be central to marketing plans for Mazola.

The latest development in the oil market as a whole is the sophistication of the own-label offering, with Sainsbury's and others now offering a range of single source oils, including corn. Obviously this represents a new challenge to Mazola, but it also offers an opportunity to compete as a strong brand in an increasingly discriminating market-place. It can only be to Mazola's benefit that it has already begun to distinguish itself from the blended oil/commodity area.

APPENDIX – THE SCOTTISH PHENOMENON

As stated in the text, Scotland's brand share rose by about 5 per cent between 1983 and 1984. Unlike the rest of the UK, where promotions on Mazola are nationally controlled, there were regional promotions in Co-ops, Symbols and Independents in Scotland throughout this period. Figure 14 overleaf shows Mazola's position in Scotland between 1983 and 1984.

As shown by the share of stocks figures, Mazola had had excellent in-store presence throughout 1983 and the early part of 1984, with its share of stocks in Scotland over *twice* the level its shares would justify. As a result of this and the price promotions in the spring and autumn, its share rose throughout 1983. It continued to rise until the end of March during which time there was a further price promotion early in 1984. (Note sell in and price reduction in April.)

As a result of this sales force activity, the share in Scotland rose despite the absence of advertising. After the end of March, share in Scotland declined again from 14.5 per cent to around 11.5 per cent but this decline is disguised by our yearly calculations.

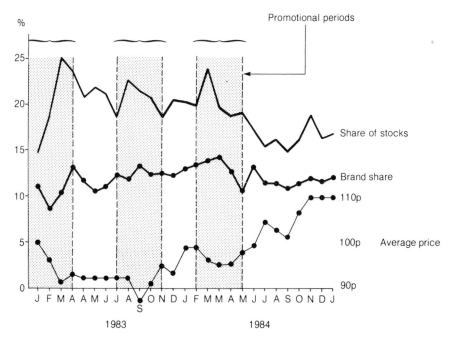

Figure 14. *Scotland – effect of stock/price promotions*
Source: MGS/CPC

8
Marketing Sleep:
The Relaunch of Karvol

INTRODUCTION

It could be said that there are two distinct if not separate effects of advertising: a short-term effect which stimulates additional sales over a defined and limited period of time; and a longer term effect which contributes to the more enduring 'saleability' of a brand.

This paper sets out to demonstrate how a brand made vulnerable through restricted distribution, and a fragile consumer base, used highly creative advertising to achieve short-term sales growth and also contributed to the longer term brand development and 'saleability'.

Background

Throughout the 1980s, there has been a steady trend by the British consumer towards self medication. This means dealing with everyday minor ailments with a non-prescription medicine.

This trend has been helped by the present Government. In an attempt to reduce escalating NHS costs, they have been committed to encouraging greater personal responsibility for healthcare.

In 1985 the 'Limited List' was introduced in order to prevent certain brands, considered to have a price premium, from being prescribed. Most of the brands had 'Over The Counter' (OTC) equivalents (ie similar products, which could be sold to the consumer without a prescription). Consequently manufacturers began to invest heavily in advertising in order to build consumer brands, and create consumer demand, rather than rely on doctor recommendation. At the same time, increasing numbers of drugs were made more freely available to the consumer. Brands originally with 'P' or 'Pharmacy Only' status (restricted to sale by a pharmacist, and therefore kept behind the pharmacist's counter) were able to switch to 'GSL' or 'General Sales List' status, so allowing them to be positioned out front in the pharmacist's store, and sold in other outlets.

The net effect of these changes has been the creation of a highly favourable environment for the growth in household medicines with 'GSL' status.

Whilst pharmacies have benefited, and have continued to dominate total sales, the real growth opportunities have moved to the other retailing outlets. The virtual sales monopoly once enjoyed by pharmacies has given way to increasing competition from the major grocery multiples and from drugstores.

The challenge for any healthcare manufacturer has been to ensure that its brands survived in this changing healthcare environment, and to take advantage of future retail opportunities thrown up by the changes.

The Opportunity for Karvol

Karvol had originally benefited from the trend towards self-medication. As a nasal decongestant, it comes in the form of small gelatine capsules containing a mixture of natural oils, such as menthol and cinnamon. When sprinkled onto bedclothes warmed through body heat, the oils provide a steady release of aromatic vapours. These clear and soothe a blocked nose throughout the night, helping easier breathing and so aiding sleep.

Karvol operates in a market sector with the somewhat tortuous definition of 'Children's Non-Ingested Decongestants', known more familiarly, if not correctly, as 'Vapour Rubs', given the format of a number of products in the sector. The market definition originates more from the trade than the consumer, since historically brand choice has depended on the pharmacist. Apart from Karvol, the key brands include Vicks VapoRub, a well known family brand, and Snufflebabe, a vapour rub positioned as a decongestant for very young babies. It also includes Olbas Oil, the brand physically most similar to Karvol given its liquid format and its method of use (also sprinkled onto bedclothes). Olbas' difference lies in its natural herbal positioning, and its use of a dropper bottle, rather than capsules, which allows for a more liberal use of liquid. This market has recently been benefiting from the significant advance in the incidence of colds (Figure 1).

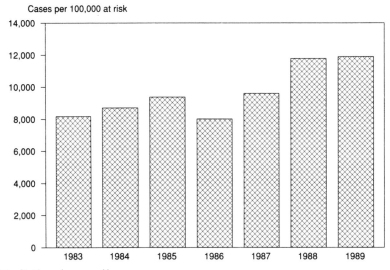

Cases per 100,000 at risk

Figure 1. *Rate of incidence of common cold*
Source: CDSC

ORIGINAL KARVOL PACKAGING

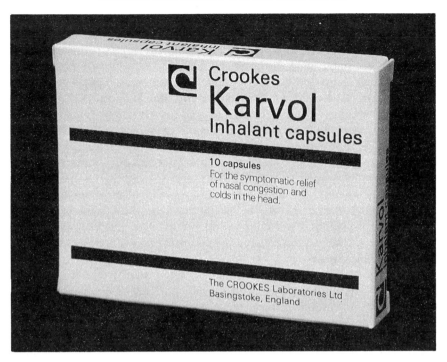

RE-PACKAGING OF KARVOL

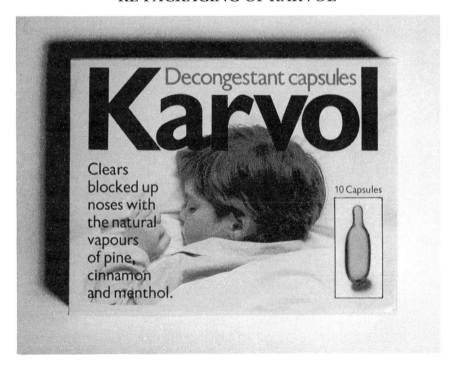

History of the Brand

Karvol itself has not always been a child's brand. It was originally launched in 1951 as a decongestant for both adults and children. Packaged in an ethical, non-pictorial pack and receiving little, if any, consumer support, it depended on a fifth of its sales coming from doctor prescription.

However, by the early 1980s, the brand's franchise was found to be strongest amongst mothers with children. The reason for this is partly explained by the format of the product itself. The use of capsules ensures a safe method of application for young children, since it avoids direct contact with a child's delicate skin. The capsules also ensure correct application of a single night's dosage, and so provide extra reassurance for an anxious parent. And the intricate method of opening the capsule (snipping the top off with scissors), together with its small size, give the product a quality of preciousness appropriate to a child's brand.

In the winter of 1981/82, in order to exploit its strengths, Karvol was relaunched with consumer packaging featuring a sleeping child. For the first time the brand was supported by a 30 second TV commercial featuring a six year old child being given Karvol by his father.

The campaign originally ran nationally, and sales grew. Following the introduction of the 'Limited List', the brand suffered a sharp drop in sales. However, the brand continued to receive yearly advertising support, and pack sales regained their momentum. In the winter of 1986/87, the pack of 10 capsules was joined by an economy pack of 20. Sales responded accordingly with 24% growth in real revenue over the following two years.

THE PROBLEM

By 1988 the brand was performing well. Karvol was experiencing year on year growth in a static market (see Figure 2).

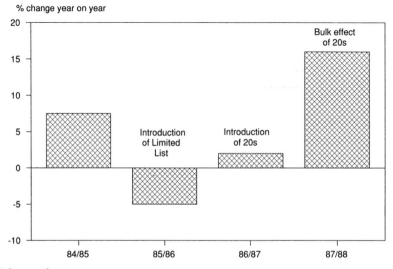

Figure 2. *Volume growth year on year*
Source: Nielsen

Karvol was also brand leader in pharmacies and enjoyed high levels of pharmacist recommendation (see Table 1).

TABLE 1: BRANDS RECOMMENDED BY PHARMACISTS
FOR CHILD USAGE

	%
Karvol	75
Vicks VapoRub	52
Snufflebabe	15
Olbas Oil	2

Source: HIPPO Research 1987
Base: Pharmacists
Note: Numbers add up to over 100% since pharmacists
are able to recommend more than one brand

It was felt, however, that the brand was vulnerable. First of all, most of the recent growth had come through distribution gains for the 20s pack. This had now reached over 70% distribution and hence could not be relied on to provide further 'easy' growth.

Secondly, Karvol was the only inhalant to possess 'P' status. In contrast, its competitors have always been registered as 'GSL' brands, allowing them far greater access to consumers.

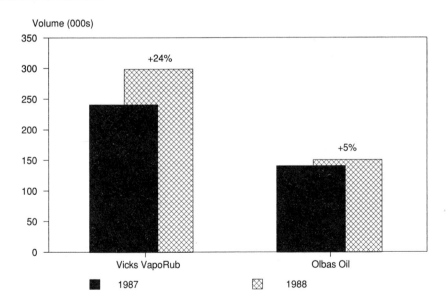

Figure 3. *Performance in grocery and drugstore of Karvol's competitors*
Source: AGB

While Karvol benefited from the medical credibility bestowed on the brand as a result of pharmacist control, it also meant that future growth for the brand would be restricted in sales. And despite pharmacies accounting for around 80% of the market, it was evident that drugstores and groceries share of sales had grown significantly over the last few years (+90%: AGB, Nielsen and Crookes' Estimates). Karvol's competitors were not only available in more outlets, but accessible to the mother shopping on a more relaxed, everyday basis. An omnibus survey had revealed that 60% of adults with children 0 – 9 bought decongestants 'just in case', in advance of any symptoms (RSGB 1987). There was a danger, therefore, that Karvol would increasingly miss out as a regular purchase, and instead become a distress purchase for extreme occasions.

While Crookes had little data available on the groceries/drugstores sectors, it did indeed appear that both Vicks VapoRub and Olbas Oil were benefiting from their presence in other outlets, and had increased sales considerably over the previous few years (Figure 3).

But perhaps one of the greatest concerns regarding the brand's future existence was the threat of Karvol's uniqueness being challenged by the launch of a 'me-too' capsule, already in possession of 'GSL' status, and thus able to be more widely distributed.

Marketing Objectives

The long-term objective had to be the acquisition of 'GSL' status for the brand, in order to fight back at its competitors (both existing and potential), and to bring in new users. This meant passing stability tests, possible product reformulation, and a lengthy application for the licence. It was estimated that, at the earliest, 'GSL' status would be achieved by mid 1990.

The short-term objectives were therefore to maintain Karvol's growth as a 'P' status brand, whilst at the same time start laying the foundations for expansion into a new distribution network. It would be difficult for Crookes to extend the brand since, as a pharmaceutical marketing company, their links with groceries were not as strong as with pharmacies. If groceries and drugstores were to consider stocking Karvol in two years' time, it was necessary to ensure its position as a clear brand leader, and use this to justify its consideration by the trade. Both of these objectives meant a strengthening of Karvol's brand leadership within pharmacies, and the development of a distinct consumer benefit.

They also meant a high level of advertising support. In the 'P' status medicines market advertising plays a fundamental part in supporting sales. Without advertising, brands are dependent on pharmacist recommendation and existing users. The pharmacist, however, in his role as salesman, can be easily influenced in his choice of brand by perceived consumer appeal. And existing users, of children's brands like Karvol, quickly move on to new brands as their children grow older.

An advertising to sales ratio of c17% is therefore the norm for this market, with some brands spending up to 30%. In fact before the new campaign, Karvol's advertising to sales ratio was almost 21%.

It was decided that advertising investment had three roles to play:

1. To support existing volume (because without it a 'P' registered brand such as Karvol would decline rapidly).
2. To boost short-term sales.

3. To support long-term investment, allowing Karvol to venture successfully into the 'GSL' market.

It was accepted that with such a high advertising to sales ratio it would be unlikely that any investment would pay for itself through short-term incremental sales growth. However, Crookes believed in the long-term potential of the brand, and took the decision to invest in it as necessary. It was agreed that specific short-term targets would be set which would establish a significant dominance for Karvol over its competitors. These were:

1. To increase volume share from 31.8% to 33%.
2. To increase brand awareness in line with the more famous VapoRub.
3. To encourage a corresponding increase in trial and penetration.

The Options

There were a number of options, however, as to how these objectives could best be met by advertising. The brand's strengths appeared to lie mostly amongst mothers of younger children. By contrast, Vicks VapoRub had for years successfully maintained a family positioning, and had as a result generated usage across a far wider age span. Olbas Oil also had a broader marketing proposition, and concentrated its advertising on adults (Table 2).

TABLE 2: MAIN USAGE BY BRAND

	Karvol %	VapoRub %	Olbas %	Snufflebabe %
Children				
Under 3	24	3	2	62
3–5	21	6	3	31
6–10	11	7	2	5
11–15	7	8	4	—
Adults 15+	38	77	89	—

Source: RSGB 1987
Base: All adults

At the other end of the age spectrum, Snufflebabe had adopted its own tightly defined positioning as a rub for young babies (particularly up to the age of one). However, Snufflebabe was a tiny brand with only around 2% value share of the market, and so was not considered a serious competitor. The option for Karvol was whether to compete with Vicks directly on a family usage basis, or to define its target user more precisely.

The Decision

Qualitative research confirmed that the brand's strengths of preciousness and cosseting made it most appropriate as a younger child's brand. Toddlers were naturally the focus for considerable parental concern. Whilst older children were considered more self reliant, once able to speak and to express their feelings fairly clearly, a younger child was felt to be particularly helpless and vulnerable. And this generated a greater level of anxiety amongst mothers.

'They can't tell you what's wrong'.

'The first time they get a cold, you think it's the end of the world, because you've never been through it before'.

'It's easier as they get older because they sit up more and they don't seem to congest as much by that time, and you've got used to them having colds, but their first..., to me it was as if she had something she could die of...' (Winstanley Douglas Research, 1988).

Already, amongst loyal users of the brand, Karvol was regarded somewhat as a guardian angel, looking after the child during the night in the mother's absence.

'You look after (the child) during the day, Karvol takes over during the night' (Winstanley Douglas Research, 1988).

Of all the brands, only Karvol possessed such a high level of cosseting values. The decision was taken therefore to build on its emotional potential as a 'carer' for younger children, and so reposition Karvol single-mindedly as a decongestant for toddlers aged under three.

Despite the danger of limiting usage further by losing older children, it was felt that the opportunity outweighed the risk. There still remained considerable untapped potential for the brand amongst younger children; the RSGB Omnibus survey had revealed that only 22% of adults with children under three years old had bought the brand in the previous 12 months. And it was also not forgotten that population trends were indicating a likely growth in the number of young babies of up to 11% during the 1990s.

DEVELOPMENT OF ADVERTISING

The Role For Advertising

Any change in positioning demanded a change in advertising. The research had indicated that the previous film had failed to portray either a genuine problem or a clear benefit from using Karvol. The execution featured a six year old child, clearly able to communicate his symptoms and therefore lacking the helplessness and vulnerability necessary to set up the problem. The need was to make the problem more dramatic, and demonstrate Karvol's ability to offer a distinct solution. At the same time, the advertising had to capture all the emotional and rational benefits of using Karvol.

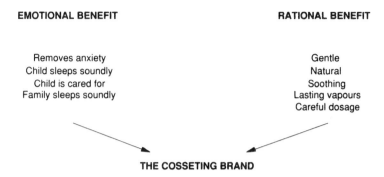

EMOTIONAL BENEFIT

Removes anxiety
Child sleeps soundly
Child is cared for
Family sleeps soundly

RATIONAL BENEFIT

Gentle
Natural
Soothing
Lasting vapours
Careful dosage

THE COSSETING BRAND

Creative Development

Television was chosen as the best means of capturing the key emotional properties of the brand. A script was developed which grew directly out of an understanding of the mother's emotions, and her actions at various stages whilst caring for her child.

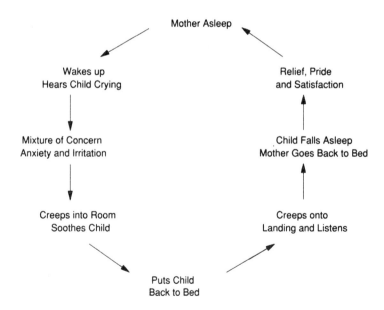

Mother Asleep

Wakes up
Hears Child Crying

Relief, Pride
and Satisfaction

Mixture of Concern
Anxiety and Irritation

Child Falls Asleep
Mother Goes Back to Bed

Creeps into Room
Soothes Child

Creeps onto
Landing and Listens

Puts Child
Back to Bed

The script focused on a helpless one year old throughout, playing on the natural instinct of mothers by highlighting the vulnerability of a disturbed child. Unlike the previous campaign the drama of the situation was clearly resolved by the child visibly falling asleep before the viewer's eyes. There was no voice over, only the sound of a child's tearfulness turning to gentle breathing. The respondents were able to understand both the rational benefits (child falls asleep) and emotional benefits (child cared for), of the brand. Moreover, the ad was found to be highly enthralling and captivating.

Media Activity

A breakfast and coffee time media strategy was chosen as one that would provide an extremely rich opportunity to reach 'housebound' women. In the first year the finished film ran from November to March, to coincide with the winter sales peak. The weighting was staggered, with the bulk of the campaign running from December to February, and with a total spend of £448,000.

Because of the resulting uplift in sales, the ad was repeated in the winter of 1989/90, this time running from January through to March, and with a slightly increased spend of £548,500 to keep in line with media inflation.

For the second year there was some concern that the breakfast/coffee time strategy might exclude working mothers. As a result, a single page press ad, depicting a distressed child, ran in *Mother & Baby* for two months prior to the second winter burst with a spend of £50,000. It was hoped this use of a secondary medium might extend the Karvol message throughout the autumn/winter season and also provide further reassurance to the more anxious mothers.

To announce the new advertising to the trade a double page spread ran twice in *Chemist & Druggist* the autumn prior to the first year's activity. A further single page trade ad ran twice in the autumn of 1989.

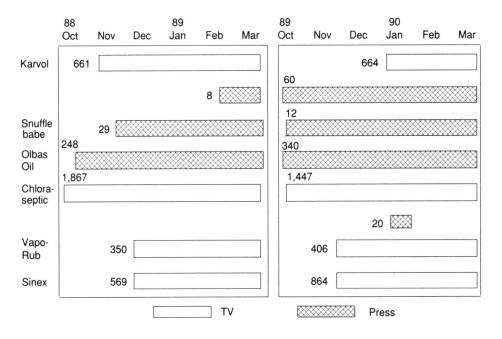

Figure 4. *Advertising expenditure – £000s*
Source: Media Register

'BABY'

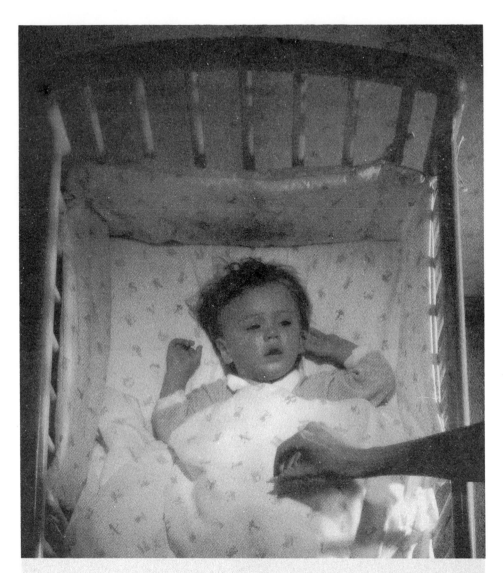

Give your child Karvol and you'll both have a peaceful night.

A blocked nose means a sleepless night for your child and a worrying one for you.

Fortunately a child's nasal congestion can be cleared simply and effectively with Karvol.

The natural vapours of pine, cinnamon

and menthol work through the night to help a child breathe easily.

*One capsule dabbed on to your child's bedclothes will help unblock a stuffy nose.

Just what you need for a good nights sleep.

Behind the best names.

Karvol. Says goodnight to a child's blocked nose.

* See pack for details. Available from your pharmacist in packs of 10 and 20.

Competitive Activity

Karvol was not the only brand to be supported. Olbas Oil, VapoRub and Snufflebabe advertised over the two year period. VapoRub would also have indirectly benefited from advertising for Vicks Sinex and Vicks Chloraseptic. The full media schedule is shown in Figure 4 (see p96).

Further Support

As further support to the repositioning, a new pack design was developed. The older child originally featured was replaced by a visibly younger child of 18 months. The new packs only began to be stocked during the summer sell-in of 1989. They were therefore only present for the second year's activity.

MEASURING THE EFFECT OF THE CAMPAIGN

An analysis of sales over time had indicated that the brand was already performing well. The key question to be asked was: had the repositioning been effective not only in growing the brand in pharmacy, but also in preparing it for future expansion?

We analysed sales of Karvol and its competitors from November/December 1983 to January/February 1990, as measured by Nielsen (bimonthly data). Our findings were as follows:

Sales

The new campaign started running in November 1988. Karvol's sales immediately increased, and in the first month alone achieved an increase in capsule sales of 27%

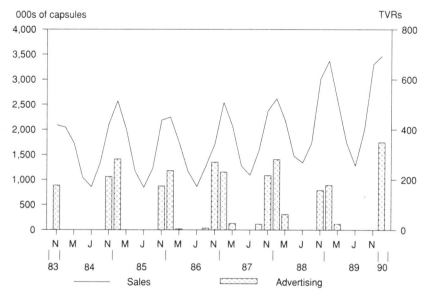

Figure 5. *Sales versus advertising*
Source: Nielsen, BARB

year on year. Altogether over the advertised period the brand experienced an increase in sales of 21.3% on the previous year.

For the following year, sales exceeded the winter 1988 peak, so that the 1989/90 sales were a further 7.1% up on the previous year (Figure 5).

Rate of Sale

Rate of sale had been static over the preceding three years for both Vicks and Karvol. With the launch of the campaign, however, Karvol's rate of sale saw a 19.1% increase for January/February 1989 vs January/February 1988, whilst Vicks remained static.

The following year saw a slight fall of 2.9% possibly affected by the reduction in share of voice (Figure 6).

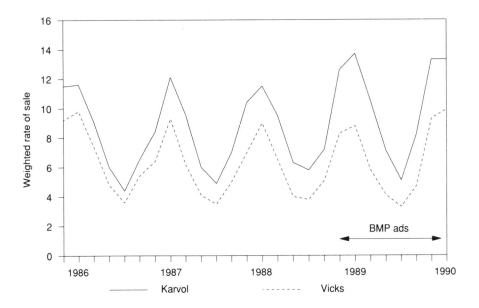

Figure 6. *Rate of sales in GB pharmacies*
Source: Nielsen

Share

Although some of the sales growth was undoubtedly due to market growth, the advertising also appeared to have a significant effect on share. To arrive at a true picture we needed to make an adjustment for the two pack sizes; we have therefore treated 20s as equivalent to two 10s. From this it can be seen that market share rose when the ad went on air, and fell back slightly as share of voice declined (Figure 7).

In analysing market share we found that Olbas Oil, which had been included in Nielsen's data since July 1984, had a slightly different seasonal pattern to the other brands in the market, and in particular to Karvol. Its sales were more seasonal than Olbas, reflecting the different usages of the two brands (Figure 8).

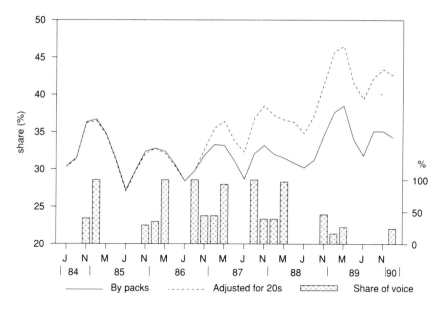

Figure 7. *Karvol market share, by volume share in GB chemists*
Source: Nielsen, BARB

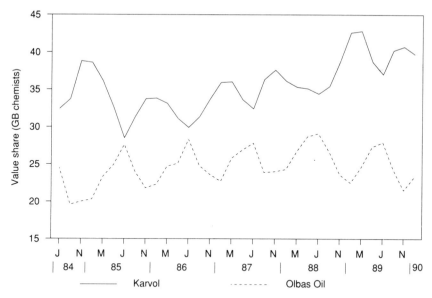

Figure 8. *Seasonality of sales, Karvol versus Olbas*
Source: Nielsen, BARB

Both qualitative and quantitative research show that Karvol is more exclusively used for colds than Olbas, and is more likely to be bought for young children. In contrast Olbas Oil appears to be used mainly by adults, and is also used for hay fever in summer months. Attempts to include Olbas' price, distribution or advertising in our subsequent analysis failed to show any significant effect on

Karvol's sales. We concluded that Olbas was not behaving as a true competitor. We therefore reverted to the original pre-1984 Nielsen definition, and excluded Olbas from our analysis.

In the first year of the campaign the objective of attaining 33% MAT share was more than achieved, with share rising to 39% whilst the advertising was on air. Despite losing share of voice in the second year, Karvol held on to an MAT share of over 36%.

Karvol remained brand leader, and, indeed, widened the gap between itself and competitive brands. It appeared to have taken share at the expense of Vicks.

Regional Analysis

Although Karvol's weight of advertising was fairly even across the country, Vicks' was more variable, and as a result Karvol's share of voice showed some regional variations. This enables us to correlate share of voice with gain in market share. In so doing we can see broadly that during the first year of advertising, the higher the share of voice, the greater the gain in market share (Figure 9).

This is further evidence to suggest that the advertising was responsible for the growth in sales.

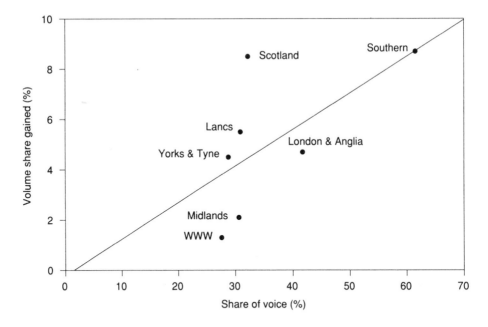

Figure 9. *Share gains versus share of voice, GB pharmacies 1988/89*
Source: Nielsen, BARB

HOW THE ADVERTISING WORKED

Consumer reaction to the advertising supports the hypothesis that the advertising was a contributory factor to share growth.

Reaction Amongst the Target Audience

There is no doubt that Karvol's advertising succeeded in generating high levels of awareness for the brand amongst the target audience. After the first winter's advertising, awareness rose to its highest level ever and, indeed, higher than any other brand in the market, despite the competitors having their own advertising support (see Tables 3 and 4).

TABLE 3: SPONTANEOUS ADVERTISING AWARENESS

	Pre 1st Burst Nov 88 %	Post 1st Burst Mar 89 %	Pre 2nd Burst Dec 89 %	Post 2nd Burst Mar 90 %
Karvol	9	18*	6	23*
Vicks VapoRub	6	7*	3	10*
Snufflebabe	1	1	1	1

Source: ISL
Note: * denotes a significant increase at the 95% confidence level.
Base: Mothers of children under three

TABLE 4: PROMPTED ADVERTISING AWARENESS

	Pre 1st Burst Nov 88 %	Post 1st Burst Mar 89 %	Pre 2nd Burst Dec 89 %	Post 2nd Burst Mar 90 %
Karvol	23	49*	24	52*
Vicks VapoRub	9	12*	8	18*
Snufflebabe	2	3	4	4

Source: ISL
Note: * denotes a significant increase at the 95% confidence level.
Base: Mothers of children under three

Advertising awareness recall rose further when prompted with a show card. 82% of our key target recognised stills taken from the commercial.

TABLE 5: PROMPTED BRAND AWARENESS

	Pre 1st Stage Nov 88 %	Post 2nd Stage Mar 90 %
Karvol	75	84*
Vicks VapoRub	90	78
Snufflebabe	61	47

Source: ISL
Note: * denotes a significant increase at the 95% confidence level.
Base: Mothers of children under three

The increase in advertising awareness coincided with a similar increase in brand awareness. Amongst mothers of children under three, prompted brand awareness grew by 12% to 84%, a gain which, for the first time, made Karvol the most well-known brand in the sector for our target audience, overtaking the historically more famous VapoRub. We had exceeded our second objective of raising awareness in line with Vicks (Table 5).

Not only did the advertising appear to affect brand awareness but it also seemed to have achieved the more difficult objective of gaining trial for the brand. Claimed usage in the last six months for Karvol doubled from 22% of mothers (with children under three), up to 40%, putting usage of the brand amongst our core target now well above that of Vicks (Figure 10).

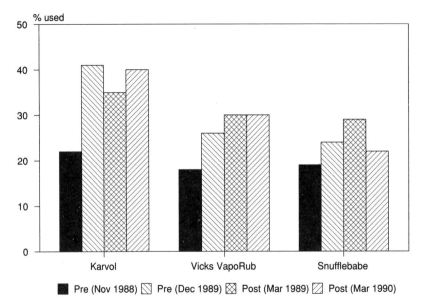

Figure 10. *Brands used in last six months*
Source: ISL
Base: Mothers of children under three years

Propensity to use also grew significantly; from 49% to 68% after the first year's advertising. It settled at over 60% of the target, indicating a level of goodwill towards the brand which is greater than that of Vicks (Figure 11).

That we can attribute the growth in usage to the success of the campaign is supported by the target's claimed reason for choice of brand. Karvol is the only brand to show significant advertising influence. After the first burst of advertising, 33% of the target asserted that advertising had influenced their choice (Figure 12). Whilst this declined after the second year of the campaign, there was a proportional rise in the percentage claiming to have 'always used the brand'. It would appear that as mothers became more familiar with the brand, so the conscious impact of the commercial on their actions declined accordingly (Figure 13).

Despite tightly defining our target as mothers of children under three, we were encouraged to discover that the advertising appeared highly effective amongst mothers of older children. Prompted advertising awareness reached 47% amongst mothers of children 3 – 5, and 44% amongst those of children 6 – 9.

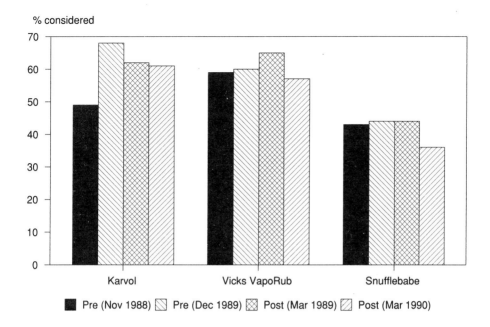

Figure 11 *Brands would ever consider using*
Source: ISL
Base: Mothers of children under three years

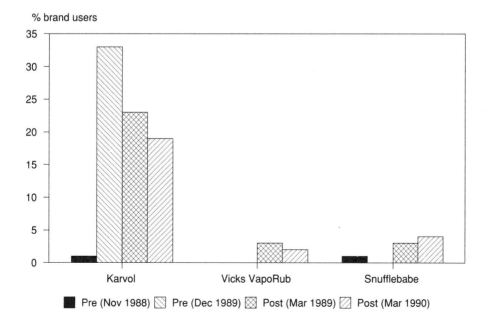

Figure 12. *Chose due to advertising*
Source: ISL
Base: Mothers of children under three years

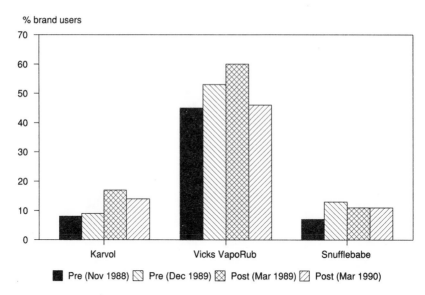

Figure 13. *Chose because always use*
Source: ISL
Base: Mothers of children under three years

There was also a significant increase in the percentage who would consider using the brand: up to 58% of mothers with children 3 – 5, and 49% of mothers with children 6 – 9.

And as a further indication of the success of the brand's intended repositioning, we looked to an impact on image. Over the last two year period, Karvol's role as a decongestant for young children has become more firmly established amongst all mothers (Table 6).

TABLE 6:   PROMPTED IMAGE DIMENSIONS

	Pre 1st Burst Nov 88 %	Post 1st Burst Mar 89 %	Pre 2nd Burst Dec 89 %	Post 2nd Burst Mar 90 %
Is suitable for young children	47	53*	54	57
Is particularly for adults	7	4	3	5*

Source: ISL
Note: * denotes a significant increase at the 95% confidence level.
Base: Mothers of children 0 – 9

The strengthening in brand image as 'one for young children' by March 1989 could only have come from advertising, since the new packaging had not been introduced at this stage.

We concluded therefore that the advertising had not only helped generate high levels of brand awareness, but had also established the desired repositioning, and encouraged purchase.

Influence on the Trade

The response of the Crookes Healthcare salesforce to the commercial was extremely positive. The advertising enjoyed a misty-eyed reception at the 1989 Annual Sales Conference. It was evident that the salesforce responded to the ad not just on a professional, but on a human, emotional level as well. As one rep said:

> 'This just finishes me off every time – it just makes me want to be back home with my kids'
> Crookes Healthcare Sales Conference, Bournemouth 1989.

Feedback from the salesforce over both advertised periods suggests that retailers were also responding well to the ad. It was considered successful in highlighting Karvol's unique younger child positioning to the trade, and justifying pharmacists' recommendation of the brand.

Further Indication of Impact

Some further peripheral evidence of the effectiveness of the campaign can be found in Appendix 1.

ISOLATING THE ADVERTISING EFFECT

Although Karvol's sales growth, and the very positive movements in additional measures of consumer response implied the campaign's effectiveness, there were other factors which could have assisted the sales increase.

To isolate more completely the effect of advertising, we carried out an econometric analysis investigating relative contributions to Karvol's growth of pricing, the introduction of the 20 pack, favourable demographic trends, competitive activity, the pattern of colds in the population, and the advertising itself.

The Growth in the Number of Children with Colds

Karvol's sales are slightly more sensitive to both the incidence of colds in the population and to changes in the numbers of children in its key target group.

Both of these increased over the last three winters, and thus contributed a relatively small proportion of Karvol's growth. Figure 14 shows the net effect of both these changes.

Price Variations

Another potential contributor to Karvol's growth was the decline in real price over the last period. This price decrease resulted from both the real price per pack having fallen and the 20s (which are cheaper per capsule than the 10s) making up a larger proportion of sales (Figure 15).

However, the model indicates that Karvol is not exceptionally price sensitive. A 1% decrease in the real price per capsule leads to only a 0.6% increase in Karvol's share of the market (by value).

At the time when the decline in real price was having its maximum effect, it was only contributing 1.9 incremental share points (July/August 1989). No statistically significant effect of competitive pricing was found.

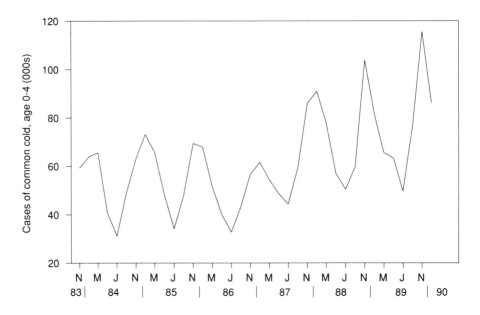

Figure 14. *Colds among young children*
Source: CDSC, CSO

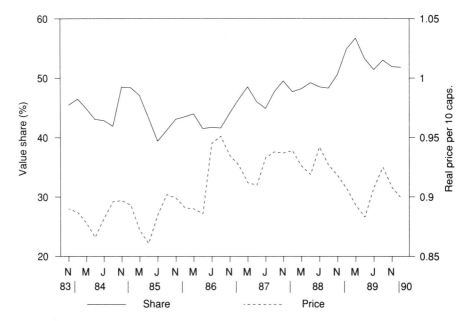

Figure 15. *Karvol share versus price in GB chemists*
Source: Nielsen

Launch of the 20s

The launch of the 20s contributed substantially to Karvol's growth between late 1986 and mid 1988 whilst their distribution was growing rapidly. Some of this was a result of their lower price/capsule (incorporated in the price effects discussed above), and some a result of the larger share of front stocks they helped to occupy (Figure 16).

However, since mid 1988, the distribution of 20s has grown more slowly, increasing from approximately 70% to 80% sterling. Model simulations show that this has added only 0.4% share points in the last two years.

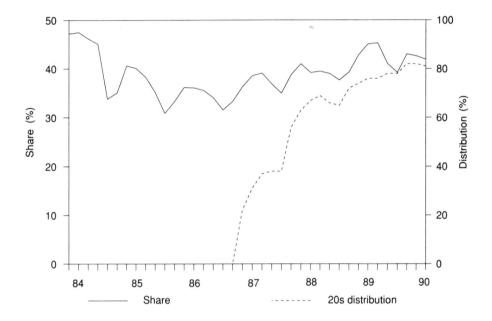

Figure 16. *Karvol share versus 20s distribution, GB pharmacies*
Source: Nielsen

Impact of New Packaging

It was not possible to use the econometric analysis to disentangle any effect of Karvol's new packaging as its introduction coincided with Karvol's autumn press advertising.

But, intuitively, as even at the time of writing the new packs have yet to gain full distribution, they can only have had a limited impact on growth.

Promotions

Because Karvol is a 'P' status medicine, it is unable to run promotions directly connected with the brand (such as price discounts, money-off coupons etc).

During the two years of advertising, a leaflet and book of Nursery Rhymes were used as prizes/mailouts in a number of competitions run in *Mother & Baby*. The uptake of the material, however, was minimal.

Advertising

The above sections indicate that some of the growth in Karvol's sales must be attributed to factors other than advertising.

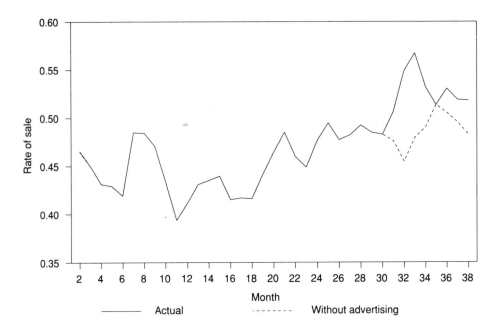

Figure 17. *Advertising effect*

Figure 17 shows Karvol's actual sales plotted against the model's projections for sales levels had there been no advertising. This demonstrates that the new campaign has been the largest contributory factor to Karvol's recent growth, and has led to Karvol achieving its highest ever brand share (over the period for which we have data). In fact the model suggests that 61% of the incremental volume over this period can be attributed to the advertising. Furthermore, whilst the old campaign generated an extra 1.9 share points/100 TVRs, overall the new campaign has been four times as effective per TVR.

Additionally, whilst any gain generated by the old campaign could be easily negated by an equivalent burst of Vicks advertising, this is not true of the new campaign. If both were to advertise simultaneously with 100 TVRs, the model shows us that Karvol would still make some share gain.

Finally, the BMP advertising proved roughly four times as effective as Karvol's previous advertising, with the sales up-lift being larger and lasting longer. Figure 17 shows the effect on Karvol's market share.

The econometric study confirms that Crookes' attempt to reposition Karvol as a young child's brand has been successful, since from the model, Karvol's sales appear now to be more sensitive to the increase of colds amongst young children (0 – 4) than other brands in the market.

SUMMARY

The econometric analysis has demonstrated very clearly that despite a number of variables acting in Karvol's favour, the one which has had by far the greatest impact on sales in the last two years is the new BMP DDB Needham advertising campaign.

As regards short-term sales effects, the advertising was the overriding factor in growing the brand, and not only achieving but exceeding the short-term share target.

Crookes's stated objective for Karvol was to achieve and maintain 33% volume share (of all 'Vapour Rubs') in GB chemists. This target has already been substantially exceeded: in March/April 1989, Karvol attained a share of 38.5%. A year later, even with a substantially lower share of voice, volume share is still well above target at 35.8%.

As for broader and longer term effects, we have already seen a strengthening of the brand's franchise amongst its newly focused target audience. And finally we have seen evidence to suggest that this stronger franchise is already restricting competitive activity – particularly launches aimed at our target audience.

THE FINANCIAL CONTRIBUTION OF ADVERTISING

Many of the effects of the advertising campaign are difficult to value in terms of financial contribution. For example, in January 1990 we saw the launch of a copy-cat version of the Karvol product, called Flurex. This product is also an oil in a gelatine capsule, but has 'GSL' status. And it retails at a lower price than Karvol. However, this new brand appears to be experiencing difficulties in gaining sales and indeed distribution. By May 1990 Flurex had achieved only 15% distribution against Karvol's 100% and a bimonthly volume share of c0.7% against 35.8% for Karvol. We believe that the success of the Karvol advertising must have played a part in restricting the growth of this rival. Unfortunately, it is impossible to put a financial value on this.

However, we can provide quantified proof of the new campaign's profitability in other ways.

For the two years previous to the BMP campaign, Karvol had an annual advertising to sales ratio of 21%. As previously mentioned such a high figure is not uncommon for a 'P' registered product. Even with an advertising to sales ratio of this magnitude the brand was profitable.

As we have seen, in the two years since the BMP campaign first started to run, sales went up, producing an increase in average annual revenue of c30%. In addition this occurred against a background of lower advertising expenditure – in fact 28% lower.

Hence the advertising to sales ratio for Karvol has fallen from 21% to 11.1% since the campaign began. Without disclosing actual profit data, it must be clear that since the brand was profitable on its previous advertising to sales ratio then it must be even more profitable when this falls to c11%, while volume and turnover are still increasing.

Finally we have already shown that 61% of the sales uplift was directly attributable to the advertising (as were substantial cost savings since ad spend went down). It is therefore fair to conclude that the profit increase was largely due to the new advertising.

CONCLUSIONS

Karvol has now gained its 'GSL' licence, and by November 1990 will have started to negotiate its introduction into drugstore and grocery.

The short-term effect of Karvol's new advertising on sales and share has been significant. But it is in the long run that its broader effects will be fully appreciated. With its strengthened franchise, and strong consumer allegiance, it now has the opportunity to take advantage of wider distribution, and a wider consumer base.

APPENDIX 1

Further Indication of Impact

1. *Awards* – The new campaign won a Lion D'Or at the 1989 Cannes Advertising Film Festival. It was also a winner in the Pharmaceutical section at the 1989 Eurobest International Advertising Awards, and was shortlisted for a D&AD in March 1989.
2. *Additional Publicity* – The first trade ad received further publicity in a *Campaign* feature on trade press advertising. With the focus of the article being the general low quality of trade advertising, the ad received welcome praise:

> 'Another BMP ad I admire is for Karvol, a medication to help you sleep....'

> 'With all the other ads around shouting about how everyone will find their multimillion pound TV campaign so riveting, this one must have really taken people by surprise in a totally relevant way'. Mike Shafron, 12th May 1989.

APPENDIX 2

Econometrics

Karvol's sales have been modelled from November/December 1983 to January/February 1990 using bimonthly Nielsen data (GB chemists). Sales volume (in packs) is not an accurate measure of the brands true performance, since it does not reflect the increase in the number of capsules sold after the introduction of the 20 capsule packs in 1986. We therefore chose real revenue as the dependant variable for the model. This is in fact closely correlated (99.8%) with the number of capsules sold, and has the advantage that it enables us to construct meaningful measures of market share.

Since July 1984, Olbas Oil has been included in the vapour rubs market as defined by Nielsen. However, as previously shown, Olbas Oil has a different seasonal pattern of sales to Karvol, and its price, distribution and advertising were shown to have no statistically significant effect on Karvol's sales. We therefore concluded that Olbas Oil does not behave as a true competitor to Karvol and reverted to the pre-1984 definition of the market.

Using this definition, we regressed Karvol's real revenue on that of the market (together with the other marketing variables), and found that the model could be restricted to a model of the market share:

	Result	Critical value
F Test on linear regression	0.52	4.35

The model of Karvol's market share was estimated by ordinary least squares regression, and performs well against a range of standard statistical tests for both fit and specification. The actual and fitted values are shown below.

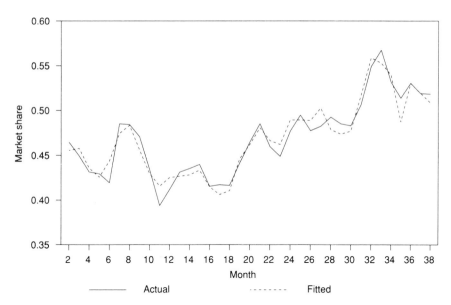

Figure 18. *Karvol revenue share model*

Statistical tests	Result	Critical value
R^2	0.920	—
R^2 (adjusted)	0.900	—
Standard error of the regression	0.028	—
Sum of squared residuals	0.022	—
Durbin Watson	2.000	—
LM(1)	0.160	3.84
LM(4)	3.750	9.49
Arch(1)	0.280	3.84
Arch(4)	2.380	9.49
Variance ratio test	1.420	2.91
CHOW (parameter stability)	1.010	2.30
CHOW (post sample predictive failure)	1.520	2.55

Interpretation of Price Coefficient

If a is the price coefficient in a value share model, it can be shown that, for a market of fixed value, the volume elasticity with respect to price is $1 - a$

This may be a slight under-estimate for a large brand, where an increase in price may actually depress the size of the overall market. On this basis, Karvol's price elasticity is about 1.6.

Forecasts for March/April 1990

When the model was constructed, data was only available up to January/February 1990. However, by making some reasonable assumptions about the likely behaviour of the independent variables, it was possible to forecast that Karvol's revenue share would rise again in March/April 1990, as the remainder of the advertising effect filtered through. The forecast brand share was 53%. When data finally became available, the prediction was confirmed: share rose to 52.8%, well within the standard error.

Advertising Effect

The table below shows Karvol's sales volume as measured by Nielsen, and how much of this is attributable to the new advertising.

Year (to April)	Sales (Packs)	Sales due to new ads
1987/1988	969,230	—
1988/1989	1,125,730	128,863
1989/1990	1,173,310	91,870

Hence the new campaign was responsible for 61.2% of the volume growth seen over the last two years.

It is estimated that, allowing for Nielsen pick-up, the advertising will have generated a total of £531,131 extra sales at RSP by the end of May 1990. This represents the combined effects of press and TV advertising. By and large it has not been possible to separate the two, because they tend to occur simultaneously. However, during October/November of 1989, BMP ran a press ad in the absence of TV, and it has therefore been possible to isolate its effect. This increased market share by an extra 2.4 share points during the autumn period.

APPENDIX 3

Analysis of 'P' Status Brands

The table below shows the advertising expenditure and sales for thirteen 'P' status brands.

Brand	Sales £000	MEAL spend £000	Advertising to sales ratio (%)
Nurofen	8,800	2,341	26.6
Solpadeine	4,400	922	21.0
Benylin	17,150	1,122	6.5
Actifed/Sudafed	7,350	1,222	16.6
Nightnurse	6,800	488	7.2
Sinutab	4,500	367	8.2
Oxy 10	1,900	548	28.8
Dulcolax	880	262	29.8
Senoket	4,220	248	5.4
Arret	1,700	291	17.1
Preparation H	2,000	301	15.1
Germoloids	1,760	284	16.1
HC45	1,320	345	26.1

The average advertising to sales ratio of these brands is 17.3%. The table below shows how much Karvol would have to spend to achieve a similar ratio.

	Turnover	Implied ad spend
1988/89	£2,600,000	£449,667
1989/90	£2,900,000	£501,886

9
Clarks' Desert Boots

INTRODUCTION

Clarks are one of the most established and respected shoe manufacturers in the UK. Their main stronghold is in the children's/infants' shoe sector resulting in Clarks having strong associations with quality and good fit. (To mothers, these are key criteria when choosing shoes for their children's delicate and deformable feet.)

In the men's shoe market, Clarks' main line is their range of air-cushioned-sole shoes. These shoes are targeted at men who buy shoes for comfort rather than style, and tend to sell predominantly to the 35+ age group. Consequently, Clarks have a relatively weak franchise amongst the more fashion-conscious younger male market.

In addition to the air-cushioned-sole range, Clarks produce a number of low-volume lines, amongst them the Desert Boot. This case study attempts to demonstrate how advertising played a role in making Desert Boots the first shoe that Clarks have sold to fashion-conscious men.

In effect, it describes a low-risk test of both the power of advertising and the flexibility of the Clarks brand name. More importantly, we believe this case study demonstrates how, in the absence of a research budget, an innovative and broad-minded attitude to research can allow a successful strategy to be developed and the consequent advertising to be evaluated convincingly.

History

The Desert Boot was 'invented' by Mr Nathan Clark in the early 1940s. Whilst in Burma on the staff of a West African brigade, Nathan was briefed by Mr Bancroft Clark to keep an eye open for any new designs which might have origins in the area. In response, he developed two designs from footwear he saw in India and Burma. One was the 'Chupplee' men's sandal, the other was the 'Desert Boot'.

The idea for the Desert Boot came from the crêpe-soled rough suede boots which officers in the Eighth Army were in the habit of getting made in the Bazaar at Cairo. Apparently, the origin of the Desert Boot can be traced back further, to the officers of the South African Division, and from them back to the Dutch Voertrekkers' footwear, 'veldschoen'.

On Nathan's return to Street in Somerset, he found that no samples had yet been made from the sketches and patterns he had sent to Bancroft. Bill Tuxill, the talented pattern-cutter of the time, was very overloaded with his regular sampling work. Every time Nathan went to see how his Desert Boot was coming on, he would see the sketches on Bill's back shelf and Bill would say with some embarrassment, 'Yes, Mr Nathan, I will get on with them next thing.' In the end, Nathan cut the patterns himself.

When the trial sample was put before the stock committee (which decided which shoes would get into the lines) the universal comment was that 'they would never sell'.

However, being in charge of overseas development, Nathan was free to offer Desert Boots to overseas markets. In 1949 at the Chicago Shoe Fair, Oskar Schoefler, the fashion editor of *Esquire* magazine, took an interest in them as a new and widely applicable type of casual footwear.

As a result of extensive editorial cover in early 1950 the Desert Boot became established in America and Canada and was a principal volume item for Clarks.

In 1965, after 15 years of large volume sales in the USA and Canada, Lance Clark decided to bring the Desert Boot to Europe. The Desert Boot took off and formed the basis of various European Clarks' wholesale companies. In France in particular, Clarks became a household name, and all boots of the type, whether originals or copies, became known as 'Les Clarks'.

In Britain, however, sales remained quite sluggish. The crêpe-soled suede boot (or 'brothel creeper') became part of the mod uniform of the 1960s (its sole didn't scratch the running boards of scooters!) but the proliferation of different makes and the lack of support for the Clarks original limited the Desert Boot's potential.

In the mid- to late 1980s it was observed that Clarks' Desert Boot had become an élite fashion item in Italy, snapped up by stylish Italians to wear with their Armani suits. This was perceived as an indicator of potential in Britain – all that was needed was a little push.

The Recent Brand History

To preserve gross margin confidentiality we will consistently present sales of Desert Boots in index form, and profit figures in actual form.

However, the absolute sales of Desert Boots are quite low, certainly when compared to many of Clarks' other lines. In fact, penetration of Desert Boots is well below 0.1 per cent of the male adult population. This point is made, since it greatly influenced both the strategy (which may of course change as penetration grows) and the budget.

Since 1980, sales of Desert Boots had been fairly constant (see Table 1), although there were signs of some growth since the decline in 1981–82.

Alongside this reasonably static and quite low sales picture was reasonably static and quite low distribution. Distribution was (and still is) largely restricted to Clarks-owned sites in large towns and city centres.

TABLE 1: INDEXED SALES OF DESERT BOOTS, 1980–86

1980	1981	1982	1983	1984	1985	1986
100	77	73	94	109	122	118

Note: All sales figures are ex-factory.

DEVELOPING THE ADVERTISING STRATEGY

Given the size of the budget, it was impossible to justify any consumer research to verify the existence of an opportunity for Desert Boots. We needed to talk to young style-conscious men without spending any money. Fortunately, we realised that a reasonable sample of our perceived target audience was working for the agency in the creative department. Whilst certainly not a truly representative sample, we believed that talking to them would be a lot better than doing nothing at all. They became the guinea-pigs on which our hypothesis was tested. Following discussions with the majority of them, either singly or in pairs, we were convinced that the potential for Desert Boots amongst this audience was real.

Thus, from our study of Desert Boots' performance in Europe and discussions with the creative teams we had identified and verified a tightly defined target audience: Male style leaders − young men who were at the forefront of fashion; men who wore certain items of clothing before they became trendy.

The role for advertising was to communicate to our target audience that Clarks' Desert Boots were a valuable part of a truly fashionable wardrobe.

The advertising objective was to turn Clarks' Desert Boots into a cult by presenting them to our target audience as a highly stylish fashion item.

At this point we spoke to the media department. We had identified our target market, but what medium could reach them within the constraints of our budget?

Choosing the Medium

Given a media budget of £30 000 and a sparse but nationally distributed target audience, the media department was given the task of finding a medium that would allow us to reach as many of this target audience as possible whilst providing an environment that gave our style claim credibility. They came up with a selection of 'style' magazines; publications that, whilst lacking readership research and having quite low circulations, were qualitatively the strongest contenders for our target audience. Their editorial covered the latest developments in fashion and music and tended to reflect an innovative and original stance towards both. They captured precisely the young style leaders we were aiming for. In addition, they provided a route of relatively low capital cost, allowing us to buy 28 double-page-spread insertions. The title list included: *The Face, ID, Arena, The Wire, Blitz* and *The Manipulator*. The campaign ran in early spring 1987.

The Creative Strategy and the Ads

Once we had convinced ourselves of the broad opportunity for Desert Boots we needed to finalise the creative strategy for the advertising. First, we examined the 'nostalgia' route — harking back to the days of the mods. What we found when we discussed this with the creative teams was that impressions of the mod era were largely negative. The mod 'uniform' which we would instantly be tied to if we followed this route was currently seen as drab and unfashionable and mods themselves were seen as rebellious, post-pubescent teenagers driving scooters because they were too young for a car licence.

In addition, we realised that the fact that Clarks' Desert Boots were the original desert boots gave us 'classic' credentials without the need to hark back to a bygone age.

What we looked at instead was a route based on what we knew about the way Italians wore Desert Boots. We arrived at a contemporary 'casual formality' positioning for the shoes, for example an Armani suit worn with a T-shirt.

We were now in a position to write the creative brief. The proposition: 'Clarks' Desert Boots are the originals' was felt to be necessary but subsidiary to the main thrust of the brief, which centred around the mood and tone of the ads. The creative team was asked for press ads for Desert Boots that were 'contemporary style on a page'. The creative idea it came up with was to feature a man wearing one Desert Boot whilst his other foot was bare, with the line:

'There is only one Desert Boot. Clarks. The original.'

The photography was to be in black and white, the accepted currency of high-fashion photography, and the photographer was to be Helmut Newton. Helmut Newton was chosen not only for his track record of atmospheric, intriguing and somewhat erotic photography but also for his interactive value. Together with the creative team, the shots for the ads were developed on location, with Helmut Newton's experience and perfectionism ensuring that the shots, and thus the finished ads, fully met the mood and tone requirements of the brief.

EVALUATING THE CAMPAIGN

Given the size of the advertising budget and the unfortunate fact that any money for research would have to come from the media budget, the effectiveness of this campaign has to be evaluated without recourse to quantified data from intermediate variables, such as attitudes towards Clarks or pre- and post- awareness of Desert Boots.

We feel that this is unfortunate in the sense that the case is less complete without these variables but that it is not a problem in proving the effectiveness of the advertising. In short, it is still possible to isolate the advertising effect on sales and to show that the incremental profit generated by the incremental sales exceeded the advertising cost — the fundamental definition of advertising effectiveness.

ELIMINATING OTHER VARIABLES

Distribution

Distribution of Desert Boots has historically been restricted to city centres and large towns, as these were the only locations where the rate of sale justified the shelf space taken up by the shoes. The distribution strategy for Desert Boots was largely unaltered for 1987, for two reasons. Firstly, to maintain some sense of exclusivity through limited availability, and secondly because the highest concentration of our diffuse target market were located in these areas. The only changes in distribution for 1987 (which were marginal in terms of increased sales and number of outlets) were directly attributable to the advertising. In fact, these new distribution points highlight another aspect of the strategy that went entirely to plan.

In order to boost the style credibility of Desert Boots, it had been hoped that through approaching a limited number of high-fashion menswear shops with proofs of the ads and the media plan, these shops would be persuaded to stock Desert Boots, thus allowing us to run the ads with a line stating 'Available from Woodhouse, Jones, Blazer ... etc.' − a strong endorsement as far as our target market were concerned. Fortunately, some of these shops did decide to stock the shoes (Woodhouse, Paul Smith, Jones and Harrods, for example), and we were able to run the ads with their valuable endorsement under the pack shot.

Thus, the only change in distribution for 1987 was the addition of a number of high-fashion shops in London, which between them accounted for less than 2 per cent of total Desert Boot sales.

We talked to the buyers at Woodhouse, Jones and Harrods:

'We stocked them during the advertising campaign.'

'The ad was stylish enough for us to stock them.'

'I think to look at they're brilliant, really first-class ads. I bought a couple of pairs myself not long after seeing them.'

Price

The price of Desert Boots has not been altered other than by changes in line with RPI. In 1987 the MRP was £29.99. It is difficult to assess whether any relative price change has occurred over the years, not least because the Desert Boots competition (in 1987) is very difficult to define since we believe the shoes were being purchased as fashion items and not from necessity, i.e. 'shall I get a pair of Desert Boots or a new shirt?'

If in 1987 price relative to other fashion items became an important variable, this can only be because the advertising positioned Desert Boots in competition with other fashion items and hence is an advertising effect anyway. We have, however, no hard data on how Desert Boots' price relative to the 'average' fashion item affected sales, though we do know that their absolute price did not change (other than with inflation) across the measured period.

THERE IS ONLY ONE DESERT BOOT

Clarks

THE ORIGINAL

THE EFFECT ON SALES

Having shown that distribution and price were constant (within limits directly related to advertising) it is difficult to find any other variable except advertising that actually varied across the period 1980–87.

The total advertising spend was zero in 1980–86, and amounted to £72 000 in 1987, of which £28 500 was spent on media. Clearly, from the relatively constant sales in 1980–86, any other variable that did influence sales was also relatively constant across that period. We couldn't find any variable other than advertising that suddenly changed in 1987 and that could affect sales to the degree shown in Figure 1.

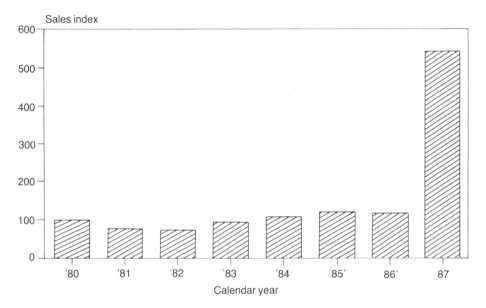

Figure 1. *Sales of Clarks' Desert Boots, 1980–87*

Incremental Profit

If we follow the trend in sales from 1984 to 1986 and assume that the 1987 sales index would be 120, we can calculate the gross profit on the additional 423 advertising-related sales index points. This incremental gross profit amounts to £141 980 or £69 980 after paying for the advertising (including production).

With a spend as low as £72 000, the production budget accounted for an unusually high proportion — around 60 per cent of the total. If, purely as an academic exercise, we ignore the production cost, and evaluate the financial effectiveness of the £28 500 media spend it is enlightening to note that each media pound spent generated £4.98 of incremental gross profit.

INDIRECT MEASURES OF ADVERTISING EFFECTIVENESS

As mentioned earlier, quantitative measurement of intermediate variables was not financially viable. However, there are a number of qualitative measures that further support our claim that advertising was the sole mover in generating the spectacular sales increase for Clarks' Desert Boots.

Shop Managers' Survey

We carried out a telephone 'survey' of Desert Boots stockists. Although not intended as anything other than an encouraging indicator, the following quotes are representative of the responses we obtained:

'The branch I came from didn't stock Desert Boots and when the ad was appearing people came in with it and asked for them.'

'We've had a couple of people bring the ads into the shop and ask if we've got them.'

'I get about two or three people a week asking for them.'

'More people asked for them rather than browsing and picking things off the shelf.'

PR Generated by the Ads

For Clarks to run ads like these generated a good deal of media interest and an enormous amount of free PR.

The biggest coup in terms of PR generated solely by the advertising was a five-minute feature on *Network 7*:

A self-conscious cult programme came to the delight of advertisers in the form of Channel 4's Sunday spectacular *Network 7*. To watch the first series of *Network 7* you needed an honours degree in hipness.

(Stuart Cosgrove, *The Listener*)

In terms of targeting, *Network 7* was ideal. The feature elaborated on the history of the Desert Boot from its 'invention' by Nathan Clark through to its emergence as a style-leaders' fashion item in 1987. It included an interview with Paul Leeves, our creative director, and a discussion of the ads. The feature resulted from an approach made by the *Network 7* producer to Clarks, precipitated by his seeing the ads.

In addition, almost all the national newspapers made some comment *about the advertising*, for example:

'Move over Doc Martens, the Desert Boot is back.' (*Today*)

'The Desert Boot has all the qualities of the style object ... and a profile just begging to be raised.' (*Sunday Telegraph Magazine*)

In the *Daily Mirror*'s White Hot Club feature on 'in' and 'out', Desert Boots were said to be 'in'.

Even the advertising trade press was moved to make comment:

'They achieve the seemingly impossible task of making Clarks' shoes appear pretty macho. All credit for seeing the erotic potential in an item of clothing I had previously associated only with bespectacled train spotters.' (*Campaign*)

It is impossible to determine precisely how many sales were attributable to this PR rather than directly from the advertising. It is possible, however, to assert that *all* of the Desert Boots free PR was generated *directly from the advertising*. It is therefore, in a sense, unnecessary to concern ourselves with the question of whether the PR generated sales, since the PR itself was an advertising effect.

SUMMARY

The bare facts are:

— In a year in which advertising was the only variable relevant to Clarks' Desert Boots that changed significantly, sales increased by around five times.
— The incremental gross profit generated was just under double the total advertising spend and nearly five times the media spend.
— The campaign was directly responsible for generating an enormous amount of free PR including a five-minute piece in *Network 7*, a programme directly aimed at our target audience.

FURTHER ISSUES

The limited budget set an unusual challenge for an agency the size of BMP. With no research budget, we needed to be innovative with our strategy and advertising development, sometimes trusting to nothing more than common sense and intuition. This virtual complete lack of research data leaves us with some vital questions that we cannot answer with hard facts. For example, we don't know how attitudes to Clarks and particularly Desert Boots changed following the campaign. We also cannot judge whether the Clarks branding helped or hindered the product's performance.

This still leaves what to us is the most important question of all — who bought the shoes? The answer to this question is the ultimate confirmation of the success of the strategy. It is unfortunate that we cannot conclusively answer this crucial question but we believe that the combination of the creative executions, the tightly targeted media plan, the response of the national newspapers, the replies of the shop managers and the tone of the *Network 7* feature together lead to only one possible answer — male style leaders.

WOULD IT HAVE HAPPENED ANYWAY?

There is one other 'big' question that needs addressing. Some stylish products seem to take off on their own without any obvious reason, for example Zippo lighters. Is it possible that Clarks' Desert Boots were destined to become a style item in 1987 and that the presence of advertising was just a coincidence?

For a number of reasons, we believe the answer is 'no'. First, products that suddenly become highly fashionable (such as Zippo lighters) tend to be featured editorially in highly fashionable publications. Clarks' Desert Boots were not featured in *any* editorial before the campaign ran.

Secondly, products that suddenly become highly fashionable tend to be distributed through highly fashionable outlets. Apart from a few shops in London, Clarks' Desert Boots were only distributed through (frankly) unfashionable Clarks-owned shoe shops. In any case, the distribution in fashionable shops in London only occurred because of the advertising, as we have seen.

Thirdly, *all* the PR generated for Desert Boots referred to the ads and appeared during or after the campaign as a direct result of the advertising.

Putting the arguments together suggests to us that there is no basis for assuming that Clarks' Desert Boots were destined for success as a fashion item in 1987 irrespective of advertising. Moreover, any features of the Desert Boots situation in 1987 that do tie in with 'unexplainable' success (for example 'fashionable' distribution and 'fashionable' consumer PR) were directly caused by the advertising.

Our belief is that it most certainly would *not* have happened anyway.

CONCLUSION

We hope we have demonstrated that alongside the right product, advertising has the power to give Clarks access to a new market. As a test of the flexibility of the Clarks brand name, the results are not only positive but also profitable.

At the very least, this opens up new doors for Clarks that before 1987 were considered to be well and truly locked.

10

How the Chimps Kept PG Tips Brand Leader Through 35 Years of Intense Competition

INTRODUCTION

Our story begins in 1955, the year Brooke Bond relaunched PG Tips. Prior to 1955 it had been called 'Pre-Gestive' tea, a reference to the historical importance placed upon tea's dietary and medicinal properties.

The relaunch may have modernised PG Tips image but it didn't lead to a growth in its market share. Throughout 1955 and most of 1956, it remained number four brand.

Today, 35 years on, PG Tips is not just a player in this market, but also the dominant brand leader. How has this success been achieved and maintained?

Certainly, many things have changed over this period that might have affected the brand's performance. The nature of what the British eat and drink has changed substantially, as have fashions in the tea market and our social lives in general. Two things that haven't changed, however, are the campaign that first started in 1956 and the high level of media support given to the brand ever since.

In this paper we aim to prove that PG Tips *reached* this dominant position by 1958 because of the interest generated in the brand by the chimps advertising, then that PG Tips *maintained* its brand leadership by assimilating added value which enabled it to represent a more valued purchase to consumers, even though its absolute price has always been higher than its competitors.

After proving that added value has indeed been added, we then show that it is the chimps campaign that is primarily responsible for this addition of value.

Finally, we attempt to quantify the financial contribution of 34 years of the chimps campaign.

However, first we need to introduce them.

THE CHIMPS CAMPAIGN

A Unique Property

The original idea for the 'chimps' was chanced upon when a copy writer, charged with inventing the first PG Tips commercial, visited Regent's Park Zoo in 1956. The chimpanzees were enjoying a tea-party in front of a large crowd. A few months later, the first chimps commercial was shot in a stately home and featured a chimps tea-party accompanied by a voice-over by Peter Sellers.

This sixty-second commercial was designed to boost awareness of PG Tips and develop an original and inimitable property for the brand. At the time, it was believed that, on seeing the commercial, the obvious enjoyment of the crowd at the antics of the chimps in Regent's Park Zoo would be replicated in the homes of the viewers. Thus, it was hoped to establish a stronger relationship between brand, advertising and consumers.

'Stately home' first appeared on the nation's TV screens in the autumn of 1956.

Consistency

In all honesty, nobody at that time suspected that the chimps advertising would be so effective so quickly. Within two years, the brand had toppled Typhoo from the number one slot, on the way overtaking other erstwhile giants such as Brooke Bond Dividend and Lyons (Brooke Bond).

The agency and Brooke Bond soon realised that they had a hot property on their hands. As time passed with PG Tips still retaining brand leadership, faith in the long-term potential of the chimps campaign strengthened. They quickly became so popular that Brooke Bond conducted film shows in cinemas around the country.

Consistency has been maintained ever since with similar creative executions running over the whole 34 year period. By the time of the chimps' 30th anniversary in 1986, over 100 commercials had been made.

Consistency has been maintained not only in creative style but also in media presence. PG Tips has always retained the dominant share of voice in the tea market, only varying its advertising spend (in real terms) by a relatively small proportion from year to year whereas the competitors' spends have fluctuated much more dramatically.

Relevance

It would be tempting to believe that, having cracked a winning formula so early on, the agency's task would be solely to churn out more, very similar, chimps commercials. This of course is untrue for several reasons.

First, viewers need continually to be excited by new ideas.

Secondly, the chimps have lived through a period of exceptionally rapid social change. Making sure that they continue to reflect trends in society and do not become 'dated', has required constant change within the creative vehicle.

In the late 1960s, for example, the commercials reflected the self-expression of the times with two of them showing the chimps portraying a photographer and an artist.

'STATELY HOME'

Music: 'Greensleeves'
VO: The clock strikes four. In millions of English homes that means it's teatime

Teatime with its gleaming silver and tinkling teacups

What a happy time it is and how fortunate the hostess who knows that her favourite tea is also the favourite of her friends

For no matter how elegant the manners or charming the company

no guest is ever really happy without the right kind of tea

good tea, fresh tea, tea you can taste to

the last delicious drop

'He means Brooke Bond PG Tips. B-B-B-B-Brooke Bond'

Sound: Laughter from other chimps

In the 1970s, the chimps pastiched topical events such as the oil crisis and Ted Heath's preoccupation with his yacht, 'Morning Cloud'.

And of course, clearly observed sketches on the British character have always had the potential to attract enormous interest. 'Mr Shifter' who in 1972 coined the phrase 'You hum it son, I'll play it' and the 'Tour de France' cyclist with his 'Avez-vous un cuppa?' are two examples which have become part of the common vernacular.

The campaign has also adapted to take account of competitors' tactics. For example, in response to Tetley's greater emphasis on the advantages of their teabags' '2,000 perforations', the Bond series relaunched PG Tips with new 'Flavour Flow' teabags in 1981. 'Brooke Bond', a character based on James Bond, guarded the new teabags' secret.

'Ada and Dolly' formed the core campaign over the 1983 to 1985 period and were a deliberate move back to the chimps more traditional 'kitchen sink' territory, representing a retreat from the flash and spectacle of the Bond series. 'Ada' characterised the traditional packet tea user, 'Dolly' her more modern teabag-using counterpart. The appeal of old favourites still seemed to be strong however and therefore this series featured flashbacks to 'greatest hits' such as 'Mr Shifter' and 'Tour de France'. It was hoped that this would enhance the appeal of the campaign – reinforcing the campaign's and the brand's provenance.

Since then, development of the chimps has been driven by the desire to keep them in tune with ever more rapidly changing everyday life. Chimps are no longer shifting pianos but are flying on holiday to Spain, visiting health farms, doing their own DIY, making Board Room decisions and using computers.

This continual updating of the advertising has paid dividends throughout the 34 years of the campaign. As we shall show, the advertising's fame and appeal has remained consistently high.

THE TEA MARKET: 1956 – 1989

Like many British institutions during the 1960s, tea was challenged by the new liberalisation of the times. Sales gradually went into decline as coffee became more appealing to the younger generation and consistently, albeit very slowly, since then, its growth, and that of other substitutes has eroded tea consumption.

TABLE 1: DECLINE IN TEA

	1964	1974	1984	1989
Tea volume (million kg)	156	140	130	110

Source: Nielsen

Two major structural changes have occurred over the last 34 years – the introduction of the *teabag* and the introduction and steadily growing importance of *own label* teas.

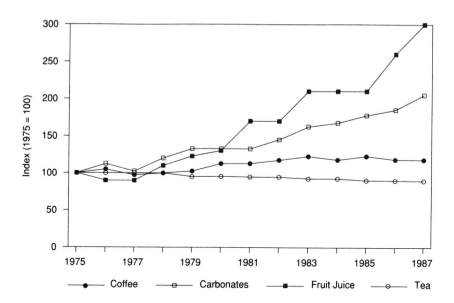

Figure 1. *Trends in drink consumption, average daily intake*
Source: NDS

The Teabag

Teabags, the single most important innovation in the market, were introduced in 1963. Their arrival heralded a format change which dominates today, accounting for 80% of the market.

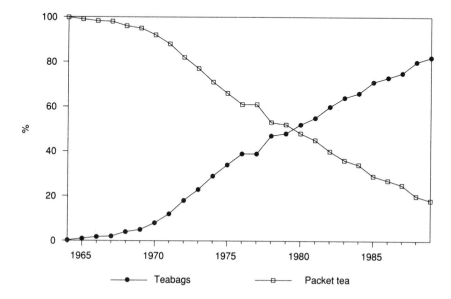

Figure 2. *The change in format, market shares of teabags and packet tea*
Source: Nielsen

The Rise of Own Label

The growth of own label and its significance in many markets is well documented. The tea market has not escaped.

It will be argued that PG Tips – the largest brand and hence the one with most to lose – has actually lost least to own label over the past 34 years.

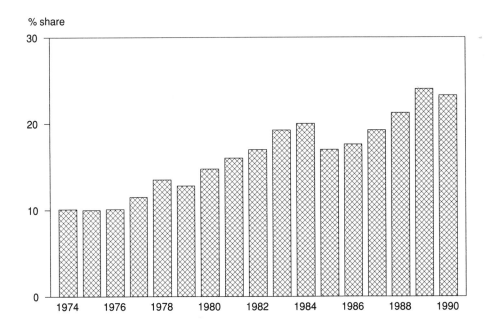

% share

Figure 3. *Own label's advances, share of total tea volume*
Source: Nielsen

PG TIPS PERFORMANCE 1955 – 1958

Assumption of Brand Leadership

PG Tips became brand leader in 1958 having been number four before the chimps campaign rolled out in autumn 1956. Although we do not possess all the data from this period, we believe that PG Tips rose from about 10% volume share in early 1956, to c. 23% by the end of 1958. This represented at the time a dramatic shift in market structure. To put it in perspective, today (and remember that the market has shrunk since 1958) a gain of 13% volume share represents approximately £50 million of extra sales per annum.

The Role of the Chimps Campaign in Achieving Brand Leadership

It has proved impossible to trace accurate sales and other audit figures from the late 1950s. However, the following analysis eliminates other possible causes and suggests that the only causal variable for PG Tips' explosive growth in these two years was the advertising.

1. *Name Change* – Prior to 1955, Pre-Gestive was already colloquially shortened to PG by consumers, possibly because the P and the G were in bold type on the packet. Thus the name change is unlikely to have been such an important factor. Anyway, the change occurred a full year before the advertising started and share did not pick up as a result.
2. *Taste Change* – The blend was not changed at the time of the first chimps commercial.
3. *Distribution Change* – PG Tips was already in very strong distribution as the number four brand (aided by Brooke Bond Dividend's pre-eminence). As own label was not widespread at this time stocking four brands was perfectly normal.
4. *Price Change* – PG Tips was sold at the same price premium to the other brands before and after the advertising broke. So the growth was not caused by advantageous pricing.

What seems much more likely is that the advertising generated large increases in rate of sale.

Circumstantial evidence for the advertising being the root cause is also provided by the fact that this explosive volume share growth coincided with the most rapid increases in penetration of ITV and the chimps were the first TV tea advertising.

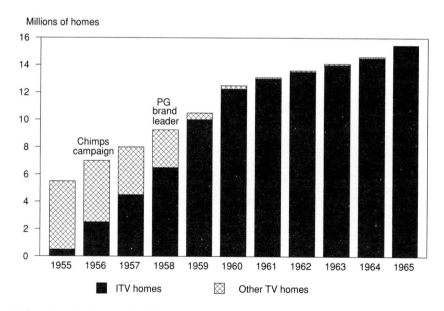

Figure 4. *The rapid growth in homes receiving ITV*
Source: ITV Association

Between 1956 and 1959, penetration of ITV grew fourfold, whereas between 1959 and 1962, it grew by only 35%.

Overall, although data inhibits our ability to 'prove' the claim conclusively, we believe that it is clear that it was the chimps TV advertising that thrust the brand from the number four slot to number one within the space of two years. Whilst the main theme of this paper is to demonstrate long-term advertising effects, we have also therefore shown that at one time the advertising had a very powerful and profitable short-term impact!

PG TIPS PERFORMANCE 1959 – 1989

Sustained Brand Leadership

Ever since PG Tips broke through into the number one position in 1958, it has maintained brand leadership with a consistently high and stable volume share. Unfortunately, we only have accurate share data available from 1968. However, this shows the robustness of the PG Tips performance from this date onwards.

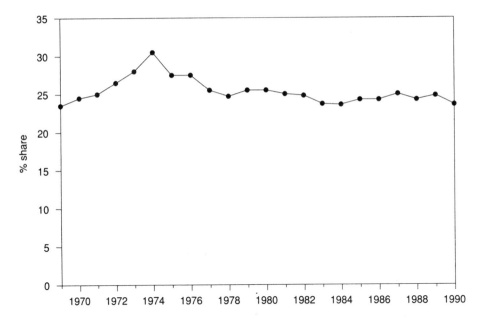

Figure 5. *PG Tips share of total tea market, year ending January*
Source: Nielsen, MEAL
Note: The unusual peak in 1974 coincided with one of the most popular ads, Mr Shifter, and with exceptional media weight

This remarkable achievement, and its rewards, should not be underestimated. The brand has faced intense competitive pressure with rival brands being relaunched (eg Quickbrew in 1986) and intermittently outspending PG Tips. In addition, every conceivable promotional weapon has been used by its rivals in an attempt to wrest away some of the PG Tips share.

The stability of the brand share over this period is evidence that these rival tactics have failed to dent PG Tips position over any significant length of time. Even when PG Tips share has dipped slightly, it has been able to bounce back shortly afterwards.

The Concept of Added Value

PG Tips has been able to maintain such consistent and dominant share leadership because it has assimilated, over the years, an increasing amount of perceived 'added value', which supplements the functional benefits of the product. We have already noted that the brand's functional benefits are essentially generic, we now intend to demonstrate that the brand possesses added non-functional values of sufficient worth to motivate consumers to buy PG Tips even when price and other factors may mitigate against such a decision.

Evidence of Added Value

The evidence that PG Tips has assimilated uniquely powerful added value over the past 34 years comes in many forms.

Branded Versus Blind Tests

Consumers find it very difficult to distinguish between the major brands in blind taste tests. For example, in 1983, when asked to rate tea tastes blind (on a scale of 1 to 7), the average consumer response for the top five brands was extremely similar – varying by only 1 or 2%.

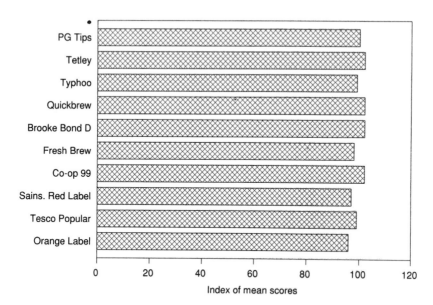

Figure 6. *Consumers find it difficult to identify teas in blind product tests*
Source: Millward Brown, May 1983

This has been the case throughout the brand's history.

However, in *branded* tests, throughout the latter part of the 34 year period, PG Tips has enjoyed the greatest preference.

Even after brand size factors have been eliminated, PG Tips is perceived to be the best tasting cup of tea.

TABLE 2: BRANDED TESTINGS

	PG Tips	Tetley	Typhoo
Best tasting cup of tea (indexed against PG)	100	85	40

Source: Millward Brown, March 1990

This indicates that the brand has indeed attained a perceived added quality which is not justified alone by functional characteristics.

Price Premium

Another significant measure of added value is whether the brand can justify a price premium and continue to sell in significant quantities while doing so – are consumers willing to pay more for a product that is functionally similar to its rivals? We have three pieces of evidence to suggest that PG Tips has succeeded in doing this.

First of all, a superficial glance at pricing data suggests that PG Tips does now command a price premium over the market average, and it does so whilst maintaining its share.

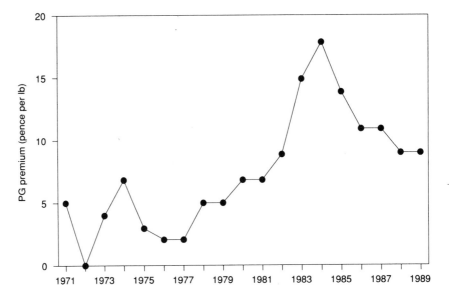

Figure 7. *PG Tips price premium vs market average at 1985 prices*
Source: Nielsen

Secondly, we have performed an econometric analysis using recent data from the teabag sector (now representing 80% of the market volume). This models PG Tips and Tetley's shares against relevant variables, details of which are given in the technical appendix.

The results show PG Tips to be much less sensitive than Tetley to price changes by both branded and own label competitors.

A 1% increase in the price of PG Tips relative to Tetley and Typhoo leads to a drop of 0.4 market share points. The effect of a similar increase in Tetley's price is much larger. A 1% increase in Tetley's price relative to PG Tips and Typhoo results in a downturn of 1.4 share points. We conclude that this is further evidence of the added value of the PG Tips brand compared with its major rivals since it implies that consumers are more likely to ignore price (in favour of other 'values') when it comes to purchasing PG Tips.

Finally, we have concrete evidence of the relative price insensitivity of the brand. In 1977, disaster struck both tea and coffee. Coffee bean and tea leaf prices rocketed. In the coffee market this provoked the introduction of cheaper, chicory based blends which grew to 30% of the market, hitting Nescafé, the brand leader, very hard.

Tea suffered too with market volume plunging by 10%. One might have expected the rapid rise in economy blends of coffee, at the expense of the brand leader, Nescafé, to be mirrored in the tea market with PG Tips. This did not happen. PG Tips retained its price premium and still held onto a 23% brand share – again demonstrating the added value justifying, even in times of crisis, a substantial price premium.

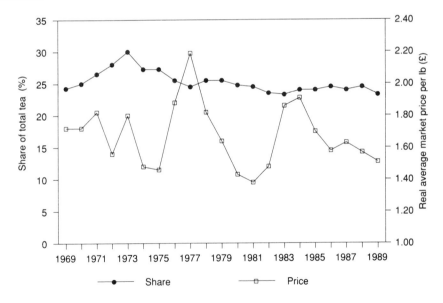

Figure 8. *PG Tips resistance to rocketing tea prices*
Source: Nielsen

Resilience in the Face of Short-term Reductions in Media Support

If indeed the brand has assimilated added values over the past 34 years, then this would suggest that it should be less sensitive to short-term declines in the level of its advertising support.

Our econometric modelling did indeed suggest that this is the case. When less is spent behind the chimps, there is only a very small decline in share in the short-term (0.07 of a share point per 100 TVRs). Similarly, when the Tetley Teafolk are on air there is only a small impact on PG Tips share (PG lose 0.3 share points per 100 TVRs of Tetley advertising), a small proportion of what Tetley gain from spending that amount.

Tetley is far more sensitive to short-term changes in advertising weight. An increase of 100 TVRs per month gives them an extra 1.7 share points. They forfeit similarly for a reduction (see appendix for technical details of how the model was constructed. The appendix also includes data from periods when PG Tips media was withdrawn for up to four months. This confirms that significant share is not lost as a result).

Given this, it is even more impressive that PG Tips can survive off air for a few months, without suffering any significant fallback in share when we know that Tetley's advertising is capable of stealing significant share (from others).

We suggest that this is a further strong indication of the existence and potency of PG Tips added value.

Having said this, there is some downside to having such strong long-term advertising effects. Gaining short-term share from increases in the chimps media weight is relatively expensive. Certainly share is also less sensitive *on the upside* to chimps advertising than Tetley share is to Tetley advertising.

Some further evidence of relative insensitivity to short-term declines in share of voice is provided by the performance of PG Tips following the 1979 ITV strike. During this period, the only advertising available was print and radio. PG Tips share of voice fell to 12.3% compared to a more usual average of 20 – 30%. Nevertheless, its share remained static at 25% that year.

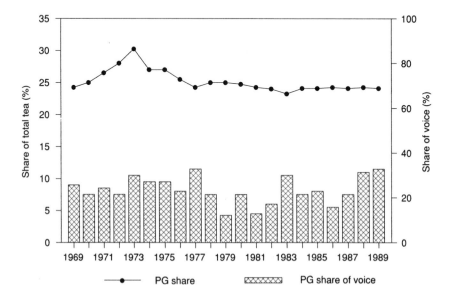

Figure 9. *PG Tips resistance to a low share of voice during the ITV strike in 1979*
Source: Nielsen

Saliency and Consumer Appeal of the Brand

PG Tips is a well known, well loved and well respected brand. All consumer audit data from the past 10 years suggests that it is consistently rated ahead of the competition on a whole raft of scores.

For example, during the whole of the 1980s, the brand has achieved higher spontaneous awareness than its nearest rivals.

TABLE 3: SPONTANEOUS BRAND AWARENESS 1981 – 1989

	PG Tips	Typhoo	Tetley
Average	100	91	58

Source: Millward Brown

In terms of perceived popularity, quality and taste, the brand continually outscores the competition.

TABLE 4: BRAND ATTRIBUTES, MARCH 1990

	Average percentage agreeing		
	PG Tips	Tetley	Typhoo
Particularly popular	100	83	83
Particularly good quality	100	54	76
Best taste	100	85	40

Source: Millward Brown

Hijacking the Teabag Sector

The teabag arrived in 1963 as the product component of the new Tetley brand. Until then, Tetley had not existed as a tea brand at all and has never subsequently introduced 'packet-tea'.

At the time, Brooke Bond were cautious and delayed introducing a PG Tips competitive product. The reasons for this delay are now slightly obscure but three explanations seem plausible.

1. Initial growth of the teabag sector was small. This suggested at the time that Tetley's innovation may have elicited little genuine consumer demand.
2. The volume implications of teabags for the market were negative. When tea is brewed with loose tea, a pot is used which usually encourages waste, and of course, an extra teaspoon of tea is used 'for the pot'. When made with teabags, it is often done in a cup, with less likelihood of waste.
3. PG Tips was already brand leader so it was not in its immediate interest to promote another sector.

Whatever the reason, PG Tips didn't introduce teabags for four years. By then, even though teabags still accounted for a relatively small share of total tea (1.4%), they had been growing by 50% year on year and it was apparent that this share would continue to grow.

Tetley, the innovator in the market, had by then established a strong brand franchise and was brand leader in the teabag sector with a share of 71%.

However, despite the strength of Tetley's position, PG Tips grew steadily and when the proliferation of teabag brands accelerated, it was Tetley not PG that lost share.

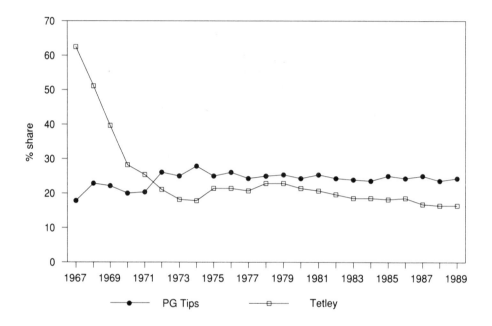

Figure 10. *Overtaking Tetley in the teabags market*
Source: Nielsen

We do not have media spend data for 1967 (the year of PG Tips bags launch) or 1968. However, during 1969, 1970 and 1971, Tetley bags *outspent* PG Tips bags on TV by 22%. Yet, by 1972, PG Tips had attained brand leadership.

The quality of Tetley and PG Tips teabags was equal. Distribution, if anything, favoured Tetley, as did price.

We conclude that this suggests that PG Tips already possessed significant added value compared with Tetley and that it was Tetley's lesser added values that made it the more susceptible of the two brands once competitive attack started in earnest.

Since we prove later that the brand's added value is largely due to the advertising, we can conclude that the advertising played a significant part in enabling PG Tips to hijack leadership in this sector.

The full significance of this is apparent when one considers that having grown from a meagre 1.4%, teabags now represent 80% of the market.

Resilience in the Face of Own Label

Own label's share of the market has grown considerably since the early 1970s as we saw earlier.

One might have expected PG Tips to have lost share to own label in proportion to the brand's size. Maybe, one would have expected it to lose even more since its price premium over own label is higher than for other brands.

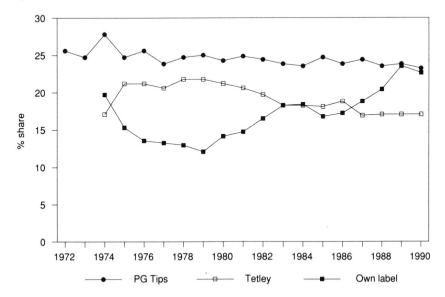

Figure 11. *The advance of own label teabags, PG Tips and Tetley vs Own label, year ending January*
Source: Nielsen

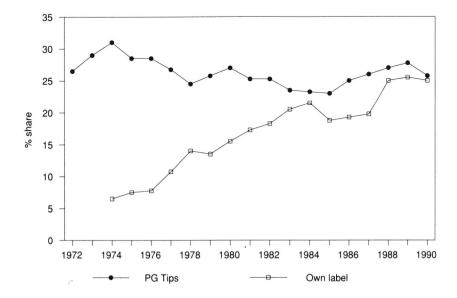

Figure 12. *The advance of own label packet tea, PG Tips vs Own label, year ending January*
Source: Nielsen

In fact, little of own label's growth has been at PG Tips expense. Instead, own label has eaten into the other brands in both packet and bags sectors.

Again, the clear conclusion is that PG Tips is more robust against price-led competition because it possesses added value compared with other branded teas. This enables the brand to offer a different, but very motivating, form of value for money to consumers.

ISOLATING THE EFFECTS OF THE CHIMPS CAMPAIGN: 1959 – 1989

We have already shown that the chimps campaign was responsible for driving the brand to the number one position in the late 1950s. We will now show that *the chimps campaign is responsible for creating the longer term added value the brand possesses.*

There are three pieces of supporting evidence for this claim.

1. We have examined all the other potential causal factors and they provide no plausible alternative explanation.
2. The long-term performance of PG Tips has been compared with that of its competitors, most of whom have declined. The only factors which can explain PG Tips resilience in the face of this are differences in creative content and the level of advertising investment.
3. Looking specifically at the chimps campaign, we have considerable 'soft' evidence showing how the advertising works. This shows direct correlations with many aspects of the brand's added values which are indirectly measurable via quantified consumer research.

Eliminating Other Factors

The key point is that many elements of the brand are very similar to those of our rivals in their offering to consumers. Hence, we can conclude that these are not primary causal factors because, if they were, PG Tips would only have assimilated added value to the same extent as its competitors. The elements which are matched by our rivals are:

1. *The Product* – PG Tips has always been an excellent product. A blend of 28 different teas, it is blended to a standard set by Brooke Bond's chief tea blender, not to a raw material price. Nonetheless, as we have seen, in blind product tests, consumers cannot tell it apart from its main competitors.
2. *Promotions* – There is no evidence at all to suggest that PG Tips has either been more promoted than its rivals or that its promotions have carried greater value. As a consequence, even if the promotions have been more effective than the competitors, surely this is a *result* of the brand's perceived added value, not a *cause*.
3. *Distribution* – Sterling distribution has been near universal for the major brands throughout much of the life of the chimps campaign. In March 1990, PG Tips, Tetley and Typhoo all enjoyed 90% plus sterling distribution. So we can exclude distribution gains.

4. *Price* – PG Tips has consistently maintained a 1% price premium over Tetley and Typhoo, its two closest rivals. Against own label, it has actually increased its premium over time – the brand was 57% more expensive than own label in September 1989 compared with 24% more in September 1971.

   Hence, price *cannot* have been a driving factor. Indeed the data suggests the opposite – that we have been able to enjoy a consistent price premium *as a result* of our added value.

5. *Packaging* – This is a more difficult variable to eliminate completely. The very nature of packaging means that the PG Tips pack is very different from its rivals – hence, it cannot easily be dismissed as a variable that is equivalent to that of other brands. Indeed, we feel that the PG Tips packaging – the tea-picker, red and green colour coding and 'PG Tips' block branding – and its consistency have played a part in building brand recognition for the brand, and its appearance must be an important factor.

   However, we also believe that the Tetley and Typhoo packaging elements are strong. It seems unlikely to us that PG Tips packaging alone could be so much more capable of adding so much value to the brand. This conclusion is circumstantially supported by the following chart which shows that claimed consumer appeal of these major brands' packs is roughly equal and certainly not significant in PG Tips favour.

TABLE 5: CONSUMER APPEAL OF PACKS 1981 – 1989

	Average percentage agreeing		
	PG Tips	Typhoo	Tetley
Has an attractive pack	100	94	114

Source: Millward Brown

6. *Repeat Purchase* – It is conceivable that consistent use of the brand will reinforce positive experience and build added value which will in turn prompt further purchase – almost a self-supporting system once it has started.

   This may be true. If it is, however, it is clear that advertising has played a role in this in two ways.

   First, the initial consumer franchise (in 1957/58) was largely attracted through the advertising.

   Secondly, we know that 'experience' of the brand in terms of all variables except advertising and packaging is matched by our rivals who have definitely not benefited in this way. Hence, if repeat purchase is a driving factor for added value then advertising is still largely responsible for this phenomenon.

Overall, this analysis leads us to believe that the only significant factors remaining which could have caused PG Tips assimilation of added value are the content of its advertising and the media weight behind it.

Comparison With Other Brands Performance

Many of PG Tips competitors have declined substantially over the last 20 or so years. The following table lists some of the losers.

TABLE 6: LONG-TERM SHARE TRENDS – STANDARD TEABAGS

	1975	1980	1985	1990
Tetley	21.2	21.1	18.1	17.2
Quickbrew	10.8	9.5	6.4	4.6
Typhoo/				
Freshbrew	11.1	9.0	6.4	7.1

Source: Nielsen, year ending January
Note: We only have historical data for Typhoo and Freshbrew
     combined

What is interesting, however, is that before their major decline, all of these brands were approximately equal to PG Tips in terms of their product qualities, pricing and distribution. Packaging of course was different, but not significantly lower in 'quality' or appeal.

The declining fortunes of each of these brands correlates instead with a strategy of *chopping and changing the content* of the advertising and with *lower support* for the advertising.

Hence, this offers further proof that advertising can have a very significant effect in this market. We would suggest that this makes it even more likely that PG Tips has added value precisely because of the more consistent support of its highly impactful creative vehicle and heavier media weight.

How the Advertising Works

Further circumstantial evidence for the part advertising has played in growing the brand's added value can be seen in analysis of how consumers react specifically to this advertising.

Awareness and Appeal

The chimps campaign has the highest level of awareness of all tea campaigns.

TABLE 7: ADVERTISING RECALL INDICES 1981 – 1989

	PG Tips	Typhoo	Tetley
Prompted recall	100	51	77

Source: Millward Brown

It is also the most efficient campaign in terms of generating awareness. According to Millward Brown, PG Tips advertising index is the highest in the market. (This is defined as the percentage gain in advertising awareness that would be produced by

100 TVRs in a theoretical TV region where no advertising had previously been shown).

TABLE 8: ADVERTISING RECALL INDICES 1981 – 1989

PG Tips	Typhoo	Tetley
100	51	67

Source: Millward Brown

Combined with the heavy media weights of the past 34 years, it is hard to believe that such an impactful campaign as this had not had a significant impact on the consumer perception of the brand's value.

In addition, we know that the advertising is well loved.

TABLE 9: ATTITUDES TO THE ADVERTISING 1981 – 1989

	Market average	Chimps
Amusing	100	139
Better than other tea ads	100	146
Would enjoy seeing again	100	162

Source: Millward Brown

Given that consumers tend to talk about the chimps as part of the brand, it seems plausible that the above data suggests that the advertising is at least partly responsible for the brand's emotional appeal which in turn is surely what the added value of the brand is built on.

We also have further evidence of the advertising's inextricable role in building the brand's added value.

Communication of specific brand benefits

The chimps advertising has always claimed in one form or another that

'There is no other tea to beat PG .... It's the taste'.

We know from consumer response to the advertising in qualitative research that the chimps campaign is 'loved'. The frame of reference for describing the campaign is always one of affection and warmth. It seems clear that the entertaining and lovable nature of the advertising enables this message of extra quality to be accepted – surely this is one direct way in which the advertising can be seen to have added value to the brand.

Assumption of Tea Values

Finally, in qualitative research, many consumers describe the advertising almost as 'a pick-me-up'.

> 'It gives me a lift after a hard day'.

This is also in fact precisely how people talk about their preferred tea. It seems that the brand and the chimps have almost become one. It is easy then to see how the appeal of the advertising which we have shown can translate into appeal for the brand.

We suggest that 34 years of such a mechanic has indeed added value, beyond functional qualities, to PG Tips.

Summary

We have previously shown that the brand has assimilated added value over the past 34 years.

Later we demonstrated that this *added value was primarily built and sustained by the chimps advertising*. Therefore we can conclude that the advertising has played a fundamental part in producing and maintaining PG Tips dominance in this competitive market.

THE FINANCIAL CONTRIBUTION OF THE ADVERTISING

Since we have shown that the advertising was primarily responsible for investing the brand with the added value it now possesses, an analysis of the financial contribution should attempt to quantify financially this added value. The methodology to do this is not completely available to us. However, we can quantify three specific consequences of the power of the advertising and the added value it has generated. These instances alone suggest that the advertising has paid for itself many times over.

Financial Benefits of Long-term Brand Leadership

Without the short-term effectiveness of the chimps campaign from 1956 to 1958, it is unclear how PG Tips could have grown share substantially because the three brands above it at the time were all strong. Once it had achieved the number one position, we have already shown that the advertising played a primary role in maintaining that dominance.

Therefore, one way to evaluate advertising's contribution is to consider what revenue would have been lost if PG Tips had continued as the fourth brand.

From this it can be deduced that the chimps have helped the brand achieve an extra £2,000m sales over this 20 year period alone.

Brooke Bond are understandably unwilling to disclose margin data, but even on quite conservative estimates, the profit generated is much higher than the total of the amount spent on media and production over the whole 34 year period. The costs over the last 20 years at 1985 prices have been £86m (as measured by MEAL) on media and £6m on production.

Financial Benefits of Price Premium

It is possible that the above scenario shows the campaign's profit contribution in too positive a light. Maybe the brand would have grown without advertising or with a campaign run on a much lower media spend (although we doubt this). However, another way to evaluate the chimps' contribution is to look at the revenue generated over the 32 years since the brand reached number one, by the price premium that we believe that the advertising supported. If we assume that PG Tips could only have charged average branded prices to maintain its volume without the chimps, the extra revenue is still some £125m (at 1985 prices) over the last 20 years alone.

Financial Benefits of Hijacking the Teabag Market

Finally, we can look at the revenue generated by being able to assume brand leadership in the teabag market compared with what might have happened without the chimps.

If we assume that without the chimps, PG Tips teabags would have remained second brand to Tetley teabags with a share equivalent to the current number two brand, then PG Tips would lose £200m of revenue (at 1985 prices) which it gained because it assumed the number one position in 1972. This ignores the advertising costs of supporting the number two brand which would significantly increase this loss.

Summary

Whichever of these methods is used, the advertising's effect over the 34 year period more than justified its cost.

SUMMARY

Overall then there can be little doubt that PG Tips has been tremendously successful over the past 34 years. Brooke Bond has had the marketing foresight to continue to invest in rather than just milk, such a strong brand.

As a result, we have seen that PG Tips has remained brand leader over the whole of the period whilst fighting off fierce competitive challenges particularly in the form of Tetley's teabags and the growth of own label. Not only that, but it has remained price leader as well.

We have also seen that Brooke Bond have done this by investing the brand with added value that prompts consumers to continue buying even when more functional qualities of the brand suggest that other brand choices would be at least as satisfactory in purely functional terms.

This is perhaps the definition of what differentiates a true brand from a product.

And we have demonstrated that the chimps advertising has been the primary generator of this added brand value. Without it, or with advertising only as effective in the long-term as other tea brands it seems extremely unlikely that PG Tips would have been able to fight off such strong competitive activity.

Finally we have seen that quantifying the financial contribution of the advertising is difficult, but three methods have been used to show that it has generated a financial value for the brand well above its cost.

CONCLUSION

Brooke Bond have created in PG Tips a brand that has enormous value to consumers. As a consequence, more consumers choose it compared with its rivals even though it sells at a price premium.

In addition, the brand's perceived value is so strong that it can actually *exploit* a *rival's* innovation. In a market place where technical barriers to entry are very low, this ability is vital for the brand's long-term maintenance of leadership. After all, no brand, not even PG Tips, can have a monopoly on successful innovation over a long time period.

We believe that there are two key lessons to be learnt from all this, which are inter-related:

1. The importance of foresight. In maintaining brand leadership, a brand is going to encounter unexpected and unplanned for competitive activity. The only way to guarantee successful repulsion of these attacks is to have *already* built added values into the brand. Waiting until the threat is specifically known is costly and could be fatal.
2. The importance of consistent advertising support. If the paper has shown nothing else, it has shown that *consistency* in a very strong creative vehicle and in high levels of media weight can ensure the brand does indeed become invested with added value and can pay back dramatically over the long-term.

Taken together, these two points suggest the critical part treating advertising as a long-term investment can play in building and maintaining a brand's strength. PG Tips is and will continue to be a testament to that.

TECHNICAL APPENDIX

Ideally we would have wished to construct a very long run econometric model to try and test some of our hypotheses about whether, as PG Tips continued to advertise, its response to marketing variables was changing over time, eg whether it was becoming less price sensitive or less vulnerable to competitive activity. Our only available long-run of data however was annual and was not sufficient therefore in terms of the number of available data points to start constructing a complex model.

So, in order to investigate PG Tips responses, we tested our hypotheses 'cross-sectionally'. That is we constructed two models, one of PG Tips and one of

Tetley, and made comparisons of the market share responses of the two brands to the various pressures in the teabag market. From consumer data we knew that differences between the products were imperceptible and thus that any difference in terms of response to price etc was not a result of product difference.

The two models were estimated using 'ordinary least squares' on monthly Nielsen data from its start at the end of 1985 to December 1989.

For reasons of confidentiality, we do not wish to report the exact structures of the models. Both models, however, fitted the data well and performed very acceptably on a range of statistical tests. They included variables like branded competitive price, own label price, own label distribution, own and competitive advertising and the introduction of any line extensions/packaging changes.

In pricing terms, the models were similar in structure; the overall impact of price changes however differed markedly with PG Tips being much less sensitive to price than Tetley. Their response to advertising was quite different. Tetley was much more volatile, exhibiting marked short-term blips as a result of advertising but which died away quite quickly.

The following statistical tests and diagnostics for the fit and specification of both models were carried out and reported: R^2, standard error of the regression, sum of squared residuals, DW, Lagrange multiplier tests (portmanteau tests for higher order autocorrelation) with up to 1, 4 and 12 lags, ARCH tests for auto-regressive heteroscedasticity (1, 4 and 12 lags), the variance ratio test for homoscedasticity and the two Chow tests for post-sample predictive failure and for parameter stability and homoscedasticity respectively.

Both models have subsequently continued to predict the market well.

11

Knorr Stock Cubes

How Thinking 'Local' Helped CPC Develop Advertising which Toppled the Brand Leader

INTRODUCTION

This paper sets out to demonstrate how, in a world of increasing focus on '1992', 'pan-European' strategies and 'global brands', thinking locally can still pay handsomely!

It shows how CPC exploited distinctive, local characteristics, ie home-made soup-making in Scotland, to develop a campaign that has become akin to popular Scottish folklore, and against all the odds, taken Knorr to brand leader in the Scottish cube market.

BACKGROUND

Knorr Stock Cubes were launched in the UK in 1954, as the first real alternative to Oxo. In many ways Knorr could hardly have been more different.

1. Whilst Oxo had its *own* distinctive flavour, Knorr cubes (available in beef or chicken) had a more authentic meaty taste, enhanced with herbs.
2. Oxo tended to mask other flavours with its own particular taste: Knorr more subtly *enhanced* other flavours.
3. Oxo was a 'dry' cube which could be crumbled into cooking. Knorr had a 'moist' format and required dissolving in boiling water before addition.
4. Knorr was launched at a significant price premium (+200%) relative to Oxo.

In effect, Oxo was a flavour and colour additive. Knorr was more akin to real stock.

Knorr's Position by Mid 1970s

Some 20 years after launch, Knorr had carved a small but profitable niche in the UK cube market.

TABLE 1: UK VOLUME SHARE 1975

	%
Knorr	7.8
Oxo	89.6
Others	2.6

Source: Nielsen

Usage

Whilst Knorr's characteristics of subtlety and lightness made it particularly appropriate for chicken dishes (casseroles and soups), the more robust flavour of Oxo was particularly suited to red meat (casseroles, minces and gravies). As a result, Knorr volume was biased towards its chicken cube, with Oxo volume biased towards its beef cube.

TABLE 2: UK CUBE MARKET PROFILE, 1975
(VOLUME)

	Total Market %	Knorr %	Oxo %
Beef	84	42	88
Chicken	16	58	12

Source: Nielsen

Attempts to Grow Knorr 1970 – 1977

Knorr was regularly supported by national TV advertising during the 1970s, with the proposition:

'Only Knorr stock cubes have a subtle enough flavour to truly complement the flavour of poultry and meat'.

TABLE 3: KNORR PENETRATION AND VOLUME SHARE
1970 – 1975

	1970 %	1974 %	1975 %
UK Penetration			
Total Knorr	14.5	13.7	13.2
Red Oxo	54.7	60.8	61.7
Chicken Oxo	18.9	17.6	19.2
UK volume share			
Total Knorr	7.8	7.9	7.8
Total Oxo	89.6	89.8	89.6

Source: Nielsen, TGI
Base: All UK housewifes

These attempts to grow the brand, however, met with little success.

Factors Holding Back Knorr Growth

In competing with Oxo, Knorr faced a challenging task!

1. It is difficult to overestimate the strength of the emotional bond between the British public and Oxo. Oxo was, and still is, one of the truly great food brands, enjoying both huge loyalty and unquestioning, almost ritual purchasing behaviour.
   The following comment was typical:

   'I don't know really why I use Oxo – I just do. Mum always used it I suppose, so I do too'.

2. People *liked* the strong, beefy taste of Oxo. Most people, therefore, saw no potential benefit from a more subtle tasting alternative.
3. Knorr's 'non-crumble' format was unfamiliar.
4. Knorr was much more expensive than Oxo.

In addition, even if Knorr *could* increase penetration, clearly its *nature* excluded it from the real volume of the market, which Oxo dominated – red meat casseroles and gravies.

Thus, whilst Knorr was left little choice but to play the same game as Oxo, the odds seemed heavily stacked in Oxo's favour.

KNORR'S POSITION IN SCOTLAND IN 1975

Although the cube market in Scotland as a whole behaved similarly to the UK, Knorr's position in Scotland was very different. As a result, Scotland accounted for over 25% of Knorr's total volume.

TABLE 4: CUBE VOLUME SHARE 1975

	UK %	Scotland %
Knorr	7.8	35.2
Oxo	89.6	62.2
Others	2.6	2.6

Source: Nielsen

Behind this difference lay an activity firmly entrenched in Scottish tradition, the making of home-made soup!

HOME-MADE SOUP IN SCOTLAND

In a region characterised by long, cold winters, and where family budgets were traditionally stretched, it is not difficult to see how home-made soup became so firmly rooted in Scottish heritage. As one respondent described her grandmother's lifestyle:

'It was economy cooking then; big families, pots of broth and potato stovies'.

In many ways, home-made soup seemed to form the backbone of the family – always there as a warm welcome, and a powerful expression of the 'provider' role which Scottish women strongly adhered to.

'The pot was always boiling on the stove'.

'I remember coming home from dances and having a bowl of soup'.

Quantitative data strikingly confirmed the role home-made soup continued to play in Scottish family life.

TABLE 5: HOME-MADE SOUP-MAKING, 1977

	Scotland	Rest of UK
% housewives claiming made any home-made soup in past 4 weeks	91	14

Source: Marplan, April 1977

How was Soup Made?

At the heart of a good soup, was good stock. Stock was made by simmering meaty bones in a large pot for a number of hours. After this, the liquid would be drained off to form the 'base' of the soup, to which vegetables or meat were then added.

Traditionally, women would obtain bones free from their local butcher for soup-making. Any left-overs, like chicken carcasses, would also find their way into the stock pot (the Scots were not ones for waste!).

How did Soup-Making Influence Knorr's Position in Scotland?

1. Stock making was a time-consuming business. Bones needed to be boiled for several hours and this process needed on-going attention. With Scottish women living more busy lives, they were less willing than their mums to 'spend all day over the stove'.
2. It was becoming increasingly difficult to obtain bones for soup-making. Many women complained that their butchers simply didn't seem to keep bones like they used to and bones certainly weren't easy to find in supermarkets!

Despite no previous soup-related promotional activity for Knorr cubes, 'discoverers' of Knorr felt they had found a genuine alternative to bone-boiled stock, which both looked and tasted like home-made. Oxo, with its distinctive taste and dark colour, did not.

This explained Knorr's strength in Scotland.

DEVELOPING A NEW STRATEGY FOR KNORR IN SCOTLAND

Research in 1977 in Scotland revealed both an untapped opportunity, and a cause for concern.

A Growth Opportunity for Knorr?

Many Scottish women, it seemed, had not yet discovered Knorr. When we talked to them, we found they were very interested in Knorr's benefits over home-made stock. However, they clearly felt somewhat guilty at the prospect of using a convenient alternative. If we could assure them that Knorr gave results as good as the real thing, it seemed we could exploit this potential. Quantitative research confirmed this opportunity.

Despite home-made soup accounting for half Knorr cube volume in Scotland, *only 25% of all home-made soups contained any cube at all* (Marplan 1977).

A Long-Term Threat to Knorr?

Younger women, in particular, seemed to be making home-made soup less often. It seemed very possible that these women were starting to adopt a more UK pattern of behaviour, only making soup when left-over carcasses were available, and otherwise using packet or canned soup.

Outside soup-making, Knorr's product characteristics clearly left it ill-equipped to challenge Oxo. If Knorr could not retain a soup-based 'foothold' in cupboards, there was a real danger of being squeezed out completely.

To sum up, we identified a real opportunity for Knorr to grow volume by actively exploiting Scottish soup-making. This potential growth, however, could only be realised if, in the long-term, Scottish women maintained their desire for home-made soup.

1977 – A NEW MARKETING STRATEGY FOR SCOTLAND

Knorr's most competitive positioning outside Scotland seemed to remain one of focusing on its more subtle flavour contribution in the context of casseroles. Soup-making was infrequent and a 'real stock' claim had little relevance – most women had never made real stock in their lives!

We decided to be bold, and to tailor a new strategy specifically to Scotland. Instead of playing the same game as Oxo – we were changing the rules.

MARKETING OBJECTIVES

We set out to exploit Knorr's unique competitive benefit in Scotland, to grow sales, share, and via maintaining our price premium over Oxo, to increase profit. We hoped to achieve this by:

Primarily
1. Increasing frequency of usage of Knorr in soups among existing Knorr users.
2. Encouraging trial of Knorr in home-made soups by non-Knorr users.

Secondly
3. Maintaining levels of home-made soup-making.
4. Increasing Knorr usage in other meals.
   (Qualitative research suggested that once Knorr was in cupboards, usage tended to spread to other dishes).

THE CREATIVE BRIEF

Advertising Objectives

1. To reinforce existing users' perceptions of Knorr as a genuine alternative to home-made stock and so encourage more frequent usage in soups.
2. To make more women aware of the benefits of Knorr cubes in home-made soup-making and so encourage them to try Knorr cubes in soups.
3. To maintain the frequency and appeal of home-made soup-making.

Proposition

Because stock made with Knorr stock cubes is as tasty as home-made stock, but more convenient, they are particularly suitable for making soup.
   NB: Convenience in this sense meant more than just time-saving. It embraced the broader issues of no mess, no need to have key ingredients (eg a chicken carcass) etc.

Tone

This needed to reflect the cultural context of soup-making in Scotland, ie everyday, family cooking.

Target Market

All home-made soup-makers (over 90% of housewives in Scotland).
   We knew that our target felt a degree of guilt at the idea of 'cheating' by using stock cubes – we therefore needed to assure them that Knorr produced stock that was as good and wholesome as the 'real thing'.

Executional Guidelines

We decided to feature Knorr Ham Cubes – a flavour introduced in 1974. Ham cubes were sold predominantly in Scotland, where they were particularly popular for making Pea and Ham soup.

THE CREATIVE SOLUTION

BMP produced a creative idea called 'Monday Night' – centred on two Highland friends, Hughie and Jamie.

The men were so naïvely innocent of the cooking process that they could only assume that chicken the night before inevitably meant chicken soup the night after.

They were left totally bewildered when Hughie's wife somehow managed to create a wonderful Pea and Ham soup the next day. Her little secret – Knorr Ham Stock Cubes.

PRE-TESTING THE CAMPAIGN

'Monday Night' was qualitatively tested – with extremely positive results. The campaign was felt to be perfectly in tune with Scottish values: the wry humour, the ignorance of the men about cooking, and the value attached to good home cooking. The message was felt to be relevant and appealing to both Knorr users and non-users. The campaign clearly showed the potential to meet our stated advertising objectives.

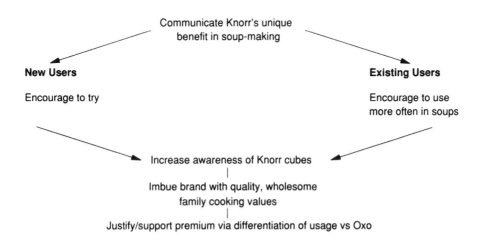

Figure 1. *How the campaign would work*

'MONDAY NIGHT'

'What d'you think the wife's cooking tonight Hughie?'
'Oh, I don't think at all – chicken soup. We had chicken soup yesterday.'

VO: Hughie doesn't know his wife uses Knorr Stock Cubes.

Boiling water over a Knorr Ham Stock Cube gives a delicious meaty tasting base for lentils and beans.

'This'll be the chicken soup then?'

'No Hughie, this'll be the pea and ham.'

'mmm. pea and ham...'

'How was your soup last night Hughie?'
'Oh delicious and the remarkable thing was it wasn't chicken, it was pea and ham.'

'Pea and ham from a chicken, now that's clever.'

VO: Knorr Stock Cubes – good soup and no bones about it.

From Small Beginnings...

Few people could have predicted, back in 1977, that we were embarking on a campaign which would still be running 13 years later! Few could have imagined the extent to which Hughie, Jamie and friends would touch Scottish hearts.

'Pea and Ham from a chicken' quickly became a national catchphrase. Phil McCol (the actor playing Jamie) became a 'celebrity' over-night. And even now, women in groups talk about 'Pea and Ham' cars (Morris Minors!) and 'Pea and Ham' roads (winding Highland roads!).

CAMPAIGN DEVELOPMENT HISTORY

1977 – 82

'Monday Night' ran annually from the winter of 1977/78 until 1980. The CPC account then moved agency, where it was recommended that given the strength of Knorr cubes in Scotland, all available monies be deployed behind more aggressively trying to grow Knorr cube volume in the rest of the UK – where sales remained static.

As a result, Scotland received no support after December 1980 until the winter of 1982, when BMP regained the account.

Analysis at this time revealed indications that Knorr's hold had begun to slip in Scotland.

TABLE 6

	1980 %	1981 %	1982 %
Knorr volume share	39.1	39.1	35.1
Knorr penetration	39.2	38.6	34.5

Source: 1980/81 Nielsen, 1982 NMRA, TGI

It was decided to re-air 'Monday Night' in December 1982, with a 'holding' objective.

In 1983, the strategy in Scotland was re-evaluated.

1983

Research concluded that whilst the soup-making strategy was still the optimum route for Knorr in Scotland, and whilst 'Monday Night' was as popular as ever, some younger women were beginning to feel it portrayed Scottish life in a somewhat negative way. The *appearance* of Hughie's wife was the main cause of this criticism.

'She really annoys me – she looks very old fashioned – a 'wee wifey' in her pinney'.

The wife's role as a 'provider' was clearly not contentious – Scottish women respected this. It was agreed to develop a new execution within the same campaign which updated the *look* of the wife, rather than her *role*. The objectives of the advertising remained the same.

A new creative idea, 'Moira', was developed. Jamie and Hamish were seen lamenting the apparent sad demise of their hen 'Moira', as they approvingly ate a fine Cock-a-Leekie soup – only to be interrupted by 'Moira' miraculously appearing in the door-way!

Pre-testing confirmed 'Moira' as tremendously appealing and clearly having the potential to refresh the campaign as intended. 'Moira' ran for the first time in December 1984.

1984 – 1989

One interesting finding from developing 'Moira' was that Hamish's more contemporary looking wife seemed to set 'Monday Night' back in context – to the extent that both executions ran in tandem until 1989.

'Monday Night' was then replaced by 'Hen Night', which brought the campaign raucously up to date. Hamish is seen proudly relating how his wife had gone all the way to Inverness for a hen night – such was her dedication to finding just the right hen for his soup. Instead we see her catching a stripper's sporran to the strains of 'What's New Pussycat?'!

This idea received a tremendous reception in research (with lots of cock-a-leekie jokes!). The idea of the wife using a stock cube for her *own* benefit (ie, so she could get out) while, importantly, the men still enjoyed a great tasting soup, was clearly a very modern expression of Knorr's 'real stock' benefit.

'Little do they know we're not at home slaving over their soup!'

'It's brilliant – even better than the Pea and Ham one'.

'Hen Night' ran with 'Moira' in November/December 1989.

MEDIA

The media strategy has been broadly similar since the beginning of our campaign: a burst of activity focusing on the key Knorr cube sales periods in Scotland (ie November, December and January) at an average weight of 1,000 housewife TVRs.

Some years have differed slightly. If additional advertising monies have become available at the end of the CPC fiscal year, it has been agreed to deploy them in Scotland to give the campaign an additional 'kick' at the beginning of the soup-making season.

'MOIRA'

'This is a great drop of Cock-a-Leekie Hamish'
'Aye, she was a fine wee bird was Moira'
'Best soup I've ever tasted'
'Aye, she never let us down, even to this day. I miss the eggs though.'

VO: What Hamish doesn't know is that his wife uses Knorr Stock Cubes.

Simply pour boiling water over a Chicken Stock Cube and you've a delicious meaty tasting base

for Cock-a-Leekie soup without the bones.

'Och, it's how she would have wanted it.'
'Aye, I suppose...'

SHOT OF CHICKEN AT DOOR

'Moira?'

'Moira...'

VO: Knorr Stock Cubes – good soup and no bones about it.

'HEN NIGHT'

'On your own tonight Hamish?'
'Aye, Elspeth has gone to Inverness for a hen night.'

'All that way just to pick up a chicken?!'
'Aye, she doesn't make the best soup in the Highlands for nothing'

VO: Hamish doesn't know his wife uses a Knorr Stock Cube to make a delicious meaty base

for Cock-a-Leekie soup

'Probably spent hours deciding on just the right hen for your soup'
'Aye well, that's devotion for you'

MUSIC STARTS: Tom Jones, 'What's new Pussycat'

MUSIC CONTINUES

MUSIC CONTINUES

MUSIC FADES OUT...

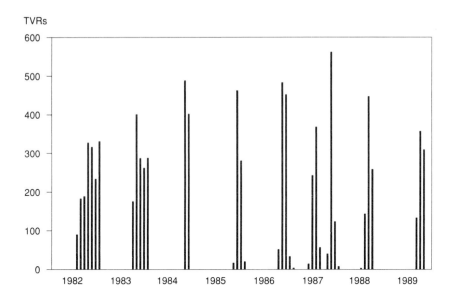

Figure 2. *Knorr housewife TVRs in Scotland*
Source: 1981–90 BARB

EVALUATING THE CAMPAIGN

We have faced a number of difficulties in evaluating this campaign.

1. Stock cubes sales are highly seasonal. Knorr sales in Scotland (due to the soup-making bias) are even more so. We have thus had to attempt to remove the effect of seasonality from our analysis.
2. Knorr has been supported every year in Scotland (as has Oxo), with the exception of 1981. As such, there is little inbuilt variability in the advertising data to help in isolating advertising effects.
3. In the year Knorr received no advertising, the retail audit company was changed – altering pick-up on both market and brand level. Our *sales* trend analysis has thus largely focused on the period since 1981.
4. Bovril cubes were launched nationally in 1978, which introduced a considerable change in the structure of the cubes market, at the same time as the start of the Knorr campaign in Scotland.
5. Research budgets only allowed ad hoc tracking of usage behaviour in Scotland.

In spite of these difficulties, we are able to demonstrate how:

— Sales and share increased steadily over the 13 years from introduction of our campaign, to the extent that Knorr is now *brand leader* in Scotland.
— Knorr's volume gains have resulted from long-term changes in soup-making behaviour which exactly match those set out in our advertising objectives.
— Behavioural changes and hence Knorr's growth, were a direct *result* of our Scottish campaign and would not have occurred in its absence.

KNORR SALES IN SCOTLAND, 1977 – 1990

While the cube market has remained static in Scotland over the 13 year period studied, Knorr sales have steadily increased.

At the end of 1989, Knorr became volume brand leader in Scotland for the first time.

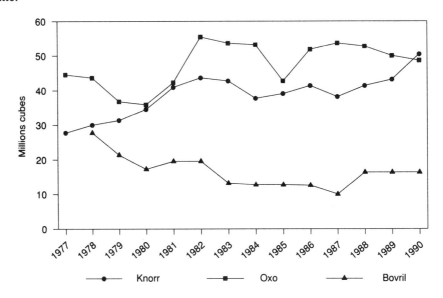

Figure 3. *Cubes volume Scotland*
Source: Nielsen 1977–81, NMRA 1982–90

TABLE 7: VOLUME BRAND SHARES

	1977 %	1981 %	1989 %
Oxo	60.6	40.5	43.7
Knorr	37.4	39.1	45.8
Bovril	—	18.8	5.5
Others	2.0	1.6	5.0

Source: 1977 & 1981 Nielsen, 1989 NMRA

Because of Knorr's continued price premium relative to the rest of the market, the volume share in 1989 equated to a value share of almost two thirds of total market value.

Knorr cubes are now a £4m brand in Scotland – more than twice the value of Oxo (NMRA, 1989).

Effect of New Varieties

Two new varieties of Knorr cubes were successfully introduced in 1984 (lamb and vegetable).

However, these varieties still account for less than 14% of annual volume in Scotland. The best selling varieties (chicken and ham) have both steadily grown in volume by more than 40% since 1984.

Therefore, overall brand growth is due to core variety growth, not just new introductions.

WHERE DID KNORR GROWTH COME FROM?

Bovril cube volume has been in long-term decline as its distribution has steadily been eroded. Bovril cubes are very similar to Oxo in both flavour (strong, beefy) and format ('dry', crumbly) – as such it seems highly probable that Bovril's volume is being picked up by Oxo. This has therefore 'buoyed up' Oxo sales and share.

What seems to be emerging in Scotland is not *one* cube market but two!

— A soup-making cube market (Knorr) which is increasing.
— A non soup-making cube market (Oxo/Bovril) which is declining.

Although we don't have quantitative data to validate this hypothesis, it seems the most probable scenario from both sales and qualitative data.

Thinking back to our objectives, this is exactly what we would expect to see if advertising was working as we planned.

We were not expecting Knorr volume to be gained primarily from other cubes at all – our 'competitors' were either bones or convenience soups. We would therefore expect additional Knorr cube volume to be largely incremental to the rest of the market.

This would also seem to explain why Scotland is increasing its share of all cubes sold in the UK, soup-making being the only major difference between the two markets.

SOUP-MAKING BEHAVIOUR IN SCOTLAND, 1977 – 1990

Long-term trends illustrate that the behavioural objectives of our advertising have been met.

Home-made soup has remained popular in Scotland

Home-made soup-making has not collapsed in Scotland as we feared.

TABLE 8:   TOTAL HOME-MADE SOUP OCCASIONS IN SCOTLAND
(MILLIONS OF OCCASIONS)

1981	1985	1986	1988	1989
57	53	61	56	59

Source: Family Food Panel, Winter/Spring

Neither has home-made soup lost out to more convenient versions.

TABLE 9: HOME-MADE SOUP IN SCOTLAND
PERCENTAGE OF ALL SOUP OCCASIONS

1981 %	1985 %	1986 %	1988 %	1989 %
47	47	45	45	48

Source: Family Food Panel, Winter/Spring

We had a particular fear that a new generation of women would reject making soup. This has not occurred.

TABLE 10: PERCENTAGE OF HOME-MADE SOUPS MADE BY YOUNGER WOMEN

Age	1981 %	1988 %
17–34	17	19

Source: Family Food Panel, Winter/Spring
Base: Home-made soup occasions

Therefore, the long-term platform on which Knorr depended, ie home-made soup-making, remained stable. We achieved our first objective.

With the home-made soup-making platform stable, cube usage in soups has increased.

There has been a dramatic increase in both the number of Scottish women who regularly use cubes in soups, and in the number of soups made with a stock cube.

The possible scenario whereby women only make soups when they have a left-over carcass available does not seem to have materialised.

TABLE 11: PENETRATION OF CUBES AMONG HOME-MADE SOUP-MAKERS IN SCOTLAND

	1977 %	1983 %	1986 %
Ever use cubes in soups	25	35	48
Always use cubes in soups	22	27	43

Source: Marplan 1977, Schlackman 1983 & 1986
Base: All housewives in Scotland

Our second objective of effecting a long-term increase in cube usage within home-made soups has been met.

TABLE 12: PENETRATION OF CUBES IN HOME-MADE SOUPS IN SCOTLAND

	1977 %	1986 %
Soups containing a cube	25	47

Source: Marplan 1977, Schlackman 1986
Base: All home-made soups in Scotland

Knorr usage within soups has increased

A growing proportion of soups contain a Knorr cube. Knorr is the dominant brand of cube used in soups – by 1986 accounting for nearly 75% of all 'cube soup occasions'. This has led to a dramatic increase in the penetration of Knorr in soups.

TABLE 13: PERCENTAGE OF ALL HOME-MADE SOUPS
CONTAINING A KNORR CUBE IN SCOTLAND

1977 %	1986 %
24	35

Source: Marplan 1977,
Schlackman 1986
Base: All home-made soups in Scotland

We have achieved another of our objectives.

Knorr usage in other dishes has increased

Having gained a presence in cupboards via soup-making, Knorr cubes are increasingly being used in other dishes.

TABLE 14: KNORR USAGE IN OTHER DISHES

Using in casseroles			Using in gravies			Using in mince		
1981 %	1983 %	1986 %	1981 %	1983 %	1986 %	1981 %	1983 %	1986 %
41	63	74	20	41	50	N/A	21	23

Source: SRA 1981, Schlackman 1983 & 1986
Base: Knorr buyers in Scotland

We have therefore met our final behavioural objective – that of increasing Knorr usage in meals other than soups.

In Summary

Long-term behaviour has changed exactly as we planned in our advertising objectives.

It appears that the home-made soup-making platform has been maintained, and Knorr has been able to capitalise on this, in a way which has increased both penetration among soup-makers (as shown earlier) and frequency of use (see Table 15).

TABLE 15: AVERAGE NUMBER OF KNORR CUBES USED
PER YEAR PER USER IN SCOTLAND

1977	1981	1986	1989
41	58	63	78

Source: Nielsen 1977, NMRA 1981/86 &
1989, TGI

We hope by now to have demonstrated that we have met our sales and share objectives for Knorr and that these were achieved via behavioural changes exactly as planned.

It could well be argued that all this is completely unrelated to the advertising. We will now show that this is not the case.

EVALUATION OF 'INTERMEDIATE' DATA

Appeal

This campaign is hugely popular. It is always discussed spontaneously in groups and despite the high exposure, women never seem to tire of seeing it.

Hughie, Hamish and friends are perceived as charmingly naïve, but totally believable – people have taken them to their hearts.

'That ad's been out for years and we're still laughing at it'.

'I come from the West Highlands and I know these people. I know lots of people like that and I just relate to them'.

'It's a nice humour as well – very sort of dry – a Highland humour'.

This is supported by tracking data. 60% of women recalling the Knorr cubes advertising in Scotland in 1989 stated that they liked it (50% higher than the Millward Brown average).

Awareness

1. Knorr's 'Base Level' of advertising awareness, as measured by Millward Brown, has more than trebled over the monitored years. This is a rough

measure of awareness 'credit' – the higher the base level, the longer the campaign would be remembered after it stopped.

2. Spontaneous awareness of Knorr cubes has steadily increased over the period tracked, and in 1989 moved above that of Oxo.

   As media spend has remained relatively static, it seems that we are benefiting from an accumulating advertising effect; with each new burst building on the success of the former. (NB: As we will discuss later, econometric modelling supports this view).

3. Absolute levels of advertising awareness are also very high. Photoprompted awareness of Knorr advertising in Scotland stood last year at over 75%, with two thirds of those aware remembering the brand correctly.

Communication

The campaign clearly communicates the proposition of good, natural stock, ideal for soup-making.

TABLE 16: COMMUNICATION (SPONTANEOUS)

	%
Tastes as good as the real thing	30
Makes good soup without the bones	25
Quick and convenient	20

Source: Millward Brown, November 1989 – January 1990
Base: All recalling Knorr cubes advertised in Scotland

Knorr Imagery

The imagery of Knorr stock cubes in Scotland is one of goodness and wholesomeness – not a convenient cop-out!

TABLE 17: KNORR STOCK CUBE IMAGERY

	Scotland %	UK %
Makes a good stock	89	76
Suitable for home-made soup	94	80

Source: Millward Brown
Base: All Knorr users

In Summary

The advertising seems to have met all of its 'intermediary' objectives – generating awareness for Knorr cubes and communicating their benefit via a very popular, high profile campaign (and at much lower levels of TVRs than our largest competitor).

TABLE 18: SCOTLAND TVRs, 1982 – 1989

Total Oxo	Knorr
16,136	8,876

Source: BARB

PROVING THE CONTRIBUTION OF ADVERTISING

We have shown how Knorr sales and share have grown as a result of behavioural changes, in exactly the way we planned. We have also shown how we have met our advertising objectives, in terms of 'intermediate variables'. The question now is, did our advertising *cause* these changes?

There are two methods by which we will answer this question:

1. By eliminating other variables.
2. By validating our hypotheses through an econometric model.

ELIMINATING OTHER VARIABLES

Distribution

Sterling distribution has remained constant for both Knorr and Oxo at nearly 100% since our advertising began, thus it cannot have been a significant catalyst for change.

Packaging

There have been only very minor modifications to packaging.

Other Activity

There have been no significant PR or promotional campaigns over the period. CPC have intermittently developed press campaigns for Knorr to a 'rest of UK' strategy (ie, non soup-making). These have of course run in Scotland, but research has consistently suggested they have limited relevance to Scottish women.

Although Knorr markets other products in Scotland, any activity during the advertised period has been on a national level.

Meat Consumption

Meat consumption has remained constant in Scotland since 1979. There seems no indication therefore that a decline in 'left-overs' has resulted in an increased need for cubes in soup.

Pricing

Knorr has, in real terms, become better value relative to Oxo by about 10%, over the period analysed. We would hypothesise however than the influence of this is probably relatively small, for two reasons:

1. The absolute premium of Knorr is still very significant. Qualitative evidence suggests that for people for whom price is important, the reduction of a few pence per packet for Knorr would make minimal difference to purchase intention.
2. Knorr is not primarily competing with Oxo or any other cube – certainly not in the key usage area of soups.

As we show later, econometric modelling confirms that Knorr price has minimal influence on sales.

In Summary

We find it difficult to see what factor, other than our advertising, could have produced the behavioural and sales effects which we planned and have achieved in Scotland.

VALIDATING OUR HYPOTHESES THROUGH AN ECONOMETRIC MODEL

In order to validate our conclusions concerning other possible causal variables, and in turn *quantify* the sales contribution of advertising, we constructed an econometric model.

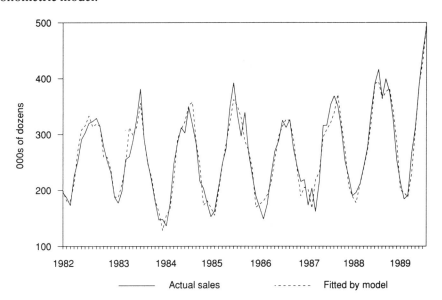

Figure 4. *Knorr Stock Cubes volume sales – actual vs fitted*
Source: NMRA

The technical details of the model are appended, together with appropriate tests to demonstrate its statistical validity.

Figure 4 shows Knorr's actual sales volume and the model's fit to it. The model explains 94% of the variation in Knorr sales from September 1982 to January 1990.

The model investigated the influences of the following factors on Knorr sales over the period 1982 to 1990:

1. Pricing and distribution for Knorr, Oxo, Bovril and own label.
2. New Knorr varieties.
3. Seasonality.
4. Knorr, Oxo and Bovril advertising.

Pricing

Knorr sales were found to be remarkably price insensitive. The decline in real price since 1982 would seem to have contributed only 1.6% of Knorr volume over the period studied.

No impact of competitive pricing was found.

Distribution

This had no significant effect on Knorr sales.

New Knorr Varieties

Introduction of new Knorr varieties was found to have minimal influence on sales.

Seasonality

Temperature was found to be the key seasonal variable. More cubes will be sold in a cold winter, the reverse in a hot summer.

However, the model found that although temperature accounts for slight variation in the seasonal peaks from year to year – it was not responsible for generating the long-term sales volume increases that we have seen for Knorr.

Quantifying the Contribution of Advertising

After isolating the effect of all other variables, the model was able to quantify the direct contribution of advertising as *12.5% of total Knorr volume* in Scotland, over the period September 1982 – January 1990.

This means that advertising alone is responsible for *90%* of Knorr's volume increase over this same period (the remainder is due to price).

The model also confirmed our hypothesis that the sales volume directly attributable to advertising was growing from year to year.

UNDERSTANDING HOW THE ADVERTISING WORKS

Shorter and Longer Term Effects

In our evaluation of this campaign, two 'levels' of effect have emerged.

1. *Short-term Effects:*
    These mirror the timing of the advertising bursts and produce discernible short-term uplifts in sales. This is a result of an immediate behavioural response, advertising increasing both immediate purchasing of Knorr cubes, and also usage of those cubes already in the cupboard at home (resulting in re-purchase a short time later).

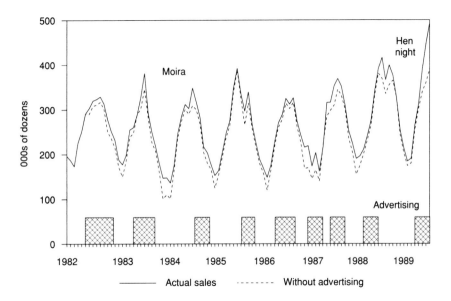

Figure 5. *Knorr stock cubes volume sales, actual versus without advertising*

The introduction of new executions seems to have effected a particularly marked short-term uplift in sales over the advertised period.

Awareness data mirrors this pattern of short-term response.

2. *Longer term Effects:*
    Even though the model was not specifically set up to measure a genuine, long-term accumulating effect of advertising on sales, the previous figure shows:

    —   Each burst produces a sales effect with a very long 'tail' (to the extent that there is no point during any year when advertising is having no effect on sales).
    —   Sales are always above the level preceding the last burst, when the subsequent burst of advertising takes place.

As we have seen, this pattern is reflected in both brand and advertising awareness data. Awareness is steadily building over time, despite an almost constant level of media weight.

It seems, therefore, that advertising effects are by no means restricted to the short-term. Instead, there seems to be a 'building' effect over a longer period of time.

This longer-term effect has undoubtedly played a key role in the success of the campaign – enabling us to achieve a significantly higher level of return over the 13 year advertised period than we would perhaps otherwise expect to achieve from a low absolute level of media spend.

It is interesting to speculate whether Knorr could have realistically achieved long-term volume growth, without the benefit of these carry-over effects.

PROFITABILITY

We have shown that advertising directly contributed 12.5% of total Knorr cubes volume in Scotland, from 1982 to 1990.

On the basis of the following factors:

1. The profit generated by this additional volume
2. An average annual media spend of £110,000 (BARB)
3. Low production costs, as a result of the stability of the campaign

the advertising paid for itself 1.8 times over.

NB: Although we couldn't apply the model to data prior to 1982, it is probable that advertising generated similar levels of incremental profit *before* this date.

However, even if, before 1982, advertising had no effect at all, subsequent incremental pay-back has been at a level which *alone* ensures profitability of the overall campaign (from 1977 to 1990).

The Real Value of the Advertising

In estimating that advertising directly generated 12.5% of total Knorr volume (1982–1990) the model had to assume that had the campaign never run, there would have been no adverse market trends working to reduce Knorr's sales.

However, as we have seen, we believe this assumption to be highly optimistic.

Our research in 1977 clearly highlighted the likelihood that home-made soup-making and cube usage within it would gradually decline. A decline in Knorr volume would inevitably follow.

The *real* contribution of our advertising to CPC profit is therefore likely to be considerably higher.

THE IMPLICATIONS OF ADOPTING A 'LOCAL' STRATEGY

We have proved that our advertising successfully generated incremental profit for CPC in Scotland.

Fundamental to this success was our decision to adopt a 'local' strategy.

Only by doing so could we effectively exploit a unique competitive benefit, ie Knorr's suitability for making home-made soup.

Only by thinking 'local' were we able to 'change the rules' and consequently topple Oxo to become brand leader.

A comparison with the performance of Knorr cubes in the rest of the UK confirms this view.

Continued support (on a 'more subtle flavour' platform) has encouraged some volume growth for Knorr, but this growth has largely been flavour and distribution-led.

Oxo still massively dominates the market.

TABLE 19: VOLUME BRAND SHARES

	Scotland %	Rest of UK %
Knorr	45.8	10.3
Oxo	43.7	74.6
Bovril	5.5	10.8
Others	5.0	4.3

Source: NMRA, year to January 1990

SUMMARY

CPC adopted a bold, new strategy when they agreed to develop advertising for Knorr cubes which specifically targeted Scotland, in order to exploit and defend a unique competitive advantage.

We have shown that these objectives have been very successfully achieved.

Since its inception in 1977, a famous, long-running campaign has developed – the effects of which have built year on year, with the result that Knorr now outsells all other cubes in Scotland.

The advertising worked exactly as we planned:

— By helping to maintain Scottish women's commitment to making soup.
— By encouraging more Scottish women to use Knorr cubes more often in their home-made soups.
— And by fuelling increased use of Knorr cubes in other meals in Scotland.

Most importantly, not only has the advertising *worked*, it has also demonstrably contributed to overall CPC profit.

CONCLUSIONS

We acknowledge that we have set ourselves a difficult task – that of proving that *only* by developing advertising to meet the specific needs of Scotland, were CPC able to defend and grow a vital proportion of their total business.

We feel convinced however that this is so and it is only thanks to Hughie, Hamish and friends, that Knorr is now brand leader in Scotland.

Maybe sometimes *only* thinking and acting 'local' can pay.

TECHNICAL APPENDIX

An explanation and validation of the econometric model

For reasons of space and confidentiality, this is an abbreviated version of the technical appendix submitted to the judges.

Stock cubes are essentially a store-cupboard item of which consumers tend to hold several weeks supply. Advertising may not therefore necessarily prompt any immediate purchase but simply encourage faster use of existing stores.

This led us to develop the hypothesis that any Knorr advertising potentially had two effects, one reducing the existing level of stores in consumers' cupboards, the other prompting actual purchase at, or close to, the time of advertising.

We developed the following theoretical model which relates the quantity purchased in any four-weekly period to a range of marketing factors, both Knorr and competitive, to consumers' *usage* and expected usage in that period and to the *change in household stores* between any one period and that prior to it.

The Theoretical Model

(1) $Q_t = a_0 + a_1 S_t + a_2 E(U)_t + a_3 T + a_4 P + a_5 A$

Q = quantity purchased, S = consumers' stores at the beginning of the period, E(U) = expected usage, T = temperature, P = price, A = advertising, for both Knorr and competitors.

(2) $S_t = S_{t-1} + Q_t - U_t$
(3) $U_t = b_0 + b_1 T + b_2 A$
(4) $E(U) = f(T)$ proxied by $c + c_1 T_t + c_2 T_{t-1}$
ie expected usage in period t is a function of temperature.

By rearranging equation (2), substituting for household stores in equation (1) and taking first differences, we obtained a theoretical equation linking Knorr sales in any four-weekly period to usage, store levels and marketing activity. In order to estimate the model, the empirical specification necessarily differed from this theoretical one in two minor respects.

We used the model to test the following hypotheses:

1. That the model specification is appropriate.
2. That as stores increase, quantity purchased will decrease, all else remaining equal.
3. As temperature increases, stores will be depleted less quickly and less will be bought.
4. As advertising increases, stores will be depleted.
5. As temperature rises, purchases fall.
6. An increase in price leads to a drop in sales.
7. An increase in advertising leads to an uplift in sales.

The final empirical model was estimated by non-linear least squares using four weekly NMRA retail audit data over the period July 1982 to January 1990 – 99 data points. The advertising data was in TVRs, the source of which was BARB. The model includes an additional advertising term for the recently introduced 'Hen Night' film which appears to be working harder than previous films and a dummy variable for a most unusual data period in February/March 1984.

The coefficients of the model all had signs consistent with the above hypotheses, demonstrating the appropriateness of the model. Apart from the 'Hen Night' campaign which was significant at the 90% level, all of the variables were significant at the 95% level. The model passes a range of diagnostic tests indicating that the data supports the theory. The reported statistical tests were: R^2, $\overline{R}^2$ standard error of regression, sum of squared residuals, Durbin's h-test, Lagrange multiplier tests (portmanteau tests for higher order autocorrelation) with up to 1, 4 and 13 lags, ARCH tests for auto-regressive heteroscedasticity (up to 1, 4 and 13 lags), the variance ratio test for homoscedasticity, Chow (parameter stability), Chow (post sample pred. failure), Q test (Box-Cox) 13 lags.

12

Quaker Harvest Chewy Bars

How Advertising Established the Leading Personality in an Emerging Market

INTRODUCTION

This paper demonstrates the contribution that advertising has made to the success of a major new product – Quaker Harvest Chewy Bars.

Our central theme is that advertising was an important element in the brand's differential advantage because it endowed Harvest Chewy Bars with a *clear personality* that has set them apart in a competitive market-place.

BACKGROUND – THE GROWING CEREAL-BAR MARKET

The trend in the 1980s towards healthier eating has radically reshaped many staple food markets, initiating many dynamic growth sectors such as muesli, wholemeal bread and margarine. Possibly the most dynamic of these has been cereal bars. After humble beginnings in health food shops, cereal bars have grown 32 per cent per annum over the last five years (NMRA). The grocery market is now worth £37 million at RSP.

The establishment of cereal bars as a mainstream grocery item is largely due to the initiative of Quaker Oats Ltd. The company, a UK subsidiary of an American parent, is engaged in the production of grain-based breakfast cereals, pet foods and spreads.

Eager to employ their cereal manufacturing expertise in other markets, Quaker had observed the considerable success of cereal bars in the USA, where the market originated as a spin-off from 'granola' breakfast cereals. Analysis in the UK had shown considerable potential for a cereal-bar product positioned as a healthy alternative to chocolate biscuit countlines (CBCLs) such as Penguin and Club.

In 1981 Quaker launched their Harvest Crunch Bar, supported by television advertising featuring the Squirrels. These were amusing, mischievous characters, attracted to the large amount of nuts in the bar. Alerted by the sound of a man innocently munching his bar they surround him menacingly and chase him into the sunset.

Harvest Crunch was immediately successful, capturing 4.1 per cent of the CBCL market in 1982. This was equivalent to 86 per cent of the cereal-bar sector, the principal competitor being Jordan's Original Crunchy.

But by mid-1986 growth in the cereal-bar market was slowing (see Figure 1). This seemed to be principally because the bars' hard, dry texture and muesli-like taste was of limited appeal: consumers' desire to eat more healthily was often overridden by their lust for more 'treaty' snacks.

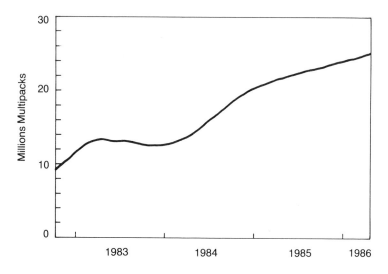

Figure 1. *Total cereal bars volume*
Source: NMRA

THE OPPORTUNITY FOR A CHEWY BAR

By mid-1980 Quaker had developed the technology to manufacture a soft, chewy cereal bar overcoming the known consumer problems of dryness and taste. The opportunity existed to launch a new product that would substantially grow the market, maintaining Quaker's dominant position. Three key issues influenced the marketing of this bar:

1. Whilst there would have been wider potential for the brand in CTN outlets (confectioners, tobacconists and newsagents), Quaker's focus as a grocery company made it prohibitive to launch the brand outside supermarkets.
2. Desire to minimise direct attrition of Harvest Crunch Bars, yet to capitalise on the known strengths of the 'Harvest' brand.
3. Anticipation of future competitive threat and the consequent need to establish a defensible brand property.

The decision was taken to launch the new product in the same format as Harvest Crunch Bars (five bars, flow-wrapped) and to christen it Quaker Harvest Chewy Bar.

MARKETING OBJECTIVES

The company devised the following marketing plan, appropriate to achieving desired volume and profit targets:

1. Achieve the first-year volume target necessary to establish a profitable long-term brand franchise.
2. Gain consumer interest and trial in Harvest Chewy Bars, generating 7 per cent trial immediately following launch, rising to 9 per cent one year after launch.
3. Minimise volume attrition of Harvest Crunch Bars.

(N.B.: Confidentiality dictates that we cannot reveal exact case volume targets. However, we are able to go on to show the actual volume achieved as a percentage of the target.)

THE ADVERTISING BRIEF

In response to this business strategy defined by Quaker we formulated the following advertising brief:

Objectives:

1. Encourage trial of Quaker Harvest Chewy Bars.
2. Harness the mainstream health values of Harvest Crunch Bars yet clearly differentiate 'Chewy' in terms of texture.
3. Specifically, generate 60 per cent prompted brand awareness following launch, rising to 65 per cent after one year.

Target Audience

Housewives who feel guilty about the snacks they feed their families and would feel happier offering a healthier alternative. Some will have tried and rejected hard cereal bars.

Proposition

All the established values of Harvest Crunch Bars (healthy, fun, popular) but a different eating experience − soft, moist and chewy.

CREATIVE DEVELOPMENT

The brief called for the introduction of a new product proposition into the established context of 'Harvestness'.

Qualitative and quantitative research into the brand in 1985 had shown the Squirrels advertising property to be integral to these Harvest values. People readily associated the characters with a quest for nuts and other natural things, so forging a clear link between the creative idea and the nature of the product. Perhaps more importantly, the fun and irreverence of the advertising had lent Harvest an image of accessibility and widespread appeal as opposed to the bible-thumping evangelism of many other health products.

Squirrels advertising was still enjoying high awareness some three years after it had last appeared on network television, demonstrating its appeal and memorability as a branding vehicle. We judged that using it to support the new Chewy Bar would generate immediate awareness and appeal as well as having a 'halo' effect on the existing Crunch product.

Clearly this was a strong case for launching the chewy bar with Squirrels advertising. However, to date the association of Squirrels with nuts had been used to suggest a crunchy texture. There was concern over the ability of the Squirrels vehicle to communicate a *new*, chewy message. Furthermore, in the first commercial it was the noise of the bar being eaten that attracted the Squirrels' attention. With a soft, chewy product this would not logically occur!

The creative challenge was thus to find a way of retaining the Squirrels and the underlying storyline of their chasing after the bar and yet clearly communicate a chewy texture. A key guideline here was not to illustrate chewyness in a way that derided crunch bars.

The solution appears deceptively simple in retrospect: Twist the 'noisy' idea around and make the Squirrels' inability to hear the product the central message of the advert. The resulting 30″ script, 'Wrapper', involves our reluctant hero feeling particularly smug since his new soft and moist Harvest Chewy Bar is so quiet to eat that it doesn't wake the snoozing Squirrels. Misadventure occurs again however, when he inadvertently alerts the Squirrels by noisily throwing his wrapper into a waste-paper bin.

Qualitative and quantitative pre-testing of the script found it to be highly impactful and likeable and to strongly communicate the chewy proposition as illustrated in Figure 2.

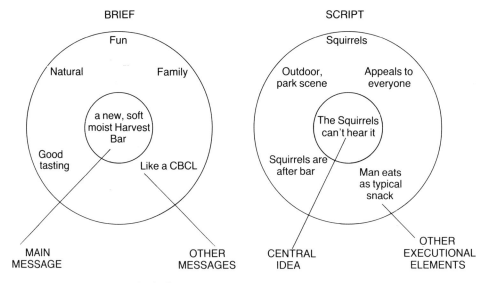

Figure 2. *Comparison of advertising brief and 'Wrapper' script*
Source: BMP

Accordingly we decided to proceed with 'Wrapper' as our launch advertisement.

QUAKER — HARVEST CHEWY BAR
"WRAPPER"

SFX: Snoring
You're witnessing a very
dangerous experiment.

This man will attempt to eat a
cereal bar within earshot of ...

... the Squirrels.
Is he barmy?
No, he's chewing a new Harvest
Chewy Bar.

Yes, conclusive proof. These new
moist and chewy Quaker Harvest
Chewy Bars are extremely quiet.

SFX: Boinnnggg!
SFX: Jaws music.

Oh oh!

MEDIA STRATEGY AND SCHEDULE

The need to generate maximum trial build and trade impact dictated a 'burst' media plan, at weights thought sufficient to achieve our awareness targets.

In order to monitor early production of Chewy Bars and optimise the marketing mix it was necessary to test-launch the bar into a single ITV area. London was duly selected, being the area with highest propensity to purchase cereal bars (a 153 index of NMRA volume over net homes). A further benefit London offered was its status as *the* major area in the eyes of the trade.

Following launch in London, the brand was rolled out nationally and the 'Wrapper' commercial exposed on network television at the summer peak of the cereal-bar market. At this stage commercial activity in the market had become intense, resulting in lower than anticipated share of voice. Consequently, support in 1988 was brought forward to February–March with the aim of pre-empting further competitive presence. A full media schedule is shown in Figure 3.

THE SIGNIFICANCE OF COMPETITIVE ACTIVITY

In an examination of the Harvest Chewy campaign it is vital to illustrate the significance of competitive activity in the market.

At the time that Quaker were developing their Chewy bar, there was very little competitive activity, and Harvest held the strongest market position. However, Quaker were not the only ones to be attracted by the chewy opportunity. The market rapidly attracted several major players. 'Jump' from General Mills had been launched in 1985 under a 'fun' positioning. This was followed in 1986 by three further competitive test launches; 'Solar' from United Biscuits (the closest bar in format to Harvest), Mars' 'Tracker' and 'Appleford's Cluster' from Lyons Tetley (both of which emerged as slightly more adult, 'countline' snacks).

In addition a more indulgent 'chocolate enrobed' sector was established by 'Jump in Choc' and Rowntree's 'Novo'.

The key advantage of competitive brands over Harvest lay in distribution. Many of them, with the support of larger companies, achieved high grocery distribution. In addition, Cluster, Tracker and Novo had the benefit of wider distribution through CTNs, offering a greater 'impulse' trial opportunity.

As a result of this increased competition, total media spend grew massively in 1987, topping £7.7 million, nearly three times the 1986 figure. In addition, several brands achieved national roll-out in the summer months of 1987, with the result that much of that year's activity occurred within the space of a few weeks. This left Harvest Chewy outspent, fighting heavy competitive advertising for consumer attention (Figure 3).

BRAND PERFORMANCE

Targets for the Harvest brand had been set without allowance for such an over-whelming level of activity (particularly from Tracker).

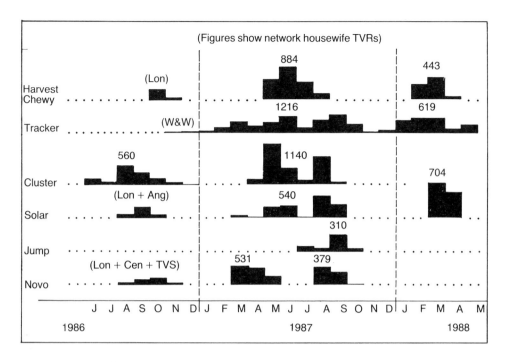

Figure 3. *Competitive media activity*
Source: BARB

Despite this, in its first full year of national distribution the brand substantially achieved its sales target (96 per cent of target volume ex-factory).

Cumulative trial of the product, measured on the TCA panel, reached 6.8 per cent of all households by March 1988. Making allowance for panel pick-up (a 30–50 per cent underestimate by company reckoning) it seems that the target level of 9 per cent trial one year from launch was exceeded.

Curiously, prompted awareness of Harvest Chewy stood at only 37 per cent in March 1988, substantially below the first-year target of 65 per cent (a figure from which volume targets had been calculated). We discuss reasons for this discrepancy later.

Concerning attrition, gains/loss analysis (AGB) revealed that only 5 per cent of crunch volume was 'lost' to Harvest Chewy. For its part Chewy attracted 82 per cent of its sales from sources other than crunch bars, clearly enlarging the market. The overall effect of this performance was, despite competitive onslaught, to maintain Quaker's leadership of an enlarged cereal-bar market (see Figure 4).

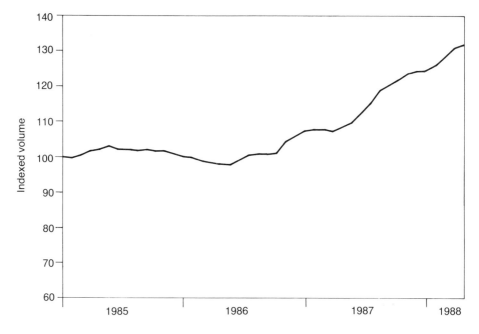

Figure 4. *Total Harvest volume*
Source: NMRA

EVALUATING THE EFFECTS OF ADVERTISING

Isolating the effects of advertising in any new product launch poses considerable difficulties. Changing distribution, pricing and the inherent impact of any new product appearing on shelf all obscure the true role of advertising in the mix.

In this case these traditional problems have been exacerbated by the changing pattern of competitive activity. It has proved necessary to look at our brand's performance not only in isolation, but also relative to the competition, bearing in mind that in an expanding market it is possible for anyone who has exhibited growth to claim success.

Despite these difficulties, a comprehensive database together with the additional advertising burst in the test market has allowed us to examine more closely the advertising effect as follows:

1. Analysis of observed audit data since launch to explain *sales behaviour* in both the London area and nationally.
2. Analysis of *competitive activity* and its probable effects on our performance.
3. Construction of a *computer model* of sales to reconcile the various influences and further increase our understanding.
4. Examination of the link between advertising and *trial* gaining.
5. Assimilation of evidence from consumer research regarding the *recall and relevance* of the advertising.

Sales Behaviour

Since Harvest Chewy's launch into the London ITV area in September 1986 the brand has been supported by three bursts of advertising. Its share of the London chewy-bar market over this period is illustrated in Figure 5.

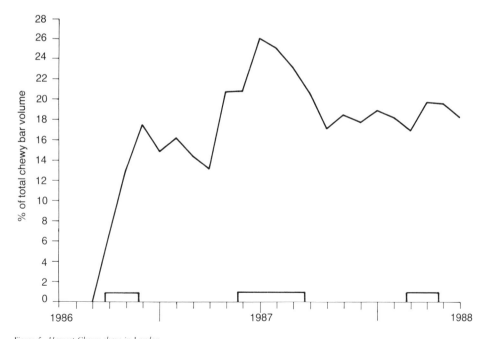

Figure 5. *Harvest Chewy share in London*
Source: NMRA

Although peaks in share correlate with the pattern of advertising there are a great deal of other interrelated variables influencing this data. Potentially most significant of these is the pattern of Harvest Chewy's distribution (Figure 6). This shows steady distribution gains together with major expansions at the periods of test launch and national roll-out.

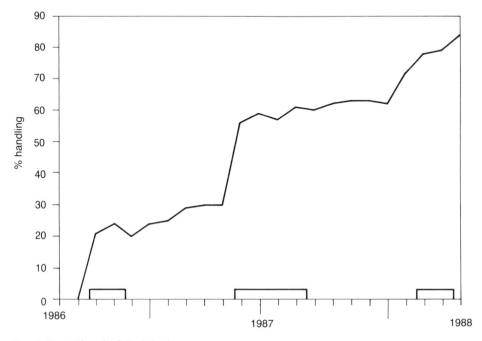

Figure 6. *Harvest Chewy distribution in London*
Source: NMRA

In order to remove the effects of distribution we can analyse sterling-weighted rate of sale (volume sold per point of distribution – a measure of the rate of consumer purchasing), as shown in Figure 7.

This data reveals more obvious peaks that correspond with advertising and other marketing activity. We can infer little about any advertising effect during the launch burst: the appearance of Harvest Chewy on shelf for the first time would have created its own interest. In addition there was a big sales force push together with an on-pack 'taste guarantee' promotion.

We find ourselves on surer ground on subsequent advertising bursts, observing an apparent correlation with rate-of-sale uplifts. However, to be more conclusive we need to evaluate any other variables that may potentially have influenced sales:

Distribution: Both the *quantity* and *quality* of distribution have been eliminated. However, it is conceivable that an uplift could have been created by the listings gain in two major supermarket chains, stores known to have relatively high rate of sale for all cereal bars. Initial trial in these outlets may explain the 'blip' in Chewy

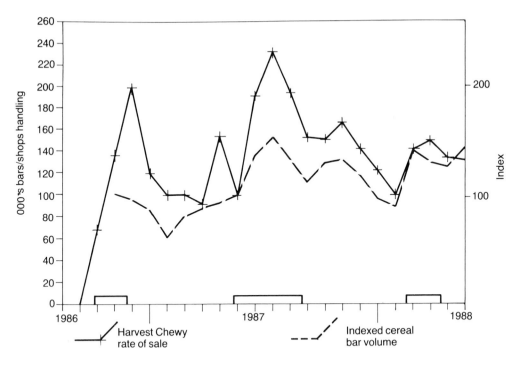

Figure 7. *Harvest Chewy rate of sale: London*
Source: NMRA

rate of sale in April 1987. However, this would be a 'once and for all' effect that would not influence subsequent results.

Seasonality: The 'natural' seasonality of the chewy-bar market is impossible to discern, given that the market has been shaped since its outset by brand launches. However, we hypothesise a seasonality identical to the total cereal-bar market. This demonstrates that whilst the winter troughs and summer peaks influence the rise and fall of Chewy's rate of sale, the magnitude of the summer peak alone is insufficient to explain the July highpoint.

Pricing: If anything, price would have had a negative influence on rate of sale, as it rose by 9 per cent in summer 1987. Furthermore, a fall before Christmas 1987 seems to have had no positive effect. Over the third advertised period pricing was static.

Promotions: As mentioned earlier, a consumer promotion accompanied launch of the brand. A second on-pack promotion in autumn 1987 (not overlapping with any advertised periods) does seem to have had a sales effect. There were no other promotions over this period.

Competitive activity is discussed in a later section. Packaging, product formulation and other variables were all unchanged over the analysed period.

This analysis gives us a strong inference of the sales effect of advertising in London, even if only by the removal of other possible factors. Examination of rate of sale for the brand nationally reveals a similar pattern (Figure 8). The summer peak suggests the relevance and distinction of the total marketing package overall, if not the advertising specifically. However, during the second national burst in February–March 1988 rate of sale again rose at a time when pricing and other marketing variables were constant. It seems that the more modest performance here may be explained by strong competitive activity, which merits discussion in its own right.

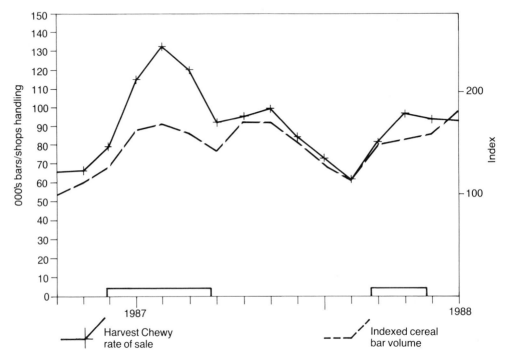

Figure 8. *Harvest Chewy rate of sale: national*
Source: NMRA

Effect of Competitive Activity

Despite a relatively late roll-out, Harvest Chewy rapidly achieved brand leadership over its initial launch and advertised period. Since then, the only brand to have consistently outperformed Harvest is Mars' 'Tracker' (see Figure 9).

However, Tracker has outspent Harvest Chewy on advertising by a factor of 50 per cent, as well as achieving higher levels and wider channels of distribution.

Throughout March and April 1988, Solar reduced its price by 17 per cent (thus selling 30 per cent below the market average), advertised this price heavily on TV and mounted a strong trade drive generating an 81 per cent increase in front stocks. The result of this blitz was a doubling of Solar's rate of sale. Solar had

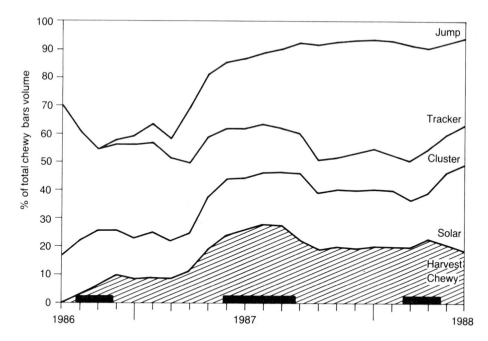

Figure 9. *Chewy bar market volume shares*
Source: NMRA

emerged as our closest competitor in product, positioning and usage terms. It seems likely that much of its incremental volume therefore would have come at the expense of Harvest. However, the promotion coincided with Harvest Chewy's third advertising burst. It is notable that, far from suffering, Harvest's brand share was slightly increased at 21 per cent, despite Solar's assault.

Straight observation of audit data and judgemental elimination of other variables seems to give strong inferential evidence of a link between advertising and sales. However, given the doubts and ambiguities created by such a dynamic marketing environment, we turned to sales modelling to investigate possible effects more fully.

Econometric Modelling

Modelling a market with such a short and turbulent history posed several particular problems:

1. To generate a more reliable data set and to give the model more 'experience' of Chewy Bar sales, we pooled audit data across regions, so increasing the number of data points from 20 to 151.
2. To better separate the closely correlated effects of Harvest Chewy advertising and seasonality, we first modelled the total chewy-bar market and (reasonably, we feel) imposed *its* seasonality on Harvest Chewy sales.
3. To understand the influence of competitive activity we included the advertising

of all major brands in our model of the market, as well as expressing Harvest Chewy sales solus in relation to competitive activity.

We found that two major factors explain the growth in the total chewy-bar market: rising aggregate distribution (five major brands), and total chewy-bar advertising (five major brands). A number of factors in turn contribute to rising distribution.

TVR for TVR, none of the five advertised brands grew the market any more than any other. Tracker, however, spent considerably more than either Harvest or Solar and as a consequence contributed more to the final total.

Approximately 15 per cent of total chewy-bar sales since December 1986 were directly attributable to advertising.

Since launch, rising levels of Harvest Chewy's sales are explained by:

Harvest advertising	21%
Tracker advertising	4%
Harvest distribution growth	44%
Underlying market growth trend	14%
	83%

Seasonality, relative price, and an initial but low distribution base are key contributors to the remainder.

The effect of Harvest advertising. Harvest advertising began to increase Chewy sales in the four-weekly period in which it appears, although in several regions the largest sales impact of the advertising came in the four-weekly period following transmission. The advertising also continued to affect sales for a number of periods after this peak, decaying at a rate of 50 per cent for each successive period.

Other Influences. Also apparent from the model is the influence of competitive advertising and price on sales.

Surprisingly, Tracker advertising marginally increased Harvest Chewy sales. This is partly a result of its disproportionately high spend, giving it a bigger influence on market growth as a whole. However, the results also support our hypothesis that Tracker is positioned differently in the market (more adult, more expensive, less mainstream).

We identified that Solar was similarly positioned to Harvest Chewy. It is not surprising therefore that its advertising tends to take sales away from Harvest.

The model also shows some degree of price sensitivity, with a 1 per cent increase in price per bar leading to a 0.5 per cent drop in sales volume. It therefore seems clear that the *combined* effect of Solar's advertising and price promotion in March–April 1988 explains Harvest's relatively low sales increase during the most recent advertising burst.

The Pattern of Trial Gain

The primary objective of the campaign was to generate trial of the brand. Special analysis of the TCA consumer panel allows us to track the number of *new* brand

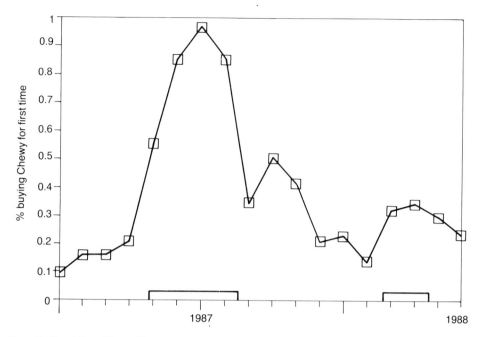

Figure 10. *New triallists of Harvest Chewy*
Source: TCA

triallists in each four-weekly period (see Figure 10).

We observe a very rapid initial build-up of trial, and correlation between trial peaks and advertising support. As with analysis of observed sales a more definitive relationship here is best demonstrated by the February–March 1988 peak. Besides advertising the only changing variable that might explain this peak is seasonality.

The ability of advertising to generate trial additional to the seasonal norm can be demonstrated by relating Harvest Chewy trial to the total level of competitive trial (Table 1). It is clear that Chewy's share of new triallists entering the market is greater over periods of advertising.

TABLE 1: HARVEST CHEWY SHARE OF TRIAL RELATED TO PRINCIPAL COMPETITORS

Pre 1st burst (Mar./Apr. 1987)	During 1st burst (June/July 1987)	Post 1st burst (Sept. 1987)	Pre 2nd burst (Jan. 1988)	During 2nd burst (Feb./Mar. 1988)	Post 2nd burst (May 1988)
19%	39%	18%	11%	30%	13%

Note:

$$\text{Harvest `share of trial'} = \frac{\text{trial of Harvest Chewy}}{\text{sum of trial of competitive brands}} \times 100\%$$

Source: TCA special analysis

Impact, Memorability and Communication of the Advertising

The advertising generated very high levels of recall. At its peak over 80 per cent of housewives claimed to recognise the commercial from a photographic prompt.

Continuous measures of claimed advertising awareness, from tracking study data, can be modelled most satisfactorily using the principle of inverse exponential decay (Figure 11). This model establishes a 'base level' of awareness (the level to which awareness would fall should advertising cease – a measure of the advertising's long-term familiarity) and an 'awareness index' (the awareness generated directly by each 100 ratings of exposure – a measure of the advertising's impact and memorability).

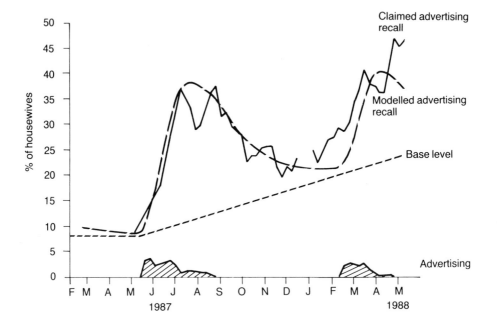

Figure 11. *Modelled prompted advertising awareness*
Source: Millward Brown

The model shows that each burst of 'Wrapper' advertising dramatically raised the base level of 'Harvest' advertising awareness, reflecting the familiarity with previous Squirrels advertising (last aired in 1982), which we identified at the exploratory stage. The campaign has thus established a base level of 24, comparable with more established advertisers like Guinness and Nescafé (both of whom spend substantially more).

Harvest's awareness index is also outstanding. The index of nine is greater than any other cereal-bar brand's and over twice the average figure across all advertised markets.

The advertising is therefore extremely memorable in both the short and long term.

Tracking study data and subsequent qualitative work also confirm the appeal of 'Wrapper': 73 per cent of Chewy buyers thought it 'amusing'.

In terms of the central communication of the ad, tracking data shows that 65 per cent of those recalling Harvest advertising following the summer burst showed clear understanding of its 'chewy' message. This figure rises to 78 per cent following the second burst (see Table 2).

TABLE 2: PRINCIPAL COMMUNICATION OF 'WRAPPER'

	Base: those recalling ad. as ...	
	'Harvest Chewy' %	'Harvest Crunch' %
Any mention − moist/soft/chewy	<u>83</u>	<u>38</u>
Quiet/quiet to eat	46	16
Chewy/chewier bar	37	13
Moist/soft/not brittle/not crunchy	33	8
Man eats bar without waking squirrels	31	17
Man eating chewy bar	18	18
Squirrels can't hear bar snap	15	9
(Throws wrapper in bin − wakes squirrels	59	37)
(Squirrels wake up	27	20)

Source: Millward Brown

Qualitative post-testing of the finished film indicated that the strength of this communication was due to its inextricable link with the creative idea of the silent bar that doesn't wake the Squirrels (as predicted by pre-testing). The quotations in Table 3 are typical.

TABLE 3: CONSUMERS' EXPLANATION OF 'WRAPPER' AD

"... and the fact that it didn't wake the squirrels up — they were still fast asleep — the only thing that woke them up was the wrapper."

Housewife, Bournemouth

"They couldn't hear him snapping the bar."

Housewife, Hull

"It's telling you you can chew it without waking them [the squirrels] up."

Harvest Crunch user, Bournemouth

"... so now I can eat my Harvest bar and not get pestered by the squirrels!"

Harvest Crunch user, Bournemouth

"... they've brought out a new bar that's quiet to eat, so you can trick the squirrels."

Housewife, Cardiff

Source: BMP group discussions

Examination of consumer data also goes a long way towards explaining how volume targets could be met whilst awareness levels for Chewy appeared low. It seems that many people referred to the brand as 'Harvest Crunch' but were now aware that this included both crunchy and chewy varieties. Although 70 per cent of those people recalling 'Wrapper' referred to the name 'Harvest Crunch', 53 per cent demonstrated clear appreciation that the product advertised was chewy. Whilst awareness of the name 'Harvest Chewy' was increased over the advertised period, it seems the major effect of the advertising was to reinforce total 'Harvest' awareness, while introducing the consumer to the notion of a new chewy Harvest bar (see Figure 12).

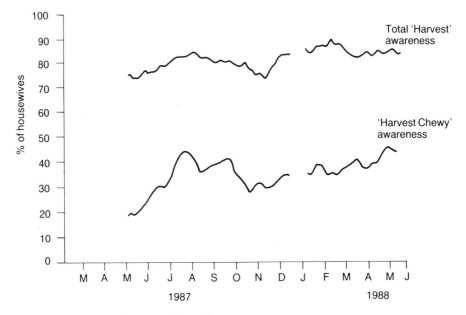

Figure 12. *Prompted awareness of Harvest and Harvest Chewy*
Source: Millward Brown

It seems that the strong franchise created by 'Harvest Crunch' (many people use the name almost as a generic for the cereal-bar category) means that it was ambitious to expect to establish 'Chewy' as a brand name in its own right.

HOW DID THE ADVERTISING WORK?

It seems clear from analysis of sales and recall/communication data that there exists a strong relationship between the advertising being seen and understood, and the product being purchased. However, such evidence is no more than 'guilt by association' unless a credible and convincing case can be made for advertising *causing* incremental sales.

It is our belief that a strong causal effect did exist, because the advertising imbued the brand with a strong personality substantially different from and more appealing than that of competitors, despite their similarity in other respects.

By developing the existing Squirrels advertising, 'Wrapper' was able to sustain the values of 'Harvestness' while establishing the new product format.

The nature of these values can be uncovered by both quantitative and qualitative market mapping. In this case such an analysis has uncovered an interesting discrepancy between the results from quantified image data and qualitative group discussion work.

Quantitatively derived 'correspondence analysis' maps link Chewy clearly with middle-of-the-road family health values (Figure 13). (Confidentiality prevents us from identifying competitive brands here.)

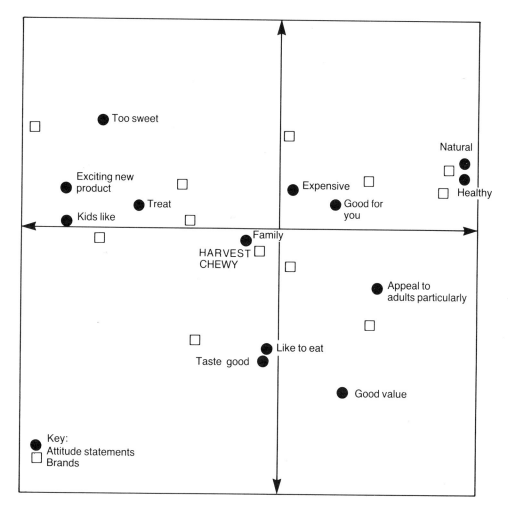

Figure 13. *Quantitative correspondence analysis map*
Source: Millward Brown

Traditional interpretation of these maps is that a central position is a weak one, offering little differentiation from competitors. However, what this method fails to demonstrate are the more intangible variables of effectiveness — the likeability and 'for-me-ness' of the brand. Here qualitative discussions were able to determine that Chewy was one of only three brands in the market with anything of a focused personality, and *the* brand that offered most personal identification and appeal to our target audience.

By strongly and creatively projecting the fun, lovable, 'everyone's favourite' values of the Harvest brand the advertising has been able to generate a clear brand personality of fun, charm and likeability. Graphic evidence of this is reflected in the difference between liking the *brand* best (with brand names prompted) and *product* preference scores (with products presented 'blind') as shown in Table 4. This

TABLE 4:   COMPARISON OF BRANDED PREFERENCE WITH
BLIND PRODUCT LIKING

Index =	% of brand triallists claiming to like that brand best
	Blind product preference rating (relative to mean)

Harvest	97
Cluster	64
Tracker	41
Solar	31
Jump	21

Source: Millward Brown

quantitive measurement of the appeal of the various brand personalities clearly sets Harvest above the rest.

It seems that advertising has involved the product with strong emotional values that exist beyond its purely physical product characteristics. Such values are of course inherently more defensible and seem to have contributed much to our competitive advantage so far.

CONCLUSIONS

1. Advertising can be directly attributed to the achievement of some 21 per cent of Harvest Chewy's sales. We are not at liberty to reveal here any details of Quaker's profit margins. Suffice it to say that the substantial achievement of the brand's first-year volume targets has ensured a profitable basis for *future* business.

2. Advertising has done this by lending the brand a clear and well-liked personality which has established the new Chewy product and maintained Harvest as the leading brand in the market. Clearly this personality has considerable long-term value.

3. The advertising's status as the most enjoyed and best recalled in the market has allowed it to work despite a media effort much diluted by competitive spends.

4. At this stage we cannot definitely establish the contribution of advertising towards building a strong brand franchise in terms of trade support and consumer loyalty. However, there are strong suggestions that without its support the brand would not be so established in the intensely competitive market.

TECHNICAL APPENDIX: THE ECONOMETRIC MODEL

Notes on the Methodology

1a. Clearly there are always problems in modelling the behaviour of new brands, first because it can be difficult to capture the growth process adequately, and secondly because the dynamics of responses to changes in the independent variables may not have settled down. However, econometric models (unlike time-series models) do not have as a prerequisite stationary data. It is legitimate to capture growth within the movements of its contributory variables. As long as the classic linear regression Gauss−Markov conditions hold (i.e. that the variance of the residuals is constant) the fact that the dependent variable is increasing over time is not important. The results of the variance ratio test reported later show that this model satisfies that condition.

1b. Evaluating the effects of advertising in a seasonal market with limited time series can produce biased and mis-specified inferences. However, from an analytical point of view we were fortunate that advertising had taken place at differing times and weights at the regional level.

This facilitated the pooling of time-series and cross-sectional data (using Zellner's seemingly unrelated regressor methodology) which allows the imposition of regional cross-equation restrictions. Furthermore, this methodology not only has the benefit of allowing a more general approach to the analysis but enabled us to make use of considerably more data than would have been the case had sales been analysed at national level.

2. Four-weekly regional sales data for Harvest Chewy bars were pooled to give a total sample of 151 observations (nine regions). Given very different sales levels across regions it was necessary to normalise the sales data before it could be combined into one sample.

The source of the market data was NMRA.

3. The timing of Harvest Chewy advertising at the seasonal peak made it difficult reliably to separate the pure effects of seasonality from those of advertising. We therefore modelled the underlying seasonal pattern for the total chewy-bar market (which had had some counter-seasonal advertising) and took it as the norm for Harvest Chewy. (There was no a priori reason to assume that Harvest Chewy sales were any more or less seasonal than the market.)

We had slightly less data than would have been ideal for this exercise − a little under two years'. However, the results we obtained corresponded very well to the seasonal pattern of the crunch bar market, so we felt that they were sufficiently reliable to go ahead with.

Main Findings

Variations in Harvest Chewy Bar sales were explained by variations in (in no particular order).

A constant term
Harvest Chewy price relative to average chewy-bar price
Harvest Chewy sterling distribution
Harvest Chewy advertising
Tracker advertising
Solar advertising
Time trend
Market seasonality

In general, the effect of price and distribution changes and of Tracker's advertising was the same in all regions. The effect of Harvest and Solar advertising varied slightly from region to region. Wales, however, appeared exceptionally advertising sensitive to both Harvest and Solar advertising — three times that of the next highest region. We can offer no convincing or logical explanation for this and the possibility remains that it is a spurious result.

Yorkshire responded strangely to distribution changes. The growth profile of Harvest and of the total chewy market in Yorkshire is untypical. Harvest followed Tracker into this region, and because the market was already established initial sales levels were very high (which reflects in a very high intercept term estimated for Yorkshire). More recently chewy-bar sales in Yorkshire have been virtually static or declining. A separate dummy variable has been included for Yorkshire distribution to prevent its untypical effect biasing other coefficients.

Model Specification

Harvest Chewy's growth is represented by growth in its own distribution and by the time trend and Tracker advertising which together capture the underlying market growth.

The preferred specification for the Harvest chewy sales model is as follows:

Dependent Variable = Harvest Chewy sales (000s bars) normalised

Independent variables	Coefficient	t-statistic
Constant term	0.95	10.51
Relative price	−47.64	−9.75
Sterling distribution	1.04	12.23
Yorkshire & Dist. (incremental effect)	− 2.46	−9.91
Tracker adstock	0.019	2.66
Harvest ad (TVRs)*	1.00	10.16
Harvest adstock (−1)*	1.00	12.95
Solar TVRs	1.00	6.87
Solar TVRs (−1)	− 0.035	−3.19
Time trend	1.11	3.67

* The regional coefficients for Harvest TVRs and adstock, Solar TVRs and the constant term were weighted together by region as follows:

	Constant	Harvest TVRs	Harvest adstock (−1)	Solar TVRs
London	24.56	−	0.07	0.08
TVS	19.98	0.09	0.09	−
Wales	16.90	0.31	0.30	−0.21
Midlands	31.74	0.03	0.12	−
Anglia	28.75	0.08	0.09	+0.05
Lancashire	6.20	0.05	0.08	−
Yorkshire	186.07	0.03	0.07	−
Tyne Tees	33.88	0.12	0.06	−
Scotland	32.52	0.07	0.10	−

Retention rates for both Harvest Chewy and Tracker adstocks were 0.5 (four-weekly carry-over). Results of tests for the specification of this model are:

R^2	= 0.90
S.E. of regression	= 11.32 (Mean of dep. var. = 71.64)
DW statistic	= 1.71
Sum of squared residuals	= 18059
F statistic	= 156.48
Variance ratio test	= $f(63,66)$ = 1.412
(Critical value above which this would fail = 1.53)	

The model had a tendency in some regions to make large prediction errors when sales levels were very low (i.e. just post-launch). This almost certainly reflects the quality of the data at these points as much as the specification of the model itself. In a modelling exercise of this type, precise interpretation of the model can be difficult. As great care has to be taken not to read too much into results, they are better treated as a 'broad brush' depiction of the market than a finely detailed analysis.

The following post-sample predictive failure tests, dropping data for a region at a time, demonstrate the general applicability of the final model to all regions:

1. Without Scotland
    $f(16,125)$ = 1.65   CV = 1.75
2. Without Scotland, Tyne Tees
    $f(31,110)$ = 1.53   CV = 1.55
3. Without Scotland, Tyne Tees, Yorkshire
    $f(45,96)$ = 1.24   CV = 1.54
4. Without Scotland, Tyne Tees, Yorkshire, Lancashire
    $f(60,81)$ = 1.25   CV = 1.48
5. Without Scotland, Tyne Tees, Yorkshire, Lancashire, Anglia
    $f(77,64)$ = 1.05   CV = 1.53
6. Without Scotland, Tyne Tees, Yorkshire, Lancashire, Anglia, Midlands.
    $f(92,49)$ = 0.87   CV = 1.60
7. Without Scotland, Tyne Tees, Yorkshire, Lancashire, Anglia, Midlands, Wales
    $f(111,30)$ = 0.75   CV = 1.68

(Space constraints necessitated omitting the 'actual and fitted' chart from the Appendix.)

13

Alliance & Leicester: Advertising for Success in the Financial Market

MARKET BACKGROUND

Building Societies

Building societies have grown spectacularly since World War II, holding 75 per cent of outstanding mortgage loans and accounting for over 50 per cent of personal liquid financial assets. Behind this success has lain a history of direct and indirect governmental control over their competitors, notably the high-street banks.

The 1980s have been a buoyant period for the building societies' traditional markets. Home ownership and mortgage demand has continued to grow, while increasing affluence has fuelled the savings market.

But this period has also seen an immense change in their competitive environment. The high-street banks now actively seek mortgage business while new financial organisations, like The Mortgage Corporation, effectively undercut building-society lending rates by using wholesale rather than retail funding (i.e. international finance markets rather than the domestic retail savings market).

In the savings market, too, building societies are experiencing 'new competition'. During those years of economic growth the British public saw a popularisation of the world of finance – through the media, backed by the Government. The man in the street became aware of the FT index, as well as scandals in the City. At the same time he was also made aware of new investment opportunities like unit trust products, and of the Stock Market itself with the massive Government privatisation programme beginning with British Telecom in 1984. Meanwhile, the high-street banks became far more active in the savings market, recognising that they must cross-sell additional services to existing customers to maintain their large branch networks and profitability.

The Building Societies Act implemented in January 1987 saw further fundamental change in their environment. This Act relaxed the legal framework under which societies operated – allowing them to offer a much wider range of services, for instance to provide unsecured loans, sell a wide range of insurance products and issue credit cards.

For building societies then there were both tremendous opportunities and substantial threats; competition was hotting up, but their markets were buoyant and they had greater freedom of competition.

One response to this new environment has been an increasing general interest in marketing, and in advertising in particular. Media spends on financial products, specifically in the building-society sector, have risen dramatically — making it one of the fastest-growing advertised categories in the last seven years (Table 1).

TABLE 1:   BUILDING SOCIETIES' TOTAL MEDIA SPEND (PRESS AND TV)

	1980	1984	1987
£000s	20 949	60 197	86 849
Index	100	287	415

Source: MEAL

Yet another response has been the huge increase in merger activity amongst the societies. In 1980 there were 273 individual building societies operating in the UK. By the end of 1987 this had been reduced by well over 100.

The Alliance & Leicester

The Alliance & Leicester Building Society is the result of such a merger. In October 1985 the Alliance Society (ninth-largest) joined with the Leicester (tenth-largest) to form the sixth-largest society — the Alliance & Leicester.

Against the background of growing competition, there was obviously a need to inform the public of this major new force in the consumer finance market-place.

To achieve this, the TV campaign 'Bright Ideas' was developed. This consisted of three films, one announcing the merger, the other two concentrating on specific products — the BankSave Plus and Gold Plus accounts. These films aimed to position the society as 'The big Society with bright ideas', i.e. the society with innovative and unique products. It was hoped that this would fight the common consumer perception that all building societies are essentially the same. It would position the Alliance & Leicester as a different sort of society and give the consumers a *real reason* to choose it.

During the campaign, prompted awareness of the Alliance & Leicester peaked in June at 56 per cent but remained behind pre-merger awareness levels of the Alliance Society (which averaged 62 per cent throughout 1985).

Further, qualitative advertising research suggested the campaign might not be working as well as anticipated. It highlighted the lack of confidence and general apathy amongst most building-society users. Interest in specific product details is limited to a few, largely older consumers, those with large lump sums to invest, who will shop around in the high street and through the press for the best savings rate available. The vast majority of people, however, see building societies as 'safe', cosy places to put their money — geared to ordinary folk rather than the financially sophisticated, and offering emotional and financial security. The 'Bright Ideas' campaign was thus based on the wrong premise. Consumers sought predictability rather than innovation and found product-specific advertising generally irrelevant and hence lacking in impact.

For 12 months from autumn 1986 a press advertising campaign was run to promote specific products by appealing to those investors interested in products with high rates of interest. By adopting a distinctive house style it was hoped that this would contribute to overall brand awareness and imagery, although clearly, press would be a slow medium through which to build these.

Meanwhile, exploratory qualitative concept and ad testing was undertaken to help understand the requirements for a mainstream television campaign for the society. This research confirmed that the role for TV advertising is to appeal to the vast spectrum of building-society users, who are not specifically interested in products or rates, but come to building societies for security, safety and customer care.

This research also made very clear that consumers see building societies as very similar, sharing these essential core values to a greater or lesser extent. Those societies with whose names people were most familiar were seen as big, reliable, respectable and safe, and generally having first claim on 'core values'.

From such societies, consumers unconsciously form a candidate list which they feel is safe to choose from. Final choice could be influenced by a range of factors including, typically, convenience or personal recommendation. The last point at which the society can itself influence customer choice is inside the branch itself, with branch staff service.

Thus it would seem that awareness, saliency and the positive brand imagery that accompanies these measures are key to a society's success.

THE PROBLEM FOR THE ALLIANCE & LEICESTER

The problem had a number of facets. Since the merger in 1985, awareness levels and brand imagery measures had fallen behind the levels the society expected for its size. By August 1987, prior to the campaign, spontaneous awareness was at 14.2 per cent, while prompted awareness was 53.6 per cent, placing the Alliance & Leicester ninth in the league of building-society awareness (Source: FRS), when it should have been sixth-largest, given its asset share (defined by fixed assets, i.e. branches, buildings owned and so on, liquid assets, and outstanding mortgages and other investments).

In addition, market share of net building-society receipts (receipts minus withdrawals) fell at the beginning of the year, necessitating a strong marketing drive at branch level. In May and June the Society offered a limited-issue Investment Bond with very attractive rates of interest (but therefore a reduced margin between those and what it could earn on mortgages).

Furthermore, the Alliance & Leicester had traditionally enjoyed a 'cost of funds advantage', i.e. the average interest rate it paid each month on savings had been lower than the industry norm. Since the merger this advantage had consistently been eroded as the Society was forced by increasing competition to offer better interest rates, resulting in a downward pressure on the Society's basic profit margin.

Thus, by autumn 1987 there was a strong need for an effective TV advertising campaign to increase the saliency of the Alliance & Leicester in the market, and in the long-term influence saving and mortgage business but without the need to increase the Society's cost of funds.

ADVERTISING OBJECTIVES

The overall objectives of the advertising were to help fulfil the marketing objectives through raising the saliency of the Society, thereby putting the Alliance & Leicester more frequently on to consumers' candidate lists when wanting to open savings accounts or take out a mortgage, and increasing the loyalty of existing Alliance & Leicester customers.

The short-term objective for the campaign was to achieve:

— spontaneous awareness of the Alliance & Leicester of 25 per cent by the end of 1988.
— prompted awareness of 70 per cent by the end of 1988.

The business effects of a corporate TV campaign of this nature were felt to be primarily long term — building the future of the Society. No specific business objectives were therefore set, but it was hoped that some short-term indication of an advertising effect might be seen — even though in such a complex market it might be difficult to isolate.

OBJECTIVES

In the light of increasing competitiveness within the market-place the Alliance & Leicester's overall marketing objective for 1987–90 is at least to maintain its current market share of building-society assets — and if possible to improve it. This may not, at first sight, appear to be a demanding objective. However, throughout the 1980s it has been the very largest societies that have gained asset market share at the expense of medium and smaller societies.

The final objective, of great importance to the Society, was the effect on its branch staff. Following a merger of two organisations, it was especially important to engender loyalty and sense of belonging and pride amongst the staff, particularly given their vital role in portraying the image of the Society and in converting sales in the branches. Thus it was important that the staff themselves should enjoy and like the advertising and identify with its public image.

Media Strategy

For an advertising campaign to achieve major shifts in awareness of a 'brand' in a relatively short time, the most obvious media choice must be television — only this can offer the impact necessary to the campaign.

The awareness levels of the Alliance & Leicester during the previous year of press advertising demonstrated that even a distinctive press style can only shift awareness slowly, and is therefore more appropriate for specific product advertising.

The aim of the TV campaign, then, was to increase awareness of the Alliance & Leicester so that it became far more of a 'household name'.

In order to support the Alliance & Leicester's national branch network, a national advertising campaign was planned. TV area share allocations were based on a number of criteria:

— Alliance & Leicester branch regionality.
— Alliance & Leicester branch penetration compared with other building societies.
— Potential monies by TV area, expressed in terms of both savings and mortgages.

This produced a cost-effectiveness for each TV area, based on area cost per thousand after share negotiations.

Target Market

The audience for the advertising was not just existing Alliance & Leicester members but potential customers. Given the ubiquitous nature of the savings market, and the enormous variety in the nature of accounts, this translates into a target of 'The General Public', i.e. all adults. However, the Alliance & Leicester investment holders show a skew towards ABC1 adults — 58.5 per cent of their investors (Table 2).

TABLE 2:   INDEX OF ALLIANCE & LEICESTER SAVERS v. ALL
BUILDING SOCIETY SAVERS

AB	145
C1	112

Source: TGI

For this reason a media buying strategy of all adults was adopted but with a minimum conversion to 80 per cent ABC1 viewers.

Timing

Following several years of the Government's privatisation campaign, the limited amount of seasonality apparent in the savings market has been masked. The mortgage market, however, is traditionally buoyant in spring and autumn. The national campaign was therefore planned to begin in September 1987 with a second burst in November in selected regions. A second national burst was timed for February 1988, continuing through to April.

Creative Development

It is the task of the advertising to create a high impact for the Alliance & Leicester across an extremely wide target audience. This task is made the more difficult because all building-society advertising is perceived by the public as being, for the most part, over-serious and dull.

In addition to creating impact, an advertising vehicle was required that positioned the Society as big, warm and friendly — something the ordinary man in the street can identify with; and as possessing the core building-society values of safety and security.

In summer 1987, a campaign was developed based on these key findings and taking into account the changing climate of consumer attitudes to financial markets. In particular it focused on the new, fashionable competitors in the market, such as stocks and shares, unit trusts and so on, exploiting not only these new forms of investment but the 'new investor' himself, who at his worst might be derogatorily described as an over-clever 'yuppie'. This character is then contrasted with someone everybody can identify with, 'the common man'.

The vehicle for the advertising was a new, young comedy team — Stephen Fry and Hugh Laurie. The 'trick' of the ads is to flatter the wisdom of the common man — Hugh Laurie — in choosing the Alliance & Leicester. In each execution Laurie wins out over the bumbling Fry, who dabbles unsuccessfully in complicated and perilous new investments (the 'Golf' and 'Restaurant' executions) or whose mortgage goes drastically wrong and forces him to live in a 'shoe box' ('Flat' execution).

Throughout the films Laurie's safe, secure choice, the Alliance & Leicester Building Society, is endorsed. In this way the Society is effectively positioned as owning these core building-society values. In addition, Laurie is portrayed as the truly clever investor — the one who really understands the financial world today. A sentiment very much in tune with the climate of the time and one neatly summed up in the advertising end line:

'You get a smarter investor at the Alliance & Leicester'.

The scale of the media spend and the use of three different films was felt to go a long way towards giving the impression of a large, ubiquitous society. However, to support this feeling, branches of the Alliance & Leicester were featured in the executions — always 'just around the corner' — even on a golf course. This also gave the opportunity to feature the distinctive logo of the Society — an important aid to branch recognition in the high street.

By using Fry and Laurie's highly original and distinctive brand of humour, it was hoped the advertising would rise above the apathy generally associated with the sector and prove impactful and enjoyable. Further, it was hoped the humour would cut across age barriers and have wide general appeal.

EVALUATION OF THE CAMPAIGN

Brand Awareness

The primary advertising objective of the campaign was to raise awareness and saliency of the Society, and improve the Alliance & Leicester's score across a range of image dimensions.

So, young Mostyn. Joining us on the top floor eh? Be nice to have a bit of cash to play with, I should imagine.

Well, I've just invested , .'. Investment, Mostyn, is a lot like Golf . . .
. . . . Now think of this ball Mostyn, as your cash . . .

. . . and let's call the flag your dividend shall we?
Now prices swing up . . . and down.
So you must strike while the iron is hot.

But you don't get all these complications at the Alliance & Leicester.

Just a good rate of interest, ... and branches everywhere

Looks like your investment's hit rock bottom, Sir.
Humour, Mostyn is something you won't be needing on the top floor.
You get a smarter investor at the Alliance & Leicester.

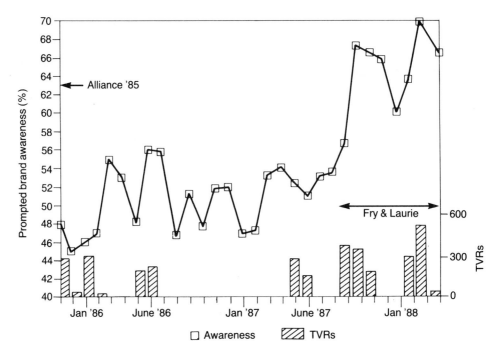

Figure 1. *Prompted brand awareness and TV ads, November 1985–April 1988*

Figure 1 tracks the monthly prompted brand awareness figures for the Alliance & Leicester since the merger in October 1985.

It can be seen that the first burst of the Fry and Laurie campaign coincided with a sharp rise in awareness. This fell away in December and January, but rose again sharply during the second burst in February. By March 1988 prompted awareness had reached 70 per cent — so meeting early the targets set for the end of that year.

Spontaneous awareness, and so saliency, also rose in response to the TV advertising campaign (see Figure 2).

By March 1988 then, the Alliance & Leicester had risen to No. 6 in the prompted awareness league from No. 8 in April of the previous year. Similarly, in the spontaneous awareness league they rose to fifth in March 1988 from seventh.

The case for the Alliance & Leicester's brand awareness being affected by the recent TV campaign is supported by considering the pattern of their advertising awareness during this period. Figure 3 shows spontaneous and prompted TV advertising awareness responding sharply during the bursts, both more than doubling during the first burst.

Following the encouraging results of the first burst, a simple econometric modelling exercise was carried out to assess the relationship between advertising and prompted brand awareness. (The spontaneous awareness data was judged not sufficiently robust to model, due to its smaller sample sizes.)

The model investigated the effect of the Alliance & Leicester's press and TV advertising, taking into account past levels of awareness.

It explains 79 per cent of the variation in prompted brand awareness over 1986

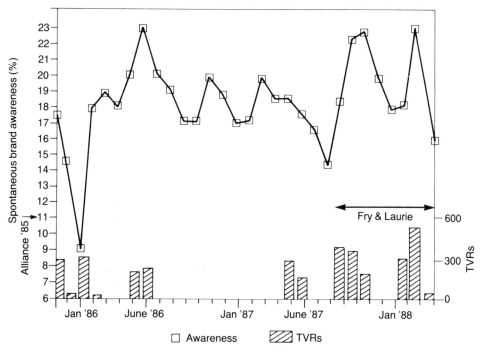

Figure 2. *Spontaneous brand awareness and TV ads, November 1985–April 1988*

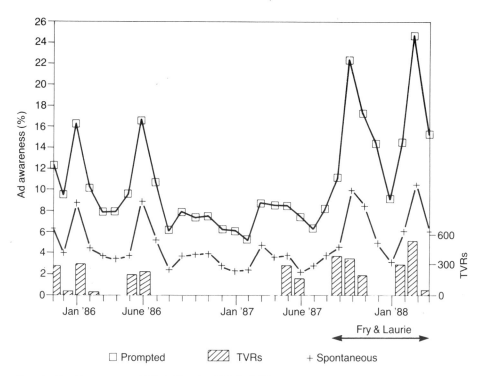

Figure 3. *Advertising awareness and TV ads, November 1985–April 1988*

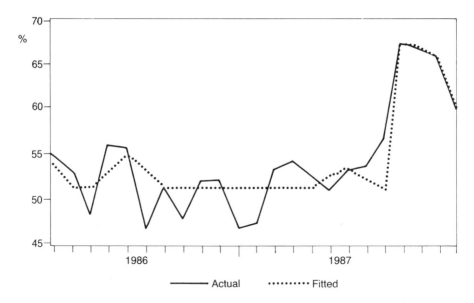

Figure 4. *Alliance & Leicester prompted awareness (actual v. fitted)*

and 1987. Figure 4 compares awareness predicted by the model with actual awareness achieved.

Only TV advertising was shown to have any effect in increasing prompted awareness over 1986 and 1987, which supports the role for TV advertising in building the brand, and press advertising for tactical promotion of specific products to those people actively seeking rates.

The first burst of advertising was shown to have shifted the base level of prompted awareness (i.e. the residual level the Society achieves in the absence of advertising or other marketing activity) from an estimated 51 per cent to 58 per cent, suggesting that the advertising was indeed achieving its task of building 'the brand'.

Brand Imagery

It was hoped that the Alliance & Leicester would increase its score over a range of brand imagery dimensions in line with its overall increase in awareness. These dimensions would include reputation, and friendliness, which are of key importance for the vast majority of building-society users.

Quantitative research, carried out on behalf of the Alliance & Leicester by Survey and Fieldwork International, monitored a series of image dimensions for the Society before and during the first burst of the campaign. This survey involved street interviews in towns containing a branch of the Alliance & Leicester. It showed a consistent improvement in scores across the bank of imagery data – implying that the overall image of the Society is improving along with awareness (Table 3).

While a short-term business effect was not directly anticipated, these results did

TABLE 3:   BRANCH LOCATION SURVEY: IMAGE OF BUILDING SOCIETIES

Base	August 517 %	Oct./Nov. 384 %	
Agree that A & L:			
Has a good reputation	48	55	*
Has personality	20	31	**
Gives straightforward advice	28	38	**
Has sense of humour	15	37	**
Has modern outlook	39	54	**
Gives better rate of interest	8	12	**
Is friendly and helpful	31	38	*
Speaks my kind of language	22	32	*

*   Significant at 95% significance level
** Significant at 99% significance level

Source: Survey and Fieldwork International

suggest that the recent campaign may have influenced receipts and mortgage advances.

However, because of the wide variety of economic factors that may affect a building society's performance — and of course the dramatic effect of the stock market crash during this period — it is impossible to draw any firm conclusions from simple observation of net receipts and mortgage advances (Figure 5). Econometric analysis was thus used to isolate advertising's contribution.

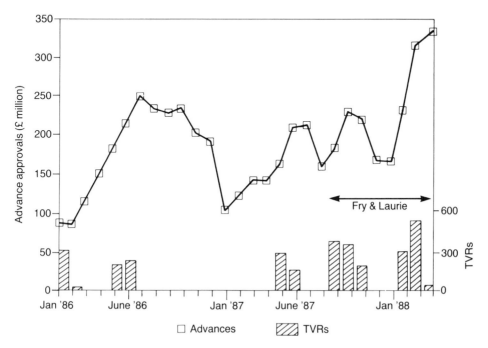

Figure 5. *Net mortgage advance approvals and TV ads, January 1985 – April 1988*

THE ECONOMETRIC ANALYSIS

A detailed explanation of how the analysis was performed is given in the Appendix. Preliminary work showed that the Alliance & Leicester responds to the influence of factors external to the building-society market (e.g. economic factors) to the same extent as the top 16 societies as a whole. We have therefore analysed the variation in the level of their net receipts in terms of these overall movements in top-16 net receipts and any prevalent marketing factors.

Whilst it is money earned on mortgage advances that finally generates profits for the Society, mortgage advances are only monitored at time of approval. For a number of reasons, wide variations in time can occur between this approval and the original customer application. This makes it difficult to relate mortgage advances to the timing of advertising, and for that reason net receipts are the subject of the model.

The key marketing factors for consideration in this market are:

Interest rates − A & L and competitive (top-16 average)
TV advertising − A & L and competitive (top-16 total)
Press advertising − A & L and competitive (top-16 total)
Access conditions
Distribution − number of branches.

Interest rates are many and varied in this market, differing not only from society to society but within a society from one account type to another and even dependent on the account balance. The building societies themselves each calculate the average interest rate that they have paid across all their accounts in any one month. This average rate is weighted by the total balances in a particular type of account and clearly provides the most comprehensive measure of each society's competitive rate position at any point in time. We used this average rate to measure the Alliance & Leicester's rate competitiveness and the average rate paid by the top 16 societies in total as a measure of competitive interest rates.

Television advertising was measured in TVRs, press advertising in terms of £ spent (MEAL).

It was not possible to compile and summarise any measure of competitive access conditions (period of notice necessary if withdrawals are not to receive an interest penalty) as they are extremely diverse and no logical system exists whereby they might be weighted together. The Alliance & Leicester did however considerably worsen their access conditions in January 1988, when those of other societies remained unchanged, and we were able to measure the impact of this.

Apart from an initial shake-out immediately after the merger, the number of Alliance & Leicester branches has changed very little over the last two years. Branch numbers would not therefore contribute in explaining net receipt movements and were excluded from the analysis. Figure 6 shows Alliance & Leicester actual monthly receipts plotted against our model's estimates of receipts, given the factors it incorporates. It explains 89 per cent of the variation in net receipts since January 1986, in general fitting the data reasonably well but having a tendency to wrongly predict during major privatisation issues.

In any month these factors are (in no particular order):

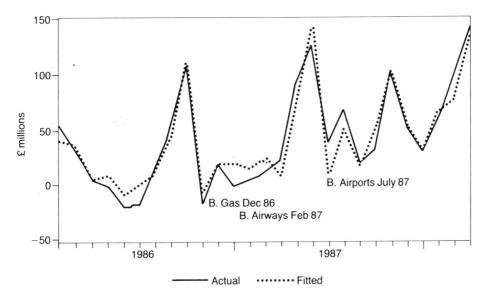

Figure 6. *Alliance & Leicester net receipts (actual v. fitted)*

1. Share of top-16 receipts

The model estimates that the Alliance & Leicester receives 6.8 per cent of total top-16 net receipts plus or minus an amount resulting from their own or competitive marketing activity (6.8 per cent is however statistically equivalent given confidence limits to their actual top-16 asset share of 6.63 per cent). Therefore, their underlying share of top-16 net receipts is directly proportional to their size.

2. Interest rates

Relative interest rates were very important. Equivalent interest-rate changes by the A & L and its competitors have equal and opposite effects. Only a short-term effect of interest-rate changes was evident. This reflects the intense competition and the difficulty of maintaining a rate advantage for any length of time.

3. Advertising

Press: It was not possible to separate the effect on the Alliance & Leicester's receipts of either the Alliance & Leicester or competitive press advertising from the effect of their respective interest-rate movements. As most press advertising tends to be informative of rates, this was not surprising. It does however make it impossible to assess its cost-effectiveness independently!

Television: Even though the Fry and Laurie television campaign is a relatively recent one aimed principally at the long-term building of the Alliance & Leicester brand, it has already had considerable success in generating extra receipts for the Society. (In contrast it was not possible to establish an effect on receipts of the earlier 'Shadows' campaign.)

The impact on receipts of the Fry and Laurie campaign begins to occur in the month following transmission of the advertising. Thirty per cent of any one month's impact continues to affect receipts in the following month, i.e. two months or more after the advertising was screened.

The first burst of the campaign included the stock market crash in October 1987. The Alliance & Leicester's receipts then shot ahead of the market during November with the net result that (all else remaining equal) a higher volume of receipts came in (TVR for TVR) during this first burst than during the second burst in February–March 1988.

How far can we realistically attribute this to advertising? All competitive activity in terms of total market movements, interest rates and advertising have already been explicitly accounted for in the model. There was no change in the Alliance & Leicester's access conditions, neither did their branches suddenly mushroom. The only variable in the marketing mix substantially different from its historic level at that time is advertising. Whilst there may be an element of fortuitous timing in this, it would none the less seem to be a real effect of advertising.

Over the two bursts of the Fry and Laurie campaign, model simulations show that the £2.6 million spent by the Alliance & Leicester on television advertising generated an extra 28 per cent additional receipts for them. Sixty-six per cent of this was during the first burst, 34 per cent during the second.

There is typically a gross margin of 1.5 per cent between interest paid by the Society on deposits and that charged on mortgages. This means that the £2.6 million advertising budget has already generated an extra £2.18 million gross margin. On average, however, savings balances remain with the Alliance & Leicester for three years generating this 1.5 per cent in each of these three years – an ultimate total of 4.5 per cent of the original receipts due to advertising.

Against such a long-term anticipated payback period, to have virtually covered the advertising costs in only eight months is a substantial achievement. At the end of three years it will have paid back several times.

4. *Changed access conditions – January 1988*
These led to a drop in net receipts, all else remaining equal, of £27.9 million.

How is the Advertising Working?

CREATING BRAND AWARENESS

To investigate the way in which the campaign is working to create awareness for the brand, an extensive qualitative post-test of the advertising was undertaken in November 1987.

This consisted of eight standard group discussions of eight respondents each, conducted in Scotland, Newcastle, Sutton Coldfield and London, amongst men and women ranging from 18–60. All were building-society users, either with savings accounts or mortgages. Overall the campaign was very much enjoyed and seen as appealing and humorous. This element of fun and humour appeared to be working, as hoped, to raise the ads above the category of what is perceived as 'boring' low-interest financial advertising. So the humour worked to create the impact and involvement necessary to raise awareness of a brand in this sector.

The response to the advertising was fundamentally affected by people's attitudes to Fry and Laurie. The majority enjoyed the characters and their very distinctive brand of humour. They understood the nature of the caricature relationship between them, with Fry the 'funny man' and Laurie the 'straight man'.

Their involvement in the advertising was enhanced by the fact that they could identify with Laurie − and feel the ads actually vindicated their personal decision to play safe and save with a building society. Many would actually relate anecdotes of reckless friends − like Fry − who would try to be 'too clever' with their money.

The richness and complexity of the executions added to these people's enjoyment, so that respondents would wish to see the ads again to enjoy more of the humour.

PRODUCING BUSINESS RESULTS

The following model depicts how the campaign might be hypothesised to work (amongst new and existing account holders).

NEW ACCOUNT OPENERS		EXISTING A & L INVESTORS
Stage 1	Awareness	Reminding
Stage 2	Put on candidate list	Engender loyalty
Stage 3	Enter branch	
Stage 4	Converting enquiries to business	

Advertising potentially has a role to play at Stages 1 and 2 in creating awareness, and at Stage 4 by motivating the branch staff.

We have already discussed qualitative evidence for the success of the campaign in generating awareness, what about the other stages?

Figure 7 considers net new account openings and would indicate that the Alliance & Leicester certainly performed well over the advertised period. However, a lack of equivalent industry figures for this measure makes it impossible to estimate the market share achieved. Further, comparison against previous years' performance is difficult because of changes in the savings market as a whole, for example more flexible building-society accounts are now in competition with traditional bank current accounts.

Further, research findings do provide circumstantial evidence to account for the mechanism of the advertising effect on new account openings.

The study held across towns where there was an Alliance & Leicester branch before the beginning of the campaign and during the first burst showed the Alliance & Leicester improving in the number of mentions it scored on the question: 'Which Building Society would you open another account with?' If the argument that building societies are viewed as essentially 'the same' holds, then gaining a position on someone's 'candidate list' would be a key factor in determining choice of society. Gains in candidate-list mentions during the advertising could then lead to business gains for the Alliance & Leicester.

The Alliance & Leicester moved in league position from seventh to fourth amongst all adults (see Table 4). Interestingly it also moved from third to first amongst respondents aware of the Alliance & Leicester − suggesting that this effect was not *solely* dependent on increasing awareness of the Society, but was the result of an improvement in overall image of the Society (see Table 5).

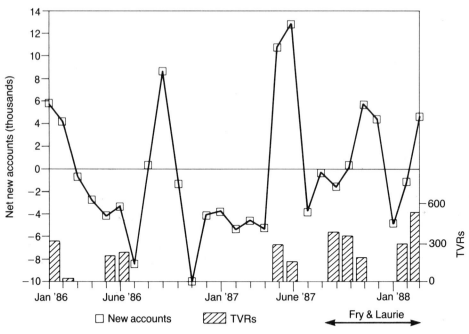

Figure 7. *Net new accounts and TV ads, January 1986–March 1988*

TABLE 4: TOTAL MENTIONS OF BUILDING SOCIETIES RESPONDENTS WOULD OPEN
AN ACCOUNT WITH. 1: ALL RESPONDENTS

League	Aug. 1987 %	League	Oct.–Nov. 1987 %
1. Abbey National	17	1. Halifax	16
2. Halifax	16	2. Abbey National	12
3. Nationwide	10	3. Nationwide	11
4. Leeds Permanent	8	4. A & L	10
5. Bradford and Bingley	6	5. Anglia	7
6. Woolwich	6	6. Leeds Permanent	6
7. A & L	5	7. Woolwich	6

Note: Alliance & Leicester results significant at 99% confidence level.
Source: Survey and Fieldwork International

Further evidence of the effect of the advertising on new accounts openings comes from a survey conducted by the Alliance & Leicester within its branches, before the advertising (24–29 August) and during the advertising (26 October–7 November).
Investors were asked how they had heard of the Society (Table 6).
This was accompanied by an impressive rise in awareness recorded in the same survey of Alliance & Leicester TV advertising amongst new investors.

	Aug.	*Oct./Nov.*
Awareness of A & L TV advertising (all new accounts)	26%	60% —

TABLE 5: TOTAL MENTIONS OF BUILDING SOCIETIES RESPONDENTS WOULD OPEN AN ACCOUNT WITH. 2: RESPONDENTS AWARE OF THE ALLIANCE & LEICESTER

League	Aug. 1987 %	League	Oct.–Nov. 1987 %
1. Halifax	14	1. A & L	15
2. Abbey National	12	2. Halifax	14
3. A & L	9	3. Nationwide	11
4. Leeds Permanent	8	4. Abbey National	9
5. Nationwide	7	5. Anglia	8
6. Woolwich	5	6. Woolwich	6

Note: Alliance & Leicester results at 99% confidence level.
Source: Survey and Fieldwork International

TABLE 6: RESULTS OF INVESTOR SURVEY

How had new investors heard of the Society?	Aug. %	Oct.–Nov. %
From family/friends	20	14
Noticed branch	21	12
From advertising	11	19
From professional adviser	3	5

Base: August – 250. October–November – 258.

There would seem to be some evidence then of a connection between the advertising and new account openings. It is, however, impossible to estimate the scale of this effect, and to what extent the business success may be due to existing customer activity.

A final mechanism by which the advertising may affect customer behaviour is the influence of the campaign on the Society's staff at branch level. This would affect new account openings, and possibly existing members. It was an important objective for the A & L that the staff themselves should feel positive towards the campaign. It was felt that this would build staff loyalty and motivate them in their day-to-day relationships with their customers.

A self-completion questionnaire was therefore sent to 1668 members of staff during November 1987, asking their opinion of the advertising. The questionnaire also sought their 'front-line' views of how their business might have been affected in the past month. The results were very encouraging, with a strong majority enjoying the advertising and feeling that the A & L as an organisation is making progress. There was also an impression from the staff that business had increased, with more people coming into the branch and more new enquiries (Table 7).

It would seem that increased awareness and business levels have fulfilled their objective in helping to motivate branch staff and thereby increase branch efficiency.

TABLE 7:   BRANCH STAFF SURVEY

Have staff seen the new TV ads?	
Yes	91%
No	9%
Do they feel the A & L is making progress?	
Agree	53%
Disagree	24%
Has the number of people entering the branch increased?	
Yes	46%
Stayed the same	50%
No, decreased	3%
Has the number of enquiries increased?	
Yes	45%
No, stayed the same	51%
No, decreased	2%

SUMMARY

The TV advertising campaign launched in September 1987 had a tough job to do for the Alliance & Leicester. Prompted awareness of the merged society was only 54 per cent, less than pre-merger levels for the Alliance Society, and placing the Alliance & Leicester in a league position of ninth when by asset size they should have been sixth.

The aim of the campaign was primarily to reverse this trend. Over a relatively short period (seven months) awareness leaped up to peak at 70 per cent, a league position of sixth. This achievement is all the more remarkable in the context of the difficulty of the advertising sector in which the campaign operates. Financial advertising is seen by most as turgid and boring − to create impact for a financial brand is a much harder task than within a sector such as drink or food that inherently interests and involves the watcher. The Fry and Laurie campaign cleverly took advantage of the mood of the times to create this involvment for *itself*, despite the product category.

The business success of the campaign, as isolated by the econometric analysis, was unexpected for what is essentially a long-term brand-building campaign.

It is extremely impressive then that during the advertised period the campaign contributed 28 per cent of the Alliance & Leicester's net receipts. This has already almost paid for the TV campaign, with the prospect of generating considerable additional profits over the next two years.

APPENDIX

General

Alliance & Leicester Net Receipts – How we modelled their movements

Typically the Alliance & Leicester's performance is compared to that of the top 16 building societies as a whole with their asset share of 6.63 per cent being the basis on which comparison is made (i.e., all else remaining equal, they should take in 6.63 per cent of top-16 net receipts). That tradition has been maintained here with the Alliance & Leicester's net receipts being analysed in relation to those of the top 16 building societies as a whole.

Building society net receipts, both for the market as a whole and for individual societies, can gyrate wildly from month to month influenced by a range of economic factors and by activity in the banking and other financial sectors. Which are the key influential factors and exactly what they contribute is very complex and would therefore be extremely difficult to measure with any confidence. There is however no a priori reason to expect any of these 'external' influences affecting the market as a whole to effect differing impacts on individual societies other than in proportion to their own base share of the building-society business.

In general, where this type of assumption is valid, an analysis of market share can provide a relatively straightforward means of investigating the impact of any marketing activity. The validity of this assumption can in fact be tested by regressing one product's sales on those of the total market and on a number of relevant marketing variables. Market share may then be a data restriction arising naturally from this regression. Total market sales act as a scaling factor and embodiment of the influence of all factors external to the market. If appropriate (i.e. the product in question is not affected more than the market by these external factors), both sides of the equation can be divided by total market sales to give market share, which is then expressed purely in terms of marketing factors.

In this market, because there are months where net receipts can be negative, the traditional calculation of market share is inappropriate. Whereas 3 per cent of a positive total market net receipt might be viewed as underperformance, only 3 per cent of a subsequent outflow of funds (negative net receipt) would be highly desirable! A scale of market share in this market is not therefore symmetric.

We were however able to use the principle outlined above to test whether the Alliance & Leicester's receipts followed the general pattern of the market. This showed that on average, the Alliance & Leicester received 6.8 per cent of top-16 building-society net receipts in any month (which then rose or fell depending on their own or competitive marketing activity).

As the Alliance & Leicester's asset share is actually 6.63 per cent, this was close enough, given acceptable statistical error, to indicate that our initial assumption that the Alliance & Leicester was subject to external factors in proportion to its own share of top-16 business to be fully justified (95 per cent confidence limits are 5.2 per cent to 8.4 per cent). Yet because, as explained, market share is meaningless, total market receipts remained on the right-hand side of the equation as a scaling factor and as an explainer of the overall market gyrations.

This meant that in attempting to isolate the effect of television advertising we were estimating a regression equation of the form:

A & L net = Total   + A & L interest + Competitive Interest rate + advertising
receipts   market   rate
              net receipts

Technical

DATA AND SOURCES

1. Net receipts for the Alliance & Leicester and the total for the top 16 building societies.
    Source: Alliance & Leicester/Building Societies Association.
2. Average interest rate paid on deposits − Alliance & Leicester/Top 16 average.
    Source: Alliance & Leicester/Building Societies Association.
3. Television advertising − TVRs. BARB weekly TV audience report.
4. Press advertising spend − MEAL.

TECHNICAL DESCRIPTION OF THE MODEL

We estimated a model of the Alliance & Leicester's net receipts using the technique of ordinary least squares.

The model performs satisfactorily on a range of statistical tests for its *fit* and *specification*. It does however exhibit relatively large errors at times when there are privatisation share issues. British Gas in December 1986, British Airways in February 1987 and British Airports in July 1987. BP, coming in the wake of the stock market crash, was a relative non-event and does not show up.

The model was estimated using monthly data from January 1986 to April 1988 (27 data points after allowing for lagged responses to interest-rate changes etc.).

The final preferred model was tested down from the following general form:

> *In any period* −
> A & L net receipts = + C
> > + Top-16 net receipts
> > + A & L average deposit-rate lags (0 and 1).
> > + Top-16 average deposit-rate lags (0 and 1).
> > + A & L TV advertising lags (0, 1).
> > + Competitive TV advertising lags (0, 1).
> > + A & L press advertising lags (0, 1).
> > + Competitive press advertising lags (0, 1).
> > + A & L bond issues (M./J. 87 and A./S./O. 86).
> > + A & L changed access conditions.

Press advertising is interest-rate dominated and as such its effect was inseparable from movements in interest rates themselves.

Competitive TV advertising by the top 16 building societies had no systematic identifiable effect on the A & L.

The final preferred model explains 89 per cent of the variation in the Alliance & Leicester's net receipts between January 1986 and April 1988. All the parameters are well defined at the 95 per cent level and the model performs satisfactorily against a range of other statistical tests.

The following mnemonics have been used:

C	Constant or intercept term.
ALNR	Alliance & Leicester net receipts (£ million).
T16NR	Total net receipts of the top 16 building societies. (£ million)
ALRI	Alliance & Leicester average deposit rate (%).
T16RI	Top 16 average deposit rate (%).
RI	Relative interest rate ALR1/T16RI.
DRI	RI − RI (−1).
BI	A & L bond issue in May−June 1987.
LF3	Adstock of TVRs for A & L's Laurie and Fry campaign (retention rate from month to month = 0.3).
ACC	Dummy variable for A & L's changed access conditions.
SMC	Effect on A & L over and above that on the building-society market of the stock market crash.
DD	= 45.24 SMC − 27.87 ACC.

ORDINARY LEAST SQUARES EQUATION
The equation of the preferred OLS model is as follows:
Dependent variable is ALNR

Variable	Coefficient	t-statistic
C	−10.573	−2.06
T16NR	0.068	7.89
DRI	5136.7	7.12
BI	87.928	7.80
LF3 (−1)	0.039	1.95
DD	1.000	3.16

Standard diagnostic tests for the *fit* and *specification* of this model are as follows:

R squared	0.91
R̄ squared	0.89
Durbin−Watson statistic	1.92
S.E of regression	15.18
(mean of dep. var. 40.18, S.D 44.8)	
Sum of squared residuals	4838.43

LM (1)	0.06	C.V. = 3.84
LM (4)	0.51	C.V. = 9.49
ARCH (1)	1.52	C.V. = 3.84
ARCH (2)	2.24	C.V. = 9.49
Variance ratio test	3.09	C.V. F(11,7) = 3.60
Chow – Parameter stability	1.81	C.V. F(6,21) = 2.57
Chow – Post-sample predictive failure	0.68	C.V. F(7,21) = 2.49

14

Alliance & Leicester
First Time Buyer Mortgages

INTRODUCTION

During a boom year in 1988, clouds were growing on the horizon of the mortgage market. All forecasts pointed towards a tough 1989 with mortgage supply far outstripping demand. Profitability was seriously threatened.

This case study attempts to demonstrate an unusual use of advertising; namely, to change the purchasing process for a particular product. In this case, first time buyer mortgages.

In essence, it shows how an understanding of the basic needs of a market enabled the Alliance & Leicester and BMP to develop advertising that, through altering the purchase process, fundamentally changed the structure and profitability of the Alliance & Leicester's first time buyer business.

BACKGROUND TO THE MORTGAGE MARKET

The mortgage market showed steady growth during the 1980s. In particular, this growth was driven by:

1. Abolition of the Bank of England 'corset' controls allowing entry into the market of the clearing banks.
2. The consequent increase in competition leading to mortgage suppliers having to court demand rather than vice versa.
3. The reduction in the base rate of tax from 33% to 25% and the highest rate from 83% to 40%.
4. The consequent increasing demand fuelling steady house price inflation that, like many other asset markets, was self-sustaining (at least short-term). Average house prices rose by over 80% between 1981 and 1987. In real terms, this represented an increase of nearly 30%.

In 1986 and 1987, the mortgage interest rate began to fall and, as with the stock market, property became seen as an investment that couldn't lose. In 1988, house buying fever continued. Multiple tax relief* was abolished (in the budget in April) for purchases after August. At the same time, the mortgage interest rate dropped to 9.5% (its lowest level since 1978). Demand was such that the average house price rose by nearly 25% across the first eight months of the year. And then, over three months, the mortgage interest rate rose by 34% to 12.75%. In combination with the sudden drop in demand post-August caused by the pulling forward of around 50,000 loans (Bank of England estimate) to beat multiple tax relief abolition, the bubble seemed about to burst (cf Stock Market crash 1987). Indeed, October 1988 saw the first reduction in absolute average house prices for almost a decade.

Forecasters were predicting a gloomy future:

'We would now argue forcefully that this heady atmosphere of euphoria and complete confidence in the housing market has been replaced savagely with an atmosphere of uncertainty and even fear as the severe turns of the screw...take effect.
The current consensus is that turnover will be down 50% on 1988 in the coming year. This unprecedentedly severe depression in the housing market is going to have grave consequences for the strategies and profitability of financial service companies' (PA Consulting Group).

BUILDING SOCIETIES IN THE MORTGAGE MARKET

The sudden emergence of strong competition in the mortgage market caused major problems for all building societies. In particular, the varying cost of wholesale funding versus retail funding**(building societies almost wholly depend on retail funding) sent the share of mortgage lending accounted for by building societies plunging from the 'traditional' 80%+ to 50% by 1987. The building societies fought back through competitive rates and new products. Deferred interest, capped, fixed rate and discount mortgages appeared.

By 1988, they had clawed back to around 60% share of the market. Despite this loss of share during the 1980s, the overall market growth more than compensated in terms of volume. In 1980, building societies lent c£9 billion. In 1988, this had risen to c£41 billion.

Amidst the doom and gloom of the 1989 forecasts, there was one sign of hope. The sudden huge rises in the bank base rate gave the building societies the chance to lag the increase in their interest rate on retail investments and thereby profitably undercut bank mortgage rates on the basis of cheap retail funding. Even if the market as a whole was about to plunge, at least the building societies would get a larger share of whatever was around (A & L, DoE).

* Tax relief on the first £30,000 of a mortgage had historically been granted per person rather than per property (except for married couples). Hence, two people getting a joint mortgage on a single house were entitled to tax relief on £60,000. In the 1988 budget, the Chancellor announced that from August, the £30,000 would apply per property rather than per person. This removed the tax advantage for multiple purchasers and made many change their plans so that they would beat the August deadline.
** Wholesale funding basically involves funding lending activity using money from the international finance markets. Retail funding involves funding lending activity with your customers' savings. The relative price of money from these two sources (ie the interest rate the bank/building society has to pay in order to get it) varies according to the domestic and foreign economic climate. During the mid 1980s, wholesale funding tended to be cheaper, favouring the banks over the building societies.

TYPES OF BORROWERS

Borrowers in the mortgage market fall into two sectors – owner occupiers (ie people who already have a mortgage) and first time buyers (FTBs).

Each year, these two sectors are of roughly equal size, each accounting for 50% ±2% of the total market.

In all other respects they differ enormously.

Owner occupiers are an extremely heterogeneous group, ranging from a couple with a new baby who need an extra bedroom to a 65 year old retiring to a bungalow by the sea. They tend to be reasonably confident about mortgages since they have been through it all before and hence tend to be either highly price conscious or highly inert (ie stick with the lender they are already with). They are generally quite unprofitable lending targets since they will already have an endowment policy (ie little commission to be made).

In contrast, FTBs are a fairly homogeneous group. The vast majority (c80%) are aged 20 – 40 and in social classes C1 C2 (c70%). In terms of lifestage, they are almost all either young independents, nearly-weds or newly-weds.

The idea of borrowing, what is to them an enormous sum of money, is quite daunting and they are consequently less likely to be purely price sensitive. They are also a potentially more profitable group through commission earnings on new endowment policies.

For these reasons, the Alliance & Leicester chose to focus their 1989 mortgage activity on FTBs (J Levin, *House Purchase Decision*, A & L, DoE).

DIRECT VERSUS INDIRECT

In addition to the owner occupier/FTB segmentation, borrowers can be classified according to whether they come to you direct (ie via a branch) or indirect (ie via an intermediary/broker).

A direct FTB is by far the most profitable borrower of all. Almost always, a direct FTB will arrange not only the loan but also his endowment policy and household insurance policy with the building society, resulting in the building society getting all the commission. Consequently, a direct FTB is over twice as profitable as an indirect FTB (or any owner occupier borrower).

In addition to being highly profitable, direct FTBs are believed to be of further value since they tend to be more loyal and more susceptible to cross-selling of other products.

'You get a better rapport since you chat to them about their whole situation and they trust you more' (Alliance & Leicester Branch Manager).

In the light of these attractions and the forecast decline in volume (and hence profit) in the market, the Alliance & Leicester chose to concentrate specifically on attracting FTBs to them *direct*.

'With the forecast cooling of demand in 1989, direct FTBs will be very important – not only from the insurance commission that can be won but because they become our 'existing borrowers' for the future' (A & L Marketing Plan 1988).

It was felt that a new product targeted purely at FTBs would be needed as a vehicle to attract FTBs to the branches. (Once in the branch, it was up to the branch staff to offer them the mortgage most suited to their individual circumstances from the Alliance & Leicester's portfolio of mortgages and this might well not be the new product).

DEVELOPING THE PRODUCT

Extensive qualitative research was carried out amongst potential and recent FTBs. The research showed:

— All borrowers describe the process of buying a house as a major, traumatic event.
— The whole experience is frightening since it is unknown territory.
— FTBs find their main problem is not knowing where to find guidance.
— Overall, they simply seek reassurance. (BMP, *Mortgage Concept Research*; IMR, *Large Mortgage Research*; J Levin, House Purchase Decision).

Based on this research and the requirement to attract FTBs direct, the Alliance & Leicester developed a product that was reasonably price competitive, gave a physical manifestation of help and advice and was only available through branches.
Specifically, the Smarter Starter mortgage offered FTBs:

— 0.5% off the mortgage rate for the first year.
— 100% mortgage if necessary.
— A filofax filled with useful advice – 'The Homebuyer's Planner'.
— A mortgage guarantee card – ie a card confirming their mortgage offer.

The product was made available in branch in January 1989 and was planned to run until December 1989.

BUSINESS OBJECTIVE

To maximise profitability of the Alliance & Leicester first time buyer mortgage business.

MARKETING OBJECTIVES

1. To secure at least asset share of the FTB mortgage market.*
2. To significantly improve the proportion of FTB business that is direct.

THE ADVERTISING STRATEGY

Existing qualitative research suggested that the basic need of the FTB was not centred simply on the cheapest deal possible but rather on reassurance/help and advice.

The research on the product itself suggested that Smarter Starter was not seen as *significantly* better than the competitive offerings. Consequently, it seemed unlikely that the product points alone would be sufficient support for the product followed simply by a statement 'only available from Alliance & Leicester branches'.

The key objective of attracting people direct to branches suggested that we should take a closer look at the way in which FTBs went about choosing the source of their mortgage. Further qualitative research was undertaken to gain an understanding of the FTB mortgage purchase process.

In summary, the research showed that, in general, FTBs got their mortgage from one of three sources:

1. The estate agent in-house broker.
2. The building society with which they already have a relationship.
3. The default option of Halifax or Abbey National, ie FTBs who had no good reason to go to any particular society tended to end up with the one they had heard of most and hence trusted most. Eventually, the majority ended up going to the 'Big 2'.

In addition, there were three key findings of the qualitative research that proved to be the inspiration for the advertising strategy. These were:

1. There was an overwhelming belief amongst FTBs that 'First you find the house you want then you get a mortgage'.
2. Almost every FTB accepted the first mortgage he/she was offered. Indeed, the first 'father figure' they came across tended to make the sale.

'Most respondents appeared not to have gone through the formalities of seeing a building society manager before looking at property. Once they'd found a property they were then very susceptible to an estate agent offering to sort out the details of a mortgage. Most respondents were very happy to take the line of least resistance, which could well mean taking a mortgage from the first person to offer them one' (Pegram Walters Associates).

---

* Asset share is defined on the basis of the Alliance & Leicester's share of the total fixed assets of all building societies. In effect, it represents the Alliance & Leicester's 'expected share' of any building society market. Asset share is an extremely slow-moving variable. Across the time period of this paper it can be treated as static. The Alliance & Leicester's asset share is 6.6%.

3.   Their major worries as far as mortgages were concerned were quite simplistic:

—   Will anyone give me a mortgage?
—   If yes, how much will they lend me?

Desk research confirmed most of the qualitative findings. Firstly, that a growing number of FTBs were indeed being snapped up by the increasing number of estate agents with brokers in-house:

TABLE 1

Mortgage arranged	% FTB mortgages arranged through estate agent/broker
Pre April 1986	11
Apr 1986 – Sep 1987	19
Oct 1987 – Oct 1988	24

Source: A & L

Secondly, the fact that most societies have always performed close to asset share in the FTBs market suggested that there was a proportion of FTBs that tended to use the society with whom they already had an investment relationship.

Thirdly, the 'default option' conclusion was confirmed by the disproportionate number of direct FTBs at both Halifax and Abbey National. Indeed, the data below on the UK's top five building societies tend to support the hypothesis that, in general, the bigger the society is, the better it does amongst these 'floating' buyers.

TABLE 2:   FTB MORTGAGES OPENED OCTOBER 1987 – OCTOBER 1988

	% who came direct	% asset share
Halifax	61	28
Abbey National	73	22
Nationwide Anglia	48	17
Woolwich	36	8
Alliance & Leicester	34	7
Total market	51	100

Source: Financial Research Survey/DoE

(NB The remaining 25% of FTBs (who didn't go direct or to estate agent/brokers) sourced their loans from independent advisors, their local authority or claimed not to remember what the source was.

The FTBs going through independent advisors represents the more sophisticated/confident end of the FTB market. They were not likely to be influenced by advertising since they went to the advisor precisely to let him/her find them the best deal. Those going to the local authority were buying their council house. Neither group were part of our target market.

The 'don't knows' we can only speculate about).

From the research, we constructed a simplified model of the FTB mortgage purchase process:

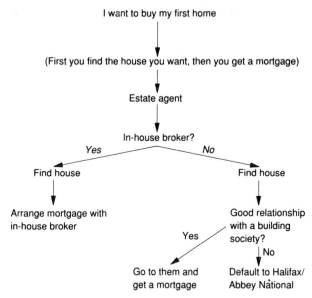

From this, we decided that ideally, the advertising should get people to come direct to the Alliance & Leicester by:

— Giving a good reason not to use the estate agent/broker.
— Giving a good reason to come to the Alliance & Leicester rather than your existing building society.
— Giving a good reason to come to the Alliance & Leicester rather than default.

The only way we could do this was to get the Alliance & Leicester into the flow chart above the estate agent. In other words, make the Alliance & Leicester the first 'father figure' FTBs came across.

When we put together all the key findings, the solution became clear:

1. FTBs need reassurance.
2. The key things they want reassurance on are:

   — Will anyone give me a mortgage?
   — How much will they lend me?

3. *They believe (wrongly) that before you can get an answer to these questions you have to find a home.*
4. They tend to accept the first mortgage they are offered.
5. We want them to come to us first.

↓

'Get your mortgage sorted out before you find a house'.

What we had arrived at was a positioning that we hoped would turn the purchase process on its head by inverting the key attitude that caused it ie:

I want to buy my first home

First you find a mortgage, then you find a house

Alliance & Leicester

Mortgage sorted out   (They've said they'll give
                         me a mortgage)

                        (They've told me what
                         I can afford)

Estate agent

Find house (finalise mortgage)

Furthermore, we were inverting the purchase process by offering FTBs exactly what they needed. The worries of buying their first home were weighing heavily on their shoulders. The Alliance & Leicester were offering to remove some of those worries and, what is more, were offering to remove them *now*, before they'd found a home.

It is worth noting that the idea of 'sorting your mortgage out first' is *not* a product specific feature of the Smarter Starter mortgage. In other words, we believed we had found a proposition for the Alliance & Leicester itself rather than simply a product specific proposition.

THE CREATIVE BRIEF

Advertising Objectives

— To attract FTBs to come to the Alliance & Leicester direct.
— To continue to build awareness of the Alliance & Leicester.

Strategy

By communicating that at the Alliance & Leicester you can get your first mortgage sorted out before you find a house.

Target Market

FTBs, 20 – 40, C1C2. Unconfident; frightened about the whole process of buying their first house.

Proposition

It's never too early to get your first mortgage.

Support

You can do it before you find your house.
Product points:

—   0.5% off.
—   100% mortgages.
—   Home buyers' planner.

Guidelines

This ad must change the way FTBs believe you have to go about getting a
mortgage. Currently, they think they have to have found a house and had an offer
of £x accepted before they can go and try to borrow £x from a lender. We need to
convince them that they can get their mortgage worries out of the way *before* they
start the traumatic process of house buying. The product points are additional
'sweeteners' and should be dealt with as such. They must not be allowed to cloud
the main thrust of the ad.

THE AD

The ad had to attract FTBs direct whilst fitting into the campaign using Stephen Fry
and Hugh Laurie that had been running since 1987.
   The creative team took the proposition literally and wrote a script that involved
using 12 year old boy lookalikes for Fry and Laurie with Fry and Laurie's real
voices dubbed on. The ad was called 'Young Ones'.

THE MEDIA STRATEGY

The ambitious nature of the marketing and advertising objectives together with the
requirement to build awareness quickly so as to maximise response in a tough year
meant that TV was the natural medium.
   We targeted C1C2 adults aged 20 – 40 and aimed for programmes that
maximised their conversion versus all adults.
   The advertising was deployed in two bursts.

Burst 1: 6/2/89 – 19/3/89; 579 60 second Adult TVRs; £1.8m.
Burst 2: 22/5/89 – 30/6/89; 311 60 second Adult TVRs; £1.2m.

Client: Alliance & Leicester *Title:* Young Ones

VISION

SOUND

In the sitting room of a country house two boys of about twelve years of age sit in large chairs having an earnest discussion.

One of them bears an uncanny resemblance to Hugh Laurie, the other is an exact twelve year old replica of Stephen Fry.

The young Fry puts down a frothy drink with a curly straw sticking out of it and leans forward in his chair.

Boy Fry: So Mostyn, you've decided to start thinking about your first mortgage.

Boy Laurie: Yes, well actually I've already got one.

Boy Fry: Have you? Bit quick off the mark aren't we?

Boy Laurie: Yes, well at the Alliance & Leicester you can get your mortgage sorted out before you've found a home.

Boy Fry: Really.

The young Fry lifts his glass and the straw sticks up his nose.

Young Laurie stands up casually, takes something out of his inside pocket and hands it to the young Fry.

He realises his mistake and hands him a Smarter Starter pack from another pocket.

Young Fry flicks through the filofax.

Young Laurie paces the room as he speaks.

He walks up to a built-in bar and picks up a cocktail shaker.

Boy Laurie: Yes, saves wasting time once you have found a place, and they give half percent off your first year's repayments, they'll even give you one of these.

Boy Fry: Big Ears Goes Fishing?

Boy Laurie: What? Oh, here.
Its got everything you need to know about buying a house.

Boy Fry: Hmm! You don't think you're a bit young to start worrying about mortgages do you?

Boy Laurie: Well I think there comes a time in a man's life when he has to leave behind his wild, reckless years and face up to his responsibilities like a mature and sensible adult.
Another milkshake?

Boy Fry: Oh don't mind if I do.

Boy Laurie: Choccy topping?

Boy Fry: Oh I don't know.

Boy Laurie: Go on!

Boy Fry: No I couldn't.

Boy Laurie: Course you can.

Boy Fry: Oh well perhaps just a little bit.

Boy Laurie: (Fades) That's what I like to hear.

Cut to Alliance & Leicester logo.
Super: Building Society.
Freephone 100

MVO: Get your mortgage before you've found your house and be a smarter investor with the Alliance & Leicester.

'YOUNG ONES'

RESULTS

Background*

The basic market picture has already been dealt with. The actual figures are listed in Table 3.

TABLE 3: NUMBER OF LOANS ADVANCED (000s)

	1985	1986	1987	1988
Market total	1,450	1,620	2,000	2,100
Building Societies	1,090	1,230	1,047	1,230

Source: DoE

* The Alliance Building Society and the Leicester Building Society merged at the end of 1985. A single computer system/data base was not fully operational until towards the end of 1986. The specific data we required for this case study (ie FTB/owner occupier splits; direct/indirect splits) are therefore only available for 1987 onwards. Hence, we will in general be dealing only with the period 1987 – 1989 (inclusive).

An added complication is that monthly data was unavailable for 1987 and 1988 (apparently, getting hold of it would involve about a week of mainframe computer time) hence, econometric modelling was not feasible since we would only have 12 data points. We hope that (as you will see), there are a sufficient number of clear indications of the advertising effect without it.

Against FTBs, The Alliance & Leicester had a particularly successful year in 1988 (see Table 4). This strong performance was largely caused by two factors:

1. The abolition of multiple mortgage tax relief. This pulled purchases forward particularly in the Midlands and the South where house prices dictated that FTB purchases were very often based on more than one income. The Alliance & Leicester are particularly strong in the Midlands and the South (the Alliance originated in Hove, the Leicester (obviously) in Leicester).

2. In 1988, the Alliance & Leicester was the only building society offering a 1% discount on a FTB product through intermediaries. This was an effective short-term way to buy market share. In both 1987 and 1989 the Alliance & Leicester was offering products through intermediaries at price parity with other major societies. (As we shall see later, increased discounting in the market in 1989 meant Smarter Starter was actually *more expensive* than its competitors).

TABLE 4:   NUMBER OF FTB LOANS ADVANCED (000s)

	1987	1988
Building Societies	505	580
A & L	27.05	40.20
A & L share (%)	5.36	6.93

Source: DoE, A&L

However, in both 1987 and 1988 the profitability of this FTB business was strongly affected by the proportion who came from indirect sources. Although the Alliance & Leicester's performance here looks poor versus the market average, we have already seen that compared with societies of similar size, this performance is quite normal.

The 1988 figure for both the market and the Alliance & Leicester illustrates the effect estate agents were having on direct business compared with 1987.

TABLE 5:   PERCENTAGE OF FTB ADVANCES DIRECT

	1987	1988
Building Societies	55	51
A & L	39	34

Source: FRS, A&L

As predicted, the overall market plummeted from 2,100,000 advances in 1988 to 1,300,000 in 1989, a drop of 38%. However, the retail versus wholesale funding advantage mentioned earlier meant that the building societies were less badly hit. Even so, the total number of advances through building societies dropped by 23% from 1,230,000 in 1988 to 950,000 in 1989.

Within the FTB market, the Alliance & Leicester managed to achieve their first marketing objective of gaining at least asset share, despite the backlash swing of business away from their areas of strength due to the pulling forward of multiple purchases from 1989 into 1988.

TABLE 6: NUMBER OF FTB LOANS ADVANCED (000s)

	1987	1988	1989
Building Societies	505	580	498
A & L	27.05	40.20	34.80
A & L share (%)	5.36	6.93	7.00

Source: DoE, A&L

What is more exciting is the Alliance & Leicester's performance against direct FTBs.

TABLE 7: NUMBER OF DIRECT FTB LOANS ADVANCED (000s)

	1987		1988		1989	
	No	Index	No	Index	No	Index
Building Societies	278	100	296	107	259	93
A & L	10.55	100	13.67	130	18.00	171

Source: DoE, A&L

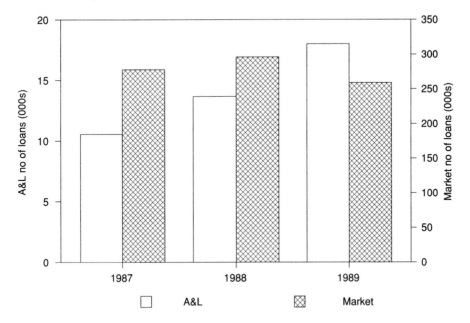

Figure 1. *Alliance & Leicester direct FTB business 1987 – 1989*
Source: A&L, DoE and FRS

What was also clear was the enormous swing in favour of direct business within the Alliance & Leicester in 1989 compared with 1988 or 1987.

TABLE 8: PERCENTAGE OF FTB LOANS WHICH WERE ADVANCED DIRECT

	1987	1988	1989
Building Societies	55	51	52
A & L	39	34	52

Source: FRS, A&L

It was quite clear that the marketing objectives (and, as we shall see later, the business objective) had been achieved. The rest of this case study deals with the evidence that supports the role the advertising played in causing this structural change in the Alliance & Leicester FTB business.

THE PERFORMANCE OF SMARTER STARTER AND OTHER SIGNS OF ADVERTISING EFFECT

Rate of Application for Smarter Starter Mortgages

Applications for Smarter Starter were made at the rate of 28.5 per day during January when the product was available with branch window support but not advertising. From February to December, applications were made at the rate of 67.7 per day. Between February and July (ie during the advertising) the rate of application was 76.5 per day (Figure 2). The poor performance of Smarter Starter in January is due only in small part to seasonality. The main reason is that direct applications were still accounting for only 33% of all applications.*

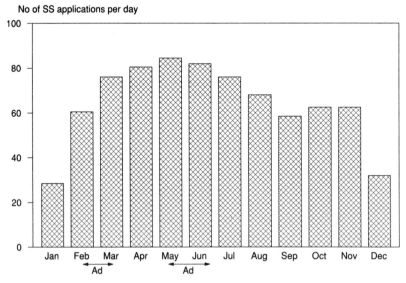

Figure 2. *Smarter Starter daily applications 1989*
Source: A&L

* The drop-off in December is due partly to seasonality and partly to the fact that the Smarter Starter advances officially terminated in December, hence branch staff were reluctant to allow applications. This is clarified by Figure 3 showing Smarter Starter advances by month.

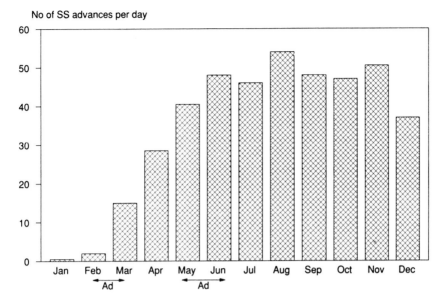

Figure 3. *Smarter Starter daily advances 1989*
Source: A&L

TABLE 9: FTB APPLICATIONS PER DAY 1989

	Jan		Feb – Dec	
	No	%	No	%
Total	120.9	100	157.4	100
All direct	40.3	33	91.9	58
Smarter Starter	28.5	23	67.7	43

It should be strongly noted that the increased demand for Smarter Starter is just a by-product of the true advertising effect which was to attract more FTBs to the branches.

Proportion of Direct Business Accounted for by Smarter Starter

Smarter Starter accounted for 73% of all Alliance & Leicester's direct FTB applications in 1989. It also accounted for 60% of all direct FTB advances. However, bearing in mind the time that elapses between applications and advances*, we can see that Smarter Starter advances were only coming through in large numbers from April onwards.

During April – December 1989, Smarter Starter accounted for 69% of all Alliance & Leicester's direct FTB advances. The remaining 30% of advances were accounted for by the Alliance & Leicester's other mortgage products (eg Professional Mortgage Plan, Fixed Rate etc). It was up to the branch staff to offer the 'right' product to the customer. Interestingly, Smarter Starter accounted

* An application is counted as a customer 'applying' to the society to be considered for a mortgage (ie filling in an application form). An advance happens when the mortgage loan is actually 'advanced' to the vendors solicitor on completion of the house purchase.

for c70% of direct applications in January as well as across the rest of the year (Figure 4) demonstrating quite clearly

1. Out of the portfolio of mortgages the branch staff could offer FTBs, Smarter Starter was the 'right' product for around three quarters of them whether there was advertising or not.
2. The additional FTBs attracted to the branches following the advertising were a reasonably representative sample of all FTBs, ie Smarter Starter was the 'right' product for around three quarters of them too.

It seems clear that the change in performance of the Alliance & Leicester's direct FTB business was advertising rather than product related.

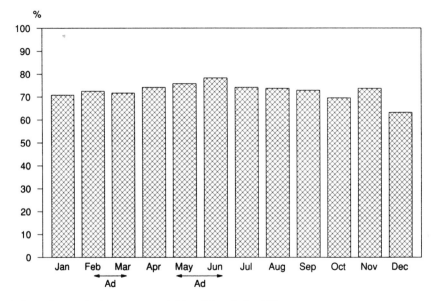

Figure 4. *Smarter Starter applications as percentage of all direct FTB applications 1989*
Source: A&L

Lag Time from Application to Advance

On average, the gap between applying for a mortgage (direct or indirect) and the advance being issued is seven weeks. For Smarter Starter (which represented 69% of direct FTB advances post the advertising), this average gap was 13 weeks. This gives the first indication that the mortgage was indeed being 'sorted out' (ie applied for) much earlier in the purchase process. The advertising seemed to be changing behaviour exactly as we had hoped it would.

The Change in Profile of Alliance & Leicester FTB Business 1987 – 1989.

Figures 5 and 6 show the huge shift towards direct FTB business that occurred when we ran the advertising. The direct/indirect profile has been almost reversed versus 1987 and 1988. (NB Due to the lack of monthly data, we have assumed

1987 and 1988 were constant throughout. There is no reason we know of to suggest that this isn't a very fair approximation to the truth).

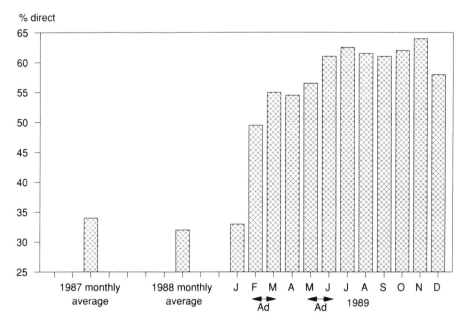

Figure 5. *Alliance & Leicester profile of FTB business, number of applications*
Source: A&L

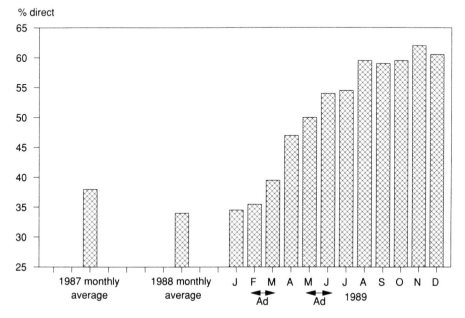

Figure 6. *Alliance & Leicester profile of FTB business, number of loans advanced*
Source: A&L

The Change in Profile of Alliance & Leicester Business in 1989

Figure 7 demonstrates a number of points quite clearly:

1. The proportion of *applications* that came direct increased immediately the advertising was on air.
2. The proportion of *advances* that came direct lagged well behind applications and didn't catch up until after April. It seems clear that the increasing proportion of direct advances is precisely as a result of the increasing proportion of direct applications that began in February.
3. Once the effect of the increasing proportion of direct applications is allowed to fully materialise (ie May onwards), the proportion of direct advances reaches 58% (cf 1987 39%; 1988 34%; market in 1989 52%).

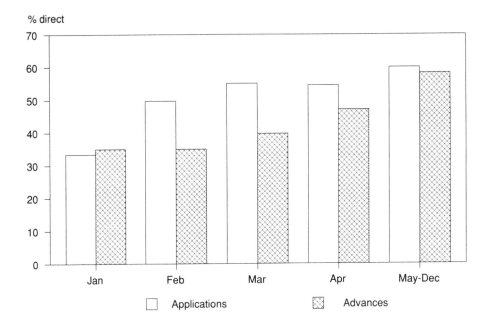

Figure 7. *Alliance & Leicester profile of FTB business, applications versus advances, 1989*
Source: A&L

The Increasing Number of Direct FTB Applications in 1989

Figure 8 shows the number of direct FTB applications made by month to the Alliance & Leicester between 1987 and 1989. The increase, starting in February 1989, is quite dramatic. If we assume that the total number of applications in the market would behave in a similar way to the total number of advances in the market then Figure 9 illustrates the change that began in February 1989 even more clearly by allowing for market growth of 6.5% in 1988 and decline of 12.5% in 1989.

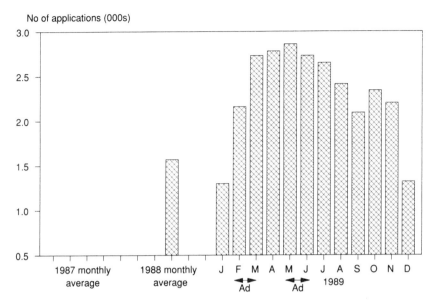

Figure 8. *Alliance & Leicester direct FTB business 1987 – 1989, number of applications by month*
Source: A&L

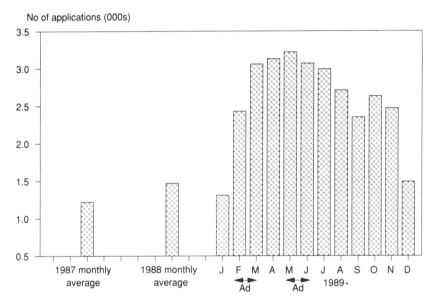

Figure 9. *Alliance & Leicester direct FTB business 1987 – 1989, number of applications by month corrected for market growth/decline*
Source: A&L

The Increasing Number of Direct FTB Advances in 1989

Figure 10 shows the number of direct FTB advances made monthly by the Alliance & Leicester between 1987 and 1989. The dramatic increase in 1989 is clear.

Figure 11 attempts to show this change even more clearly by correcting for the market growth of 6.5% in 1988 and decline of 12.5% in 1989.

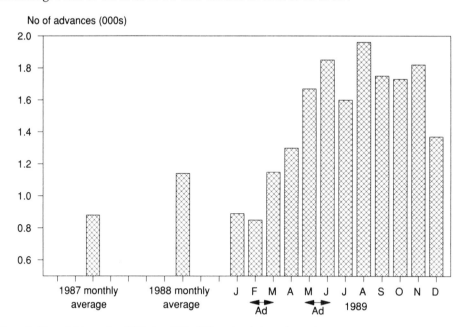

Figure 10. *Alliance & Leicester direct FTB business 1987 – 1989, number of advances by month*
Source: A&L

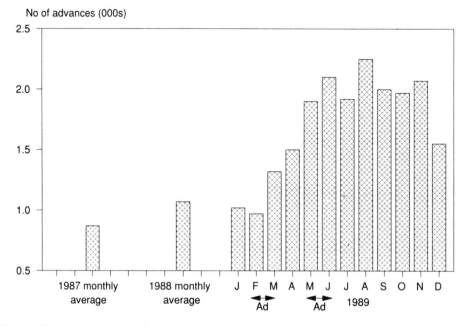

Figure 11. *Alliance & Leicester direct FTB business 1987 – 1989, number of advances by month corrected for market growth/decline*
Source: A&L

(NB Once again, the lack of monthly data has necessitated a simple averaging of the annual figures for 1987 and 1988. Whilst seasonality would serve to alter the 'shape' of 1987 and 1988 it would not alter the point the figures make).

Quantitative Post Test

The Alliance & Leicester conducted a quantitative post test of all its ads in November 1989. This was five months after 'Young Ones' had been on air.

The test was conducted in halls and involved showing each ad to a separate sample (of ABC1C2D adults, aged 18 – 65, men and women) followed by a battery of questions. Table 10 shows the results for 'Young Ones'.

TABLE 10

	Total sample %	18 – 44 year olds %
(Base	105	66)
Main message (unprompted)		
Apply for a mortgage early/ before you find a house	45	55
Easy to get a mortgage/ quick decision	21	18
Opinion of ad		
Original	82	85
Memorable	58	56
Amusing	85	91
Confusing	13	14
Seen advert before?		
Yes	89	92
Willing to see again?		
Yes	64	65

Source: Sample Surveys

All measures appeared encouragingly high. It is gratifying that advertising awareness (albeit highly prompted) is at c90% so long after the ad ran. It is also particularly pleasing that unprompted main message communication was so clear in an ad that was also so enjoyable and entertaining.

Survey Amongst Smarter Starter Purchasers

The Alliance & Leicester conducted a telephone survey in January 1990 amongst 30 people who had taken up a Smarter Starter mortgage. Whilst the base is small, the signs are still extremely positive regarding the effects of the advertising.

TABLE 11

	%
Did you get your mortgage sorted out before you started looking for a home?	
Yes	93
No	7
Were you surprised that you could do this?	
Yes	73
No	27

These two results are particularly enlightening since the advertising was the only part of the promotional mix suggesting that they sort their mortgage out first.

Respondents were then asked why Smarter Starter had appealed to them. There were five possible answers and respondents could choose as many or as few as they liked.

TABLE 12

	%
Smarter Starter appealed to me because...	
It made the whole process of buying a house easier	73
It offered me help and advice	47
It gave me half % off	23
It gave a homebuyers planner	3
It gave me a mortgage guarantee card	0

There were clear signs that we were meeting the basic need of the bulk of FTBs. Next we asked them about the advertising.

TABLE 13

	%
Did you see any advertising for the Smarter Starter Mortgage?	
Yes	97
No	3
Did you like it?	
Yes	93
No	3
Don't know	3

Despite the fact that the ad had been off air for seven months, the respondents were asked unprompted open-ended questions about main message. Their answers when taken in conjunction with their previous responses certainly suggest that the ad was influential in shaping their purchasing behaviour. Below are some representative responses.

What was the ad trying to put over?

'Never too early to go there'.

'Get your mortgage arranged before you go looking for a house' (x5).

'Start planning before you get your home'.

'Start early. It's never too early to get a mortgage'.

'Friendly and helpful. If you go there they take the hassle out'.

'Help you a lot better'.

'Simple and easy. Even a school kid could do it'.

'You feel about five years old when you start buying a house. You don't have to worry – they know everything. Do it in one fell swoop. This is the simple package'.

'Their mortgages are so simple even two kids could understand it'.

Finally, respondents were asked how they felt when they first decided to buy their first home. Again, some representative quotes:

'I had no idea. It put me off looking to begin with'.

'Frightened. Terrified'.

'I didn't understand much'.

'Not confident'.

'I didn't know what to do' (1989 Smarter Starter User Survey).

It seemed that, at least for this sample, the advertising had worked precisely as hoped. They were nervous and unconfident. They needed reassurance and help. The advertising offered it to them and they took it.

Survey Amongst Branch Managers

One of the roles of the advertising is to engender support amongst branch staff. Particularly in this case where potential customers were coming into the branch looking for an arm around their shoulder, it was important that the staff were motivated about the product and about selling it.

We conducted a telephone survey of ten area branch managers who between them were responsible for over 30 branches. The results are summarised below.*

All had seen the advertising on TV.
All agreed that 'it had worked'.
All agreed that more FTBs came into branches compared with 1988.
All agreed that more FTBs came to get a mortgage before they started looking for a house.
All agreed that through this they had significantly improved their endowment and household insurance business.

Did customers talk about the advertising at all?

'They never stopped. They joke and then they relax'.

'Yes, all the time'.

'Yes, we got jokes like, excuse me, do you sell milkshakes?'.

'Yes, we got lots of people going on about it'.

'Many would say something like, we saw the ad and we liked it'.

What did you think of the ad?

'Very proud. Lots of comment from people who had seen it'.

'I got excellent feedback. It gave a good modern image. Shows we're interested in young people'.

'We feel it's well thought out. The advertising generally has done a hell of a lot for improving our name and awareness. Smarter Starter gave a professional image – a professional society giving good advice'.

'Good. Not too staid and stuffy. A sense of humour. Not just throwing figures at you which blinds you and cheapens it'.

How do you feel the advertising worked?

'It brought the FTBs in and gave us the chance to quote to them'.

'It really helped awareness'.

'The advertising meant we got a lot more enquiries from FTBs who hadn't bought their house yet'.

'It helps you get a banter with the customers'.

'Specifically, it got people to arrange their mortgage before they got a house'.

*Three points to note: (1) We represented ourselves as a research company working for the A & L, *not* the ad agency, (2) We told the respondents that they had been randomly selected and their names would not be recorded, (3) Branch managers are not slow to complain when they are unhappy!

These levels of support and enthusiasm were a vital component of the success of the advertising. If the customer had come in looking for reassurance and help and had found instead uninspired and uninterested staff, we feel sure the results in this case study would look significantly less impressive than they in fact do.

ELIMINATING OTHER VARIABLES

Distribution

Distribution in this market changes very little over time as it is directly related to number of branches. Hence, neither the Alliance & Leicester not the competitors' distribution altered to any significant degree in 1989.

Price

The 0.5% discount offered for the first year was in fact less than many competitors were offering FTBs. In 1989, FTBs were being offered a 1% discount by building societies who between them accounted for c70% of the market. Much of the major building societies mortgage advertising was focused solely on these discounts. The Smarter Starter interest rate was 0.23% *higher* than the average for the top 14 building societies.

We would argue from this, that if anything, the product's price should have had a negative influence on its success.

Branch Window Activity

Branch window activity started in January when Smarter Starter was available without advertising support. The window material did not include any mention of 'sort your mortgage out first'. The lag time of 13 weeks between application and advance compared to the more normal 7 weeks suggests that this *was* being communicated by something. It can only have been the advertising. In addition, the window material did not appear to increase the proportion or number of applications coming direct. This did not increase until February when advertising broke.

Other Advertising

Alliance & Leicester – The Alliance & Leicester ran only one other TV ad in 1989. It was a general investment ad and received 310 TVRs in July.

The Alliance & Leicester runs press advertising sporadically throughout every year concentrating mainly on investment interest rates.

We see no reason why this would affect the direct/indirect profile of FTBs.

Competitive – The total media spend by all building societies was up by 27% in 1989 versus 1988 and the Alliance & Leicester's share of voice dropped from 9.5% in 1988 to 7.4% in 1989.

In addition MEAL suggests that Halifax, Abbey National, Nationwide Anglia, The Woolwich, The Leeds and National & Provincial were all advertising mortgages on TV in 1989 with comparable spends to the Alliance & Leicester.

If anything, the competitive advertising environment in 1989 was even tougher than in 1988.

In summary, it seems reasonable, on the basis of the evidence, to suggest that much of the Smarter Starter mortgages success and, far more importantly, *all* of the credit for the structural change in the Alliance & Leicester FTB direct/indirect profile lies with the advertising.

PROFITABILITY

What follows is a gross profit calculation for the Alliance & Leicester's FTB business in 1989. At the end of it we will take into account the advertising cost.

The average FTB loan in 1989 was £33,000. After taking into account all administration costs, discounts and, of course the cost of funding the loan, the Alliance & Leicester make a gross profit of £990 on a *direct* loan of £33,000 and £440 on an *indirect* loan of £33,000 in the first year. The difference between these two profit figures is largely accounted for by commission earnings on the endowment policy and household insurance policy.*

After the first year, the gross profits on direct and indirect loans become more similar since endowment commission earnings are a one-off commission. The annual gross profit after year one is £490 *indirect*, £540 *direct* (on a £33,000 loan).

The average FTB loan has a life of five years. However, the majority of loans are replaced immediately by a new loan for the FTBs second property. The majority of second loans are taken out with the same lender as supplied the first loan. Hence, a FTB new to the Alliance & Leicester continues to generate profit for them, on average, for well over five years. For the purposes of profit calculation, we will look at first year and five year profits only.

In 1989, the Alliance & Leicester made a first year gross profit of £25.2m from new FTBs. Taking into account the average five year lifespan of a FTB mortgage, the Alliance & Leicester will make a total profit of £97m from FTBs who came to them in 1989.

There are a number of ways in which one could forecast what would have happened in 1989 without the advertising. One route is to suggest an extremely optimistic view and extremely pessimistic view and to assume that what really would have happened in 1989 if there had been no advertising would lie between these two extremes.

In both the optimistic and pessimistic scenarios, we shall assume that the direct/indirect profile would have been 35%/65%. This is justified, we believe, by the following points:

1. The market profile of direct/indirect remained at roughly 50%/50% in 1989.

---

*The vast majority(c85%) of direct FTBs took out an endowment policy and household policy at the same time as arranging their mortgage. The profit figures take into account the c15% who took out a repayment mortgage rather than an endowment mortgage.

2. The Alliance & Leicester profile of direct/indirect was 33%/67% in January 1989 (and 34%/66% in 1988).
3. The profile of the society closest in size to the Alliance & Leicester (ie The Woolwich) was c35%/65% in 1988 and remained there in 1989.

Optimistic View of 1989 without Advertising

Same number of loans (ie 34,800) but split 35%/65%. In this case, first year profit would have been £22.0m. Five year profit would have been £92.7m.

Pessimistic View of 1989 without Advertising

Same number of loans indirect (ie 16,800) but a split of 35%/65% giving only 9,050 direct loans. In this case, first year profit would have been £16.4m. Five year profit would have been £68.8m. Hence, the additional first year profit generated by the advertising lies between £3.2m and £8.8m. Over five years, the advertising generated additional profit of between £4.3m and £28.2m. The midpoint between the optimistic and pessimistic view may give the best estimate of what really would have happened. If this is the case, then the advertising generated £6.0m of additional gross profit in the first year and will generate £16.25m additional profit over five years.

With an advertising cost of £3m, 'Young Ones' was clearly a good investment for the Alliance & Leicester in terms of mortgage profit. What should also not be ignored are the additional benefits in terms of increased customer loyalty through so many extra new branch/customer relationships.

An additional point to note is that, because of the change in direct/indirect profile, the average first year profit per FTB loan from the Alliance & Leicester was £565 in 1988 and £725 in 1989. In other words the average FTB was 28% more valuable to the Alliance & Leicester in 1989 than he/she was in 1988 despite the average size of the loan being almost identical.

SUMMARY

There were two needs to be met here. One was the FTBs need for reassurance – the removal of worries. The other was the Alliance & Leicester's need to maximise profitability in a market forecast to be significantly depressed versus the year before.

By offering to sort out the mortgage first, before you've found your house, we were able to meet both.

The FTB was worried about his mortgage *now*, the Alliance & Leicester would remove those worries *now*.

The Alliance & Leicester's need was met by the influence of this offering on the purchase process. By effectively inverting the purchase process, the advertising generated a disproportionate number of doubly profitable and far more loyal customers.

The Alliance & Leicester's FTB business generated more gross profit in 1989 than in 1988 (£25.2m versus £22.7m) despite the forecasts for the market proving to be true.

Even taking the most optimistic view of what would have happened to the Alliance & Leicester's FTB business if there had been no advertising, calculations show that the advertising was an investment that paid back within one year and will continue to generate additional profits for the Alliance & Leicester for over five years into the future. Furthermore, the 18,000 direct FTBs the society attracted in 1989 count for more than just increased mortgage profits. They represent 18,000 additional customers who have a relationship with a specific branch. The value of this in future cross-selling of investment products, further mortgages and other loans cannot even be estimated.

CONCLUSION

The magnitude of the task we set the advertising should not be underestimated. Basic logic has always suggested to FTBs that the first step they have to take in buying their first home is finding it. Only then, when they can tell the lender what it is they want to buy, would the lender tell them whether or not he/she would loan the money.

We were telling FTBs, through our advertising, that their basic logic was flawed. We were telling them that the Alliance & Leicester would sort their mortgage out now, even though they didn't yet know what they were going to buy. No wonder c75% of 'Smarter Starters' were 'surprised that they could do this'.

We needed advertising that had to fundamentally change the way they went about purchasing their first home. To do this it had to have a powerful proposition and an impactful execution. We believe the advertising we developed had both. The results certainly seem to suggest we are right.

For the Alliance & Leicester, 1989 proved to be a remarkable year. In a market that was panicking, discounted mortgages and pure interest rate advertising were the normal reactions. They, however, developed a sensible product and we promoted it in a way that made the Alliance & Leicester the society that met the true needs of the market − not necessarily the lowest rate but lots of help, lots of advice and lots of reassurance. Looking at their first year and five year profit in 1989 (higher not only than in 1988, but their highest *ever*) the Alliance & Leicester certainly think we got it right.

15

Kensington Palace

INTRODUCTION

This paper sets out to describe how Doyle Dane Bernbach addressed the problem of how to promote the Royal Palaces in the care of The Department of the Environment, and how the advertising developed and paid for itself through the incremental visitors – and thus entrance fees – which it generated.

BACKGROUND

At the beginning of 1984 the Government set up a new body called 'The Historic Buildings and Monuments Commission' (English Heritage) to look after most of the historic houses, castles, monuments in the country, which had previously been in the care of the Department of the Environment.

Six so-called 'Royal Palaces' were left in the care of the Department of the Environment. They are:

1. The Tower of London.
2. Hampton Court.
3. Kensington Palace.
4. Kew Palace.
5. Osborne House.
6. Banqueting House, Whitehall.

Prior to setting up the commission, any marketing/promotion of these buildings had been done on an ad hoc basis. It now became the aim of the Department of the Environment to produce a cohesive marketing strategy for 'the six'.

Corporate vs. Individual Promotion

The option existed to promote the palaces jointly on a 'corporate' platform or singly. The latter was felt to be the better approach.

1. There was no readily understandable way accurately to group the buildings. While they were commonly referred to in The Department as Royal Palaces – one (the Banqueting House) is actually only part of a building; Osborne is more a country house than a palace.

    A corporate terminology could mislead the consumer.

2. There was no major unifying link between the buildings. They all had, at one time, been associated with Royalty, but to a varied extent; some (Kew Palace, the Banqueting House) could not justifiably be promoted on this platform.

3. Little could be said about each separate building in an advertisement for them all.

4. The buildings differed widely in

    — Level of awareness.
    — Present number of visitors.
    — What they offer.
    — Potential to accommodate increased numbers.
    — Opening times.
    — Accessibility.

Client, COI and agency believed it made better sense to examine each in more detail as potential advertising subjects.

THE OPPORTUNITY FOR INDIVIDUAL PROMOTION

The Tower of London and Hampton Court

Both buildings needed little promotion, as they already had high awareness among tourists, and attracted large numbers of visitors.

Kensington Palace

This building offered immediate potential for an increase in visitor levels.

— It had strong links with present-day royalty.
— It was conveniently sited in Central London.
— It had the Court Dress Collection on permanent display.
— It offered considerable scope for increasing awareness that it was open to the public, so putting it on the tourist map.

Kew Palace

Again, there was limited awareness of the building, and the fact that it was open to the public. However, it was felt that less potential existed as an advertised site:

— There was nothing sufficiently compelling about the building's history, current-day attraction, or architecture to make it a major tourist attraction.

— As such, major advertising might well raise expectations to a level at which they would not be fulfilled.
— The location was less convenient for tourists.

Banqueting Hall, Whitehall

Again, while current awareness was low, its historical and current-day connections did not provide sufficient potential for development as a major tourist attraction.

Osborne House

The location of this building made its promotion rather a different proposition to that of other palaces. While each of the other five might be promoted effectively to a localised and sizeable target audience in London, the location of Osborne House on the Isle of Wight gave this palace less potential for increasing visitor numbers.

Overview

It was agreed that Kensington Palace was the building with greatest potential for generating increased visitors at the low level of funding available, and that all efforts should be put behind this single site.

ADVERTISING STRATEGY

Target Audience

This falls into two distinct categories:

— Tourists to London, both from overseas and of domestic origin.
— London and home counties residents.

Based on previous 'dipstick' research it was agreed that, of the two categories, the first one would be the most important as it appeared that the majority of visitors to Kensington Palace were tourists to London.

Objective

The advertising objective that was set was to create awareness of Kensington Palace and its attractions, and persuade the target audience to visit the site.

Proposition

Kensington Palace ranks among the most interesting places to visit in London.

Supports

— Court Dress Collection.
— State Apartments.

Executional Guidelines

Two executional guidelines were set. Firstly, in view of how the key target audience has been defined, the execution would need to be both clear and simple, enabling as many people as possible to understand its message. Secondly, it was felt that it was desirable to show both where the Palace was situated and when it was open.

MEDIA STRATEGY

The complete range of media were assessed against a number of criteria:

1. Mass coverage of all adults – both from overseas and the UK.
2. Coverage of the key campaign period at an acceptable weight. This campaign was to vary from normal campaigns in so far as tourists are a continuously moving target audience. Usually a campaign is aimed at a segment of adults who can be reached in a variety of ways – for example, through their regular readership of a paper or magazine, or via posters in their area of abode. Thus, to a certain extent, the number of people is fixed, and coverage and frequency can be built up against that fixed market. The number of tourists, however, is not fixed, as some leave, more arrive and the number coming and going varies across the year.

    Therefore, the advertising would not only need to cover as much of the prime tourist season as affordable in order to ensure the broadest possible coverage but would also have to be maintained at a relatively heavy weight as there was very limited time to build coverage and frequency.
3. Regional flexibility.
4. Cost effectiveness against the target audience.

Media Plan

The agency recommended a plan that was a combination of London Transport tube cards and four sheet posters. Research from a number of sources (BTA, TGI and London Transport's own research) showed that the tube would provide high coverage of tourists as well as reaching a large number of people who live in and around London. Furthermore, the fact that people are in effect 'contained' in the enclosed environment of the tube while they are travelling on it increases the opportunity they have of seeing the tube card, and also allows them the time to take in the necessary details (where the Palace is and what are the opening times).

The posters, a specially designed tourist package, were used to upweight the prime tourist and high turnover stations both in terms of places of interest and British Rail stations. An additional upweight was included to cover stations close to the Palace.

Due to the low level of funding available and the previously agreed requirement to maintain a relatively heavy weight, the campaign was limited to July and August, when there are the highest number of visitors to London. Indeed, it was only possible to afford posters for one month, so August was chosen, again because it had a higher number of visitors.

·KENSINGTON·
·PALACE·

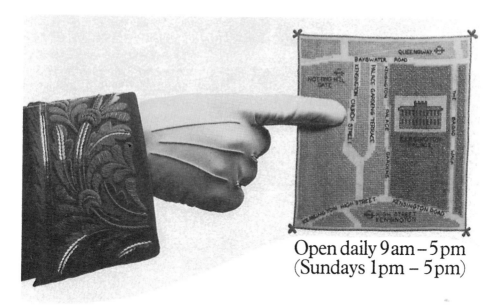

Open daily 9am – 5pm
(Sundays 1pm – 5pm)

· VISIT THE STATE APARTMENTS ·
·AND COURT DRESS COLLECTION·

Department of the Environment.

Issued by the Department of the Environment and the Central Office of Information 1985. Printed in UK for Her Majesty's Stationery Office Dd 8831469 ENV1 J0083N

THE RESULTS

The results were extremely encouraging. Admission figures were significantly up on the previous year (by over 25 000); in fact, they set new records for Kensington Palace.

TABLE 1:   ADMISSIONS FOR KENSINGTON PALACE

000s	1984	1985	% Increase
July	15.9	24.8	+ 56.0
August	16.2	26.6	+ 64.2
September	13.3	19.1	+ 43.6
TOTAL	45.4	70.5	+ 55.3

Source: DOE

Not surprisingly, August was the month which showed the largest increase in admissions as this was the period during which both the tube cards and the poster ran. Furthermore the effect of the advertising was likely to be subject to a 'time-lag'. It would take time for people to see it, for it to register and then for people to act on it. (However, in the case of Kensington Palace, this time-lag would be relatively short as tourists would only be in the country for a limited period.) Interestingly, September (by when the advertising was officially meant to have finished) also showed a significant increase in admissions. This increase was probably due to two key factors: the 'time-lag' effect of the advertising (as previously described) and the fact that many of the tube cards and posters were not taken down or replaced until a later date.

CONSUMER RESEARCH

During the campaign period it was agreed that some relatively small-scale consumer research would be conducted among visitors to Kensington Palace.
    The objectives of this research were:

1.   To find out where visitors to Kensington Palace came from.
2.   To find out how they came to know about Kensington Palace.
3.   To find out how they travelled to Kensington Palace.

The results were to be used to help in planning future activity for Kensington Palace, and secondly they were to be used as a guide to assessing the effectiveness of the advertising. The research was conducted between the 15 and 21 July, and 17 and 25 August. Sample sizes obtained were 230 and 229 respectively.
    The research showed that the overwhelming majority of visitors during this period were foreigners (94 per cent). This confirmed the necessity for making the execution clear and simple, so that as many people as possible would understand it.
    Respondents were asked where they had heard about Kensington Palace. (It should be noted that no specific questions were asked about their source of awareness of the fact that Kensington Palace was open to the public, or what had prompted their visit.)

TABLE 2: Q: WHERE DID YOU HEAR ABOUT KENSINGTON PALACE?
(SPONTANEOUS)

	TOTAL	15–21 July	17–25 August
Poster on Underground station/tube card	12.5	8	17
Poster in Kensington Gardens	11	6	16
Guide book	23.5	28	19
Leaflet	11	13	9
Friends	13	11	15
Always known	29	30	28

Source: Consumer Research

The results show that 12 per cent of people spontaneously mentioned the advertising as their source of knowledge. This is very high, given the general nature of the question and people's tendency not to mention advertising. Looking at the results over the two periods they also show the build-up of the effect of advertising.

On a prompted level the scores for the advertising increase again reflecting the build-up of the effect.

TABLE 3: Q: WHAT GUIDES/LEAFLETS/ADVERTISING HAVE YOU SEEN FOR
KENSINGTON PALACE?

	% TOTAL	15–21 July	17–25 August
Underground tube card	32.5	27	38
Underground poster	24	23	25
Historic Royal Houses (DOE)	37.5	40	35
Kensington Gardens poster	44	50	38
Visitors Guide to Central London (LT)	43.5	45	42

Source: Consumer Research

Looking at the mode of travel used to get to the Palace confirmed the appropriateness of the media chosen, as the majority of people came by foot or tube.

TABLE 4: Q: HOW DID YOU TRAVEL TO KENSINGTON PALACE?

	TOTAL	15–21 July	17–25 August
Foot	65.5	72	59
Tube	36	30	42
Bus	7.5	8	7
Car	2	1	3

Source: Consumer Research
(Note: No question was asked as to whether they had used London Transport in the last week.)

MEASURING THE EFFECTIVENESS OF THE ADVERTISING CAMPAIGN

Method

While the raw data of admission figures were an indication that the campaign had been successful, it was agreed that an evaluation of the effect of the advertising should be undertaken. The process by which this was achieved was, firstly, to produce an estimate of what the admissions would have been without any advertising, then to subtract this figure away from the actual number of admissions. The resulting figure then provided an estimate for the number of admissions that have been generated by the advertising.

In estimating what admissions would have been, the first stage was to hypothesise what, if any, variables other than advertising would have affected admissions. We hypothesised that the key variable was the number of visitors to London, in so far as it would be expected that if the number of visitors went up, then the number of people visiting Kensington Palace would go up. Then, by assuming that the same proportion of these additional visitors would know about and visit the main tourists sites, it was hypothesised that visitors to Kensington Palace would go up by the same percentage as the number of visitors to London.

Application

Using figures from the London Visitor and Convention Bureau on the number of visitors to London, and figures on admissions to another key London tourist site, but one that did not receive any advertising support (in this case Hampton Court) as a control (which should confirm our second assumption), it was possible to construct the model of the expected increase in admissions not due to the advertising.

As a further control we looked at the non-advertised and advertised periods.

TABLE 5: PERCENTAGE INCREASE 1984–1985

	Jan–June	July–Sept
Visitors to London	+ 16.8	+ 5.2
Admissions to Kensington Palace	+ 16.2	+ 55.2
Admissions to Hampton Court	+ 11.6	+ 11.4

Source: London Visitor and Convention Bureau DOE

This data confirmed our hypotheses. Admissions during the non-advertised period to both Kensington Palace and Hampton Court were in line with the increase in visitors to London. During the advertised periods, admissions to Hampton Court and visitors to London also went up roughly in line, but admissions to Kensington Palace increased significantly more. However, as there was some variation between the percentage increase in London visitors (+5.2) and admissions to Hampton Court (+11.4) it was decided that both figures should be used to provide a 'high' and 'low' estimate.

The next stage was therefore to take the admission figures for Kensington Palace for 1984 and multiply them by one plus the percentage increase figures which would give us the estimate for admissions had there been no advertising.

i.e.   (a)   1984 Admissions × 1.052
        (b)   1984 Admissions × 1.114

Admissions to Kensington Palace during the July–September period 1984 were 45 400 and therefore the two estimates were:

(a) 47 760
(b) 50 575

Subtracting these two figures from the actual number of admissions to Kensington Palace July–September 1985 gave the estimate for the increase that was attributable to the advertising.

Our estimates were therefore:

(a) 22 740
(b) 19 925

Cost-Effectiveness

The next stage was to use these results to prepare an evaluation of the cost-effectiveness of the campaign. To do this, we multiplied the estimated increase in admissions due to the advertising by the average price of admission (i.e. accounting for the proportion of concessionary tickets sold) and then subtracted the known cost of the advertising from this figure. This calculation demonstrated that the incremental admissions generated had more than paid for the cost of the advertising – in the case of the 'high' estimate by as much as 20 per cent more and in the case of the 'low' estimate by 5 per cent more.

It should be noted that, for this campaign, this cost-effectiveness calculation is much simpler that it would be for many other campaigns as what was being promoted here was a service and not a product, and that therefore there were no additional costs involved with the increase in admissions. (There was no need to produce extra goods or indeed to take on extra people to staff Kensington Palace).

Furthermore, if anything, the calculation may be an underestimate of the cost-effectiveness as it does not take into account the additional revenue, and profit, which were generated at the Kensington Palace souvenir kiosk from the increased number of visitors.

IMPLICATIONS FOR FUTURE CAMPAIGNS

Given this excellent result there seems no reason why, given similar support, Kensington Palace should not once again prove a potent attraction.

There are a number of reasons for this view:

— The universe is likely to be new.
— Visitors to London, at the time of original planning for 1986, were again expected to the high.
— Among the visitors to Kensington Palace foreign visitors dominate admissions. Given this bias with the new universe, it seems more immediately productive to concentrate resources in this area.

However, in the plans for 1986 it was recommended that in addition to the London Transport tube cards and four sheet posters there should be a selected package of four sheet posters in the vicinity of the Palace. This recommendation was based on the consumer research that highlighted the proportion of visitors who arrived on foot, and the hypothesis was that this should help encourage 'impulse visitors' who are strolling in the vicinity.

16

The GLC's Anti 'Paving Bill' Campaign: Advancing the Science of Political Issue Advertising

INTRODUCTION

This paper seeks to demonstrate the effectiveness of a GLC advertising campaign which aimed to counter the Government's Local Government (Interim Provisions) Bill. The Bill became known as the 'Paving Bill' because it 'paved' the way for abolition of the GLC by cancelling the GLC elections scheduled to take place in May 1985, provided that the main abolition legislation had by that time passed into law. The Bill sought to place control of the GLC in the hands of councillors nominated by the Government from May 1985 until the following year, when the authority would cease to exist and new arrangements for London's local government came into force.

The paper will attempt to demonstrate that the advertising stimulated widespread opposition to the proposed legislation – among the public, within the media, and within Parliament. Partly through the mechanism of public opinion polls, it will be shown that the advertising stimulated and influenced media coverage of the issue, thus consolidating and intensifying opposition to the Bill. The paper will hopefully demonstrate that this created the climate in which the Government's original proposals were overturned by Parliament.

For, although the Bill reached the statute book in July 1984 and thus secured the abolition of the GLC elections, it did so in amended form. The interim provisions, whereby control of the GLC was to be placed in the hands of nominated councillors, was defeated by the House of Lords and the Government was forced to grant the elected Council a stay of execution for an additional year.

In one sense this achievement may seem 'small beer'. Yet it will be shown that the scale of what the advertising achieved in stimulating public and media opposition to the Government's proposals, in transforming the issue from one of obscure local government administration into a matter of genuine and popular concern, in pushing the issue up the political agenda and in undermining confidence in the Government's local government reforms, was unique. Its effectiveness in achieving all the above is without parallel; the advertising must surely be regarded as one of the most significant campaigns in British advertising history.

DEVELOPING A ROLE AND STRATEGY FOR ADVERTISING

To demonstrate the effectiveness of the anti 'Paving Bill' advertising it is necessary to understand how it was intended to work, and what it was designed to achieve.

When Boase Massimi Pollitt started to work with the GLC in January 1984, there was an urgent need for a judgement on what advertising might accomplish. From the beginning, qualitative research proved vital. Throughout the period from January to July 1984, the agency conducted 38 group discussions among Londoners of all political persuasions. This proved invaluable in understanding popular attitudes to the issue, in developing a strategy, and later advertising executions. In January quantitative and qualitative research revealed that abolition was of low interest to Londoners and that attitudes towards it largely reflected party political loyalties[1]. Negative perceptions (for long fostered by the press) that the GLC was synonymous with 'Red Ken', the squandering of money on dubious minorities and irresponsible meddling in national politics as demonstrated by the invitation of IRA leaders to County Hall, were both more salient and widespread than knowledge of the body's technical functions and responsibilities[2].

Against this background a number of advertising objectives were agreed.

1. Given the Government's massive majority of over one hundred in the Commons, the strategy would have to persuade the Government that the political costs of the unpopularity that would result from pursuing its policy would outweigh any benefits of getting the proposed legislation on to the statute book without amendment[3].

2. In order to popularise and enliven the 'Paving Bill' issue, advertising would have to demonstrate to people that 'democratic rights' lay at the heart of the debate. In January 1984, Boase Massimi Pollitt's qualitative research identified that 'democracy' had the potency to popularise the debate in a non party-political manner and to outweigh existing prejudices against the controversial Labour-controlled council[4]. The agency's qualitative research proved invaluable in 'hot-housing' arguments, and facilitating assessments of the various strategic options. It could thus be predicted that presenting abolition as a constitutional issue about the rights of every Londoner to control the running of the city promised to convert Conservative voters to opposition to the proposed reforms. This was vital if the Government was to be dissuaded from its proposed reform. The advertising was thus to perform the bold task of *changing the grounds of the debate* and of establishing new grounds on which opponents of the Government's policy could win.

3. All of this was dependent on a vision of *how the advertising could work* in a political marketplace where the public is daily bombarded with the views of political commentators and politicians. Clearly, the commerical media value of this would be many times the media budget for any advertising. And so the advertising campaign was *designed to excite, influence and work in conjunction with other media*. The advertising would have to win other media, and also politicians, over to its point of view if its influence was not to be swamped.

Thus the campaign was intended to function as a catalyst, setting in motion a series of influences which would surround the Government and convince it that to continue to pursue its proposed reform was increasingly unwise. Conservative Party activists would become alarmed, Conservative MPs and Lords would express their concern, and all of this would put pressure on the Government. This may be represented diagramatically:

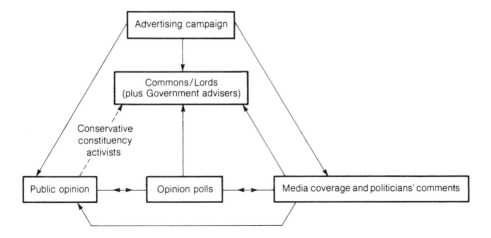

Figure 1. *Model of how the advertising could work*

It was a bold plan; arguably nothing like it had ever been attempted before. But would it work?

CRITERIA FOR MEASURING THE ADVERTISING'S EFFECTIVENESS

The fact that advertising was designed to excite, influence, and work in conjunction with other media and the utterances of politicians themselves makes it difficult to identify its effects in isolation. Advertising effectiveness can nevertheless be demonstrated against a number of criteria, namely:

— By demonstrating that the advertising was seen by the public, the media, and the politicians.
— By demonstrating that a change in public opinion, which was reflected in opinion polls, and a related change in press coverage of the issue, can be explained only by the advertising. (To this end, extensive use is made of the MORI tracking study, conducted periodically among a representative sample of adult Londoners, and which measured awareness of the advertising and attitudes to abolition.)
— By demonstrating that the political decision makers believed that the proposed legislation had become unpopular, and that this was linked to the advertising. The understandable unwillingness of the Government and its Parliamentary supporters to be drawn on these issues force us to rely on the views of those close to, or with expert knowledge of, the political decision makers.

The Government's ulitmate decision to press ahead with the abolition of the GLC elections, and later the abolition of the GLC itself, in the face of massive opposition from the public and 'expert' opinion, was of course its choice. At the end of the day the Government runs the country, not advertising. However, the anti 'Paving' campaign appears to have done everything that could reasonably have been expected from it, and more.

THE EFFECTS OF ADVERTISING: VISIBILITY

The salience of the advertising campaign among the public, the media and the politicians is unquestionable. The campaign started in early March, with poster locations throughout London and two press bursts during the month. Posters ran continuously until the end of June. By the beginning of April 1984, 52 per cent of adult Londoners claimed to be aware of the advertising without any visual prompting. By May this had risen to 63 per cent. Prompted awareness of the specific creative executions, copies of which are in the Appendix, was equally positive, as Table 1 reveals.

TABLE 1:   PROMPTED AWARENESS OF SPECIFIC
EXECUTIONS

	(Have you seen this advertisement?)		
	April	May	July
	(817)	(1048)	(1032)
	%	%	%
'From Now'	26	40	36
'Kind of Place'	23	40	42
'Petition'	19	28	27
'Dustbin'	n/a	25	31
(Other)	–	–	28

Source: MORI Tracking Study 1984

With such high awareness of the campaign among the general public, it followed that among political commentators and politicians, to whom the advertising was particularly heavily targeted through media-buying policy, awareness must have been almost universal. All the available evidence supports this notion of saturation coverage and universal awareness[5]. Advertisements like 'What kind of place is it that takes away your right to vote and leaves you with no say?' and 'Dustbin' thus became familiar reminders of the democratic issue. The press not only commented on the advertising but quickly came to treat it as an issue in its own right[6].

NEXT YEAR ALL LONDONERS' VOTES GO THE SAME WAY.

If the Government has its way there won't be any GLC elections to vote in next year. **SAY NO TO NO SAY.**

Politicians were also clearly aware of the advertising. Not only was it commented upon in the House but reports of this were carried in the press[7], and Government ministers spontaneously mentioned the advertising in public interviews[8]. In April Patrick Jenkin, Secretary of State for the Environment and the Government minister charged with seeing the 'Paving' and abolition legislation through Parliament, announced that the Government was considering the introduction of legislation to prevent local authorities spending ratepayers money on advertising 'for political purposes'. 'We have never seen a campaign of this sort before', he exclaimed[9].

THE EFFECTS OF ADVERTISING: THE MECHANISM OF CHANGING PUBLIC OPINION

It can clearly be demonstrated that there was a marked change in public attitudes to the abolition of the GLC and of the GLC elections within the period in question, and that this can be directly linked to the advertising. Londoners' opposition to the abolition of the GLC and of the elections to it grew markedly between January and the beginning of April 1984, as Table 2 demonstrates.

In the period from January until the beginning of April, when the MORI fieldwork was conducted, the press had devoted relatively little attention to the GLC issue. Such coverage as there was had not as yet, and on balance, become critical of the Government's proposed reforms, as Table 3 indicates. One month of the anti 'Paving Bill' advertising had been the only strong influence warning of the anti-democratic consequences of the proposed legislation and it must be largely credited with having achieved these significant shifts of opinion, particularly in relation to the cancellation of the elections. Support for this contention is to be found in the MORI survey among the majority of the country's TV and national press political editors. Despite the natural inclination, among such a sample, to minimise the effects of advertising, 71 per cent claimed that the advertising campaign had played a significant role in increasing public opposition to the 'Paving Bill'.

It was vital that the advertising should stimulate and influence media coverage of the issue. It was essential that the advertising confirmed the core issue of democratic rights for journa-

TABLE 2:   APPROVAL AND DISAPPROVAL OF THE GOVERNMENTS
PLANS TO:

		Jan (420) %	April (817) %	May (1048) %
1.	*Abolish the GLC elections*			
	approve	16	14	13
	disapprove	55	70	69
	no opinion/don't know	29	16	17
2.	*Abolish the GLC*			
	approve	19	18	17
	disapprove	50	62	64
	no opinion/don't know	30	20	18

Source: MORI Tracking Study

lists and political commentators, and persuaded them that the public was motivated by it – in particular by means of opinion polls. Thus press and television coverage would become critical of the proposed legislation; this would both unnerve the Government and further strengthen public opposition to the reform. There is clear evidence that all of this actually occurred.

Regrettably, detailed content analysis of television coverage is in practice impossible. However, such an analysis of the national press and London's own *Evening Standard* newspaper reveals that press coverage of the plans to abolish the GLC and its elections increased markedly from the beginning of April 1984. From that date the press coverage also became, on balance, markedly more critical of the Government's proposed reform and performance on the issue. Table 3 demonstrates this. It is based on an analysis of national newspapers, and measures coverage of the GLC issue using tabloid page sizes as the standard unit of measurement.

TABLE 3:   ANALYSIS OF PRESS COVERAGE OF GLC

(*Note*: Units of measurement are full tabloid page size equivalents)	Jan	Feb	Mar	Apr	May	June
Abolition issue						
critical of legislation	3	6	8	18	22	28
neutral	4	2	4	6	6	4
supportive of legislation	4	5	6	2	4	3
Coverage of other aspects of GLC (traffic planning, women's committee, minority groups, etc.						
supportive of GLC	2	2	4	1	8	4
neutral	3	3	4	2	9	1
critical of GLC	2	2	2	2	6	12
Coverage of Ken Livingstone as individual personality						
pro	2	2	2	3	12	6
neutral	1	1	1	2	–	–
anti	3	3	3	1	2	2

The last week of March was key to this change, and the role of London's *Evening Standard* and its publication of a public opinion poll revealing increasing public opposition to the Government's proposed reforms appears to have had a seminal influence[10]. Henceforward, and from April to June, the publication of further opinion polls revealing ever stronger public opposition to the Government's proposed reforms attracted immediate and widespread press coverage that was highly damaging to the Government's case[11]. It seems likely that this regular flow of opinion poll information consolidated and intensified opposition to the proposed legislation among both public and politicians, and within the press.

Interesting support for the view that it was the advertising which initially motivated both the public, and then the media, by persuading them that democratic rights lay at the core of abolition, and that once converted the media simply reinforced this perception, is to be found in a MORI survey among most of the country's leading television and national newspaper political editors[12]. This evidence confirms that it was the advertising which converted press and television to the view that abolition was an important public issue and that 'democratic rights' lay at its core.

It has proved impossible to ascertain what influence the much-publicised movement of public opinion may have had on the critics of the proposed legislation within the Conservative party and in the House of Lords. Clearly, it can only have been an encouragement. Detailed content analysis of the press reveals that the parliamentary rebellions of senior Conservatives such as Heath, Pym, Rippon and Gilmour, and rebellions in the Lords at various stages of the Paving Bill's progress, each excited immediate and major splurges of publicity that were highly damaging to the Government's case[13].

Thus it can reasonably be claimed that from the beginning of April increases in, and con- solidation of, opposition to the proposed legislation is founded on several interconnected factors – namely the nature of the press (and TV) coverage, the vociferousness and stature of the eminent critics of the legislation, the advertising, and the effect of the published opinion polls. It has also been shown that it can only have been the advertising which first stimulated public opinion, the opinion polls, and press and television coverage in an anti 'Paving Bill' direction, and so triggered the whole mechanism of opposition.

While politicians and the quality press talked of abolition almost exclusively in terms of democratic principle, qualitative information and detailed content analysis of the press reveal that first the public, and later the tabloid or popular press, also saw the issue in broader, emotional, and human terms. There was a growing feeling, even among Conservatives, that the Government was abusing its power, behaving dictatorially and selfishly, and arrogantly attempting to eliminate an organisation merely because of its political colour. The advertising was praised for capturing and projecting this feeling in March 1984[14]. Its wit and use of popular views about the remoteness, insensitivity and unaccountability of central Govern- ment seem to have helped position the GLC as being 'of the people'. In such circumstances the British public empathised with the underdog – there was growing emotional sympathy with Ken Livingstone, who was increasingly positioned as the defender of democracy and Londoners' rights.

The advertisement 'If you want me out you should have the right to vote me out', featuring Ken Livingstone, seems to have played on, and helped foster, these sentiments. Certainly it seems that advertising must have played a major role in creating these new and more positive feelings towards the GLC and its human face, Ken Livingstone[15]. Again, the press seems to have followed, rather than championed, this change of public mood – although in responding to it, it confirmed and consolidated Livingstone's new status[16]. In the coming months, the

"IF YOU WANT ME OUT YOU SHOULD HAVE THE RIGHT TO VOTE ME OUT."

Everyone's entitled to their view. The British constitution says you express it through the ballot box.

That's the law.

Unfortunately the Government doesn't like the law as it stands in relation to the GLC.

Today the first bill relating to the abolition of the GLC gets its second reading in the House.

It's devised to wipe out next year's GLC elections. Whether you're Labour, Tory, Liberal or SDP, you'll have no say.

Not since the last World War has your statutory right to vote been withdrawn in this way.

And it's a cynical dismissal of public opinion.

In a recent MORI poll 61% of Londoners of all political persuasions said no.

Only 22%, by the way, said yes.

In every straw poll, overwhelming public opinion has said no to abolition.

On 26th March Tom King the Conservative Secretary for Employment outlined in the House the elementary rights of people to register their vote without interference.

That was in relation to the Trade Union movement.

This Government steadfastly refuses to apply the same principles to the rights of 7 million Londoners.

You may hold the view of course,

that they were voted into power democratically and have the right to do as they wish.

But, nowhere in the Tory manifesto was there a mention of abolishing your right to vote in local elections.

Ask yourself why the Government is intent on doing away with the GLC in the first place.

There has not been a single proposition motivated by the desire to improve London.

What you might have heard have been outbursts.

"Red Ken spending our money on weirdos again."

(For the record less than half of one

per cent of GLC expenditure is allocated to all minorities.)

Don't let bigoted arguments of this kind blind you to the real issue.

This country's centuries old democratic tradition is at stake.

Local Government is one of the checks and balances which safeguard us against the abuse of central Government power.

And it would be an abuse of power for any Government to abolish a democratic institution such as a local authority, simply because it did not like the incumbent administration.

SAY NO TO NO SAY.

press sometimes seemed surprised at the degree of popularity with which it now credited him, and the extent of its own volte-face.

> Only last year the plan (Abolition) seemed accepted as a popular and justified modernisation of local Government. . . . Yet today abolition is regarded on almost all sides as a gratuitous personal attack on a noble democratic institution. The GLC's left-wing leader, Mr Ken Livingstone, whose more lunatic activities and expenditures so delighted the Tories at the last General Election has emerged as the apostle of electoral freedom, despite having never led any party to victory at any poll. His financial irresponsibility, IRA sympathies and ratepayer support for gay co-operatives are forgotten as he covers London with posters calling on the citizenry to defend their vote.
>
> *The Economist*, 19 May 1984

In conclusion, it has been demonstrated that a marked change in public attitudes to the abolition of the GLC and its elections can be attributed to the advertising. It has also been demonstrated that the advertising – in part through the mechanism of public opinion polls – influenced media coverage of the issue which, in turn, seems to have consolidated and intensified opposition to the Government's proposed legislation[17]. The advertising triggered this opposition by convincing the public, the media, and perhaps many politicians, that the issue was one of democratic principle. It also stimulated emotional sympathy with the GLC 'underdog' in what it portrayed as its unequal and hence unfair fight with central Government.

Such principle and feeling was capable of transcending party political loyalties and converting Conservative voters to opposition to the proposed reform, as the MORI Tracking Study confirmed.

TABLE 4: ATTITUDES OF CONSERVATIVE VOTERS TO GLC ABOLITION

	January %	May %
Disapprove	26	34
Approve	42	44
Neither/nor ⎫ Don't know ⎭	32	21

THE EFFECTS OF ADVERTISING: IMPACT ON THE DECISION MAKERS

Beyond all reasonable doubt the advertising campaign and the other media coverage which it influenced had the effect of undermining Conservative Party and Government confidence in the legislation, and created the climate in which the Bill was defeated by the Lords on 28 June 1984.

Attempts to question Conservative MPs and members of the House of Lords on the impact of the anti-abolition campaign on their own attitudes and behaviour have proved abortive. Non-co-operation was the predominant reaction. Clearly there are vested interests which work against admissions of being influenced by outside 'propaganda', and also party political considerations that might also taint any responses. Given these problems, the best opportunity to ascertain MPs' opinions in a vaguely unguarded way – namely through MORI's annual omnibus to a representative cross-section of members of Parliament – yielded a remarkable result. Over one hundred MPs were sampled in June 1984 and asked whether they considered abolition of the GLC and metropolitan county councils a vote winner or vote loser. Opposition party members unanimously claimed that it was a vote loser: 43 per cent of the representative sample of Conservative MPs claimed it was a vote loser and only 42 per cent claimed it was a vote winner.

There is considerable circumstantial evidence to indicate that the advertising, and the opposition to the proposed legislation which it helped stimulate, produced a lack of confidence in the proposed legislation among Conservatives in Parliament, so creating the circumstances in which the Paving Bill was defeated and amended. It is only reasonable to assume that Parliamentarians were more than aware of the increasingly critical press coverage of the issue and the numerous published opinion polls revealing ever stronger opposition to abolition which appeared between March and June 1984. In addition MPs must have been aware of the declining percentage of Londoners who, according to published opinion polls, declared an intention to vote Conservative in either a General Election or a GLC one, and who contrasted with relative stability in voting intentions elsewhere in the country[18].

We cannot know what 'behind the scenes' pressures were placed on the Government by Conservative Party members concerned by the Government's course. However, concerns about the threat to Conservative Party fortunes in the capital may explain the efforts of leading London Conservatives to counter the GLC's propaganda, and their public criticism of the Government for not doing so[19].

In the circumstances we must rely on the opinions of those with expert knowledge of the politicians. The country's television and national newspaper editors were in no doubt that the advertising had directly persuaded the political decision makers that abolition was an unpopular reform[20].

But perhaps the final words should belong to Patrick Jenkin. On being ousted from the Cabinet in 1985, he claimed that Cabinet colleagues had failed to support him over local Government reforms because they had recognised the growing unpopularity of the proposed measures.

CONCLUSION

Despite the difficulties of establishing causal relationships, there is clear evidence that the advertising was widely seen, shifted public opinion, influenced media coverage of the Paving Bill and thus created the climate in which the Government's original proposals were overturned by Parliament so that the GLC achieved a stay of execution. In the longer term, the campaign may be judged to have helped stimulate a renewed public and opposition party commitment to the restoration of democratically-elected metropolitan authorities.

Demonstrating the cost-effectiveness of the campaign in terms of conventional commercial profit is clearly impossible. In the political market-place, public and party attitudes may be regarded as the bottom line – and no exact financial value can be placed on these. Perhaps the closest we can come to demonstrating the campaign's 'value for money' is in the calculation that the commercial value of the positive media coverage of the issue which the advertising appeared to stimulate was many times the advertising budget.

The anti 'Paving Bill' advertising, and the anti-abolition campaign, of which it formed a part, have been profoundly significant. The widely acknowledged effectiveness of the campaign has undoubtedly given further impetus to the fast-growing corporate advertising sector. More importantly, the campaign has actually extended perceptions of the power and influence of advertising itself – in particular in its ability to influence other media. In addition, trade unions and other bodies, not traditionally associated with the skills of marketing and advertising, show increasing interest in such activities. Advertising and market research must rise to the occasion and demonstrate the skills that are required. In particular there is a need to advance access to, and hence content analysis of, television news and current affairs programmes.

APPENDIX: REFERENCES AND NOTES

1. The MORI tracking study of a representative sample of all adult Londoners revealed that half of them (56 per cent) spontaneously mentioned abolition when asked of Government plans concerning the GLC. On prompting, awareness of the plan rose to four-fifths (81 per cent). Qualitative research indicated that these figures were in a sense highly misleading: for even among those aware of the issue it was of very low interest. The GLC, like other Government bodies, was felt to be remote, its functions were not understood, and its fortunes were thus a matter of popular indifference.

   When prompted, 50 per cent opposed abolition and 19 per cent supported it. People rationalised these responses on a wide variety of grounds as the following figures indicate.

REASONS FOR ATTITUDE TO ABOLITION

	Attitude to abolition	
	Approve %	Disapprove %
The GLC do a good job	3	29
Save money/stop waste of money	50	1
Fares would go up	–	23
Services would deteriorate	1	10
Ought to keep local government authority/autonomy	1	1
Need an overall body for London	–	10
Why change it/OK as it is	1	9
Because of the leader/politics	21	1
Don't know	3	5

Source: MORI January 1984

   Qualitative research helped to explain why opinion reflected party-political loyalties. Those who disapproved of abolition often simply disliked change or were motivated by Labour party loyalties. Concern that services, and in particular public transport, would deteriorate were common among the latter. Those who approved of abolition were often Conservative party voters who believed it would save money by ending the profligate expenditure of 'Red Ken' on dubious minorities.

2. Academic support for the fact that the media made Ken Livingstone one of the most vilified people in public life is to be found in C. T. Husbands, 'Attitudes to Local Government in London' *London Journal* II, (1), 1985. The most recent quantitative confirmation of the widespread public ignorance of the GLC's responsibilities and activities was to be found in Harris Research Centre, *Survey of Public Opinion in London* (June 1983).

3. The intention was that the Government would then be widely seen to have lost the popular, and hence moral, argument for its policy. For it to have then persisted on its original course would thus threaten to undermine its popularity and authority, and prejudice its future electoral fortunes. It would also have promised to excite rebellion within the party. The threat of such a scenario might induce the Government to drop or radically amend its schemes.

4. The qualitative research conducted in January 1984 revealed that respondents had largely forgotten that the GLC Council was democratically elected by all Londoners every four years but, when reminded of this, and that the legis-

lation thus meant the loss of their vote and hence control over how London was governed, they objected vehemently. This perception seemed to transform attitudes to the issue: suddenly the Government was felt to be sacrificing the democratic rights of the citizen through its desire to abolish one GLC administration out of political spite. In this context, its policy immediately became less acceptable and objections became quite emotional and intense.

5. For example, the MORI survey among the majority of the country's TV and national press political editors reveal 100 per cent awareness of the campaign.

6. The cost and ethics of the campaign became the subject of numerous articles, many of which were lengthy and boasted vaguely sensationalist headlines (for example, *The Daily Telegraph*, 24 March 1984 and 16 April 1984; *The Times*, 4 June 1984; *Evening Standard*, 21 June 1984; *Daily Mail*, 21 June 1984; and *Daily Express*, 21 June 1984).

   Some of these sought out and published the comments of the GLC's advertising managers. When the *Daily Mail* obtained an advertising strategy document it made a 'scoop' of the story (*Daily Mail*, 23 March 1984).

   Readers letters on the subject of the advertising were published (for example, *The Times*, 21 April 1984; and *Daily Star*, 24 April 1984).

   Indeed the campaign seems to have stimulated interest in the broader issue of political advertising in general, a subject on which eminent advertising personalities expressed their views in the press (for example, Winston Fletcher in *The Times*, 20 June 1984).

7. *Hansard*; and for examples and reports of this in the press see *The Times*, 5 and 10 April 1984. MPs letters on the subject of the advertising were published in the press, for example the letter of Richard Tracy (Conservative MP) in *The Daily Telegraph*, 10 April 1984.

8. For example, interview with William Waldegrave, the Environment Minister, in the *Evening Standard*'s 'Great Debate', *Evening Standard*, 22 March 1984.

9. *Financial Times*, 19 April 1984. Other papers carried the story, for example *The Times*, 19 April 1984.

10. On 22 March, London's *Evening Standard* newspaper began a series of articles under the banner of 'The Great Debate' to 'bring home to Londoners the momentous issues involved' in abolition. The initial article paid tribute to the vigour of the anti 'Paving Bill' advertising. On 26 March it published a MORI opinion poll, commissioned by the paper, which revealed that public opposition to abolition of the GLC had grown to 61 per cent of adult Londoners while only 22 per cent approved of the Government's plans. Other papers were quick to report the survey results (for example *The Times*, 27 March 1984; and *The Guardian*, 27 March 1984) and from that point onwards coverage of the abolition issue in the national press became distinctly more critical of the Government's position. On 27 March both the *Evening Standard* and *The Guardian* paid tribute to the 'masterly' and 'skilled' advertising campaign of the GLC which was credited with having achieved 'substantial shifts' in public opinion. Other journals were quick to link the results of this poll to the advertising (for example, *The Economist*, 7 April 1984). On 30 March the *Evening Standard* concluded the 'Great Debate' by saying that 'This House Supports the Retention of the GLC'.

11. For example, the April MORI poll commissioned by the GLC was published by the *Evening Standard*, 16 April 1984. The paper claimed that the 62 per cent who opposed abolition was 'not necessarily a direct result of the massive advertising campaign to keep the GLC'.

   A MORI poll, commissioned by the GLC, of voters' opinions in Finchley and Greenwich which revealed that 66 per cent of the Prime Minister's Finchley constituents opposed abolition was reported in *The Economist*, 14 April 1984.

   An Audience Selection poll which found that 54 per cent opposed abolition of the GLC and only 15 per cent favoured it, was reported in the *Financial Times*, 16 May 1984 and in *The Guardian*, 16 May 1984.

   The May MORI poll, commissioned by the GLC and which found that 69 per cent of Londoners opposed the cancellation of the GLC elections and that 64 per cent opposed abolition, was reported in *The Daily Telegraph*, 8 June 1984 and *The Guardian*, 8 June 1984.

   A Harris poll, commissioned by 'The London Programme', and which indicated that Ken Livingstone would win a by-election with an increased majority, was reported in *The Times*, 22 June 1984.

12. The survey was conducted by MORI in June 1986. Twenty-four interviews were achieved, a sample which represented 80 per cent of all leading political editors and journalists working for television and the press. In the context of the fact that such a sample of 'experts' must have a natural inclination to deny that they were influenced by advertising and to minimise its effects in comparison with the power of their own media, the results are remarkable. Of those interviewed, 71 per cent claimed that the advertising had been influential in persuading the media to see abolition of the GLC as an important public issue. Even more remarkable was the fact that 67 per cent of the sample claimed that political journalists and commentators had not initially seen the issue as one of democracy versus central government control, and that 50 per cent of the sample claimed that they had come to see the issue in this light as a result of the advertising campaign.

13. The parliamentary rebellions that won such adverse publicity for the Government's proposals may be listed as follows:

— In early April there were press reports of the opposition of the Tory Reform Group and of the intention of various senior conservatives (notably Heath and Pym) to oppose the legislation.
— On 11 April, Heath led 19 other Conservative rebels who voted against the 'Paving Bill' on its second reading.
— On 10 and 11 May, Heath led two revolts during the Bill's committee stage on the floor of the Commons.
— On 23 and 24 May, there was chaos during the third reading of the Bill as a result of the 'filibustering' of the SDP Liberal Alliance.
— Press speculation in early June that the Lords would inflict injury on the Bill came to fruition when, on 11 June, there was a Government majority of only 20, despite extensive and controversial whipping, on an amendment condemning the Bill as a dangerous precedent.
— On 28 June the Bill sustained its most notable setback – the Lords passed an amendment preventing the Government from cancelling the GLC elections until the main Bill abolishing the Council had received the Royal Assent, and voted down the 'interim provisions' whereby the GLC would have been controlled, from May 1985 until early 1986, by councillors nominated by central Government.

14. Qualitative research conducted in March 1984 revealed this feeling that the Government was abusing its power, and abandoning all sense of fair play. Qualitative research conducted on a regular basis throughout the period revealed that such feelings grew stronger in the following three months. Central Government was taking something away from London against the wishes of the majority of its citizens and, even among those who otherwise favoured abolition, this was felt to be wrong.

Although the MORI tracking study is of limited relevance here, the available quantitative data is at least consistent with the claims, and indicated that the relevant shift in recorded opinion had, for the most part, already taken place by the end of March. By 2 April the number of Londoners claiming that the proposal to abolish the GLC had made them think less of the Government had risen from 43 per cent (January) to 54 per cent: by July the figure had risen to 57 per cent. The April figures also revealed that, of those who had seen the advertising, 68 per cent disagreed that the Government was trying to abolish the GLC in the interests of Londoners and 62 per cent agreed that it was really trying to abolish the GLC to silence a political opponent: among those who claimed not to have seen the advertising the scores were 59 per cent and 47 per cent respectively.

Thus in March there were extremely positive reactions to the Ken Livingstone execution, even among Conservative opponents of the GLC, during its qualitative pre-testing: two months before such an execution would have been unthinkable.

15. No influence, other than the advertising and the opinion polls which it influenced, can explain the conversion. In March the press had still not begun to treat Livingstone favourably. Nor had it publicised any activity of Livingstone which was likely to court public favour. Support for this comes from the MORI survey of the country's national newspapers and TV political editors (for details of survey see footnote 12): 92 per cent of those interviewed believed that the advertising had been effective in causing the public to sympathise with the GLC.

16. Detailed content analysis of the press reveals that the change in coverage of Livingstone can be dated with surprising precision. In mid-March the flow of critical press articles came to a stop. The timing coincides with the appearance of the advertising campaign, and the first burst of press executions. There then followed a period when Livingstone received little, although on balance more favourable, coverage. Then, in May, his new status was recognised. The event which first gained him extensive favourable coverage was the opening of the Thames Barrier at which his mother, Ethel, an avowed monarchist, met the Queen. Virtually every national newspaper devoted extensive coverage to the story. 'Red Ken' had become 'Our Ken': the publication of a book on his life and interviews with his mother provided the press with much human interest material on the man with a long history of reptilian pets.

The press still found an outlet for its criticism of the GLC's left-wing policies. In May and June there was much more extensive, and on balance more critical, coverage of items such as the GLC women's committee, the Talgarth Road traffic experiment and the GLC's attempts to pressurise Zola Budd into an anti-apartheid statement. However, this was now visibly separated from the issue of abolition and the champion of Londoners' democratic rights, 'Citizen Ken'.

17. Further evidence of the compound and interrelated impact of media coverage, opinion polls, and the advertising in stimulating opposition to abolition of the GLC and its elections is to be found in a MORI survey conducted in July 1984 which compared the views of Londoners to those of residents within the other metropolitan County Councils that were also to be abolished by the legislation. Of Londoners, 80 per cent were aware of the plans to abolish the

GLC whereas only 47 per cent of those interviewed in the other Metropolitan authorities were aware of the intended fate of their own councils. Among those aware of the abolition threat, opposition was much more intense in London: 50 per cent of Londoners 'strongly disapproved' of abolition of the GLC whereas only 32 per cent of those in the other areas 'strongly disapproved' of the plans to abolish their own authorities.

18. These trends are authoritatively documented in C. Husbands, op. cit.

19. In June John Wheeler, London's senior Conservative MP publicly attacked the Government for its failure to counter the GLC's 'effective "save us" fight', and to outlaw its advertising campaign (*Evening Standard*, 27 June 1984). The same week Lady Porter, Conservative Leader of Westminster City Council, admitted to the effectiveness of the GLC's advertising campaign when she claimed that Londoners had been 'conned' by it at the launching of an organisation of Tory politicians and businessmen called 'Efficiency in Local Government' which aimed to counter the GLC's propaganda. (*Financial Times*, 19 April 1984).

20. For details of the survey see footnote 12. The results were again quite remarkable. In resonse to the question of what had persuaded the political decision makers that abolition was an unpopular reform, 75 per cent of those sampled in the MORI survey claimed it was the advertising. This score was exceeded only by the 83 per cent who mentioned the opinion polls. Amazingly the editors gave the media comment about the issue a score of only 67 per cent.

17

Home Protection

How advertising helps fight crime

THE ROLE OF ADVERTISING

This study is concerned with an advertising campaign to improve the security of households by encouraging the installation of window locks with the ultimate objective of reducing the number of domestic burglaries.

The following statistics illustrate the scale of domestic burglary.

— Over 340 000 'burglaries in a dwelling' in England and Wales were reported to the police in 1981. This represents about 10 per cent of all indictable crime recorded by the police and is one of the major categories of crime with which they have to deal. It also means that approximately 2 per cent of homes were burgled in 1981.

— The figures almost certainly underestimate the total number of actual and attempted burglaries; the scale of the dark side of crime is unknown but the 1972 and 1979 General Household Surveys suggest that some 30 per cent plus of burglaries are unreported. The British Crime Survey, the data from which are now being analysed, will give a clearer picture.

— The reported value of goods stolen was over £100 million and averaged £440 per burglary in 1980. These figures coincide with payments in 1981 made by members of the British Insurance Association of £106 million and an estimated average claim of £300 to £500. Again these are likely to be underestimates given under-reporting and/or inadequate insurance cover.

— Most burglaries are not solved; in 1981 72 per cent of police-recorded offences were not 'cleared up'.

These bare statistics are enormous in their scale and cost to the community; however they say nothing about the misery that a burglary causes to the victim: the disruption to the physical and emotional security of somebody's home cannot truly be assessed but it is not uncommon for victims to move from their house.

Faced with this enormous problem, it is advisable to consider how advertising can help solve or at least diminish it. The short answer is that it cannot; the causes of crime are inevitably complex (and largely unknown) reflecting a multiplicity of economic, political and moral factors. It is judged unlikely that advertising could directly influence the activities of burglars and thereby bring about a reduction in crime. It does, however, seem more feasible to tackle the problem from the perspective of the potential victim and address the issue of how their actions can reduce the incidence of burglary, or at least the risk of they themselves being burgled. The essential philosophy underlying this approach is that individuals are in a position to protect themselves because improved domestic security reduces the risk of burglary. The obvious qualifications to such an approach are:

(a)   Domestic security is only adequate to the level of skill and determination displayed by the burglar. However, most burglaries are committed by sneak thieves, those who are looking for the more vulnerable and easier 'targets'. Against such attackers, simple precautions are likely to act as an effective deterrent.

(b) The second qualification to this approach is that one man's security may be another man's downfall. If one dwelling is sufficiently secure to deter a burglar, it does not of course preclude a neighbouring less secure dwelling from being attacked instead.

However, these two qualifications do not invalidate the commonsense hypothesis that a more secure home is less likely to be burgled, and that provided sufficient homes are made secure there is some probability that the incidence of the crime itself may, in the long term, be reduced.

CAMPAIGN OBJECTIVES

There are, of course, a large number of security precautions that a householder should take to minimize the risk of burglary. These range from the simple – ensuring doors and windows are closed and locked when the house is left empty – to the more complex (and possibly expensive) such as installing burglar alarms.

It was decided that window locks should be the principal security measure featured in the advertising campaign, for the following reasons:

(a)   Windows are the most common point of entry for burglars.

(b) The installation of window locks acts both as a practical deterrent in making forced entry more hazardous, requiring glass to be broken or frames forced; and as a visual deterrent to prevent an attempt being made in the first place.

(c)   Window locks are relatively inexpensive, available through ironmonger and DIY outlets, and can be installed fairly easily by anyone with a minimum proficiency in DIY.

(d) While the main objective of the advertising was to encourage the installation of window locks, it was hoped that this would not preclude some spin-off effect on other security measures.

Thus the primary and behavioural objective of the advertising campaign was *to encourage householders to install window locks*.

In addition to this primary objective, a secondary campaign objective was to encourage and stimulate the activities of others concerned with advising the public about domestic security. These included:

— Crime prevention officers within each police force division and the lay crime prevention panels that have been set up by most forces.

— Lock manufacturers, wholesalers and retailers, persuading them to stock, feature and, ideally, promote window locks.

This supportive objective is analogous with, for example, the way in which an advertising campaign can act as a stimulus to sales force and retailer in the area of packaged goods to increase the distribution or shelf displays of a particular product. In this instance, this objective was to be achieved by press releases prior to the campaign, consultation with the appropriate organizations and trade federations and the provision of promotional material such as window stickers, radio tapes, miniature posters etc. reflecting the overall campaign theme.

In summary, the objectives of the campaign were to encourage householders to install window locks and to act as a focus for the supportive activities of the police and suppliers/retailers of window locks.

CAMPAIGN DETAILS

Target Audience

The target audience for the campaign was defined as *all householders*, for three reasons:

(a)   75 to 85 per cent of houses do not have window locks. (It is important to emphasize that window locks are not the same as 'catches' with which all windows are conventionally fitted.)

(b)   Qualitative evidence suggested that both men and women were likely to be involved in the decision to install and purchase window locks: women, who are more emotionally concerned about burglary, providing an important stimulus to purchase; men, more 'matter of fact' in their comments, being more concerned with the choice and installation of window locks.

(c)   It seemed wrong to exclude in creative or media terms any sub-group given the objective and nature of the campaign offering advice about self-protection.

Advertising Strategy

The underlying principle behind the advertising strategy was to arouse the public's fear of the risk and consequences of burglary, and to demonstrate window locks as an effective deterrent to the burglar. The basic model for this advertising strategy was to highlight and dramatize the problem – burglary – and to offer a solution to that problem – installing window locks.

From initial qualitative research, it was evident that the prospect of burglary was viewed with considerable alarm. In particular, the invasion of the house, the loss of property and the expectation of vandalistic behaviour were all felt to be among the worst aspects of burglary; the experience of burglary was frequently likened, particularly by women, to that of rape.

These understandable anxieties appeared to be a powerful way of dramatizing the prospect of burglary and by doing so to position window locks as a simple and easy solution to the problem. This juxtaposition of the horror of burglary with the simplicity of the solution appeared to be a route to overcome two commonly-expressed attitudes.

1.   Fatalism ('burglary happens to others, it won't happen to me'). If presented in a credible and convincing manner, it was believed that showing the full horror of burglary would break down this barrier.

2.   Helplessness ('There's nothing you can do to stop a determined burglar'). The point of
     the campaign was to say that there *was* something that could be done – the solution was
     to install window locks.

It was felt that this combination of 'fear arousal' and positive advice would be the foundation
of a powerful advertising strategy acting synergetically. Either on its own was likely to be a
far weaker proposition: fear arousal alone merely resulting in increasing the public's feelings
of helplessness and fatalism; positive advice lacking the necessary impact to make it seem
worthwhile.

     However, while this primary and emotional strategy appeared to be likely to succeed in
encouraging the installation of window locks, it was evident that some more information-
based communication was required in order to overcome certain concerns. These included
the availability of window locks for different types of window, their cost and ease of
installation. While the advertising was expected to tackle these issues, it was felt they were
to an extent subsidiary to the primary strategy outlined above: if enough people were
sufficiently aroused by the advertising and absorbed the message about window locks, they
would tend not to require reassurance on these dimensions. Also it was hoped that the other
activity stimulated by the campaign through Crime Prevention Officers, retailers etc. would
help in overcoming these concerns.

     Figure 15.1 represents the advertising strategy diagrammatically.

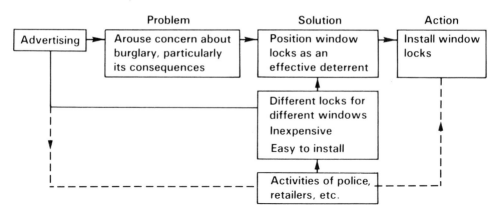

Figure 15.1   *Advertising model*

Creative Executions

From the requirements of the strategy and target audience a mixed media schedule was
adopted: television to consolidate high media impact with the necessary dramatic qualities,
press to convey more detailed information about window locks, and posters to act as
reminder medium.

     From the exploratory qualitative research mentioned above a campaign was developed
with the common theme: 'A window is always open to a thief. Unless it's locked.' The
campaign included:

(a)   Two television commercials, one highlighting the physical and emotional consequences
      of being burgled ('Scars'), the other showing a potential burglar menacingly stalking
      a house but being thwarted by the presence of window locks ('No windows').

How a thief could get to know you. Intimately.

A window without window locks is an open invitation to a thief.

All too easily he can let himself in and start looking through your personal belongings.

But he can be discouraged by window locks, like those we've illustrated.

Take the simple lock designed for wooden sash windows.

They cost £4 a pair and take only minutes to fit if you do it yourself.

The window security bolt is sold at most D.I.Y. and hardware shops in a choice of colours, so it won't spoil the looks of your window frames.

The push lock is specifically designed for side or top hung casement windows, whether they're aluminium or wood.

And the transom lock is made to protect metal and wooden windows.

If you're not sure which locks would make your windows most secure, ask the Crime Prevention Officer at your local Police Station.

His advice is free and he'll be pleased to help you avoid letting a burglar get to know you.

A window is always open to a thief. Unless it's locked.

ISSUED BY THE HOME OFFICE

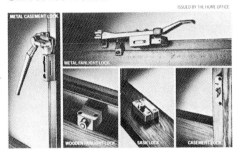

(b)   Three press executions all of which provided more detail about the costs, availability and ease of installation of window locks.
(c)   One poster which appeared on 4- and 16-sheet sites in residential areas.

Media Summary

The campaign ran in the Granada and Yorkshire television regions in two bursts from October to November 1981 and from January to February 1982. In both bursts, television and press were simultaneous to achieve maximum impact and synergy; the posters appeared in February to act in a reminder role and to supplement the somewhat lower strike rate of this second burst.

Total campaign expenditure was £360 000 which equals a national equivalent expenditure of approximately £1 600 000, assuming that national press publications are substituted for the enforced use of local press in the two regions.

CAMPAIGN RESULTS

Methodology

Given the principal objective of increasing the installation of window locks, it was decided that this behavioural measure should be assessed through the establishment of a *retail audit* of hardware/ironmonger/DIY outlets in the advertised areas for the duration of the campaign. In addition a random sample *survey of householders* was carried out to assess behaviour, attitudes and advertising awareness.

The research programme was underpinned by two methodological principles:

(a)   Frequent monitoring, to establish the effect of each burst of advertising and thus involving four fieldwork stages, before and after each advertising burst.
(b)   Advertising versus control area comparisons to establish that changes in the advertised areas were not due to other unknown factors. The control area chosen was the non-overlap Midlands television region.

The rationale for these two projects was to be able to synthesize hard sales data from the retail audit with any observed changes in the public's behaviour or attitudes. Although the technique of a retail panel is itself not new, it should be noted that it represents a departure for the Central Office of Information and Home Office in their methodology of campaign evaluation. Its use was justified not only because of the tangible advertising objective of increasing the penetration of window locks, but also because it was likely that the campaign effect might be insufficiently large to be shown with any statistical confidence in a household survey.

Purchases of Window Locks

The results of the retail audit (Figure 15.2) were dramatic, with sales of window locks showing, from similar initial levels, a large and statistically significant increase of 128 per cent in the advertised areas compared with the control area.

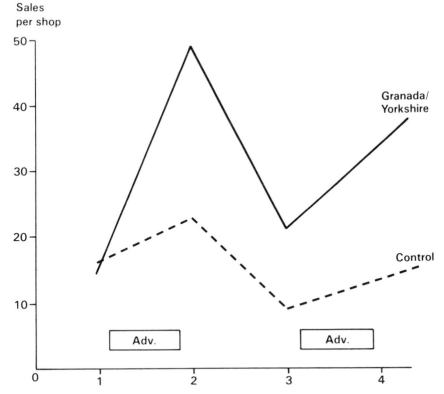

Figure 15.2 *Window lock sales per sample shop*

Commenting on these results we can observe:

(a) A short-term increase of 127 per cent in Granada and Yorkshire at the end of the first burst compared with a small but statistically insignificant increase in the control area.

(b) In both areas a decline of similar proportions (approximately 60 per cent) in period 3, probably explained by the fact that this period covers the two months of November and December. However, sales in Granada and Yorkshire continued above their pre-advertising level (compared with a lower level in the control area) and therefore were maintained at similar levels as Table 15.1 illustrates.

TABLE 15.1:   INDEX OF SALES IN ADVERTISED
AREAS

Period	Control area %	Advertised areas %
Pre-1	100	95
Post-2	100	212
Pre-3	100	227
Post-4	100	252

(c) Increases in both advertised and control areas after this second burst of advertising, with sales in Granada and Yorkshire returning to a level only slightly lower than that following the first burst.

It has been possible to substantiate the evidence of the retail audit through other indirect evidence. In the advertised areas eight out of the 25 sample shops claimed to be out of stock of at least one brand of window lock (compared with four out of 25 in the control area) suggesting that demand exceeded supply. Subsequent telephone interviews with eight major window-lock wholesalers confirmed not only evidence of increased demand but also, in four instances, of supply difficulties with at least one manufacturer.

The demonstration of higher levels of sales of window locks measured during and between bursts of advertising presents a prima facie case for the effectiveness of the campaign. Moreover, other measurable factors do not explain the higher sales levels.

— MEAL records no advertising expenditure by security device manufacturers during the campaign.
— Some Crime Prevention 'fillers' were screened in both advertised and control areas. (Fillers are public service films screened at the discretion of the television contractors.) However, the control area, Midlands, screened more fillers (475 adult TVRs) than either Granada (395 adult TVRs) or Yorkshire (99 adult TVRs) *and* their subject matter will not have featured window locks specifically.
— Reports from Crime Prevention officers on their own activities, media coverage, retailer support etc. have not yet been analysed, so that we are unable to assess the extent and impact of such activity. However, as mentioned earlier, an objective of this campaign was to help to create a momentum that would aid the efforts of those organizations concerned with domestic security and thus such activity may be seen as a direct result of the campaign rather than an independent variable.

In overall terms, then, it would seem that the campaign was the only known variable that could explain the sales increase of 128 per cent.

Intermediate measures

Confidence in the efficacy of the campaign can be further increased by examining intermediary measures and specifically by assessing the advertising model outlined earlier (Figure 15.1). In particular we can examine five elements, drawing on the results of the household survey.

ADVERTISING AWARENESS

There seems no doubt that the campaign was noticed by the public. Spontaneous awareness of advertising in the last three months (Table 15.2) increased significantly from 33 to 78 per cent with a small drop in the period between bursts.

TABLE 15.2:   PERCENTAGE CLAIMING TO
HAVE SEEN ANY SECURITY/BURGLARY
ADVERTISING IN THE LAST 3 MONTHS

Period	Granada / Yorkshire %	Control %
Pre-1	33	39
Post-2	68	48
Pre-3	58	43
Post-4	78	52

Prompted recognition of the campaign (Table 15.3) using photographs of the creative material suggested that 93 per cent recognized some element of the campaign, with television dominating recall.

TABLE 15.3:   PERCENTAGE CLAIMING TO RECOGNIZE

Period	Any %	TV %	Press %	Posters %
Post-2	75	70	32	15
Pre-3	75	64	38	16
Post-4	93	86	53	27

As a digression on monitoring advertising recall, we expect some claimed recognition of advertising which people are unlikely to have seen. For example 50 per cent of householders in the area without advertising claim to have recognized some part of the campaign and 15 or 16 per cent in the advertised areas claim to have seen the poster before it appeared. In this instance, we believe the problem of incorrect recall may have been exacerbated by the theme of anti-burglary advertising which is socially and 'morally' positive and which may have resulted in people wanting to recall a campaign they had not in fact seen.

CONCERN ABOUT BURGLARY

The advertising model discussed earlier indicated the need to heighten personal concern about burglary. However, the household survey suggested that there was very little change over the period (Table 15.4).

TABLE 15.4:   PERCENTAGE AGREEING WITH 'I AM VERY WORRIED ABOUT BEING BURGLED'

Period	Advertised areas %	Control %
Pre-1	59	56
Post-2	61	51
Pre-3	55	63
Post-4	60	59

The campaign appears to be exploiting the generally-held perception of the risk of burglary rather than causing more people to believe that they are more likely to be burgled. Obviously, risk assessment is made up of a complex interrelationship of factors (experience, psychology, environment, etc.) and the advertising campaign appears to be *reinforcing existing beliefs* rather than changing them and to be providing a new and positive course of action – namely installing window locks.

WINDOW LOCKS AS AN EFFECTIVE DETERRENT

This conclusion is reinforced by the fact that, over the campaign period, the proportion of the public agreeing with the statement 'Window locks will deter sneak thieves' increased compared with a small decline in the control area (Table 15.5).

TABLE 15.5:   PERCENTAGE AGREEING WITH 'WINDOW
LOCKS WILL DETER SNEAK THIEVES'

Period	Advertised areas %	Control %
Pre-1	58	76
Post-2	67	65
Pre-3	67	70
Post-4	71	68

KNOWLEDGE ABOUT WINDOW LOCKS

The public's knowledge about window locks (availability, cost, ease of installation) did not appear to change; however this disguises the fact that there were a large number of the public claiming to 'not know' and of those giving an opinion, most expressed a positive view.

It is believed that, while this aspect of the advertising strategy warrants further consideration, the prime motivator lies less in educating the public about window locks than in providing a powerful trigger to take action.

WINDOW LOCK INSTALLATION

Finally, the household survey measured both actual and intended installation of window locks. Claimed installation of window locks showed no significant change; however, measuring this behavioural change would have required substantially larger sample sizes than those actually used (200 to 220 per area per check). For this reason, the use of the retail audit was justified as a more cost-effective method of establishing a change in behaviour against the stated advertising objective.

However, Table 15.6 shows increases in the number of people claiming they were 'likely to install window locks in the next 6 months'.

TABLE 15.6:   PERCENTAGE CLAIMING TO BE LIKELY TO
INSTALL WINDOW LOCKS IN THE NEXT 6 MONTHS

Period	Advertised areas %	Control area %
Pre-1	7	12
Post-2	18	13
Pre-3	11	11
Post-4	14	13

It is interesting to observe the similarity of trend in the advertised areas with the audit data: namely a larger initial increase than was shown after the second burst. Although not statistically significant the changes in periods 3 and 4 do, in relation to periods 1 and 2, mirror the findings of the retail audit (Table 15.7).

TABLE 15.7:   PERCENTAGE CHANGE PERIOD ON PERIOD

Period	Sales (audit) %	Intention to install %
Post–2	+217	+157
Pre–3	−57	−38
Post–4	+85	+27

In concluding this section on strategy evaluation the evidence suggests that the advertising 'worked' according to the model discussed earlier.

— The advertising was noticed.
— Window locks were seen as an effective deterrent by an increasing number of people.
— Claimed intention to install did improve, which on the basis of the retail audit, appears to have been translated into action.

However, in one particular area – concern about burglary – the model requires some amendment. Concern among the public about being burgled does not appear to have increased. We would conclude that the advertising has worked by reinforcing existing beliefs and providing a positive focus for action for those who, already somewhat concerned, seek assistance and advice in the protection of their homes.

This hypothesis is supported by Table 15.8 which demonstrates that those who are concerned about burglary show a higher claimed intention to install window locks and that this proportion increases after each burst of advertising.

TABLE 15.8:   PERCENTAGE CLAIMING TO BE LIKELY TO
INSTALL WINDOW LOCKS IN GRANADA AND YORKSHIRE

	Total %	Concerned about burglary %	Not concerned about burglary %
Pre–1	7	9	5
Post–2	18	22	10
Pre–3	11	12	11
Post–4	14	17	10

From Table 15.8, it is possible to estimate how and on whom the advertising worked. If we start with 1000 in the target group, we can say that, before the campaign began, 600 expressed concern about burglary whereas 400 did not. As Table 15.8 shows 9 per cent of the 'concerned' (54) and 5 per cent of the 'unconcerned' (20) claimed they were likely to install window locks.

After the first burst of advertising, there was no change in the number professing concern about burglary but there was an increase in intention to install of 13 per cent among the 'concerned' and 5 per cent among the 'unconcerned'. Among our 1000 target, these translate into an extra 78 and 20 respectively; Figure 15.3 illustrates the advertising model diagrammatically.

Advertising does not seem to have worked by simply moving people through a hierarchy of effect i.e. from unconcern to concern, and from concern to action. Lock sales increased,

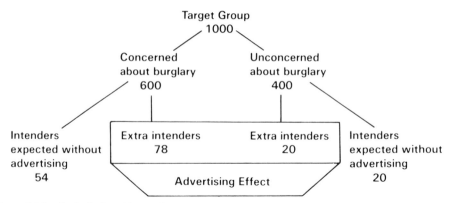

Figure 15.3   *Revised advertising model*

yet the number concerned about burglary did not. Our model suggests that 80 per cent of extra 'intenders' came from those already concerned, and that 20 per cent of 'intenders' came from the 'unconcerned' who did not pass through the intermediary stage of concern about burglary.

ASSESSMENT OF THE CAMPAIGN

Unlike other, commercial case histories, the contribution of advertising cannot be demonstrated by reference to profitability – spending money to make money. Notwithstanding this difficulty, we believe some attempt to justify the expenditure of public funds should be made.

The retail audit suggests that more than twice as many window locks were sold in areas with advertising as would otherwise have been the case. Assuming that retail distribution and consumer purchasing patterns were similar this would imply that for every 100 households who would have bought window locks a further 120 did so as a result of the advertising. On a national basis, tentative estimates suggest that about 130 000 households would have installed window locks in the mid–October to mid–February period and that the campaign would have increased this by about 170 000 households to 300 000.

Furthermore there is some evidence that the campaign would have some additional longer-term effect as window lock sales in the period between bursts remained at a higher level in the areas with advertising than in the control area (see Figure 15.2 and Table 15.1).

It is believed that this level of achievement, when set against the media expenditure, is highly satisfactory. To have more than doubled the numbers of households purchasing window locks is itself a major achievement; if their installation has prevented a burglary from being committed a number of costs have been saved as a result of the campaign: the average property loss of £400, the emotional cost to the family concerned and the police time and resources involved.

Finally, the advertising has been judged to be sufficiently successful to justify a national campaign in 1983.

18
Chip Pan Fire Prevention 1976–84

INTRODUCTION

In 1981 there were 21 deaths and 1 372 injuries caused by 15 000 chip pan fires. The key question was whether advertising could do anything to reduce this catalogue of personal tragedy, or whether accidents were unavoidable.

This paper sets out to demonstrate that advertising can, and did, affect the number of accidents and thus make a valuable social contribution.

Background

The number of deaths and injuries caused by chip pan fires has been mentioned already; however, the scale of the problem is wider than human cost alone.

Chip pan fires are the biggest cause (31 per cent) of domestic fires and result in over £8 million of property damage, and this is only the tip of the iceberg, since the vast majority (95 per cent) of chip pan fires are unreported. Furthermore, chip pan fires represent a cost to the taxpayer in terms of emergency services such as the Fire Brigade, the National Health Service, and the Police.

Against this background of waste and human anguish, the Home Office (HO) and the Central Office of Information (COI) asked the agency to put forward advertising recommendations 'to reduce the death, injury and damage caused by chip pan fires'.

THINKING BEHIND THE ADVERTISING STRATEGY

A reduction in casualties and damage could be achieved *either* by trying to prevent accidents happening in the first place *or* by educating the public about how to contain a fire efficiently and safely so that it does not get out of control because the wrong actions are taken (eg putting water onto it or moving the pan outdoors). Both these routes would achieve the advertising objective: the 'prevention' strategy, by reducing the number of chip pan fires, and the 'containment' strategy, by minimising the injuries and damage caused, albeit without reducing the number of accidents.

Initially we examined the prevention option. The main causes of chip pan fires are *overfilling*, so that oil overflows onto the hotplate or ring when the chips are put in, and *inattendance*, when the oil can reach a flashpoint and self-ignite.

However, there seemed to be two obstacles to encouraging preventive action. The first concerned the nature of accidents. Although deep-frying is extremely common (more than 80 per cent of housewives deep-fry at least monthly), most people have not experienced a chip pan fire.

In.fact it is estimated that only about 15 per cent of households have had such a fire, and we assumed that, in general, people do *not* overfill their pans or leave them un-attended. Thus an accident can be defined as being an aberration from normal behaviour probably caused by misjudgement or distraction. We were doubtful, initially, whether advertising could stop someone from making such a misjudgement or being distracted in the domestic environment that may have contributed to it, eg being in a hurry to prepare a meal, forgetting to check the level of oil, being called away from the kitchen to answer the door or settle a crying baby.

The second problem concerned people's unwillingness to believe that accidents might happen to them personally. Our own exploratory qualitative research indicated that people recognised that a chip pan was such an obvious hazard from the point of view of burns and scalding, as well as fire, that they claimed to take extreme care anyway. This, allied to the fact that most people have not experienced a chip pan fire, encouraged the belief that accidents happen to 'other' people who are more 'careless' or 'stupid'.

In considering these twin problems – the momentary, aberrational nature of accidents and the unwillingness to take the risk of a fire personally – we concluded that the prevention route did not appear to be particularly promising. On the other hand, we felt that the containment route was more fruitful. Initial qualitative research indicated that there was ignorance about what to do in the event of a fire and uncertainty about whether, at the moment of danger, the individual would do the 'right' thing, or simply panic. Thus we concluded that the role of advertising should be to inform people about the correct containment procedure and instil confidence in its effectiveness.

However, in reflecting on this proposed strategy, it occurred to us that demonstrating how to cope with a chip pan fire was a possible way to address the prevention issue. Above all, we felt that it could *personalise* the problem in such a way that advice about how to prevent accidents was more likely to be heeded. We believed this for two reasons. First, we felt that showing someone tackling a chip pan fire would raise doubts in the viewers' minds about whether *they* could do this in such an eventuality. By raising this doubt about *their* ability to cope, we felt that advice about how to prevent a fire occurring in the first place would be welcomed. We felt that showing the containment procedure would encourage viewers to want to take more notice of preventive advice in order to avoid the greater of two evils.

The second potential benefit of this strategy lay in the tone voice in which the adver-tising could address the target audience. Rather than saying, 'Don't do this because it might cause an accident' – advice which might be rejected or ignored for the reasons outlined earlier – we wanted the advertising to say, 'Well, it's happened – unluckily – but here's what to do'. The possibility ot the advertising being accusatory, and therefore being rejected, could be replaced by advice which was unmistakably reasonable, helpful and positive.

In effect, we hypothesised that, by turning the problem on its head, we could maximise the potential benefit of the advertising.

Instead of saying:

'Don't overfill your chip pan or leave it unattended, because you may cause a fire and possibly injure youself.'

we wanted to say:

'Here's what to do if you're unlucky enough to have a chip pan fire; putting it out isn't easy, so why not remember why it happens in the first place.'

The advertising model which we postulated can be represented diagrammatically (see Figure 1).

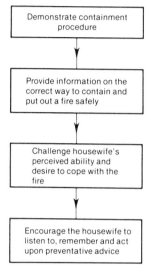

Figure 1. *Advertising Model*

CAMPAIGN DETAILS

TV was the natural choice for both media and creative reasons: it reaches the wide audience of 'all housewives' and it was the logical choice to show the containment procedure with the most dramatic impact. The campaign line encapsulated the strategy:

FIRE: IF YOU DON'T LET IT START, YOU WON'T HAVE TO STOP IT

Two 60-second commercials – 'Inattendance' and 'Overfilling' – were produced, and these have been used since 1976, although in 1982 they were edited to 40 seconds, (see pages 289 and 290 for storyboard examples). Both showed the initial cause of the fire and then the actions required to put it out:

— turn off the heat;
— cover the pan with a damp cloth;
— leave the pan to cool down.

The dramatic effect of the commercials was heightened by combining real-time with slow-motion sequences.

INATTENDANCE

If you go out of
the kitchen

and leave your
pan of cooking
fat or oil with
the heat on

it's going to
get very hot.

When it gets
hot enough

it'll catch fire.

When you notice it

the first thing

you'll have
to do

is turn off the
heat. The second
thing you'll

have to do is get a
tea towel, run it under
the tap and wring it out
until it's just damp.

The third thing you'll
have to do is place it
over the area of the fire.
And the fourth thing is
to leave it alone until
it is completely cooled
down.

Of course, if you don't
leave your pan unattended
in the first place you
won't have to do any of this.

OVERFILLING

If you fill your
chip pan more than
half full of cooking
fat or oil

it will bubble over
when you add the chips.

When it touches the
heat it will naturally
catch light.

Having started a fire
you should set about
putting it out.

The first thing you
should do if you can
reach the knob safely
is turn off the heat.

The second thing you'll
have to do

is get a towel, run it
under the tap,

and wring it out
until it's just damp.

The third thing you'll
have to do is place it
over the area of the
fire

and if you haven't already
done it, turn off the heat.
The fourth thing is

leave the pan alone for half
an hour or so ... until it's
completely cooled down.

Of course, if you don't
overfill your chip pan in
the first place, you won't
have to do any of this.

TABLE 1:	CHIP PAN FIRE ADVERTISING 1976–84
1976	Yorkshire
	Granada
1977	Granada (reminder)
1979	Central
1982	Harlech
	Tyne-Tees
1983	TVS
	Harlech (reminder)
	Tyne-Tees (reminder)
1984	London

The campaign has appeared on a regional basis in ten areas since 1976, and Table 1 shows the chronology of the advertising. The advertising has always appeared in the period January–March/April and at a national equivalent expenditure level of about £1 million. (Reminder campaigns were about half this level.)

CAMPAIGN RESULTS

Sources

The primary source for evaluating the campaign has been the Fire Statistics (derived from the reports made by fire brigades on every fire to which they are called), which are available for the six campaigns between 1976 and 1982, (data for 1983–84 not yet being available). The Fire Statistics have been analysed by the HO and the COI, and these behavioural data have been supplemented by two quantitative consumer surveys in 1976 and 1983. The rationale for the methodology and the results of combining statistical behavioural data with consumer attitudes and claimed behaviour have been written about by N Phillips.[1]

The Results

There are a number of benefits in regional advertising: the ready availability of control areas, the opportunity to experiment with different media and media weights and, with particular reference to this case history, the opportunity to see whether the advertising is working in different areas over time.

The overall results of the campaigns evaluated between 1976 and 1982 are shown in Table 2 and show 'net' declines of between 7 per cent and 25 per cent over a twelve-month period.

There is clear evidence that the advertising has been successful in reducing the number of chip pan fires. The most disappointing result is in the Central area (the Midlands). This is an area with one of the lowest incidences of reported chip pan fires per thousand households in the UK. We cannot explain why this is the case, but it implies that it is likely to be more difficult to produce an effect from a lower base.

Further analysis of the data adds credence to the causal effect of the advertising. As we would anticipate, the advertising is having its maximum effect during and immediately after the campaign.

TABLE 2:   YEAR–ON–YEAR PERCENTAGE CHANGE IN REPORTED CHIP PAN FIRES

		advertised area	control area	'net' change
1976	Yorkshire	− 20	+1	−21
	Granada	− 24	+1	−25
1977	Granada*	− 32	0	−32
1979	Central	− 2	+5	− 7
1982	Harlech	− 19	−2	−17
	Tyne-Tees			

* Six months only

Source: HO and COI

Figure 2 shows the pattern of actual fires against forecast in the 1976 campaigns and indicates that from about August the effect of the advertising was diminishing before the reminder burst in the Granada area re-depressed the number of fires.

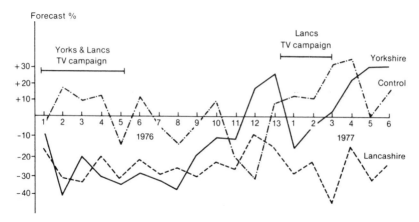

Figure 2 . *Change in the number of calls to fat pan fires relative to the forecast number*
Source: Home Office

TABLE 3:   YEAR–ON–YEAR CHANGE IN CHIP PAN FIRES 1982

	during campaign	next 25 weeks	next 15 weeks
Harlech	− 27	− 20	− 8
Tyne-Tees	− 33	− 17	− 15
control	− 6	− 2	+ 1

Source: COI

A similar pattern over time was observed in the 1982 areas (see Table 3). Further credence is added to the advertising effect if 'pure' and overlap areas are analysed separately. We would anticipate that the effect would be less in overlap areas because of reduced advertising impact (due to dual or triple ITV tuning). This proved to be the case, as shown in Table 4.

TABLE 4:   COMPARISONS OF YEAR–ON–YEAR CHANGES IN CHIP PAN FIRES IN 1982

	during campaign	next 25 weeks	next 15 weeks	total 52 weeks
'pure' areas	− 30	− 18	− 12	− 19
overlap areas	− 14	− 14	+ 2	− 9

Source: COI

Not only has the advertising produced an effect, but it has generally been cost-effective, because a 12 per cent drop in fires represents an estimated saving of £1 million in property damage alone, excluding the benefits of reducing injuries and deaths and savings to the emergency services.

Moreover, these results have been achieved with increasing cost-efficiency. The Yorkshire campaign had 2 800 housewife TVRs (circa £2 million +) and used the original 60-second commercials; by 1982 the advertising weight had been reduced by over half and 40-second commercials were being used. This represents a saving of over 70 per cent.

In summary, therefore, we believe there is a prima-facie case for the effectiveness of the advertising: different regions over a six-year period have all responded positively. The number of chip pan fires has been reduced, and this decrease translates directly into reductions in casualties and property damage.

The hypothesis that the advertising is effective is supported by further analysis of the data. The pattern of reduction over time and the differences between 'pure' and overlap areas confirm a common-sense view of how the advertising is likely to work: with greatest effect during the campaign and in pure, non-overlap areas.

In addition, it has been possible to improve the efficiency of the campaign by reducing the weight of advertising and the lengths of the commercials with no apparent loss of impact.

ADVERTISING AWARENESS AND RECALL

Our confidence that these decreases were a function of the advertising is heightened by the high levels of awareness recorded. Spontaneous awareness of chip pan fire advertising increased sharply after just one burst and was sustained at very high levels thereafter (Table 5).

TABLE 5:   SPONTANEOUS AWARENESS OF CHIP PAN FIRE ADVERTIS-ING 1976

	pre-campaign %	after first burst %	post-campaign %
Yorkshire	62	90	96
Lancashire	47	85	90
control	53	N/A	57

Source: RSL

The pre-campaign levels were caused by and correlate with levels of exposure to COI fire fillers (screened at the discretion of the ITV contractors) in 1974–75. They were not shown during the campaign, and recall and prompted awareness measures show that the paid-for advertising was what was remembered. Similarly, high levels of advertising awareness were achieved in 1983, with no evidence of a decline even four weeks after the TV advertising had stopped.

The impact of the advertising is further confirmed by the way the advertising appears to increase the awareness of chip pan fires as a potential kitchen hazard (Table 6).

TABLE 6: SPONTANEOUS FIRST MENTION OF CHIP PAN
          FIRES AS A DANGER IN THE KITCHEN

	Pre-advertising %	Post-campaign %
Yorkshire	12	28
Granada	18	33
control	10	17

Source: RSL 1976

Indeed, we are sufficiently confident of the impact and memorability of the advertising to be considering further media experimentation in the future to increase media flexibility and cost-efficiency and also, it is hoped, to reduce or minimise the 'decay' effect noted earlier.

HOW THE ADVERTISING WORKS

In theory, understanding how this campaign works does not matter: the objective of reducing chip pan fires appears to have been achieved. However, understanding can help to improve our confidence that the advertising was effective.

It is tempting to conclude from the fact that reported chip pan fires decreased that advertising prevented fires occurring in the first place. However, it is possible to explain the decrease by the containment theory: more people knew how to cope with and put out a chip pan fire as a result of the advertising, and therefore did not *need* to contact the fire brigade.

We cannot determine with certainty whether prevention or containment was the more significant, since we would need to know whether unreported fires increased or stayed the same; these have never been monitored because of the large samples sizes required. However, we believe, on the available evidence, that a combination of prevention and containment was responsible for the decrease in the number of reported fires.

There seems to be no doubt that the advertising increased knowledge of the correct containment procedure, as Table 7 shows. Furthermore, housewives' confidence that this technique would work increased to 75 per cent and, equally importantly, incorrect (and dangerous) practices declined.

However, we do not think that increased knowledge of the containment procedure *is* the sole reason for the decrease in the number of reported chip pan fires. Had it been, then we

TABLE 7:   OBSERVED REACTIONS OF RESPONDENTS TACKLING A CHIP PAN FIRE

	Yorkshire		Granada		control	
	pre %	post %	pre %	post %	pre %	post %
turn off heat	68	84	57	80	75	70
cover with damp cloth	53	74	39	75	40	52
leave to cool down	42	62	22	47	41	33
open doors/windows	5	24	5	20	7	3

Source: RSL

would expect that those fires to which the fire brigade *was* called would be more serious than before. But this did not happen: the brigades did not have to fight a higher proportion of fires, injuries were no more common or severe, and the nature and level of damage caused by fires that were reported did not increase.

Also, we believe that the decay effect observed earlier is more likely to be caused by people forgetting prevention advice than by their forgetting the 'new' information about the correct containment procedure.

Furthermore, we think that the twin 'effect' of advertising may explain the relatively disappointing results in the Central area. We do not know precisely why there should be such a low incidence of reported chip pan fires. Survey data suggest that their knowledge of the 'damp cloth' technique appears to be no better than in other areas (before advertising), so we assume that 'Midlanders' are more careful and have fewer fires. If this is the case, then the prevention advice is less relevant and the observed effect may be only a reflection of the containment component.

In summary, neither containment nor prevention alone seems to explain the reduction in chip pan fires; as a result, we believe that both were important.

CONCLUSION

The purpose of this paper was to demonstrate the effectiveness of advertising in reducing the deaths, injuries and damage caused by chip pan fires. We believe there is clear evidence that advertising achieved this objective in six monitored campaigns between 1976 and 1982.

We believe that a causal relationship has been established between advertising and the reduced number of chip pan fires and that proof of this effect is enhanced by the way in which advertising works over time, or, more accurately, by the way the advertising effect decays over time.

The creative strategy of using the containment procedure not only to inform but also to encourage preventive behaviour produced highly visible advertising and appears to have helped achieve greater public awareness of both containment and preventive practices.

Furthermore, we believe the advertising has been not only effective but progressively more efficient. The campaign now costs two-thirds less in real terms than in 1976.

This advertising campaign has had a measurable and worthwhile effect on society: savings in damage to property have generally covered the cost of the advertising and there have been additional savings in loss of life, injuries and fire brigade expenditure.

REFERENCES

1. Phillips, N., 'Measuring attitudes and behaviour – practical implications for advertising', *Admap*, March 1979.

19

Value For Money in Charity Advertising

Advertising for Amnesty International 1988 – 1990

INTRODUCTION

This paper is an account of the effectiveness of a small press campaign for Amnesty International, over the last two years. This effectiveness was achieved in a charity sector which has become fiercely competitive.

Our short- and long-term profitability derived from capitalising on an unusual feature in the charity world – membership. In the short-term, it gave us a competitive edge. Research tells us that it was tantamount to offering better 'value for money' than just asking for donations, because it offered something back. As well as outperforming other charities, we also drastically improved on the results of previous Amnesty advertising. How we executed this strategy in advertising was therefore an important factor. The full benefit of recruiting members rather than raising money accrues in the long-term, as members pay annual subscriptions and generally stay in the organisation for a number of years. Overall, we can attribute the following achievements directly to members recruited by our advertising:

— An immediate return on media spend of 106%, compared with a 29% average for all charity advertising.
— A return, in members recruited, 12 times higher per insertion than previous Amnesty advertising, in the same newspapers and on a similar strategy.
— A projected long-term return on investment, which far outstrips the return from the best commercially available interest rates.

In addition, we have a list of names from which Amnesty can generate further profit through direct mail appeals and trading, and we have raised awareness of Amnesty. These are the two ways in which most other charities nowadays justify advertising as a cost.

BACKGROUND

Amnesty International

Amnesty International was founded in 1961 by British lawyer Peter Benenson. It is a worldwide campaigning organisation which focuses on prisoners.

— It seeks the release of prisoners of conscience. These are people detained solely for their beliefs or origins.
— It works for prompt and fair trials for all political prisoners.
— It opposes torture and execution in all cases.

Amnesty has a very high success rate, for example, in 1988, 1,566 of the 4,640 prisoners whom Amnesty was campaigning for, were released.

In recognition of its work for human rights, in 1978 Amnesty International won the UN Peace Prize.

Membership

Amnesty neither seeks nor receives any government funding and relies totally on voluntary donations.

Amnesty is unusual in the UK charity sector in having a membership structure. Members pay annual subscriptions of £12.00 (individual), £15.00 (family) of £5.00 (student, under 18, claimant, OAP). Once enrolled, members receive a magazine every two months and campaigning literature. They are encouraged to write letters or telegrams on behalf of individual prisoners, take part in campaigns and join local group activities. They are also sent regular appeals for donations or for schemes such as 'Enrol a Friend'.

The Competitive Environment

In asking the public to give money to join, Amnesty is competing with all other charities. In the last four years the total voluntary income received by charities has barely increased, whereas the total spend on and total numbers of charities advertising has increased dramatically. Telethons, disaster appeals and major fund-raising events have all raised the stakes in the fight for a share of the public's mind and pocket. Figure 1 shows this fall off in income relative to advertising, using the latest information available from the Charities Aid Foundation.

Recent research has given us a clear picture of Amnesty's closest competitors. These are the other campaigning organisations such as Greenpeace and Anti-Apartheid and Third World charities such as Oxfam and Christian Aid (see Table 1). This clutch of concerns appeals to an educated liberal minority of perhaps a million individuals (calculated roughly using newspaper readership). The competition is fierce, with Amnesty having a 2.5% share of voice in 1989 according to MEAL.

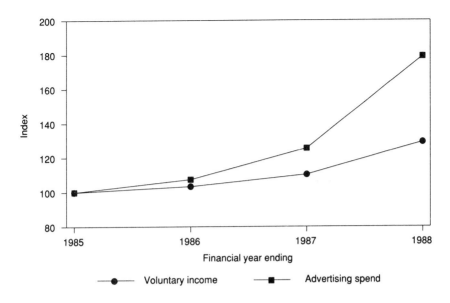

Figure 1. *Income and advertising; top 200 charities*
Source: Charities Aid Foundation, MEAL

TABLE 1: AMNESTY SHARE OF VOICE, 1989

Amnesty competitors	Spend (£000)	Share of voice (%)
ANC	64	2.0
Action Aid	547	18.0
Christian Aid	231	7.5
Disasters Emergency Committee	77	2.5
Friends Of The Earth	433	14.0
Greenpeace	674	20.5
Oxfam	214	7.0
Red Cross	258	8.0
National Anti-Vivisection	159	5.0
Save The Children	112	3.5
Shelter	93	3.0
Unicef	200	6.5
Amnesty International	77	2.5
Total	*3,139*	*100.0*

Source: MEAL

Raising Money Off the Page

Experience on charity accounts and anecdotal information indicates that many charities have given up trying to raise money off the newspaper page. Instead they use it to recruit for direct mailing or to raise awareness for other activities such as door-to-door collections. Table 2 uses Charities Aid Foundation figures to estimate that charity advertising has an average return of 29% on expenditure.

TABLE 2: AVERAGE RETURN ON CHARITY ADVERTISING

1.   Advertising accounts for 3.4% of total Voluntary Fundraising (1)
     Top 400 charities raised £127.8 million in Voluntary Fundraising (2)

Advertising income   = £4.3 million

2.   Top 400 charities spent £15.1 million in advertising (3)

Average return   = £4.3 million

£15.1 million

= 29%

Notes:
(1) Charities Aid Foundation, Household Survey 1988.
993 households were asked how much they gave and by what means. Donations in response to advertising accounted for 3.4% of total Voluntary Fundraising. ('Voluntary Fundraising' is the amount of money given by individuals, excluding legacies and covenants).
(2) Charities Aid Foundation Statistics, 1988.
(3) MEAL 1988. This does not include cinema, posters, inserts and local press advertising, which are likely to account for a substantial proportion of the 3.4% figure. On the other hand it measures ratecard costs and charities generally pay less. We have assumed these effects balance out to give a reasonable estimate of actual spend.

MARKETING AND ADVERTISING OBJECTIVES

Marketing Objectives

The fundraising department at the British Section of Amnesty has three objectives, in order of priority:

1.   To develop a large and active membership.
2.   To increase the groundswell of public support.
3.   To generate funding for campaigning, organisation and international activities.

The tools which it uses to achieve these objectives include:

—   Advertising
—   Direct marketing
—   Trading
—   Direct campaigning
—   Local activities
—   Events
—   Media relations

Up until 1988 advertising had been used almost exclusively in a subsidiary role, in publicising and selling tickets for events such as The Secret Policeman's Ball. In June 1988 we were appointed to advertise to help to meet all three marketing objectives.

Advertising Objectives

From the outset, we saw membership's potential as a fundraising tool. Firstly a new member provides a handsome £12 on joining (the average household only gave £24 in total to charities in 1987: CAF Household Survey) followed by further repeat subscriptions over a number of years. Additional profit could be made from these members through appeals and trading. Secondly membership offers 'value for money' – something back for the money you give – so it might attract more responses than just appealing for funds. We therefore made recruiting for members the primary objective.

Telephone research told us that, although awareness of Amnesty was high (82%) awareness of what Amnesty actually does was low (under 20%) (Audience Selection Telephone Research, April 1988). This convinced us that advertising would need to put across the problems Amnesty deals with, in order to recruit members most effectively. In doing this we would also be generating wider public support which was our secondary objective.

The third fundraising objective of raising money was principally to be achieved through membership subscriptions. However, we also included in the coupon a request for donations suggesting amounts from £15 to £50 so that those responding could donate more than (or if they wished instead of) the subscription.

I wish to join Amnesty International:

£12 (Individual) ☐   £15 (Family) ☐   £5 (Student, Under 18, Claimant, OAP) ☐

I wish to give a donation of: £50   £25   £20   £15   Other £ _____

Name _____

Address _____

_____

Amnesty International British Section, 5 Roberts Place, Off Bowling Green Lane, London EC1R 0EJ

Figure 2. *Coupon design*

The advertising objectives were then, in order of priority:

1.   To recruit new members off the page.
2.   To raise awareness of Amnesty's activities.
3.   To raise additional funds in the form of donations.

The primary objective was monitored by use of key codes on coupons which were entered onto the Amnesty membership computer files. We could not justify the cost of monitoring our performance against the other objectives, as our budget was so tiny.

Target Market

At the outset we had no consumer research and used a common sense definition of the target market:

—   Younger men and women.
—   Liberal minded people.
—   Having a basic awareness of Amnesty and of current affairs.
—   Readers of *The Guardian, The Independent, The Observer*.

Subsequent research among Amnesty members yields a very similar picture – the 'Lifestyle' measures yield a particularly graphic picture.

TABLE 3:   MEMBERSHIP SURVEY (SEPTEMBER 1989)

	Amnesty Members % of Total	UK Population %	Index
Age			
Under 22	24	31	77
22–34	30	19	158
35–44	19	14	136
45–54	9	11	82
55+	18	25	72
Sex			
Male	51	49	104
Female	49	51	96
Lifestyle			
Environmental concerns	66	27.5*	240
Had further education	63	12	525
Earn more than £20,000	30	15	200
Read *The* Guardian	45	3	1,500
Read *The Independent*	36	2.5	1,440

Sources: HMSO/TGI.
Note: *Definitely disapprove of aerosols.

Members therefore tend to be educated, young, liberal, professional (and middle class).

Our advertising has aimed to recruit new members from the section of the population similar to this existing member profile. This assumes a greater tendency to join among this group and is borne out by experience which shows, for example that *The Guardian* elicits a very much higher response than *The Sunday Mirror*. It will remain profitable to recruit 'close to home' while an overwhelming proportion of this group have not joined Amnesty, and this is the case at present.

TABLE 4:   READERS WITH EDUCATION PAST THE AGE OF 19

Guardian	587,000
Independent	382,000
Observer	795,000
Total	1,764,000

Clearly not all of these are typical of their papers' editorial stances but we might expect at least a million of them to be potential Amnesty members – compared with the current membership of 67,000.

There will come a time when it is no longer profitable to recruit within this niche. Our long-term objective is to recruit a much broader-based membership but in the short-term we are constrained, by the need to maximise profit, to advertise further afield only when free space becomes available.

DESCRIPTION OF CAMPAIGN

Advertising Background

Amnesty advertising has necessarily been a process of learning by doing: every pound has been needed in the front line. Where possible the direct response data has been supplemented by small qualitative programmes of research, to help us understand how the advertising was working. This research was often conducted voluntarily – without cost to Amnesty.

Because few people knew what Amnesty did (although many were aware of the organisation) and because once Amnesty's mandate was explained the majority supported it (Table 5), we decided the advertising should focus on the problems Amnesty deals with.

TABLE 5:

QUESTION: *'This is a summary of Amnesty International's aims – can you tell me how much you support them (READ CARD)?'*

Support	Total (%)
A lot	43
Quite a lot	32
Not very much	14
Not at all	5
Don't know	6

Source: Audience Selection
Telephone Survey,
April 1988

Anybody reading the papers, particularly our core titles, is confronted by a barrage of similar charity advertising. Common sense, backed up by our qualitative research, tells us that in this environment impact is the first criteria for success. Impact rests on having a visual or verbal hook:

'It says the same thing, but stops you and gets through to your emotions somehow' (BMP Qualitative, April 1990).

This is particularly difficult in Amnesty advertising as the naked representation of what Amnesty deals with is too horrible – torture, hanging, sexual abuse – and positively deters readers' involvement. We have always therefore adopted a symbolic approach, but we do find that it has most impact when the full horror is lurking just below the surface.

In this competitive environment, research has also confirmed our initial hunch that asking for more than just money – ie membership – might be an advantage. Respondents spontaneously suggested that:

'Amnesty's not like any other charities, which just want your money' (BMP Qualitative, December 1989).

Advertising has mostly recruited members aged 22 – 24. (see Table 8). Nearly all the members we spoke to in this lifestage had joined because of a general feeling that they didn't do enough 'worthwhile' things. What made them choose Amnesty was the chance to feel involved rather than 'just throwing money at a problem'. Some went as far as to describe it as 'better value for money' (BMP Qualitative, December 1989).

In recruiting members to Amnesty, we not only have to overcome ignorance of the issues, but also the general feeling among non-members that Amnesty is:

'An organisation'
'Far from home and real life' (BMP Qualitative December 1989).

We therefore needed advertising which affected people personally and made people identify with the victims – rather than just setting out Amnesty's activities. Making people identify in this way with the victims of horrible abuses has been a tough creative challenge.

Advertising Development

'Letters'
This advertising lets realistic translations of real letters from prisoners speak for themselves. In this way we hoped to achieve a very personal communication with readers. It also builds on any existing awareness of the letter-writing activities of Amnesty members.

DEATH PENALTY

IN AMERICA, HE CAN'T VOTE FOR ANOTHER 18 YEARS BUT HE CAN BE SENTENCED TO DEATH IN 10.

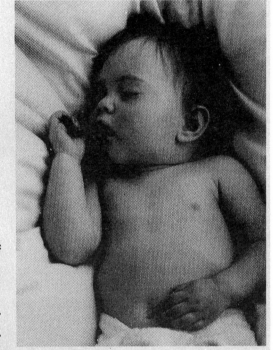

The International Covenant on Civil Rights states: 'Sentence of death shall not be imposed for crimes committed by persons below 18 years of age.'

This treaty was signed by the United States Government in 1977. Despite this, 17 states still set a minimum age below 18.

In both Indiana and Vermont, that age is just 10.

America is only one of 125 countries whose laws provide for the death penalty for ordinary crimes.

Amnesty International opposes the death penalty which is the ultimate cruel, inhuman and degrading punishment.

It seeks the release of men, women and children detained anywhere for their beliefs, ethnic origin, language or religion who have not used or advocated violence.

It is self financing and independent of any government, political faction, ideology, economic interest or religious creed.

It seeks your help to win these freedoms.

I wish to join Amnesty International: £12 (Individual) ☐
£15 (Family) ☐ £5 (OAP) ☐ £5 (Student, Under 18, Claimant) ☐

I wish to give a donation of: £100 £50 £25 £15 Other £___

Name

Address

Postcode

Amnesty International British Section, Freepost, London EC1B 1HE.

AMNESTY INTERNATIONAL

BAZOFT

FARZAD BAZOFT
AGED 31

DANA MA'RUF
AGED 14

The Farzad Bazoft case has shocked public opinion all over the World.
Equally shocking, though, has been the execution of children as young as fourteen. The imprisonment
and torture of infants of five and six has also been reported. We're investigating allegations
that methods used by the Iraqi government range from pulling out fingernails to gouging out the eyes of their victims,
cutting off noses, ears and penises. And even hanging female prisoners upside down during menstruation.
Join Amnesty International and you can help fight the methods of all oppressive governments like Iraq.
This is an appeal on behalf of Farzad Bazoft. Something the Iraqis didn't allow him.

306

To: Amnesty International British Section, Freepost, London EC1B 1HE.
I wish to join Amnesty International: £12 Individual ☐ £15 Family ☐ £5 OAP ☐ £5 Student, Under 18, Claimant. ☐
I wish to give a donation of: £100 £50 £25 £15 Other £_____
NAME _____ ADDRESS _____
_____ POSTCODE _____

AMNESTY INTERNATIONAL

'*Death Penalty*'

New advertising was developed to coincide with a major Amnesty publicity campaign against the death penalty. The 'letters' campaign could not accommodate this focus on an issue. The photographs were chosen to be visually compelling – the headlines to bring out the barbaric nature of execution.

'*China*'

An advertisement was prepared using an existing visual (*Times* cartoon) following the Tiannenman Square massacre.

'*Bazoft*'

Two advertisements were used at the time of the execution of Farzad Bazoft in Iraq. The first was all type (for speed), the second using photography of nooses as shocking symbols of hanging, followed on two days later.

Media

The space sizes have generally been 25 x 4 column – one size larger than the plethora of 20 x 2 column size charity advertisements. We wanted to stand out from all the other charity advertising. We also then had more space to create the impact and communication which was needed given the low level of knowledge about Amnesty.

The total advertising budgets available to us have been:

1988	£30,000
1989	£50,000
1990	£150,000

The successive increases are obviously a vote of confidence. By being innovative and persistent we have managed to buy at a considerable discount. In many cases it has been sight of the advertisement and our topical approach which has got us free space. This is especially true of smaller publications like the *Spectator* who have actually contacted us offering free space.

The bulk of our money has been spent on our core publications – *The Guardian*, *Independent* and *Observer*.

Figure 3 shows our spend (including production), the saving compared with ratecard and the surrounding Amnesty publicity. We learnt early on that publicity has an effect on the response – the first evidence we had of this is shown in Table 6.

TABLE 6: EFFECT OF HEAVY PUBLICITY IN DECEMBER 1988 (Running the Same Advertising)

June–Oct 88	Average Response:	Observer	119
	(Members)	Independent	122
		Guardian	98
Dec 88	Average Response:	Observer	207 (+74%)
		Guardian	148 (+51%)
		Independent	182 (+49%)

Note: PR in Dec 1988: Secret Policeman's Third Ball, TV screening of Amnesty World Tour and TV series on human rights.

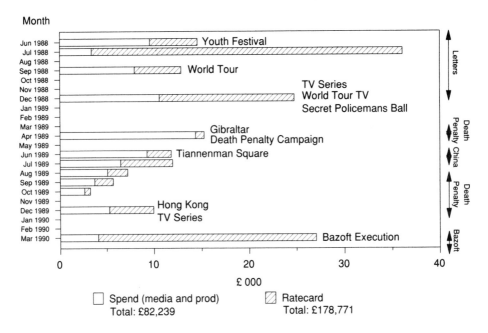

Figure 3. *Media Schedule*

While some of this effect might be cumulative – the campaign wearing in – other examples have convinced us that there is a genuine effect of publicity. This effect cuts both ways. The response in December 1989, when many people were upset about Amnesty's 'unpatriotic' publicity about Hong Kong, gives an example of a negative effect – responses fell by an average of 60% in our core publications, compared with the previous exposure of the same advertisement.

Results

A summary of costs and responses is shown in Table 7. From this we can see that advertising directly recruited 4,718 new members. A full analysis of overall effectiveness is conducted in the next section. In this section we concentrate on lessons we have learned from these results.

TABLE 7

	Inserts	Ratecard (£)	Actual cost (£)	Production (£)	Total spend (£)	Recruits
Letters (Jun – Dec 88)	22	88,222	18,050	13,446	31,496	1,852
Death Penalty (April 89)	5	15,250	10,400	3,930	14,330	780
Tiannenman (Jun – Jul 89)	4	23,742	13,200	2,532	15,732	510
Death Penalty (Aug – Dec 89)	8	26,047	14,300	2,323	16,623	903
Iraq (Mar 90)	8	25,510	1,000	3,058	4,058	673
Total	47	178,771	56,950	25,289	82,239	4,718

The previous agency advertised on a similar strategy to ours early in 1988. Their responses were recorded, as ours were, in the membership computer files, so we can compare how our advertising did in the same publications (Figure 4). This gives the cleanest measure of the relative strengths of the advertisements themselves (rather than media efficiency, which is considered later).

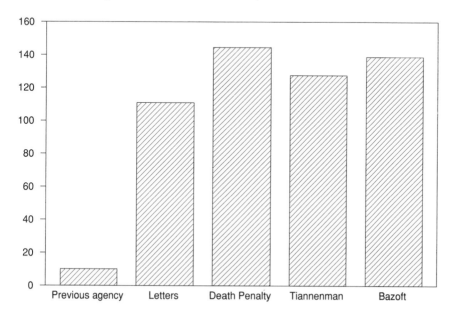

Figure 4. *Recruits per insertion, Guardian, Independent, Observer*

The 'Stones' death penalty advertisement achieved the highest return per insertion of all our advertising. It is gratifying therefore to note that 'Stones' was also rated highest by respondents in our research (December 1989) when they were asked which of our previous advertising they were most likely to respond to. And it is also interesting to note that this advertisement won an advertising creative award (Campaign Press & Poster, Silver).

The effectiveness of our advertising rests on media buying as well as creative strength. A better overall comparison of effectiveness is therefore gleaned from a graph of return in members on total cost of advertising (Figure 5). We do not have costs for the previous advertising, but a number of other interesting points arise from this graph.

1. The results for the Tiannenman advertisement fell well below the standards set by our previous advertising. Part of the blame falls to us for getting to press over a week after the event. At this late stage we had little leverage for cheap space with the press on the basis of topicality, and public interest had fallen away.

2. In March 1990 we learned the lessons from this affair and bent over backwards to get an advertisement in the papers the day after the execution of Farzad Bazoft. This approach paid off in pure responses per exposure, doubly

so as we managed to get nearly 90% of the media cost for free, and triply so as accompanying donations reached nearly £2,000.

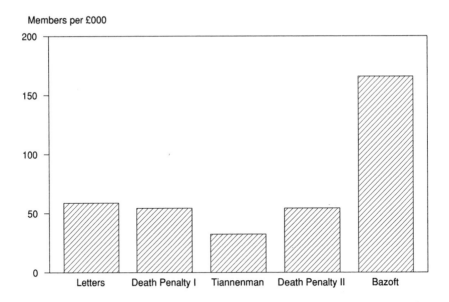

Figure 5. *Return from advertising*

As often happened with 'Letters' and 'Stones' it was sight of the advertising which contributed to our getting free space – a direct advertising effect. Smaller publications have often requested advertising which they ran for free, after seeing it in the national press.

EVALUATION AND ISOLATION OF THE ADVERTISING EFFECT

Isolation of Advertising Effect

The 4,718 new members were definitely recruited by advertising. The figure comes from return of coupons, which were only available in the advertisements – it is a clear, direct response and there is no need to isolate an effect in the normal sense.

The question could perhaps arise as to whether some of these people might have joined by other means if we had not advertised. Figure 6 shows that the annual rate of growth of membership increased once advertising began.

This graph in itself strongly suggests that advertising alone was responsible for its recruits and indeed that the advertising may have increased the effectiveness of other methods of recruitment like direct mail.

Further evidence is provided by the type of people advertising recruited. Amnesty is highly visible amongst young people, particularly students, due to events like concerts and activities at school and on campus. On the other hand the 1989 membership survey indicates that our advertising recruits are on average substantially older.

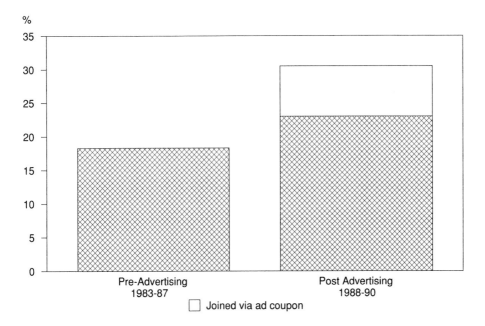

Figure 6. *Annual rate of growth of membership*

TABLE 8: AGE PROFILE BY SOURCE OF MEMBERSHIP

Base	Advertising (%) (440)	Other (%) (1850)
Under 22	11	27
22 – 34	32	30
35 – 44	26	16
45 – 54	12	8
55+	18	18

This is confirmed by the profile of membership types for advertising versus other recruits (Figure 7). Qualitative research with 25 – 44 year olds indicated a very low public profile. Given that advertising and press mentions are the principal contact for these people, and given that joining unsolicited is hard work, we would argue our advertising alone is responsible for their recruitment.

We have always recognised the beneficial effect of advertising when other favourable publicity exists. This generally pays back in increased responses and in our ability to get cheap media space by being topical (and therefore interesting to have in a newspaper). Obviously in these cases we have worked in synergy with PR. There is absolutely no evidence that our recruits would (or could) have joined in other ways. In many cases it was *only* our advertising which linked world events (such as the execution of Farzad Bazoft) with the idea of joining Amnesty.

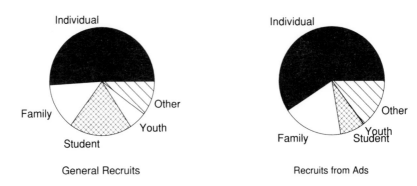

Figure 7. *Recruits by type, 1988–89*

Short-Term Pay-Back

The first issue in assessing advertising effectiveness is what return advertising has provided in the short-term. Members provide Amnesty with income in the form of fees and donations, but also cost Amnesty money in magazine and campaign mailings. Ideally we would look at the net income from members recruited by advertising. This is however not available as a separate sample so we use the total membership base, and go on to show that the advertising recruits are above average in terms of net income.

The 1989 financial report gives us the overall net income.

TABLE 9

	Membership mid-year	Income from members (£)	Net cost of mailing & magazine (£)	Net income per member (£)
1989	55,781	983,900	322,100	11.86

These figures exclude additional income from trading and donations made in response to appeals, but include any donations made with the membership application.

As mentioned above, advertising tends to recruit different sorts of people to other methods of recruitment. This has financial implications. A statistical analysis shows that the distribution of membership types is significantly different (see Appendix).

On average the recruits from advertising pay £11.00 per head in subscriptions, as opposed to the average of £9.99. And since they tend to be older (and hence wealthier), it is reasonable to assume that they will make larger donations (the Charities Aid Foundation Household Survey research confirms this view). We can scale up the £11.86, to take account of the higher subscriptions paid by advertising recruits. This gives a figure of £12.87 (11.86 + 11.00 – 9.99), which is the direct return from the advertising coupon.

It is then possible to assess the profitability of the advertising so far (Table 10).

TABLE 10

| | Immediate income | | 2nd year income | Total |
	Ads 1988/89	Ads 1989/90	Ads 1988/89	to date
Spend	£45,826	£36,413	—	£82,239
Recruits	2,632	2,086	—	4,718
Renewals	—	—	2,050	2,050
Income	£33,885	£26,856	£26,391	£87,133
Profit	–£11,941	–£9,557	£26,391	£4,894

The important point which we wanted to make from this snapshot of cashflow is that by April 1990, income from advertising had already outstripped expenditure by £4,894. All further income from these members is pure profit (allowing for administration).

It is interesting to note that a calculation of return on media spend using the accurate £12.87 figure gives a pay-back of 106% – compared with the charity average of 29%. In immediate responses, we have been nearly four times more effective than the average charity.

Long-Term Profitability

We have stated all along that the greatest benefit of recruiting members accrues in the long term. By looking at people who have joined Amnesty over the last six years and calculating the percentage now lapsed, it is possible to get a picture of the typical lifecycle of a member. Figure 8 shows that it is possible to model this life cycle accurately (see Appendix for details).

The model is an equation in which the chance of members renewing their subscription increases with every year they have already stayed.

This means that people who stay with Amnesty for more that three or four years are likely to stay for a very long time – perhaps for life. This accords with Amnesty's own experience of having a hard-core of more committed members. It is also a well-known tenet of fundraising that people give in proportion to how often they have given before to that cause.

We showed earlier that advertising recruits give more income than other recruits. It is also the case that they stay longer. Looking at the period June – September 1988 (lapsing is not recorded on the computer files until attempts over six months to retain a member have failed), we find that recruits from advertising are significantly more likely to renew their subscriptions for a second year (see Appendix for significance test).

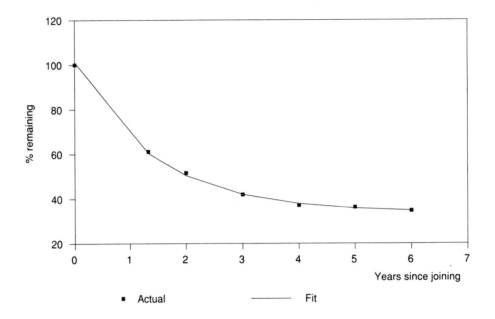

Figure 8. *Model of decay rate*

TABLE 11

	Recruits	Renewals	% Renewing
Ads	832	648	78
Non-ads	5,346	3,128	59

Once again, this is understandable. Research (BMP Qualitative, December 1989) suggests that younger members often join because of peer pressure – it's a trendy thing to do. Older members are more likely to be going against the flow of opinion (prejudices about Amnesty being left-wing etc) and so if they do take the trouble to join, it is probably because of a deeper commitment. We actively encourage recruitment of more committed members by advertising on the issues rather than appealing to Amnesty's 'badge appeal'.

With only one year's data it is not possible to produce a separate model of the life cycle of new advertising recruits, so in what follows we will assume that they follow the pattern of ordinary members. This will tend to *under-estimate* the longevity of membership, and hence future income.

We can calculate the stream of future income by looking at the member life cycle graph and using our estimate of net income per member (£12.87).

TABLE 12

Year	Ad Recruits left from year 1	Ad Recruits left from year 2	Income from recruits (£)
1989	2,632	—	33,885
1990	1,354	2,086	44,287
1991	1,133	1,073	28,396
1992	1,022	898	24,715
1993	967	810	22,877
1994	939	766	21,959
1995	926	744	21,501

Total: £197,621

Thus, after six years, we can expect a profit of £115,382 for an investment of £82,239, a return of 140%. This is a *conservative* estimate for reasons outlined above – in fact, Table 12 shows that actual performance has already outstripped these predictions.

As a comparison, consider the sort of return we might expect from an alternative investment. Suppose Amnesty were able to invest the money at the best commercially available interest rate. Table 13 shows the expected stream of income.

TABLE 13

Year	Interest rate**	Income* from year 1	Income* from year 2
1989	13.9	6,370	—
1990	15.0	6,874	5,462
1991	13.0	6,957	4,734
1992	11.5	6,270	4,187
1993	12.0	7,499	4,370
1994	12.3	8,637	4,479
1995	12.1	9,545	4,406

Total: £41,152   £27,637

Notes: * Annual return on spend in year
       ** Henley Centre Forecast, 1990.

This gives a total profit of £91,436 after six years, a return of only 119%.

Thus, even on a conservative estimate, advertising can be shown to represent a very profitable investment in the longer term.

The actual profitability will be higher than the estimate shown because:

1. Recruits from advertising stay longer than average.
2. They make larger donations.
3. Increased membership also increases the profitability of trading and direct mail appeals. On average Amnesty makes £2.80 from appeals and 92p from trading, per member, per year (Amnesty costings) – adding 30% to our profit.

4.   Members also recruit other members.
    13% of current membership joined in this way: there is a substantial 'snowball' effect which is encouraged through 'enrol a friend' schemes.

CONCLUSIONS

The key to the success of our advertising was the recognition that membership offered a competitive edge and a long-term income. The whole paper has concentrated on how effective and creative advertising used these facts to secure a large profit for Amnesty International, and indeed a larger profit than their previous advertising had generated. This gives a very one-dimensional picture of what we have really achieved. Earlier this year the agency had a visit from a man who had been arrested, imprisoned and tortured continuously for four years in Argentina. Letters from ordinary Amnesty members and visits from Amnesty delegates kept him going through his ordeal, and he believes are the only reason he is alive and free today. If one member recruited by advertising wrote one letter that saved another human being's life – how could we possibly account for that on a balance sheet?

TECHNICAL APPENDIX

Membership Profile

As outlined above, the 1989 membership survey indicates that recruits from advertising show a different age profile from other recruits (see Table 8). A chi-squared test on the age distribution confirms that this difference is statistically significant at the 95% confidence level:

$$\chi^2 = 65.5 \qquad \text{Critical value} = 14.1 \ (7 \text{ degrees of freedom})$$

An analysis of new members recruited in the period June 1988 – May 1989 shows the following breakdown by category:

Category	General recruits	Ad recruits
Individual	11,611	1,004
Family	3,156	312
Student	4,423	127
OAP	86	6
Youth	1,230	4
Reduced	2,200	240
Twin	47	1

The differences in the two distributions are highly significant at the 95% level:

$$\chi^2 = 281.7 \qquad \text{Critical value} = 19.7 \ (11 \text{ degrees of freedom})$$

Longevity of Membership

By looking at people who have joined Amnesty over the last six years, and calculating the percentage now lapsed, it is possible to get a picture of the life cycle of a member:

Date of joining	Average time elapsed*	% remaining
June 1983–May 1984	6 years	35
June 1984–May 1985	5 years	36
June 1985–May 1986	4 years	37
June 1986–May 1987	3 years	42
June 1987–May 1988	2 years	52
June–October 1988**	16 months	61
May 1990	0 years	100

* since subscriptions came up for renewal
** latest data available

It is possible to model this by the equation: $Ae^{-xt} + B$
Where:

$$Y = \% \text{ remaining}$$
$$A = 0.674$$
$$B = 0.336$$
$$x = 0.694$$
$$t = \text{time elapsed}$$

Figure 8 shows the actual and fitted values for the model, which has a remarkably accurate fit ($R^2 = 99.2\%$).

An analysis of recruits in the period June – October 1988 (the latest period for which such data is available) shows that recruits from advertising are significantly more likely to renew membership after the first year.

	Recruits	Renewals	% renewing
From ads	832	648	78
Other	5,346	3,128	59
Test statistic	8.35	Critical value	1.65

It is therefore likely that recruits from advertising will on average stay with Amnesty longer than other recruits. However, in the absence of longer-term data, it is impossible to produce a separate model for the life cycle of a recruit from advertising. We have therefore assumed for the purposes of profitability that recruits from advertising behave like all others. This will tend to *underestimate* their length of stay, and hence profitability.

20

Hogsheads Revisited:

How Advertising Helped Accelerate the Development of Aberlour Malt Whisky

INTRODUCTION

It is normally very difficult to assess the effectiveness of advertising for malt whisky until it has been running for some years.

The typical malt drinker only buys three bottles a year, is middle aged, rather conservative and not easily influenced. Retailers would normally take time to be convinced to accept a newcomer from among dozens of malts seeking distribution.

Consequently traditional advertising campaigns for malt whisky have concentrated on small spaces in specialised publications. These are run for years to gradually build awareness and an image for the brand.

Aberlour was another typical small malt whisky which had never been advertised before in the UK.

Yet its advertising campaign consisted of full colour pages in national quality daily newspapers. The advertising invited consumers to invest in a unique promotion: a hogshead (360 bottles) of Aberlour which would mature at the turn of the millennium, in 1999.

The results more than justified such a bold strategy.

175 hogsheads have been sold to date. This is the equivalent of almost three years' retail sales of Aberlour in the UK. Advertising contributed to all of the sales, and analysis indicates that its contribution was profitable.

Even more significantly the advertising helped Aberlour leapfrog over other unsupported malt whiskies in gaining distribution in major retailers such as Tesco. These listings gains mean that Aberlour's year on year retail sales since the advertising took effect have increased by 129%. The impact of the advertising has been so strong that it will now run in Holland and the USA.

This paper will aim to describe how advertising contributed to this rapid acceleration in the brand development of an obscure malt whisky.

THE UK WHISKY MARKET

The size of the whisky market in the UK in 1989 was 12.3 million cases. Most of this consumption was of household names such as Bells and Teachers, commonly known as scotches. These are the sort of whiskies which are to be found on optics in the on trade. However, growth in the market in recent years has come from whiskies which appeal to more tightly defined consumer segments. Bourbon, or US whiskey, has been a particularly buoyant sector during the 1980s as has Irish whiskey.

Another healthy sector has been that of single malts, the produce of just one distillery. They tend to be smoother to taste than ordinary scotch whisky – and more expensive to buy.

TABLE 1: THE UK WHISKY MARKET 1989

Type	Examples	Consumption Profile
SCOTCH 'Mainstream'	Bells Teachers Grants	Drunk by men lacking in confidence or too indifferent to choose any other
'Premium'	Chivas Regal Johnnie Walker Black Label	Often given as gifts, or offered at dinner parties by men who enjoy playing the generous host
Own Labels	Sainsbury Tesco	A 'pick me up' for men (and women) at home
IRISH	Jamesons Black Bush	Often the choice of those introduced to Irish whiskey by Irish friends or connections
BOURBONS	Jack Daniels Jim Beam Wild Turkey	'Trendy' whiskies drunk mainly by men in their twenties attracted to bourbon's American image.
MALTS 'First Tier'	Glenfiddich Glenmorangie	Drunk by men over 35 attracted to the discerning image of malts but lacking the time or inclination to explore the rest of the sector
'Second Tier'	Macallan Laphroaig	Post 'First Tier' men attracted by the idea of a relatively obscure malt in reasonable distribution. Small scale advertising campaigns will have stimulated awareness
'Third Tier'	Edradour Glengarrioch Tullibardine	Hundreds of malts exist which are unheard of outside a small band of devotees

ABERLOUR MALT WHISKY

Aberlour is a malt whisky from Speyside in Scotland. It is described by the authoritative Michael Jackson in his book on whisky as having 'a full rich aroma; a rounded, fruity palate; and a clean finish'. It was very much a 'third tier' malt. Prior to advertising, annual retail sales of Aberlour stood at 1,800 cases. This gave Aberlour an estimated share of the UK malt sector of 0.38%.

The whisky has a colourful background. At the turn of the century the villagers of Charlestown of Aberlour changed the name of their birthplace simply to Aberlour in honour of the whisky which they distilled. Other stories abound. Kenny, the chief brewer, for instance, attributes the drink's flavour to his bagpipes. On his rounds of the ageing cellars he plays wistful airs to sooth the whisky during its ten year maturation.

THE ORIGINAL SUPPORT PLAN

Despite being the sixth biggest selling malt whisky in the world, Aberlour had never previously been supported in the UK. In 1989 Campbells decided to support the brand here for the first time.

Drawing on previous experience in handling such whiskies, it was assumed by Campbells that the brand development process for Aberlour could not be rushed. Consumers in this marketplace seemed to need time to accept the credentials of a 'new' brand into an 'establishment' category. Opportunities for large distribution gains appeared to be limited. A realistic figure of £60,000 was allocated for the 1989 advertising budget. The marketing objective was simply to raise awareness among both consumers and in the trade.

As we shall see, this initial thinking was eventually rejected as over-cautious.

BMP DDB Needham, who were working on other brands with Campbells, were appointed as the advertising agency.

BACKGROUND TO THE ADVERTISING

Before developing an advertising plan, a qualitative research project was carried out by BMP DDB Needham. Since budgets were small it was intended to aid understanding in the development of other Campbells brands as well, but some time was taken within each of the eight extended groups to discuss Aberlour. All of the groups were conducted among ABC1 males (except one female group) ranging from 20 to 55 in age, in Scotland and in the South East of England. Three of the groups were among 'second tier' malt drinkers; one among 'first tier' malt drinkers, three among premium scotch and bourbon drinkers; one among Irish whiskey drinkers.

The qualitative work yielded four important findings concerning Aberlour:

— Confirmation that awareness of Aberlour was extremely low. During the project not one respondent claimed to have heard of it, or recognised the bottle when shown. This was not surprising in the case of scotch, bourbon and Irish whiskey drinkers, but more surprising in the case of 'second tier' malt drinkers.

— A sharper definition of the likely Aberlour consumer was developed. In addition to being male, rather upmarket and over 35, he exhibited other traits. He tended to be rather conservative in outlook and not easily influenced by new trends in society. He was interested in malt whisky, and although admitting to ignorance about Aberlour in particular, relished the idea of introducing an obscure malt whisky to friends and acquaintances who fancied themselves as connoisseurs. The fact that Macallan, for example, is matured in sherry casks to give it its distinctive taste provided him with exactly the sort of rationale he required to justify his recommendation. All in all he tended to be a good-natured sort of chap – in short a sociable would-be malt buff.

— The bulk of whisky advertising across all sectors when exposed during discussion was condemned as dull, samey and unadventurous.

— Reaction to the Macallan campaign however was markedly different. It seemed to be appealing for two reasons. The 'quirky' look of the campaign, black and white in small spaces with gently humorous copy, set it apart from other malt whisky advertising. And the media choice – many respondents recalled seeing executions in *Private Eye* – seemed to flatter the intellectual aspirations of these drinkers.

THE 'MILLENNIUM' OFFER

It was now possible to develop an advertising strategy. At this stage, however, a fresh turn to the story occurred which completely changed the communication package plan for 1989.

Campbells had developed a unique promotion. Customers would be invited to invest in a hogshead (360 bottles) of Aberlour which would mature in the year 1999. The cost would be £1,350 payable on order. Duty, shipping and VAT (if applicable in 1999) would be due on delivery.

The inspiration for the promotion came from two sources.

For many years Bordeaux wines and ports had been sold in this way – 'en primeur' as it is called. Purchase and payment are made prior to bottling and bottles are then laid down in one's own name or in the name of sons, grandchildren, godchildren, friends or business colleagues.

Secondly, celebrations were being planned for the millennium, which was a mere ten years away, and were already receiving publicity in the media. London's Ritz was receiving bookings for the New Year's Ball 1999. A table for the evening had been booked at a New York restaurant yet to be built. Concorde had been booked to allow revellers to toast the millennium not once but twice.

Strategically this felt like a very appropriate promotion for Aberlour. Potentially it could invest the brand by association with a similar prestigious stature to fine wines and ports. It was topical. And it was unique – the first time that a malt whisky had been offered 'en primeur'.

But most importantly it had radical implications for the brand development plan on Aberlour.

A CHANGE OF STRATEGY

A unique opportunity seemed to be offered by this promotion. Perhaps it could be used to speed up the lengthy process of developing an obscure malt whisky. Aberlour's support programme was re-examined. The original marketing objectives and strategy were redefined.

Marketing Objectives

Overall: To accelerate the development of Aberlour.
Specifically:
1. To increase consumer share of the retail product in the UK malt sector.
2. To gain trade acceptance and distribution of the retail product.

The marketing strategy for 1989 would be tactical.

Marketing Strategy

1. To use the promotion and its support package to help gain acceptance in the trade, and consequently increase consumer exposure to the brand.
2. To sell as many hogsheads of Aberlour as possible.

Advertising would be the main element of the support package.
   The priority was to stimulate enquiries about the offer – after all, 60 hogsheads represented total sales of Aberlour for a whole year.
   But a bold and impactful advertisement for the promotion might also offer proof to the trade that Campbells was serious in its intentions for this brand. It would position Aberlour to them as a genuinely differentiated malt whisky. This was vitally important considering the dozens of malt whiskies with a similar share of the sector to Aberlour seeking distribution.

Advertising Objectives

1. To stimulate inquiries about the 'Millennium' offer.
2. To help convince retailers that they should stock Aberlour.

Advertising Strategy

By positioning Aberlour as a significant contender within the UK malt sector through investing the brand with the credentials and status of an authentic yet distinctive malt.

The Advertising Brief

Several key elements featured in the advertising brief.

— We did not simply want Aberlour to be promoted from 'third tier' to 'second tier' status. Macallan, seemingly the most successfully advertised malt of recent years, was perceived in a different light from other 'second tier' malts.

It had a highly distinctive personality. Research indicated that a campaign which had equally different tonal qualities was also required for Aberlour in order to stand out from the unimaginative mass of whisky advertising; and that an inventive media solution would support this uniqueness.

— The offer would *not* be positioned as an astute financial investment. Astute speculators would be able to find investments which were likely to be more profitable. And we were probably talking to astute financial speculators.

— Advertising would need to feature a direct response mechanism to allow interested readers to send off for further information.

THE ADVERTISING

A short while later the concept was presented. Ian Mitchell, the distillery manager, would appear with wings in front of a hogshead of Aberlour as a 'Guardian Angel'. This was a reference to the 'angel's share', or the alcohol which evaporates into the atmosphere during maturation. Copy would run to over 1,000 words expressed in olde worlde phraseology and featuring the stories which have attached themselves to Aberlour over the years. 18th century typography would reflect these traditional values. There would be a coupon but it would blend into the overall tonal approach. The end line would be 'There are more hours in Aberlour'. There would be only one execution – full page and in colour to appear in the national quality dailies.

In the malt whisky sector, only 'first tier' malts such as Glenfiddich and Glenmorangie ever use full page advertising. This was a unique approach for such a small malt which seemed to reflect the values of our target audience.

The length of copy allowed anecdotes space to breathe. The 'onerous existence of a distillery manager' is described at length. There is conjecture that St. Dunstan, who founded the first settlement at Aberlour and went on to become Archbishop of Canterbury, may have welcomed in the previous millennium with 'a spot of private bibulation'. This was all ammunition for the 'second tier' malt drinker badly needing information so he could 'outconnoisseur' other connoisseurs.

The trade could now be provided with the evidence when they asked if Campbells were serious about putting funding behind developing Aberlour.

PR

Campbells were delighted with the advertising. They decided to use it as the basis for their PR campaign. Support material was developed, and together with a copy of the advertisement, sent to a variety of national and regional publications, and to TV and radio stations.

The PR campaign would not have been as comprehensive nor would it have been developed in this way without the advertising to support it. In particular, Campbells would not have committed to support material.

THE MEDIA PLAN

The creative treatment had already encompassed the strategic requirement for an unusual media solution. In the event, within the confines of the budget, the size of the ad and the profile of the target audience, choice was severely limited. Among quality daily newspapers ones with the best coverage of malt drinkers (apart from Glenfiddich – not the choice of the would-be buff) were chosen.

TABLE 2: MEDIA PLAN

Publication	Insertion Date	Position	Booked cost
The Times	21 October	Outside back cover (second section)	£13,500
	25 November	Outside back cover (second section)	£13,500
The Independent	11 November	Right hand page in food and drink	£14,700

The Independent insertion was in a prime site for those interested in specialised food and drink. *The Times* had an alternative position within their arts section, but all things being equal, it was judged that the effective back cover of the paper would gain more impact.

Analysis indicates that this total spend of £41,700 achieved a share of voice of the whisky sector of 1.8% in the period over which the advertising ran, and a total sector share of voice for 1989 of 0.4%.

It can be seen how loudly Aberlour had to 'shout' to be 'heard'.

RESULTS

Funds were not available to carry out any quantitative or further qualitative research. However, the analysis we can do is remarkably encouraging.

Sales of Hogsheads

The number of purchases of the 'Millennium' offer far outstripped expectations. Response was sluggish initially and by Christmas only a handful of customers had actually committed to purchase. In the next few weeks however rate of purchase considerably increased. At the time of writing (end May 1990) it has declined to one or two a week. 175 hogsheads have been ordered. This figure represents the minimum level of response. More purchasers may be left.

175 hogsheads are equivalent to 5,250 case sales. Therefore the promotion has sold almost three years' UK retail case sales of Aberlour.

Distribution

Subsequent to the advertising running two major retailers have now stocked Aberlour again who had not stocked it for 12 months. Morrisons took 90 cases and

Vauxhall Vintners 40 cases. Most significantly, however, Tesco agreed to take Aberlour into their top 200 stores for the first time. 240 cases have been sold since March 1990. Aberlour has been listed ahead of other unsupported malts with a larger share of the UK malt whisky sector, and consequently beyond the brand's expectations prior to advertising. To put this in context, Morrisons, Vauxhall Vintners and Tesco have accounted for 48% of ex-distillery sales of the retail product in 1990 to date, Tesco alone for 31%. Many other smaller retailers also listed Aberlour for the first time after the advertising ran.

Just as encouraging is Tesco's decision to *carry on* stocking Aberlour. To date they have ordered 110 cases in March, 20 cases in April and 110 cases in May. This in turn suggests consumer demand for the brand. This is particularly heartening since it justifies the decision to employ such bold marketing and advertising tactics so early on in the brand development process.

Retail Sales

These distribution gains have naturally had an effect on ex-distillery sales of Aberlour.

It seems fairest to look at the figures from the first week of January to the latest figures available (last week April). The data then begins at the first point when listings gains could reasonably be a function of advertising rather than stock ordered for the traditional pre-Christmas peak in malt whisky sales.

This analysis shows that Aberlour's year on year retail sales have increased by 129%, from 335 to 767 case sales.

Other Effects

The advertising produced some unexpected effects.

A number of rival companies magnanimously rang the marketing director on seeing the advertising and, in addition to acknowledging that Campbells had pipped them to the post by running the promotion, commented very favourably on the unique qualities of the ad itself.

At an international Aberlour conference involving marketing departments worldwide held in March 1990, it rapidly became clear that the UK had emerged as the force to be reckoned with. Both the promotion and the advertising received widespread commendation and as proof of their impact, it is now intended to run the promotion and the advertising in as many countries as possible. It is about to run in Holland and in the USA, in publications such as *The New York Times* and *The Wall Street Journal*. The idea is being adapted for use in France.

The style and content of the advertisement, but without the promotion, has also been adapted for use in magazines for international businessmen such as in flight and duty free publications.

the atmosphere.

While a rather larger portion finds its way into Mr. Mitchell.

And there's surely not a man in Scotland with a sharper nose or keener palate.

Mr. Mitchell has been steeped in malt whisky since he was but a tot.

Born in a nearby distillery, he is now a mellow sixty-year-old himself, having spent forty years at Aberlour, twenty or more as distillery manager.

Overseeing the entire process.

The first stage involves hand-picking the best Scottish ❧ barleys from as far afield as the Black Isle, Moray Coast and the milder Border region.

Once malted, the barley is dried over local Aberdeenshire peat, which gives it a *unique*, smoky aroma.

Then the barley is mashed and, using the unique waters of Aberlour's own secret spring, distilled, in stills with a shape, reminiscent, some say, of a rising swan, or perhaps, more prosaically, of a prize-winning onion.

In truth, though, it's hard to determine what exactly makes Aberlour so distinctive.

Perhaps it's to do with its location in the centre of the great malt whisky-producing region along the banks of the Spey, which seems to spawn almost as many distilleries as it does salmon.

More significantly, Aberlour is held in such high esteem in the Highlands that the inhabitants of the little settlement which is the distillery's home actually renamed the town in honour of their favourite malt.

And the reason for their regard, at least, is clear.

Because, when you buy a bottle of Aberlour Single Speyside Malt, you can be sure of its quality.

After all, Mr. Mitchell has been drinking it for ten years.

ABERLOUR Single Malt Whisky takes ten years to mature ✝ (Or so our head taster, Mr. Mitchell, would have us believe.) ⚓ ⚓ ⚓

DURING ten years of maturation, Aberlour Single Speyside Malt Whisky is kept in two quite distinct kinds of container.

One is a stout oak bourbon or sherry cask. The other is Mr. Ian Mitchell, Aberlour's taster-in-chief and distillery manager *par excellence*.

Over this period, a small amount of the heavenly nectar (commonly known as the "angel's share") naturally evaporates into

THE EXCEPTIONAL MALT FROM THE HEART OF SPEYSIDE.

ISOLATING THE CONTRIBUTION OF ADVERTISING

Sales of Hogsheads

64 purchases were accredited to people who applied via the coupon at the bottom of the ad. It seems reasonable to infer that advertising was the major influence on their decision to purchase.

In an effort to find out more about how the advertising worked we contacted a small sample of purchasers by telephone. Among those who had enquired about the offer from the advertising, most agreed that it was very clever and arresting. One was even able to quote large chunks of copy.

The other methods of finding out about the offer were being approached directly by an employee of Campbells or from the PR effort. One salesman contributed five purchasers, while the marketing department within the company persuaded eight of their friends to invest. Campbells also bought one hogshead.

The marketing department certainly made use of the advertising when selling to their acquaintances. The comments of the salesman who sold the hogsheads directly to his customers are interesting:

'There is no question the ad helped. It was a talking point. I loved the ad, I wished I had got more. It was a very funny piece. Some customers had, of course, seen the ad in the paper, but weren't interested in investing in a hogshead. I got the ad put up in some of the bars locally'.

Of the remaining 97, it seems likely that PR was the primary reason for the majority of purchases. The salient point here is that it was the advertising which provided the catalyst for the PR campaign. The coverage (see Table 3) could not have been achieved without advertising.

TABLE 3: PR COVERAGE

Media	Items	Impacts
National	15	16,640,000
Regional	33	2,147,000
Radio	7	650,000
TV	1	915,000
Trade	9	151,000
Financial	2	77,000
Total	67	20,580,000

Distribution

Proof of commitment to support in the form of a national full page advertisement in quality dailies combined with the promise of more advertising support to come, we believe are more likely to have formed a persuasive argument for listing Aberlour than a tactical promotion or its publicity drive. Advertising, promotion and PR were the only variables in the marketing mix operating over this period of fresh trade listings.

The gain of Tesco does not coincide with the normal peak for distribution gains. That comes before Christmas when the trade is stocking up, and first sales into

Tesco were not until March. Hence advertising seems to have been a causal factor in gaining distribution in, for example, Tesco.

The Other Elements of the Marketing Mix

There had been no change in Aberlour's packaging for years. No other advertising ran during 1989 or during the first four months of 1990. There was no change in pricing strategy and, although distribution data from audit sources is not available, no major gains or losses of listings prior to the advertising.

PROFIT

In assessing the overall return on Campbells' advertising investment, there are various angles to consider, some easily quantifiable, some much less so.

The first way to analyse profit is to assess the gross profit generated by sales of the hogsheads. The profit per hogshead is £800 and there were 175 purchases. Hence gross profit is £140,000. All sales of hogsheads included some advertising contribution.

It is more realistic however to consider what would have happened to the Aberlour whisky had it not found its way into the hogsheads. The answer is that it would probably have been sold off for use in blended whiskies for less profit. Hence the minimum profit generated by the sale of the hogsheads is the difference between the profit on whisky sold in the promotion and the profit on the same volume of whisky had it been sold for use in blends. This figure is £745 per hogshead. Hence when multiplied by 175 this gives an incremental profit figure for the promotion of at least £130,375.

If we consider the 64 direct response purchases which are wholly attributable to advertising, then advertising's bare minimum contribution to profit is £47,680. This figure is 14% higher than media costs (which seems the fairest measure since production costs will be amortised by using the execution outside the UK in the future).

At the very minimum, therefore, advertising was more than self-liquidating.

A true evaluation should take into account the spin off effects from the success of the offer. As we have seen, advertising played a major role in gaining distribution which in turn greatly boosted year on year sales.

However, there are also profit implications in being paid now for whisky which will not be delivered until 1999.

Campbells could always invest in their own business with the help of this 'interest free loan'.

The advantage of such a loan could, of course, be severely reduced if real whisky prices were likely to increase faster than real interest rates. But, in fact, over the last ten years, real interest rates have been on average 5.7% higher than the percentage change in whisky prices (see Figures 1 and 2). There is little evidence to show that this differential will vary significantly over the next ten years.

As an academic exercise, it should also be noted that the revenue could be invested where it is likely to yield an even higher rate of return than real interest rates. Campbells could plough this money into a relatively low risk investment, such as government bonds. Were they to perform in line with the last ten years (see Appendix), then the additional profit generated through this mechanism by advertising would be at least £115,540, based on the revenue from sales of hogsheads to date of £236,250.

To sum up, advertising more than paid for itself via the direct response to the offer, then contributed to profit gained from PR sales of hogsheads, from gains in distribution and from retail sales.

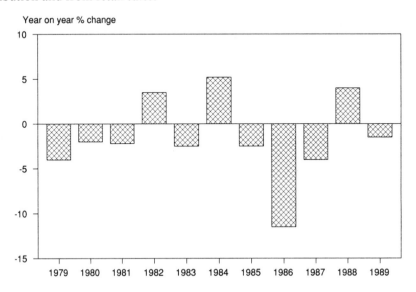

Figure 1. *Year on year percentage change in real whisky price*
Note: Price excludes duty and VAT

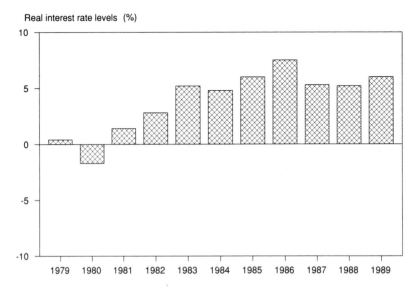

Figure 2. *Real interest rate levels*
Source: CSO

COULD THE PROMOTION HAVE BEEN COMMUNICATED AS EFFECTIVELY WITHOUT ADVERTISING?

The promotion might simply have been communicated via PR. But it was advertising which originally stimulated such a successful PR campaign.

The only other realistic way of running the promotion would be on the bottle itself. But it would have been impossible to reach the same numbers of people since Aberlour was in such patchy distribution. With case sales of 1,800 a year, since there are 12 bottles in a case, only 21,600 impacts for the promotion could have been achieved with a resulting penetration of awareness for the offer of considerably less. And a piece of stiff card around the neck of the bottle could not have projected a prestigious image which the promotion demanded.

COULD THE PROMOTION HAVE BEEN COMMUNICATED AS EFFECTIVELY IN DIFFERENT MEDIA?

The justification for larger spaces rather than smaller spaces in more magazines has already been argued. Posters cannot incorporate a direct response mechanism and such a mechanism seems justified by the results. TV does not allow whisky advertising. There is a gentlemen's agreement that it should not be transmitted on radio.

Although Macallan has recently been on cinema, theirs is a rather special case. They seem now to be attempting to broaden their franchise, having established their heartland credentials over a number of years. Significantly they did not use cinema in their early years since its target audience is younger than 'second tier' malt drinkers. Moreover the production costs of communicating such a prestigious offer would have ruled cinema out as an option.

WILL SALES BE DEPRESSED IN TEN YEARS TIME?

A theory might be advanced that in ten years time sales of Aberlour will fall heavily when the hogsheads are distributed. However, the number of purchasers is 175. At 1989 levels of 1,800 UK case sales a year, and assuming the average drinker buys about three bottles a year, the introduction of hogsheads into the market would result in sales being depressed by less than 3%. It is true that consumption of purchasers is likely to be above average, and that they are also likely to give bottles to their friends. But it is also true that the brand is likely to be consistently supported over the next ten years. Hence annual retail sales in 2000 are likely to be considerably more than 1,800. Overall, then, a future depression in sales is unlikely to be a major concern.

Moreover qualitative research indicates that 'second tier' malt whisky drinkers particularly enjoy introducing their friends to new malts. TGI analysis suggests that malt drinkers are 22% more likely to entertain than other adults. It is possible that investors in such an offer might be even more sociable. Hence it may well be that during the next ten years purchasers will want to tell their friends about the offer they have invested in and encourage them to try Aberlour (quite apart from continuing to drink it themselves). In fact it seems quite possible that the shortfall in sales occurring in ten years time will be compensated for by fresh purchasers generated over the previous ten years by word of mouth.

We like to think that the Guardian Angel in the ad now has a loyal band of disciples, eager to spread the good word.

CONCLUSION

Successful advertising achieved the immediate objective of generating sales of hogsheads for Aberlour, and in so doing more than paid for itself. It then went on to help Aberlour gain distribution in major retailers and hence greatly increase retail sales of the brand. The advertising is now helping Aberlour's marketing effort in other countries.

We hope to have demonstrated that by reversing traditional marketing and advertising thinking in the malt whisky market, Aberlour has achieved in six months what might otherwise have taken years to accomplish.

APPENDIX

TABLE 4: REAL AVERAGE RETURN ON GOVERNMENT BONDS

	Short-term	Medium-term	Long-term
1980	−4.16	−4.09	−4.22
1981	2.75	2.98	2.84
1982	4.19	4.49	4.28
1983	6.59	6.67	6.20
1984	6.29	6.27	5.69
1985	5.03	4.96	4.52
1986	6.61	6.65	6.47
1987	5.16	5.37	5.27
1988	4.76	4.77	4.46
1989	2.91	2.38	1.77

Source: CSO Financial Statistics (adjusted for retail price inflation)

21
The Launch of Tjaereborg Rejser

BACKGROUND

Tjaereborg Rejser were founded in 1950 by a Danish pastor! They are now the third largest package holiday tour operator in Europe.

Their growth is based on the simple proposition of selling high quality holidays at prices significantly below other tour operators. The cost saving is achieved primarily by selling direct to the consumer, saving ten to fifteen per cent in travel agent's commission.

The UK was a logical place for Tjaereborg to launch as it is the largest source of package holiday takers in Europe, and a market in which direct sell was embryonic. BMP were appointed in June 1977, and the company officially opened for business on 1st January 1978.

THE BRITISH HOLIDAY MARKET

The package holiday market is a volatile and highly fragmented one. 1972 and 1973 were peak years for the industry with over four and a half million holidays sold each year, but economic recession, the loss of confidence in tour operators following the collapse of Courtline, and the hot summers of 1974 and 1976 had led to a gradual decline in the market.

There were already over a hundred tour operators fighting for a share of this shrinking market, from the giant mainstream companies like Thompsons and Cosmos, to the small specialist outfits like Kuoni and Inghams.

In their first season Tjaereborg aimed to sell 25 000 holidays to consumers in the South East. In 1977 there were 1.3 million package holiday takers from this part of the country, so Tjaereborg were targeting for a modest 2 per cent share. However, as their programme concentrated on popular destinations such as Spain and Majorca, a sector in which there was severe overcapacity and fierce competition, it was evident that without their strong proposition they would have been foolish to enter the market at all.

THE ROLE OF ADVERTISING

Figures 14.1 and 14.2 illustrate the differences in method of operation between a conventional tour operator and a direct-sell tour operator.

Conventional tour operators use travel agents to distribute their brochures, and rely on

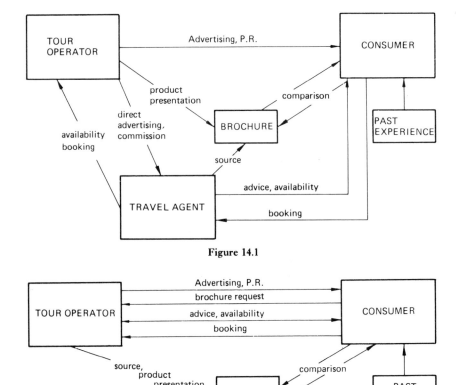

Figure 14.1

Figure 14.2

them to recommend their holidays to consumers when asked for advice. Travel agents also take bookings and collect money for conventional tour operators. The role of advertising is simply to persuade the consumer to consider that operator when choosing a holiday. It is not necessary for the advertising to inform consumers how to go about booking their holiday.

To purchase a holiday from a direct-sell tour operator, the consumer must contact the tour operator to get a brochure, and again to ask for advice or information, and again to make the booking. This is obviously more complex than dropping in on a local travel agent. The advertising thus has the dual role of creating demand and also telling the consumer how to satisfy that demand.

Figure 14.3 illustrates the important stages in the direct-sell booking claim and the role of advertising in each stage.

  (i) The advertising must motivate consumers to request a brochure and inform them how to do so.
 (ii) The consumer will compare the brochure with competitors' brochures, so it must be consistent with the advertising claims.
(iii) Holidays are a very expensive purchase and consumers are very suspicious of tour operators following the collapse of several notable tour operators in the mid-seventies. At the stage when consumers are actually committing themselves, the advertising has

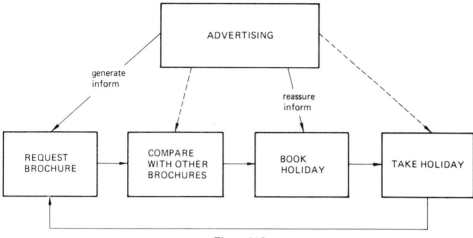

Figure 14.3

a vital role in providing reassurance about the experience and reliability of this new company.

This 'schema' provides the structure for the evaluation of the Tjaereborg launch advertising.

ADVERTISING DEVELOPMENT

Qualitative research was carried out to discover the important factors in planning and booking a holiday and consumers' reactions to the Tjaereborg proposition.

Respondents varied markedly in the thoroughness and degree of premeditation involved in planning and booking their holiday. However, it was evident that, having decided where to go and the standard of facilities required, price was the key factor in deciding which tour operator to travel with.

Not surprisingly, therefore, low price was the primary attraction of the Tjaereborg proposition. Pretesting of the initial executions, however, showed that low price alone tended to imply poor quality, a reaction heightened by the general distrust of tour operators. The best way of reassuring consumers about the quality of the holiday was by a factual explanation of how the low price is achieved. In other words, to say that by cutting out the travel agent, and thus his commission, it was possible to offer holidays of comparable quality to other tour operators, but at prices at least ten per cent cheaper.

No demographic groups stood out as particularly likely to book a Tjaereborg holiday. Inexperienced holiday takers were loath to pioneer an unknown company with a novel booking method, and thus it seemed that the discriminators of potential Tjaereborg bookers would be attitudinal rather than demographic. The target market was therefore defined as all package holiday takers, a group which is biased towards ABC1s and 16 to 44 year olds.

A mixed media schedule was used. Television was included for impact and because of the prestige attached to advertisers in that medium. The primary role of press was brochure generation, and publications with a good history of direct response were chosen for the schedule. In addition the press advertisements provided increased coverage of the primary target group, more information about Tjaereborg and a detailed explanation of the booking method. The total media budget was £83 000. The television advertising was on London and Southern during January 1978; the press insertions carried on until the end of February.

EVALUATING THE ADVERTISING

As mentioned above, the section on advertising evaluation will follow the structure outlined in Figure 14.3.

Generating Brochure Requests

AWARENESS OF TJAEREBORG

A necessary precursor to entering the booking chain is to be aware of its existence. Table 14.1 shows the results of a post-advertising awareness check of 1100 adults.

TABLE 14.1: POST-ADVERTISING AWARENESS OF TJAEREBORG

	Expenditure[3] (£)	Share of voice[4] %	Prompted awareness %
Tjaereborg (1978)	115 200	8.1	32[1]
Vingressor (1979)	196 600	8.3	17[2]

[1] Respondents intending to holiday in 1978.
[2] Respondents who have taken a foreign holiday in the last five years.
[3] MEAL.
[4] Share of 'foreign tours and holidays'.

By March 1978 32 per cent of the holiday-taking public in the South East were aware of Tjaereborg. In the same survey Thomsons, Cosmos and Cooks achieved scores of ninety plus, which is to be expected given their brand share and length of time in the market. A better comparison is with the prompted awareness achieved by Vingressor, a Swedish direct-sell company, after their UK launch in 1979.

A post-awareness check carried out in March 1979 showed that Vingressor had only 17 per cent prompted awareness, slightly over half that of Tjaereborg, despite a similar share of voice (MEAL has been used for expenditure and share of voice because of the importance of press in both launches; Tjaereborg's press/TV expenditure was split 50:50, Vingressor's 57:43) and, allowing for inflation, a 40 per cent increase in media spend.

Vingressor had the disadvantage of being second into the market. Tjaereborg's novelty, not to say notoriety, within the travel trade meant that they received considerable coverage in industry publications, consumer press and holiday programmes. This would undoubtedly have boosted awareness of Tjaereborg considerably, but, as Table 14.2 shows, advertising was still the primary awareness generator for Tjaereborg.

The post-advertising awareness check also showed that awareness of Tjaereborg was higher amongst the main target group, and moreover that ABC1s were much more likely than C2DEs to have heard of Tjaereborg first through a press advertisement, one of the intentions of the mixed media schedule.

TABLE 14.2: HOW WAS TJAEREBORG FIRST
HEAD OF? BASE: ALL AWARE OF TJAEREBORG

TV advertisement	66%
Press advertisement	11%
TV programme	10%
Newspaper article	3%
Friends/relatives	4%
On the radio	3%
Others	8%

Fieldwork International Awareness check, March
1978.

BROCHURE GENERATION

Table 14.3 shows the number of brochure requests generated by each medium.

Television is apparently more efficient than the press at generating brochures. This is undoubtedly exaggerated as the Ansaphone number was printed on the press advertisements and thus some Ansaphone responses would actually have been generated by the press.

TABLE 14.3: BROCHURE REQUESTS BY MEDIA, JANUARY/FEBRUARY 1978

Media	Expenditure (£) (actual)	Number of responses	Cost per response (pence)
London	31 637	57 053	55
Southern	10 154	9 898	103
Total TV (Ansaphone)	41 791	66 651	62
Press (coupon)	41 177	57 290	72
Total	82 968	124 241	67

More surprising is the difference in efficiency between London and Southern, with Southern roughly twice as expensive per brochure generated as London. The reasons for this are not fully understood. Although London received 70 more adult TVRs than Southern (398 against 328), the cost per thousand was identical. A partial explanation is probably that the incidence of package holiday taking is 50 per cent higher amongst Londoners than Southerners (BNTS).

There are no directly comparable response data available on either press or TV as there were no comparable advertisers. However, Thames TV have provided anonymous data about their five most successful holiday advertisers to give a yardstick against which to measure Tjaereborg's success. Table 14.4 compares these responses with the weight of the exposure of the five heaviest advertisers (there were only six major advertisers on Thames in 1978 excluding Tjaereborg). While Tjaereborg account for 8 per cent of these advertisers' total adult TVRs, they account for 48 per cent of their total brochure requests. On average the other advertisers generated 13 brochure requests per TVR; the Tjaereborg advertisement generated 143 requests per TVR.

It has been emphasized that these comparisons are quite crude because a mainstream holiday advertiser does not *need* to generate direct brochure requests through its advertising. However, when consumers do ring up to request a brochure they are told that they

TABLE 14.4: WEIGHT OF EXPOSURE AND NUMBER OF BROCHURE REQUESTS OF FIVE ANONYMOUS
HOLIDAY ADVERTISERS, LONDON, JANUARY/FEBRUARY 1978

	Weight of exposure (adult TVRs)	Number of brochure requests
A	1610	20 765
B	1093	17 974
C	949	11 534
D	617	8 928
E	494	2 273
Tjaereborg	398	57 053

Note: Except in the case of Tjaereborg, the numbers in the two columns are not necessarily related to their opposite numbers.

are allowed to ask for up to six brochures. It is significant that, when in a position to obtain a brochure by simply uttering a name, rather than walking down to a travel agent, 70 per cent of consumers who rang up for a Tjaereborg brochure asked *only* for that brochure. That this is the case, when choice is so facile, is an interesting demonstration of the power of Tjaereborg's commercial, and of Tjaereborg's proposition.

Low price was identified as the key element in the advertising strategy, and in fact a postal survey of 1000 brochure requestors, 416 of whom replied (Table 14.5), showed that low price was the most memorable communication of the commercial and the key reason for requesting a brochure.

TABLE 14.5: POSTAL SURVEY OF 1000 BROCHURE REQUESTORS

	State anything you can remember about the advertisements you saw for Tjaereborg (%)	
	TV	Press
Lower price/cheaper than other companies	45	32
Book direct/no travel agent's fee	37	26
Phone number	10	7
Just the name	2	10

	State the main reason you sent off for a Tjaereborg brochure (%)
Inexpensive/cheaper holidays/lower prices	39
Wanted to compare prices/services	23
No travel agents/direct selling	13
Wanted to see what holidays were offered	10

Fieldwork International 1978 Postal Survey.

Brochure Comparisons

The brochure is a very important, in some ways the most important, part of the overall communication from Tjaereborg to the consumer. Obviously the advertising can have no direct effect on consumers when they are comparing the brochures of different companies. However, the brochure must be consistent, in image and tone of voice, with the advertising.

To cut the cost of your holiday, cut out the travel agent.

Would you like to save 10% on the cost of your holiday?

Like £35 on a fortnight's holiday for two in Majorca?

Or £60 on a holiday in Greece?

These are the sort of savings you can make by cutting out the travel agent and booking your holiday direct with Tjaereborg.

Tjaereborg are one of Europe's biggest holiday companies, and starting this summer, they'll be taking British holidaymakers to Europe's most popular resorts.

Although Tjaereborg save you money, you won't have to give up any quality.

In fact, Tjaereborg share many of their hotels with companies that charge considerably more for the same holiday.

And all Tjaereborg's prices are guaranteed, there are no hidden charges, and there won't be any surcharges.

If you'd like to save money on your holiday, all you have to do is pick one from the Tjaereborg brochure, and book it direct, either by phoning or calling in at the Tjaereborg office.

To get your free Tjaereborg brochure, send off the coupon or phone 01-493 7232.

To cut out the travel agent, cut out the coupon.

NAME_____
(BLOCK CAPITALS)

ADDRESS_____

◆ TJAEREBORG
7–8 Conduit Street, London, W.1.

Tjaereborg press advertisement.

To ensure that this was the case the brochure was researched at the same time as the advertising; consequently it has some unusual features. The shape is landscape rather than portrait, which helps emphasize the uniqueness of Tjaereborg. The copy about hotels and resorts points out problems and faults as well as advantages, thus making Tjaereborg stand out as particularly trustworthy and honest. Finally the prices are clearly marked and 'no surcharges' is guaranteed, thus reinforcing the price claims made in the advertising.

The returns from the postal survey showed that in fact 90 per cent of brochure requestors thought that the Tjaereborg brochure was as good as or better than its competitors.

Conversion to Bookers

The final stage in the booking chain is for the consumer to ring up Tjaereborg and actually book the holiday. As the consumer is at this point committing himself to large sums of money he/she must be fairly sure that Tjaereborg are reliable and trustworthy. If in fact the advertising is effective in reassuring consumers it should be possible to demonstrate that brochure requestors exposed to the advertising are more likely to convert to bookers than requestors not exposed to it.

There were a significant number of brochure requests from outside mainstream TV-advertised areas, due in part those press insertions which were national or semi-national, but otherwise due, presumably, to national PR exposure.

Table 14.6 shows the conversion to booking ratio in TV-advertised and non-TV-advertised areas. The ratio of brochure requestors to bookers was ten to one in the former and

TABLE 14.6: CONVERSION OF BROCHURE REQUESTORS TO BOOKERS

	Number of brochure requests	Number of bookers[1]	Conversion ratio
Main advertised areas (London and South East)	94 012	9 573	9.8:1
Rest of England	27 319	1 202	22.7:1
Other areas (Scotland, Wales and overseas)	1 026	225	4.6:1
Total non-advertised areas	28 345	1 427	19.9:1

[1] 2.6 holidays per booker
2 to 3 per cent of data lost due to misaddressing.

twenty to one in the latter. Thus consumers with Tjaereborg brochures exposed to a reasonably heavy weight of advertising were apparently twice as likely to book a holiday with Tjaereborg than those who had not.

However, there is another possible explanation for these findings. In 1978 all Tjaereborg holidays departed from Gatwick airport. By and large the advertised areas are nearer to Gatwick than the non-advertised areas. In other words it could be that the product was inhibiting brochure requestors from outside the TV-advertised areas from booking, rather than the advertising encouraging bookings within the advertised areas.

To control out the product variable, the conversion ratios in six counties which are roughly equidistant from Gatwick and which all have London between them and Gatwick have been compared. Of the six counties – which are Hertfordshire, Essex, Buckinghamshire, Berkshire, Oxfordshire and Bedfordshire – two, namely Oxfordshire and Bedfordshire, fall substantially outside the London and Southern ITV areas.

As Table 14.7 shows, the conversion ratios in the advertised areas is 13 to one, whereas in the non-advertised areas it is 22 to one. This is substantial evidence that the advertising is having an influence on the final stage of the booking claim.

TABLE 14.7: CONVERSION OF BROCHURE REQUESTORS TO BOOKERS BY COUNTY

County	Number of brochure requests	Number of bookers	Conversion ratio
Hertfordshire	7 695	574	13.4:1
Essex	18 212	1 265	14.4:1
Buckinghamshire	2 180	206	10.6:1
Berkshire	2 822	328	8.6:1
Total advertised	30 910	2 373	13.0:1
Oxfordshire	2 052	69	29.7:1
Bedfordshire	1 796	106	16.9:1
Total non-advertised	3 848	175	22.0:1

WAS THE ADVERTISING EFFECTIVE?

In answer to this question, so far this chapter has looked at the mechanism of the advertising and evaluated it against such criteria as are available and seem sensible.

One fact not yet mentioned is that, although Tjaereborg targeted to sell 25 000 holidays, they actually sold 29 000, thus going 16 per cent over budget. It could be argued that this is, per se, a demonstration of advertising effectiveness. However, it also could be argued that the direct-sell operation, and the advertising which is so integral to it, was not the most cost-effective way of marketing Tjaereborg's holidays, and that a conventional operation could have been equally successful and more cost-effective.

Direct Sell

Table 14.8 lists all the marketing costs which Tjaereborg had during their first season in the UK. Apart from the cost of advertising (media and production) most of the costs relate to the printing and distribution of brochures.

The net sales value (NSV) of the 29 000 holidays which Tjaereborg sold in 1978 was £3 500 000. At £251 000 the advertising and distribution costs were 7.2 per cent of NSV.

TABLE 14.8: DIRECT SELL COSTS (£)

Advertising	83 000
Production	68 000
200 000 brochures	57 000
Postage and packaging	32 000
Handling house	4 000
Ansaphone costs	7 000
Total	251 000

BMP Estimates.

Conventional

Table 14.9 estimates the costs of marketing these same 29 000 holidays using the conventional brochures distribution mechanism through travel agents.

No advertising other than trade press is costed in, although it could be argued that a moderate amount of advertising would be advisable. However, as Tjaereborg's holidays would be such good value for money they could probably rely on consumers finding them

TABLE 14.9: CONVENTIONAL COSTS (£)

Advertising	5 000	(trade press)
Production	2 000	(trade press)
300 000 brochures	78 000	
Sales force (8)	35 000	
Launch	10 000	
Travel agents' com.	350 000	
Total	480 000	

BMP Estimates.

out for themselves and hope that travel agents would reassure consumers about their quality. A vigorous trade press campaign and a prestigious trade launch would be necessary!

There are approximately 1700 travel agents in the South East; however it would not be necessary to service them all, probably the 500 largest would suffice. A well known tour operator employs a sales force of eight and prints 300 000 brochures to cover just such a number of travel agents and the costs for Tjaereborg are based on this.

The largest new cost would be travel agents' commission, which would represent at least ten per cent of the net sales value of the holidays. The total cost of this option is therefore £480 000, which is 13.7 per cent of NSV.

The conventional operation is almost twice as expensive as selling direct, which means that Tjaereborg would have had to sell a considerably higher volume of holidays through travel agents than the 29 000 they sold direct to the consumer to make as much money.

Tjaereborg could pass on the cost of the travel agent to the consumer as do all other tour operators. It appears that if they sold 29 000 holidays this way, they would make more money as there would be no expensive media costs to bear. However, this line of reasoning is invalid as to raise the price of Tjaereborg's holidays would destroy their proposition. To sell their holidays in this situation Tjaereborg would have to segment the market on a different basis than price. For example, they could offer unusual destinations or specialize in certain destinations, though given the mainstream nature of their programme this is not really feasible. Alternatively they could build a proposition around high quality; however, for a new company this in itself would require substantial advertising support, which would be competing head on with the big tour operators without the benefits of their long established and reliable brand names.

As discussed in the introduction it is apparent that if Tjaereborg had not had a distinctive proposition, i.e. low price, they would have been foolhardy to enter the UK holiday market at all. Now it has been demonstrated that direct sell, and the advertising which is such a vital ingredient in direct sell, was by far the most cost-effective way for Tjaereborg to sell their holidays.

SUMMARY OF THE ARGUMENT

Tjaereborg had a requirement to sell 25 000 holidays; they had a mainstream programme of resorts but a distinctive proposition, namely, lower prices achieved by their means of operation – selling direct to the consumer.

Price was the key element in the advertisements which were developed for Tjaereborg. The television commercial used the distinctive 'How much?' device, while the press concentrated on giving consumers information about the quality of the holidays and the size and experience of the company.

There are three stages in the holiday booking chain: (i) brochure requesting, (ii) brochure comparison, (iii) booking the holiday. It has been argued that advertising has a major influence on (i) and (iii).

The scale of the number of requests generated by the television advertising has been demonstrated by comparison with other holiday advertisers; it was, simply, unprecedented. Moreover the percentage of solus requests has been used as evidence of the degree of interest aroused by the advertising.

The importance of the advertising in reassuring consumers that Tjaereborg are a trust-worthy company at the stage at which they are booking a holiday has been demonstrated by comparing the conversion ratios of advertised and non-advertised counties which are equidistant from Gatwick.

Finally, the cost-effectiveness of the advertising has been demonstrated by contrasting the costs and profits of the direct-sell method with the conventional operating system. It is clear that Tjaereborg would have had to sell a considerably higher volume of holidays to achieve the same return if the latter system had been used. In fact, as it was, they sold 16 per cent more holidays than they had originally budgeted to do.

DISCUSSION AND CONCLUSIONS

This case history is direct response because advertising is the means of the advertiser carrying out his business as well as the tool used for creating demand for his products. It differs from most direct-response advertisers in that with Tjaereborg a brand is being created.

The launch of Tjaereborg was the launch of a new sector of the travel industry, and it is important to establish Tjaereborg as number one in that category. The benefit of this is that with repeat bookings and increased personal recommendation from satisfied customers the need for advertising decreases over the years, making the whole operation even more profitable. This contrasts with the lot of the conventional tour operators, where the travel agents' commission is omnipresent.

When seeking to demonstrate the effectiveness of Tjaereborg's advertising it could be argued that the advertising should have generated even more brochure requests or achieved an even lower conversion ratio. However, given the finite number of holidays to sell, and even here Tjaereborg over-achieved, this argument is impossible to validate.

The difficulties of demonstrating anything at all in the real world are immense. Without areas controlled for such variables as PR, distance from Gatwick, media weight, propensity to take package holidays and so on, it is difficult to take these factors into account and impossible validly to assign causes to effects. However, the criteria of the business man are not the same as those of the empirical scientist. The fact that Tjaereborg were successful, and continue to be so, despite the opposition of the travel industry and their dire predictions of doom for Tjaereborg, setting up in such difficult times, is perhaps the best demonstration of advertising effectiveness which could be offered.

Index